ABRAHAM HOLTZMAN

North Carolina State University

with Sylvia Holtzman

AMERICAN GOVERNMENT
Ideals and Reality

PRENTICE-HALL, INC., Englewood Cliffs, New Jersey 07632

Library of Congress Cataloging in Publication Data

Holtzman, Abraham.
   American government, ideals and reality.

   "The Constitution of the United States:" p. 420
   Includes index.
   1. United States—Politics and government.
I. Holtzman, Sylvia, joint author. II. United
States. Constitution. 1979. III. Title.
JK274.H654   320.9'73'092   79-22944
ISBN 0-13-027151-9

Editorial/production supervision by Colette Conboy
Interior photos by Stan Wakefield
Cover design by A Good Thing
Cover photo by Reginald Wickham
Manufacturing buyer: Harry P. Baisley

Printed in the United States of America

10 9 8 7 6 5 4 3 2 1

Prentice-Hall International, Inc., *London*
Prentice-Hall of Australia Pty. Limited, *Sydney*
Prentice-Hall of Canada, Ltd., *Toronto*
Prentice-Hall of India Private Limited, *New Delhi*
Prentice-Hall of Japan, Inc., *Tokyo*
Prentice-Hall of Southeast Asia Pte. Ltd., *Singapore*
Whitehall Books Limited, Wellington, *New Zealand*

CONTENTS

iii

PREFACE

This book is designed for beginning students. It is written in a style that will enable them to understand and deal with the concepts, structures, and interrelationships in our political system. Although most of these students will probably take no additional work in political science, those who do will find that the concepts stressed, the approach taken to the political system, and the substantive treatment of government and politics will afford them an adequate preparation.

I start with certain assumptions that grow out of over twenty years of teaching American government and politics to both nonmajors and majors in political science.

Students should learn basic concepts. This is the only way they can meaningfully study and derive from a political science course a framework for relating to and dealing with government and politics. If students can emerge from the course with twenty of the most relevant concepts and if they can understand how these concepts relate to and help explain the American political system, then they will have profited greatly from their study.

Students should be encouraged to think. All too frequently they come into the course with simple notions, simple solutions and a propensity to memorize and compartmentalize rather than to analyze and synthesize. It is important that they see and, therefore, become accustomed to look for the complexities in problems and answers. This book seeks to aid them to become aware of and to think in these terms, and it seeks to help them see the links between concepts, political actors and institutions of power.

Students must be encouraged and helped to ask questions. Teaching students to question is one of the most difficult assignments facing a teacher. Most students do not even know how to begin to formulate a question. Although the instructor is the real key to helping students, a textbook should so present material that questions are built into the treatment of the subject matter itself. In that way students will become accustomed to dealing with political matters in terms of questions and they will find it easier to see and raise questions themselves. The teacher who uses this book should be able to build on the questions in the chapters that the students have read. I am not referring to review questions at the end of chapters, which most students ignore anyway. My emphasis is on the substantive questions of political science as they relate to the American political system.

Students learn best when what they study is meaningful and relevant to them. All too frequently politics and government remain vague and abstract "things" to students. Not only do students have difficulty with abstractions, but many times they could care less. What a textbook must do is combine both the theoretical and the abstract with the actual practice of politics and government so that the students can see how and why the two tie together.

Too many students complain that politics and government are boring subjects. A text must help readers capture some of the excitement of politics, make clear the relevancy of government to their lives, and present the fascinating problems within the political system.

The writing must be clear and not get in the way of the students' learning. It must encourage students, affording them the confidence that they can read and understand the ideas and material. Only in this way will they be willing to read further and to study.

Students today are not proficient readers. This is as true for many students in the public universities as it is in community colleges and technical institutes. All too frequently texts confuse students. The latter complain that they have to cut through too much verbiage; that they get lost and have a difficult time identifying the key points. Writing that is not clear, and sentences and paragraphs that are too long and complex, become obstacles to reading and to learning.

One challenge in writing a new text is to present sophisticated ideas in a form that students can comprehend and that will at the same time help them achieve a sense of satisfaction in dealing with the subject matter. I am not contending that learning is easy, for it involves a confrontation with concepts, terms and relationships that are generally new to students. However, the process of learning can be made easier if the material is presented in a lucid, interesting and challenging manner.

On the basis of the above criteria, I have omitted a number of traditional features of introductory texts that, I feel, get in the way of the reader: 1. all footnotes and most Supreme court cases; 2. extensive citations from the latest research studies; 3. reference to the works of the philosophers as well as to the historical roles of actors at the

Constitutional Convention; 4. emphasis on the elitist-pluralist controversy or on the failures of the American political system. I have also
confined the scope of the book to those chapters that are absolutely
essential to an understanding of American government and politics and
that fit easily into a semester-length course of study.

If this book is as helpful to students of American government and
their teachers as I hope it will be, a number of people deserve credit for
contributing to it. My wife, Sylvia, initially convinced me to write an
introductory text and then fully immersed herself in the writing as a
full-fledged co-worker. Without her inspiration and assistance, this book
would have never been written. Stan Wakefield, an old friend and my
Prentice-Hall editor, was more than generous with support and encour-
agement. And his production editor, Colette Conboy, proved exceptionally helpful.

Our departmental staff of secretaries, headed by Alois Chalmers,
suffered willingly through the many demands I imposed upon them for
typing and other assistance. And the ever-helpful staff of reference
librarians at North Carolina State University's D.H. Hill Library deserve
a special note of appreciation for their patience and diligence in answer-
ing my numerous queries.

Finally, I wish to thank my sons, Adam and Seth, who took time
away from their own busy university studies to help improve the
manuscript.

The mistakes, if any, are mine, but the credit, if any, I share
willingly with those who so generously contributed their time, effort
and skills.

Abraham Holtzman
Raleigh, N.C. 1979

CHAPTER 1

GOVERNMENT IS IMPORTANT TO EACH OF US

Government is so vital to our existence today that we cannot live civilized lives without it. This chapter is about the relationship between government, civilization, and each of us.

What is *government?* It is human machinery for making rules and regulations that affect our behavior. It provides services. It makes demands on us and imposes penalties. And it is a legitimate means for resolving conflict among us.

A famous United States Supreme Court Judge, Oliver Wendell Holmes, once characterized the demands government made upon him in the following manner: "I like to pay taxes. With them, I buy civilization." The implication of Justice Holmes' axiom—taxes buy civilization—is that we cannot afford the option of operating without government. Taxes paid to it are not only necessary but beneficial. Yet how many taxpayers are grateful to government for giving them the opportunity to "buy civilization"?

Most of the time we assume government is neither essential to nor closely involved in our lives. We tend to be unaware of the many things it does for us. Not unnaturally, its very "invisibility" leads us all too frequently to assume its irrelevance. Yet if you examine your own life more carefully you will learn that the reverse is true: Government is very important to each of us.

GOVERNMENT AND YOUR DAILY LIFE

You are being asked in this book to study about government, to understand what it does and why, and to be alert to how it may help or harm you. If you can see how government relates to you and to important aspects of your life, then you in turn will be able to relate more realistically to it. Begin by asking a question: How much does government enter into what you do each day? The answer is not as simple as you might think.

Your Water and Food

Have you ever thought about the source of your water supply? Aside from those few who rely on their own wells, most of us obtain water from local government reservoirs. Water flows into our homes because government has anticipated our needs and arranged to supply water so we may use it. In all probability you use this water without worrying whether you will have more tomorrow or whether it is safe to drink. These concerns have been removed from your consideration, leaving you free to think about other matters. Government has given you this **freedom** by assuming responsibility for the water supply and its treatment.

Similarly, most of the food you consume and the milk you drink must meet governmentally imposed health standards. When you are enjoying a meal, do you know or concern yourself with whether your food is uncontaminated? No, you take this for granted. Recognizing, however, that it cannot be taken for granted, government has intervened at the various stages of the commercial preparation of food, from the slaughterhouse and dairy to the retail merchant. Recently, the national government has even prohibited food producers and manufacturers from using certain steroid hormones and artificial additives—dyes, sweeteners, preservatives—because they might cause cancer to consumers. Government's assuming these responsibilities for protecting your health frees you to enjoy your food and to concern yourself with other aspects of life.

The "Biological" You

The relationship between you, government, and civilization can also be explored by examining a basic biological fact: Each of us produces waste. But if each of us assumed responsibility for disposing of our own waste, the resulting sanitation problems would overwhelm us. Consequently, government intervention becomes absolutely necessary. If our taxes may be said to "buy civilization," it is in part because tax-supported waste disposal systems contribute to the quality of that civilization. In the absence of such systems, the environment in our towns and cities would become so unbearable and dangerous to our health that our personal lives, our liberties, and our property would be seriously impaired.

To illustrate the relationship between you, government, and civilization, push the waste disposal model somewhat further. The amount of waste our rich industrial society produces is stupendous. Factories produce waste. Automobiles produce waste. In consuming goods, you produce waste of various kinds—glass, metal, paper, food, chemical. Not only is much of this waste dangerous to ourselves and to others in our environment, but the usual means of disposal—burying it in land, piping it into oceans, rivers, or lakes, or burning it and thereby releasing part of it into the atmosphere—either are no longer feasible in many places or are unacceptable because of their harmful effects. And the dangers inherent in the disposal of nuclear waste, as we increasingly turn to nuclear power for energy, pose additional serious problems of their own.

Waste disposal is a particularly complex twentieth-century problem. It challenges our best scientific and technological abilites. Alternative solutions not only raise questions of feasibility but invariably generate conflict. Should government be involved? Which level of government—national, state, or local—should intervene? Who should bear the costs?

Fifty or one hundred years ago Americans could not have imagined the need for government to regulate the quality of air. It was all around them and apparently inexhaustible. To suggest that air was a resource to be guarded or that government had to intervene to guarantee its cleanliness would have seemed absurd. Not until 1970 was a special unit, the U.S. Environmental Protection Agency, established in our national government to assume responsibility for setting air quality standards for the entire country.

By yourself you can do little about air pollution; by using your government you can do a lot to protect the quality of the air from those who eject their waste into the atmosphere. Only government has sufficient power and legitimacy to establish standards and to compel both individuals and giant corporations to comply. Recently, our national government passed legislation requiring automobile manufacturers to install pollution control mechanisms in new cars; a few of our state governments have for some time ordered these devices installed in old cars as well. And government is attempting to induce factories that release sulphur-laden fumes into the air to change the type of fuel they use or to install chemical "scrubbers" in their chimneys.

Those of you who like to fish and hunt, birdwatch, or swim in lakes and rivers cannot by yourself prevent the pollution of the environment that results from the indiscriminate disposal of deadly waste products by factories or cities. Nor can you alone do anything to prevent farmers from polluting waterways with the dangerous pesticides they use to

"Just keep driving around–We may come up with a solution yet"

protect crops. Too often fish and birds die, other wild animals disappear, and the waters repel rather than attract people. Because rivers and lakes are the major sources of drinking water for many Americans, the dangers are compounded still further.

Merely to request a factory manager to cease pouring his waste into a river or a boat captain to stop flushing his waste into a lake is, in most instances, futile. They must dispose of their waste, and traditional methods are both easy and inexpensive. So we have no recourse but to use the power of government. It can compel them to treat their waste or to dispose of it in other ways. They alone may have to bear the financial burden, or government may offer them a tax incentive, thereby spreading the cost among the rest of us. Sometimes local governments are the worst polluters. Only a more powerful level of government can force them to upgrade their waste treatment systems and supply aid to help them achieve this goal.

Other Areas of Government Intervention

Government involvement in your daily life is not confined to water, food protection, or waste disposal. It extends to the traffic patterns when you walk as a pedestrian or drive in an automobile. It covers the automobile itself, which must display one or two license plates or stickers and pass an annual mechanical inspection in some states. If you wish to drive an automobile or truck, you must demonstrate competence in a governmentally prescribed test. Who benefits from these regulations and the vast bureaucracy of government employees needed to implement them? Obviously, the beneficiaries include you and your family. Government regulations introduce order into what otherwise might be chaos, and they extend the area of comparative safety in your life.

To further assure your safety, the buildings you occupy at school or work are required by your local government's building and fire codes to incorporate safety features in their construction. To protect your property, the locality in which you live may be zoned by your city or county government to prevent its being ruined by undesirable types of construction or businesses. And government also helps you meet your recreational and entertainment needs through its parks, playgrounds, and community centers.

By providing a police force to keep order and prevent crimes against life and property, government enables you and others in your community to live in relative safety. Although the presence of the police is usually invisible, it is reflected in our confidence to use our homes, streets, businesses, and schools without fear. When official law enforcers cannot effectively provide this necessary minimum peace and order, our confidence is undermined and our lives, property, and liberty endangered. Freedom from fear and freedom to concern ourselves with the good things in life are diminished, and the quality of our civilization depreciates.

Why Depend on Government?

That we all depend on government—local, state and national—should be clear. This dependency is both inevitable and generally advantageous, although many people are unaware of it and some resent it. This dependency upon government also involves costs for each of us.

Our dependency upon others makes us dependent on government.   Each of us is a specialist in just a few areas of life; we are mechanics, farmers, teachers, homemakers, whatever. As a result we must depend on specialists in other economic areas for most of the goods and services we need.

To ensure that we will not be endangered by that dependency, we turn to government. Why endangered? Because almost all the specialists on whom we depend have no moral or legal obligation to us, aside from whatever they voluntarily assume or government requires. Primarily, they relate to us in an impersonal way, through money and profit. People who are bound by feelings of affection or friendship are most likely to treat each other fairly and honestly. A producer who never sees the consumer is less likely to be concerned about the individual who buys or uses his products. In this impersonal economic world in which we live, the drive to achieve success, measured by money or prestige, leads some individuals to ignore the safety and health needs of those who depend on them for goods and services. Not all producers, manufacturers, or service providers are irresponsible, of course, but enough of them are to make life sufficiently uncertain and dangerous for the rest of us, were it not for government.

The Psalmist said that humans are a little lower than the angels. It has also been said that they are only a little higher than devils. Government cannot lift us up to be angels, but it can mitigate the consequences of our being only a little higher than devils.

Our independence diminishes as our numbers increase.   Although we all treasure our independence, only those few who live isolated from their fellows can truly be independent. Proximity and numbers of people automatically impinge on our independence, reducing it drastically. Multiply the number of individuals, mass them in larger and larger clusters, and each individual becomes more and more vulnerable to the actions of others. A collective piece of machinery (government), which has both sufficient and legitimate power to order relations among us, compensates for our increased vulnerability as proximity and numbers of people cut into our independence.

Government expands our freedom—but not without cost!   By assuming responsibility for certain services and by regulating our behavior, government benefits us in at least two ways. It enables us to live healthier, safer, and more comfortable lives. And in so doing, it *frees* us so that we may concern ourselves with more desirable activities. Frees us? Yes, because we are not normally required to spend large amounts of time, energy, money, and peace of mind obtaining the protective services that government supplies us. Freed from these burdensome responsibilities, we can concentrate more easily on our work, our families and churches, members of the opposite sex, entertainment, or whatever.

Note that we cannot obtain this freedom without relinquishing something in return. At a minimum we pay two types of costs. First, we accept a reduction in our personal freedom to act absolutely as we wish: We may not dispose of our waste where we wish, drive as fast as we would like, build wherever, whatever, or however we prefer. Second, we pay an economic cost: We give up a percentage of our income to government through taxes, which means that we forfeit our freedom to spend our money exactly as we wish. This trade-off is implied in Justice Holmes' saying, "With them [taxes], I buy civilization."

Civilization, in terms of the services government provides, is costly. For example, someone has to pay for the sewage system that operates so unobtrusively under the streets, connecting plumbing lines from homes, businesses, and factories with complex waste treatment plants. Since very few individuals are willing to contribute voluntarily, or even to agree on what constitutes their fair share of the costs for this service, government must possess the power to assess the costs and compel (tax) us to give up part of our resources. By distributing costs to a large number of people, sometimes over a lengthy period of time, government can reduce the immediate burden that each of us must assume.

Everything government does has some cost. Therefore, we should always ask, especially when requesting more services or assessing present services and regulations: Are the benefits worth the costs? What alternatives may government adopt, and what are their costs? Is private action more desirable than governmental intervention, and what will that cost us?

PUBLIC GOVERNMENT, PRIVATE GROUPS, AND INDIVIDUALS

Our American society is made up of more than public governments and private individuals. It also includes private groups: an extraordinary number of social, economic, religious, ethnic, and racial groups offering to meet the particular needs of various individuals. What private groups do you belong to? You almost certainly belong to a family, most likely to a church or temple, and perhaps to an economic organization as a worker, manager, or owner. You may belong to social or fraternal groups, to leisure-oriented groups, to professional and civic groups.

What are the similarities between these private groups and the public governments—national, state, county, or city—each of us belongs to? All are made up of a number of people who have certain shared characteristics. Both private groups and public governments have boundaries for determining who is "in" and who is "out." Government boundaries are largely geographical. Church boundaries are broadly determined by articles of faith, although geography may sometimes be relevant. Families have totally different types of boundaries, ones that are defined socially, legally, and by "blood" ties.

Private groups resemble public government in their ordering of relations among their members. Corporations have their boards of directors and officers; factories, their managers and foremen; unions, their presidents and shop stewards; athletic teams, their coaches and team captains; churches their religious leaders and lay boards of deacons or trustees. These officials formulate and enforce rules, provide services, and impose punishment.

What are some of the differences between public governments and private groups? Obviously, size is not a measure of difference, since some states and counties are smaller in population than such giant corporations as AT&T or General Motors with their millions of stockholders and hundreds of thousands of employees.

A major difference is how public governments relate to their members and how private groups relate to theirs. Membership in private groups, for example, is usually voluntary. Except for minor children in families, individuals may refuse to belong to any religious, social, professional, or economic group; if they do belong, they may voluntarily leave or shift over to another such group. The right to decide whether or not to offer oneself as a member of a particular private group, to withdraw from or to remain outside it, is left to the individual.

The individual does not have this choice with public governments. It is impossible for any person to avoid coming under the rules and regulations of a county, a state, or a national government. Even if you were to move from Alaska to Florida or from Canada to Mexico, you would discover that there was absolutely no way to avoid being involved with government, whether you liked it or not. Your only choice would be in deciding on which of these governments.

Private groups also differ significantly from public governments in terms of **legitimate power.** By *power* we mean the capability to affect the lives and actions of others. By *legitimate* we mean the exercise of power that is recognized as properly belonging to those who wield it. Public government has a tremendous concentration of legitimate power. It may deprive us of our lives, liberties, or property: that is, it has the authority and capability to strip from us those precious aspects of the self that we treasure as human beings. May the family, the church, the union, the corporation legitimately take life? The answer is no. Although the family and church may have legitimately exercised such power in the past, it has long since been taken away from them.

What about liberties? Obviously minor children have restrictions imposed on their liberties by the rule makers in their families. And adults can be subjected to punishment if they engage in behavior contrary to the rules and practices of their churches, unions, or businesses. But none of these groups has the authority to imprison an individual. The power to deprive a person of his freedom of movement and association belongs legitimately only to the official public group, government.

Associated with its authority and capability for restraining liberty is government's near monopoly over the legitimate use of force. Note again the word legitimate. The right of private individuals to duel with weapons until injury or death is forbidden by government today, although it was an acceptable means for resolving personal conflict over a long period of American history. Parents may still spank their children, but any serious physical abuse of a child can lead to the arrest and punishment of the parents by government. Private police or investigators may use force to protect life or property, but they operate only with a license from and under the general rules of government. The authority to employ force against individuals belongs exclusively to government.

Government also has power to confiscate private property for public use or to regulate that property without the specific consent of its owner. Although private groups have the power to deny their members all types of services, or to deny individuals the right to belong, they may not compel their members to part with property against their will. Thus churches may levy a tithe, but if an individual refuses to pay, a church has no legitimate power to coerce that person. Union dues may be required for union membership or even job security; however, the worker willing to risk forfeiting these benefits may still refuse to pay such dues.

Differences in power are also significant in the relations between public government and private groups. Government may legitimately exercise power over the private group, but the group has no power over government. The family, for example, must have consent from state government for a marriage to be valid, regardless of the wishes of the partners or the church to which they belong. Should either partner wish to dissolve the marriage, such consent must again be obtained before a divorce can become official. What power does the family have over public government? None whatsoever. In the economic system, many businesses and professional people may not function without a license or charter from state or local governments. These governments may also regulate the conduct and even the profits of such private groups. Again, the reverse is not true. Certain religious practices may be forbidden by state or local governments, whereas no religious organization exercises power over these governments. The very existence as well as the practices of private groups may be subject to the decisions of government.

Government is at the center of the **political system.** Simple as it sounds, this observation asks you to draw a distinction between the two concepts—government and political system. In fact, it asks you to accept a paradox: Government is always political, but the political system includes more than government.

Let us make certain we understand these concepts. Government, we have said, is the human machinery that has legitimate power for making authoritative (binding) decisions for all individuals and groups in society. Who makes up this human machinery? Individuals who in their official capacities serve as legislators, judges, elected executives, and appointed bureaucrats.

The political system has government at its core but expands to include anything relating to the shaping and implementing of governmental policy, whether it occurs within or outside the framework of government itself. Thus when the people and governments interrelate with each other in any way, that interaction is political.

Most of us at one time or another interact with government either directly, indirectly, symbolically, emotionally, or intellectually. We may make demands on government or provide it with support; we may try to determine its leaders and its policies. Government invariably makes certain demands on us. Its services, regulations, or punishments affect our lives. The nature of these relationships—individuals and groups as they relate to government and government as it relates to them—is political.

The boundaries of this political system are not as precise as those of government itself. Here we are not using the term *boundaries* geographically but rather symbolically to indicate who and what are included. Private individuals and groups may direct their energies into political acts at any one time and engage in purely private acts at another. Anyone going to a Catholic mass, a professional football game, or a family reunion is engaging in a purely private activity. When that same individual participates in the Democratic or Republican party, registers to vote, pays taxes, applies for a business license, or is sentenced to a prison, he or she is involved in the political system. A group may be simultaneously engaged in both private and political behavior. For example, while some union leaders may be discussing dues and organization with their members (a strictly private and economic set of relations), others may be attempting to influence state legislators to adopt laws favoring unions in their dealings with business.

The boundaries may change as government moves out of some areas and into others. *Abortion* is defined politically as well as medically, and it used to be legally prohibited. In the 1970s the U.S. Supreme Court ruled that discontinuing a pregnancy in its first three months was strictly a matter to be decided privately between a woman and her physician. Any government regulation during this period was illegal. The Court held, however, that government might legitimately intervene after the first three months.

To summarize, the political system centers on government but also includes anything that relates to it. This set of relationships exists in an environment where individuals and groups live their nonpolitical lives. They may at any time move out of the private sphere to involve themselves temporarily or regularly in the political system, making demands on or offering support to government. So too may government extend into this private environment and move back from it, constantly changing the boundaries of the political system. The distinction between the purely private, the political, and the governmental must be grasped to understand our political system and some of the conflicts that center on it.

CONFLICT IS INHERENT IN POLITICS AND GOVERNMENT

Our political system encourages conflict; other systems do not. Because we are an open, free society, individuals and groups are more likely to voice their differences. Because we select most of our governmental leaders through official contests that actively involve the people, we encourage and institutionalize conflict. The American structure of government, as we shall see in a later chapter, is also purposely designed to foster conflict within it.

Individuals and groups naturally differ about what is good for themselves and for society. These differences in views and interests make political conflict inevitable. Although much conflict in our society is initially and essentially economic, social, ethnic, racial, or interpersonal rather than political, the degree and legitimacy of governmental power induce the contestants to bring their private claims and demands into the political system. Those who are successful in shaping the decisions and actions of government gain great advantages in resolving conflict in their favor.

Not only individuals and private groups but also officials in the different branches and levels of our government frequently disagree on public policy and administration. Conflict occurs over what should be done and how and when it should be done. Moreover, this conflict may align official decision makers in government and their allied private groups against other sets of governmental actors and their private allies.

Most of the time conflict is resolved peacefully within the rules of our political system. What these rules are and how participants in conflicts behave are aspects of the political system that you as a student must consider and that you as a member of that system may help decide.

QUESTIONS YOU SHOULD ASK

We have advanced the proposition that government is more powerful than any private individual or group. With its legitimate, almost monopolistic control over force to support it in making binding, authoritative decisions regarding our behavior, our lives, and our property, government represents the greatest concentration of power in our society. Therefore the overriding question for you to consider about the American political system is: *How should we deal with this concentration of power?*

Certain sets of questions are pertinent to your examination of the American political system. In your course of study you should raise these questions. Each chapter of this book deals with one or more of these questions and discusses some of the answers that have already been devised. But the questions are open-ended; that is, there are no definite, prescribed answers. Rather we repeatedly argue them anew in our society, fashioning different answers in the face of changing conditions and diverse groups of contestants in the political arena.

1. For what purposes should we employ our government? How far out into the environment (into the private sphere) do we wish to extend its powers? Are there certain areas of life in which governmental action should be given priority over our private values and actions?

2. What limits do we wish to place on government? Are there specific aspects of our lives that are best left to the private group and the private individual? If government's power is potentially destructive, how can we prevent that concentration of power from harming that which we deem important? How, when, where, and by what standards do we tighten the limits on the power of government?

3. How can government best be organized and arranged to operate effectively (to achieve what is intended) and efficiently (with the smallest waste of resources)? Should parts of government be kept, changed, or abandoned? Should their relations with each other be rearranged?

4. Who should participate in shaping the use of this machinery? How should this participation take place? What should and can be done to encourage participation by all who have a stake in government policy? How can the best possible people be attracted to and retained in government? Can the official holders of public power be held to ethical standards? How can the tendency of power to corrupt be minimized?

5. How should we pay for the benefits of government? Remember, nothing is free. Who should bear the costs that are involved in keeping the machinery going and in carrying out the services and benefits that government distributes?

Concepts To Study

conflict	government	power
cost	legitimacy	private groups
freedom	political system	

CHAPTER 2

THE AMERICAN POLITICAL CULTURE:
Democracy and Capitalism

Answers to the major questions we raised about government and politics in Chapter 1 are shaped in large part by the American **political culture.** This is the framework of accepted ideas, attitudes, and practices within which government operates and politics takes place. Two principal components in that political culture—**democracy** and **capitalism**—help shape the typical American approach toward government and politics.

Most Americans would characterize their society as being both democratic and capitalistic. They proudly identify with the two, believing that democracy and capitalism make their society the best in the world. It is irrelevant to argue, as some critics do, that these Americans are misinformed, that democracy has not been realized or cannot be achieved, that capitalism operates imperfectly and produces undesirable results, and that the two are basically incompatible. For it is what people believe that determines how they perceive reality.

Democracy and capitalism are fundamental belief or value systems in the United States. At an early age Americans are socialized (educated formally and informally) to accept the two as ideal types: as valid ways for ordering political and economic life. Democracy and capitalism are also seen as more than just ideal models. For most Americans they are fundamentally embodied in the institutions and practices of their society. That is, they represent what *exists* as well as what *ought* to be.

For these reasons the answers to the outstanding issues in American society are much more likely to be shaped within the context of these belief patterns than outside them. In fact, answers that lie outside the democratic and capitalistic frames of reference find few adherents and encounter either massive resistance or indifference. Unless they are cloaked in the rhetoric of these two dominant value systems, they tend to lose out in the competitive struggle for acceptance.

This does not mean that all Americans believe in democracy and capitalism, although the great majority do, or that all Americans can clearly state their beliefs and understand all the components of both concepts. What is important is that they accept democracy and capitalism as valid, essentially American attributes. It is not even necessary that they subscribe to all the components of each or apply them all in practice. It is sufficient that they identify with the basic patterns of both and see them as beneficial to themselves and to their society.

What is meant by *democracy,* and what are its essential components? What is meant by *capitalism,* and what are its essential components? To what extent are the two compatible and to what extent do they contradict each other?

DEMOCRACY: VALUES AND PRINCIPLES

Democracy is a term that represents a combination of two Greek words, *demos* (the people) and *kratos* (authority). It means rule by the people. In characterizing the government of the United States, Abraham Lincoln restated the definition as follows: "government of the people, by the people and for the people". It is not government by one individual or by a class, caste, or small permanent group but government in which the people as a whole control the power that is used in their behalf.

Although these definitions go to the heart of democratic government, they obscure key elements and leave others totally unstated. To fully understand the meaning of democracy, you must explore its fundamental value assumptions as well as its key principles.

Democratic Values

Every belief system has at its core a fundamental set of values. They cannot be proved but are asserted as a matter of faith. Thus, in a manner of speaking, democracy is a secular religion, a set of beliefs or value assumptions about human beings. Superimposed on these value assumptions are a set of principles involving relationships between government and people.

The supreme importance of the individual. Democratic theory starts with a basic assumption: the intrinsic worth and importance of the individual. Because we are human beings, each of us is valuable. Is this demonstrable? No, it is a matter of belief, grounded either in religion (our Judeo-Christian heritage views human beings as creatures of God and as reflecting the sacredness of their Creator) or in secular humanism. Since the principal emphasis in democracy is on the inherent worth of the person, government is measured by its usefulness to and respect for the individual.

Liberty or freedom. If individuals are intrinsically important, they should have the freedom to determine, insofar as possible, their own destinies. Their basic worth is lessened if they are not free to select their own goals and life patterns. Self-determination, arranging one's life with a minimum of interference from others, is possible only in a society where people have freedom, or liberty. According to democratic theory, individuals should be free to make their own choices because individuals are important and because they, better than anyone else, know their own interests and needs. Democracy assumes that individuals can make rational choices about their own futures.

Although **liberty**, or freedom, is a basic value in democracy, absolute liberty for all individuals ends up in anarchy or chaos, with an inevitable loss of freedom. Thus, liberty, or freedom, demands some government. Paradoxically the power of government to make rules and impose punishments both limits and expands freedom, or liberty. It is obvious that government rules and regulations impose restraints on the freedom of people. But what is not so obvious is that government can also advance freedom; it does so by compensating for the personal powerlessness of individuals to cope with the massive restraints that private elements of society impose upon them.

There is no secular truth. The initial democratic premises—the supreme worth of the individual and the importance of liberty, or freedom—demand still another assertion of faith: No answer to the human predicament is an absolute truth. Any claim that a specific scientific, economic, social, religious or political answer is the only possible, acceptable truth and that all others should be denied because they do not represent the truth constitutes a repudiation of individualism and freedom.

Individuals should be free to examine whatever they wish in looking for answers. All answers, and especially those adopted by governments, should be considered only tentative or provisional and should be open to challenge, even rejection. New answers should themselves be subject to reexamination, reformulation, and possible rejection.

According to democratic theory, no individual, class, political party, leader, or government has the ultimate answer, the only truth. If this were so, everyone else would be wrong and should be restrained from teaching error or questioning what was clearly truth. At that point freedom would disappear and so would the significance of the individual.

Equality of individuals. The fourth premise on which democracy rests is a belief in the **equality** of all individuals. Again, this cannot be proved.

We are born with different talents, physiques, intelligence, temperaments, advantages, and opportunities. But each of us is human, and each of us shares in the humanity of others. Each of us is, therefore, inherently equal in importance or value and equally deserving in our right to freedom.

This emphasis on equality leads to a denial of the belief that the rich are intrinsically better than the poor and that those of one race, religion, or nation are better than those of another. Because individuals are inherently equal in value, all deserve to be considered equal in worth until they demonstrate otherwise by their behavior. Government must not favor one individual or group over another. Rather it must treat each individual with the same dignity, respect, and fairness.

Democratic Principles

A number of principles emerge from the values of individual worth, liberty, no absolute truth, and equality. These principles define democratic government for us in more precise terms than "government of the people, by the people and for the people." They provide additional standards by which to judge whether or not a political system is democratic.

The bridge between values and principles of democratic government is exemplified in the Declaration of Independence, which Thomas Jefferson drafted in 1776 to argue the case of the American revolution before the rest of the world.

> We hold these Truths to be self-evident, that all Men are created equal, that they are endowed by their Creator with unalienable Rights; that among these are Life, Liberty and the Pursuit of Happiness—that to secure these Rights, Governments are instituted among Men, deriving their just Powers from the Consent of the Governed. . . .

Note that the Declaration of Independence rests upon certain assumptions, starting with the proposition that its "truths" are "self-evident."

Government exists to serve the people. The primary purpose of government, its principal justification according to democratic theory, is to protect and enhance its people: not the few, not the rich, not any privileged party or class, but the people as a whole. Government should be their servant, responsive to their wishes and concerned above all with their interests. A government that defines its purposes in these terms will more readily honor their individuality, protect their liberties, treat all as if they were roughly equal in value, and respect their right to challenge ideas, no matter how orthodox. Those who occupy positions of authority in government, and therefore wield its tremendous powers, must accept the people as their ultimate masters and the well-being of the people as their purpose for governing.

Government should be based on the consent of the governed.   In a democracy, the **consent** of the people, those who are governed, legitimizes the operation of government. Those who make the rules and impose the punishments or the rewards as officials of government do so in the name of the people. Only if the people have agreed to rules made in their name can the public officials and the rules be said to reflect the wishes of free individuals. Government must, therefore, be based on the consent of the governed.

Consent is expressed through free elections.   **Elections** afford individuals an important voice in government. By participating in free, open elections, which decide either who their public officials will be or what particular rules will be adopted, the people give their consent to government. When they vote in favor of one set of candidates over another, the people consent to elected officials employing governmental power in their name. When they vote directly on specific laws, the people give their consent to having these laws govern them.

Consent can only be given if elections allow the people a chance to make *meaningful choices* about public officials and laws. To be meaningful, the choices must be real; that is, they must offer significant alternatives. The voters must be unrestrained from fear of punishment in making their choices. Those who offer themselves as candidates for public office must be unrestrained to compete against one another, including those already in government, for the approval of the people.

If they wish to continue to exercise the power of government in the name of the people, elected officials must regularly subject themselves to a popular vote by the people. At these times the people have the power to continue them in office or repudiate them and replace them with other leaders. Those who are defeated must give up their offices to their opponents who have won the most recent expressions of popular consent.

Free, meaningful choices, competing sets of politicians, decisions made by votes of the people, regular elections, and the peaceful transfer of power to the popularly elected victors characterize what is called **representative democracy.** This is a governing system in which the people in free elections choose representatives to rule in their name.

Elections may focus on proposed laws rather than on competing sets of contenders for governmental office. When voting on the laws themselves, the people rather than their elected representatives are making the rules of government. This is called **direct democracy.** Direct democracy may exist side by side with representative democracy in the same political system. However, the larger the political system and the more diverse its population, the more likely it is to be ruled through elected representatives rather than by the people directly. Modern democracies are either completely or predominantly representative; where it exists, direct democracy only operates as an adjunct to representative democracy.

Votes should be allocated equally and to as many people as possible. Equality in democratic theory translates in practice into equality of voting power. A vote is a share of power in an election. Since elections determine who make the rules of government or what these rules shall be, each individual who is to be governed should have an equal share in that voting power. If all individuals are inherently worthy and equal as human beings, each one should have one vote, no more and no less.

Ideally, everyone who is governed should be permitted to vote on the rulers or the rules of government. However, practical considerations of maturity and responsibility mandate an electorate restricted to the adult members (citizens) of a political system. Any further restriction— exclusion of individuals on the basis of race, color, sex, age, wealth, religion, or political views—contradicts basic democratic values and principles.

The majority rules. The principle of **majority rule** is fundamental to the conduct of democratic decision making. Majority rule means a governmental system in which the principal public officials are chosen by and are responsible to the popular majority and in which rules that are voted on directly by the people are decided by a majority vote. A majority vote in an election contest is defined as a number equal to one more than half of those cast in the election.

Ideally, for government to be based on the consent of the governed, the consent of *everyone* should be necessary, and decisions should be made by the rule of unanimity. All individuals would have freely agreed to whatever rulers or rules governed them, and self-government would be fully operational. Unfortunately, obtaining the consent of everyone (**unanimity**) in election contests in a democracy is virtually impossible. **Individualism** accents differences, and these differences flourish in a free society. Questions relating to government and politics are invariably controversial and bring about conflict among people. Thus the rule of unanimity leads inevitably to *no* consent, *no* government, and *no* decisions.

A majority vote offers a practical compromise between the ideal of unanimity (incorporating the agreement or vote of every individual in the making of a decision) and the practical necessity of reaching a decision. Majorities are easy to achieve when only two candidates oppose each other or when a vote is taken on a policy issue, since there are only two alternatives. Majorities are more difficult to achieve when more than two candidates oppose one another for the same office. Consequently, a less demanding standard than a majority—a **plurality**—is often acceptable in a democracy. A plurality is less than one half of the total vote cast but more than that obtained by any other candidate. It is the most votes, but less than a majority. Plurality elections are acceptable in a democracy because, even when majorities cannot be formed, election decisions must be made.

Democratic government rests on a faith that the majority will make correct decisions at least a majority of the time. But this means some of its decisions will inevitably be incorrect. Moreover, if popular majorities and the laws enacted in their name are to govern even those who disagree with them, how can this, too, be reconciled with the importance democracy assigns to individuals and their liberty or freedom? Democratic theory resolves these dilemmas by accepting the principle of **minority rights.** Although the majority governs, it must still respect the rights of minorities.

Minorities have rights.   The principle of minority rights is critical to democratic theory and government. Individuals and groups who are not part of a majority, who have not determined the decisions of government, are fully entitled to a right to be different, to express these differences, and to be treated by government with consideration. The case for the importance of minorities rests upon the bedrock of democracy—the value of the individual, the ultimate minority, and the importance of liberty or freedom. No matter how small their number or unpopular their views, members of minorities are entitled to all the rights of members of the majority, except the right to determine election results.

Minority rights are also justified on the grounds that majorities may be wrong, that they may make poor decisions, and that they may abuse power so as to destroy the very dignity and freedom of the individual, the premise of democratic government. An assumption crucial to democracy is that those in a minority may be correct in assessing a problem and in offering answers. Therefore, they must be free to express themselves, to organize, and to attempt to persuade others to join them in becoming the new majority. They must be free to criticize the majority's representatives in government and their use of power.

Minority rights are not only crucial to the self-determination of individuals in the minority, but they may work to the advantage of the majority. By challenging the ideas and decisions of the majority, minorities tend to keep the majority more responsible and alert, perhaps even saving it from serious mistakes. And by protecting the rights of individuals and groups against government, minority rights benefit members of the majority, for they may someday become part of a minority. Their rights to express their uniqueness and to compete are thus preserved for them.

Minority rights are not confined to the politics of shaping decisions in a political system. Minority rights also limit the power of government in its treatment of people. Democratic government must treat its people—all the people—with respect and dignity; they are worthwhile, valuable components of society. Because government represents the greatest concentration of power in society, this is especially important. When government impinges on the lives, liberty, or property of individuals, government must behave toward these individuals with fairness, decency, and consideration. If you have noticed, with this point we have returned to where we began: the value assumptions of democracy. Value assumptions and principles are inextricably linked together.

Democratic Values and Principles as Standards

When we refer to democracy we refer both to a set of values concerning people and to a set of principles concerning the relations between people and government. The more a government adheres to these values and principles, the more democratic it is. The more it rejects them, the less democratic it is. Values and principles constitute a set of standards for judging government. Although no political system perfectly exemplifies the democratic ideal, a number contradict it entirely.

Democracy is such an attractive belief system to most people throughout the world that even some of the most non-democratic countries today claim to be democracies. Thus the Communist dictatorships of Eastern Europe boast that they are the true "people's democracies." But words do not make reality. Individuals in these political systems are not free to disagree with their governments and have no real opportunity to vote public leaders out of power. A permanent minority, not the majority, controls power. Although elections are held and the rights of individuals are allegedly guaranteed, these elections do not reflect any real freedom of choice, and power always prevails over rights. Instead of government being the servant of the people, it is their master. The values and principles of democracy are not honored in those political systems.

Americans refer to their political system as a democratic one. At the beginning of the republic, however, democracy was an unpopular idea, one that aroused fear and contempt. To many Americans it meant mob rule and anarchy or disorder. Only gradually were the values of democracy accepted and its principles put into practice. The democratic element in the American political system has expanded as part of a continuing struggle, for there have always been those who distrusted "the people" or who sought to exclude certain individuals and groups from political rights, denying that democratic values and principles applied to them.

Today, the values and principles of democracy have become so widely accepted that most Americans approvingly identify them with their system of government and politics. This is true despite the fact that many black Americans, Mexican-Americans, American Indians, and women in our society complain that these values and principles have never fully applied to them. What is significant is that these aggrieved groups find in democracy the proper answer to their discontent. They judge the American political system and their relationship within it by the values and principles of democracy. What they want is for the democratic system to encompass them as it has the rest of the population.

CAPITALISM

It may seem strange to include **free enterprise capitalism** as part of the American political culture. Democracy clearly concerns the relationship of people and government; capitalism is concerned with the economic system —the production, distribution, and consumption of goods and services. But from the beginning of our Republic the relationship between economic and governmental decisions has constituted one of the most controversial issues of political debate.

Recall some of the questions we raised about the relationship between government and the society in which it operates. Should there be private spheres of human activity from which government should be excluded, or should government make decisions about all aspects of society? If there is to be a private sector of life, should government still have authority to intervene? If so, for what purposes and by what means?

If we add the word "economic" whenever "private" appears, you can now begin to see the tremendous implication of these questions for economic decisions and activities. Should government divorce itself from economic matters so that they are determined entirely by private decision making? Or should government assume complete responsibility for economic decisions? Should government intervene only in certain economic areas? If so, which ones, by what means and for what purposes? The debate, as well as the answers Americans arrive at, occurs within a context of values, institutions, and practices called free enterprise capitalism.

As an ideal model free enterprise capitalism is a self-motivating, self-regulating economic system. Not only does government play virtually no part in it, but government intervention is considered to be dangerous, destructive to the effective operation of the economic system, and harmful to the well-being of its participants. Why? To answer this question, we must understand the basic features and values of free enterprise capitalism.

Individualism and liberty. Capitalism starts with the same basic values as does democracy: individualism and liberty. It argues that individuals know what is best for themselves. The emphasis in capitalism is on individuals maximizing their economic self-interest, competing with others to advance their own material well-being. For free enterprise capitalism, the primary motivating force is the competing self-interests of its participants.

According to capitalistic theory, an economic system in which individuals pursue their own self-interests will be dynamic and progressive. It will lead to better products, increased production of wealth, inventiveness, and growth, and hence the improved economic well-being of everyone. The economic system will constantly stimulate itself, accommodating itself to the needs, demands, and decisions of its millions of participants.

If the production of goods exceeds the demand for them, their prices will fall, which will benefit the consumer. Less efficient producers will be driven out of the market but may engage in the production of other products in an effort to maximize their economic well-being. The remaining original competitors will seek to improve the efficiency of their production and the quality of their goods and services in order to survive. If demand exceeds production, prices will rise, benefiting producers and increasing employment. Additional competitors will be attracted into the market by the opportunity to make money, and production will increase to take advantage of the increased profits. The prices people pay for goods and services will stabilize or fall as supply meets or exceeds demand.

Competition will lead individuals to improve their business practices and skills just as it will stimulate the production of more attractive, valuable goods and services. Competition among economic producers will force them to remain alert, keen, and interested in improving their products in order to appeal to the consumers. This reflects the importance of individualism in the theory of free enterprise capitalism.

Freedom for individual economic producers and consumers is absolutely necessary, according to free enterprise capitalism. Individuals are motivated by self-gain; if they are to remain dynamic competitors, they must be free to pursue, as they deem proper, their own advantages and to profit from their economic activity. They know best what is advantageous for themselves. Hence, any artificial or noneconomic restraints on their decisions or activities reduces competition, interferes with their ability to succeed, weakens their incentives, and hampers the production of goods and services.

Private ownership, private decisions, and private profit: primary operating principles of free enterprise capitalism. Private ownership requires that the means of production and distribution belong to private individuals, companies, or corporations, not to government. If production and distribution of goods and services are in the hands of private people, they will use them to maximize their incomes. They must have absolutely no restrictions, other than those of the free market, on their ability to make *private decisions* about prices, wages, production, consumption, interest, and capital. Capitalism assumes not only that producers and consumers know what is best for their own self-interest, but that only in this manner can economic decisions and activity benefit everyone in the long run.

Private profit undergirds the justification of private ownership and decisions. Economic entrepreneurs must be free to benefit materially from their own efforts if they are to risk capital, time, effort, and reputations in establishing and operating economic enterprises. The constant search for economic rewards will provide the incentive for producers to reduce costs, to improve products, and to become more competitive. Private profit will encourage continued capital investment in economic enterprises, which will expand employment and rebound to the advantage of all participants in the economic system.

"Government Stay Out": the other major principle. Free enterprise capitalism is sometimes referred to by a French term, **laissez faire** (lěśāfâŕ), meaning "allow [them] to do," or noninterference by government. Government should stay out of the private economic system, allowing its participants to make their own decisions and to compete freely among themselves.

The assumption of free enterprise capitalism is that government destroys initiative, motivation, competition, profit, and productivity. Government interferes with—tries to plan—what should be a naturally balanced and balancing economy based on private economic decisions. Government cannot respond quickly to economic change; individual entrepreneurs who find their property and profit at stake in their

Paul Conrad. Reprinted by permission.

"Licensing is going to lead to government confiscation of automobiles, mark my words!"

decisions can. Moreover, government is tempted to intervene for noneconomic reasons—justice, equality, health, and safety, among others. Free enterprise capitalism maintains that government intervention tends to divert economic resources into nonproductive activities. This causes private economic participants to lose their freedom to make the decisions they think proper and the profits that will induce them to be dynamic instruments for economic growth and prosperity. It also affects their incentive to take risks. Workers, too, lose their motivation to work hard and increase their productivity if decisions about wages and working conditions are made for them by government rather than in the free economic market.

According to free enterprise capitalism, if workers or business people make their own private economic mistakes, they alone are penalized by losing profits or wages, capital or jobs. But if government makes the wrong economic decisions, the entire system is endangered, for its powers affect everyone. Thus the only legitimate role for government in the economic system is a minimal one: to make certain a common currency is available; to provide courts for redress so that

private economic participants can settle their differences before an
honest broker; and to guarantee peace and security so private economic
activity can continue uninterrupted by violence and disorder.

Free Enterprise Capitalism
and the American Economic System

The values and principles of free enterprise capitalism condition the
attitudes of most Americans toward their economic system and government's relation to it. Government is viewed with considerable suspicion;
private enterprise and profit are accorded the highest respect. Just as
belief in democracy constitutes a secular religion in the United States
so, too, does a belief in the free enterprise system.

In practice, however, free enterprise capitalism differs considerably
from its ideal model, which is accepted by most Americans as a form of
secular faith. The American economic system today is a highly *modified*
form of free enterprise capitalism. Although predominantly characterized
by private ownership, private decisions, and private profit, it is, nevertheless, a mixed economic system in which both government and private
participants play a part.

Government supports certain economic competitors.   Within the business and agricultural areas of the economy, certain private entrepreneurs
have at one time or another called upon government to help them
survive. Businesses have requested and received government loans, tariff
protection against foreign competition, and financial subsidies to help
them continue their operations. Farmers have turned to government for
scientific research and for crop insurance as well as for subsidies and
loans. Workers, professionals, and consumers have also sought government intervention in their behalf. Government support for certain
economic producers and consumers, therefore, is now an integral feature
of the American economic system.

Government preserves free enterprise competition.   From within the
private economic sector have come demands and pleas for government
intervention *to preserve the competitive economy.* Large trusts and
monopolies, which have tried to take advantage of their strategic position
in the economy to maximize their profits, have at times endeavored to
destroy their economic competitors and to replace a naturally determined
market price with an artificially rigged one. To defend themselves,
smaller businesses as well as farmers and consumers have asked government to intercede to keep competition open and to penalize those who
sought to impose artificial restraints on trade or who forced artificially

determined prices upon a market. Government has been called upon to guarantee that the economy remains a free and competitive one.

Government encourages and protects some monopolies. In certain areas of the economy, government has actually discouraged competition and encouraged private monopoly. Responding to the demands of some businesses, those fearing economic chaos as a result of competition, and to the demands of consumers for regular, predictable services, government has decided that private monopoly (absolute control over the market and competition) might in some cases benefit the people and the economy. Public utilities—private businesses providing electricity, gas, water, or telephone service—were afforded total control of the consumer market by local and state governments. In return, these governments reserved the authority to determine the rates these monopolies charged, the amount of profit they made, and certain of their business practices. In other economic areas—radio and television, for example—either private monopolistic control over the market or very limited competition was ordered by the national government.

Government regulates economic decisions and actions. To insure health, safety, and morals, to protect the general public against fraud and deception, and to guarantee continued economic activity, national, state, and local governments have limited the freedom of individuals, companies, corporations, and unions to make their own decisions in the economic realm. For many varied reasons government has imposed its own standards and its rules and regulations on the economic decisions and actions of many private participants in the economy. It has intervened to regulate the quality and safety of products; labor relations, wages, working conditions, and pensions; the raising of operating capital through the sales of stocks and bonds; and in times of crisis, wages and prices.

Government tries to manage the economy. Because the free enterprise capitalistic economy often goes through boom-and-bust cycles, from economic prosperity to economic depression, government has intervened to prevent depressions or at least to reduce their severity and length. It has also intervened to prevent or control inflation. By its tax policies, its own spending decisions, and its control over the money and credit supply, the national government has attempted to *manage* the economy. At the same time, the national government has sought to reduce the adverse economic impact upon individuals of unemployment, illness, disability, and old age by providing them with special governmental support systems: social security, Medicare, unemployment compensation, and others.

Government has taken over parts of the economy.   In a few instances, governments in the United States have themselves become producers and sellers of goods and services. Governments have taken over the ownership, management, and profits of certain economic enterprises, making them totally public rather than private. This is called **socialism,** and it absolutely contradicts the values and principles of free enterprise capitalism.

Public ownership, decisions, and profits at the national level of government are exemplified by the Tennessee Valley Authority, a governmental corporation that produces and sells electricity in the private market. A number of city governments own their own water and power systems; they produce and sell these products directly to their people, often excluding private competition. Some state governments have also socialized a particular business or industry. For example, North Carolina permits no private retail business to sell liquor in bottles. Only Alcoholic Beverage Control (ABC) shops, which are owned and operated by the state government, are permitted to sell bottled liquor to the people. The profits are divided between the state government and the county governments in which ABC stores are located.

On the whole, however, the economy in the United States remains overwhelmingly in private hands. It is controlled and managed by private decisions, and the profits and losses are borne by private entrepreneurs. Virtually every major industry, almost all retail and wholesale businesses, and the entire agricultural sector operate according to the principle of private ownership, private initiative, and private profit. Government support programs and regulations permeate this private economic activity, but it remains, nevertheless, a primarily private enterprise system. Indeed, the typical American approach to the relationship between government and the economy accepts and glorifies the values and principles of free enterprise capitalism.

DEMOCRACY AND CAPITALISM

Democracy and capitalism share two values: individualism and liberty. Both belief systems accept the premise that the individual is intrinsically valuable and that individuals should be free to determine their own destinies and to pursue their happiness as they define it. Both assert the primacy of the private sectors of life, and both demand that private goals, interests, and actions be respected. In both, government exists to protect and enhance the private individual and the private life; indeed, government is to be used and judged in these terms. Beyond these two shared values, capitalism and democracy either move apart or conflict.

Democracy's emphasis on equality is not reciprocated in free enterprise capitalism. A free enterprise system makes no assumption about equality and places no value on it. In fact, this economic theory assumes that, in the economic sphere of life, individuals may start unequally, compete unequally, and remain unequal. Any action to achieve economic equality or to reduce inequality might interfere with the economic initiative of other individuals and impose excessive burdens on effective producers and consumers. Under free enterprise capitalism those who earn less profit, lower wages, or smaller incomes are assumed to be the more inefficient, ineffective producers and the less successful participants in the competitive world. Any push for equality, or less inequality, in the economic sector inevitably results in a much greater role for government, a price that the free enterprise capitalistic model rejects.

Equality in democratic theory starts with the need, indeed, the right, for equal opportunity to participate in decision making—electing representative officials or voting directly on governmental decisions— and extends to the way government should treat individuals. But does equality also mean that all persons should have approximately equal opportunities to pursue their definition of happiness? If so, how far should government intervene in the private social and economic sectors of society to help individuals achieve this equality of opportunity? Should government take an active hand in reducing inequality of conditions in wealth, social standing, health protection, job advancement, professions, and so on? How far should it go in this direction and in what areas of life? How should it operate: through inducements, punishments, government expenditures, taxation, exhortation, or mandatory law? Should government go so far as to guarantee the social and economic equality of all its people? The term *equality* is open to many interpretations that impose positive obligations on government to act.

At some point, individualism (a value shared in common by democracy and capitalism) and equality conflict. Individualism stresses the uniqueness of the person and emphasizes an individually defined "pursuit of happiness." Assumed in individualism is the notion that different persons have different degrees of ability and motivation and that opportunity and rewards should reflect differences in merit. Assumed in equality is the notion that all persons are equally valuable as human beings and that the common aspects of this value should have precedence over the uniqueness and differences among them.

Democracy and free enterprise capitalism conflict on another basic point: the notion of secular truth. Free enterprise capitalism defines itself as an absolute answer. Only by incorporating its value assumptions and by operating according to its principles can an economic system function effectively and efficiently. Only through the acceptance and operation of its principles can the values of individualism and liberty be preserved. Democracy, on the other hand, is committed, beyond its own frame of reference, to no given or absolute truth. This means that democratic theory cannot accept free enterprise capitalism or any other economic doctrine as the one and only proper way for organizing the economic system.

In its emphasis on majority rule, democracy asserts a faith in the ability of government by the majority to make wise decisions most of the time. This includes economic decisions. The majority rule principle assumes that government can at times be a positive, creative instrument in the economy. This assumption is completely rejected by the ideal model of free enterprise capitalism, which emphasizes private ownership, private decisions, and private profit and assumes that intervention by any government is automatically dangerous. Therefore, to the extent that Americans accept the legitimacy of government by majority rule and adhere to the basic values and principles of free enterprise capitalism, they hold contradictory belief systems.

The democratic commitment to minority rights is potentially both a challenge to free enterprise capitalism and a support for its values and principles. In democratic theory government must respect the dignity and self-esteem of the individual, the ultimate minority. Minority rights have traditionally been advocated as a restraint on governmental power. However, a recent shift to a positive obligation on the part of government to improve the economic conditions of individuals, so as to enhance their dignity and self-esteem, also coincides with democratic values. This shift in emphasis runs head-on into the capitalistic principle that government is a dangerous intruder and should be excluded from the economic system.

The principle of minority rights may also be used to *oppose* governmental intervention on behalf of the disadvantaged and those who have suffered from economic or social discrimination. Individual businessmen and businesswomen, farmers, or workers can justifiably claim that each one of them is a minority and that their liberty and rights as minority members of society are threatened by government's using its power over their economic decisions or property to guarantee dignity and self-esteem to others.

CONCLUSION

The questions raised in Chapter 1 and in this chapter are not easily answered. Even if you agree on the underlying values of individual worth and liberty, common to both democracy and free enterprise capitalism, you have only just begun to grapple with the questions. Do you adopt the other assumptions of democratic theory as well as the principles of democratic government and politics? If you also accept the basic values and principles of free enterprise capitalism, how do you reconcile the two belief systems? Should American democracy exclude majority rule over economic matters? Or should free enterprise capitalism be drastically modified to accommodate the values and principles of democracy? If there is to be a mix of private economy and public government, what is the proper mix? Both capitalism and democracy carry with them costs as well as benefits. Do the costs of each outweigh their benefits? If we combine the two, what benefits do we lose and what costs must we pay?

Not every American believes in democracy or in all its features, but most subscribe to democracy as being both good and American. Not every American believes in free enterprise capitalism, but most subscribe to free enterprise capitalism as being both good and American. Indeed, neither of these value systems is fully realized within the United States. But both, no matter how incomplete or modified, provide the basic framework of ideas and attitudes within which modern Americans approach the relationship between government and the individual.

Concepts To Study

consent	individualism	plurality
democracy	liberty/freedom	political culture
equality	majority rule	socialism
free enterprise capitalism	minority rights	unanimity

Special Terms To Review

capitalistic principles	democratic values	laissez faire
capitalistic values	democratic principles	no secular truth
competition	direct democracy	representative democracy
Declaration of Independence	elections	

CHAPTER 3

DESIGNING THE MACHINERY OF GOVERNMENT

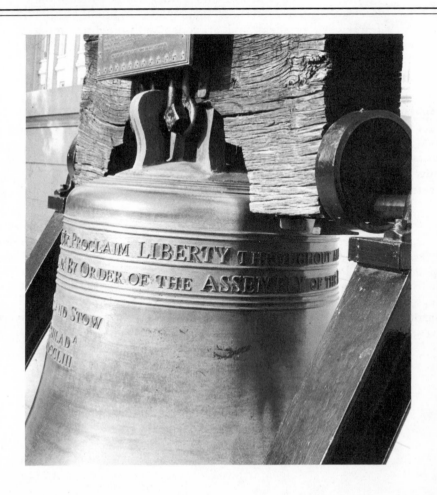

In the first chapter we considered how government relates to you and others in society. We now focus on our government as a "power package,"—how government has been put together in terms of its powers, its component parts, and its dynamic principles. And we begin to deal with two sets of problems raised in that first chapter: how best to organize government and what controls if any to place on it.

The designers of our American government were confronted with two broad sets of problems. Their first set of problems concerned how to balance national unity with diversity? How could a system of national unity be created which would permit a central government to deal effectively with national and international issues and, at the same time, preserve the integrity and independence of the local units (states). The second set of problems concerned how to control those who control power. How could effective government be established without making its leaders so powerful that they could destroy the liberties of the people?

In grappling with these basic questions, they first designed a confederate model of government and then replaced it with a federal model within a constitutional package that was both innovative and controversial. Although the constitutional-federal model is the one that continues to function today, it is still important to examine the American Confederacy, for our experience with a confederate model had a decided impact on the changeover to our present system.

MODEL ONE: A CONFEDERATE UNITED STATES

From 1781 to 1789 the United States governmental system was essentially a confederate one. A **confederation** is an alliance among independent states that establishes a minimal degree of unity among them while enabling each state to retain maximum power to itself. The basic units in a confederate system are established, independent state governments plus a very weak central government that they create and in which they participate.

The American leaders who designed the confederation during the Revolution and later fought unsuccessfully for its retention deeply distrusted a strong central government. They had revolted against just such a government in England, and that experience motivated them to move in the opposite direction. Moreover, their emotional attachment, like that of most Americans of the period, focused on the level of government most directly and immediately involved with their lives—their colonies, now independent states.

The Revolution was fought under the general direction of a **Continental Congress,** an *ad hoc* or temporary national legislature in which each of the new, independent states was represented. Its sole purpose was to provide the minimal unity and direction to ensure victory. Hence it appointed the commander in chief of the Continental armies, raised and supported troops, borrowed and printed money, and negotiated with foreign countries. The states retained to themselves the primary powers of government. No basic set of rules defined the organization of the congress, its powers, or its relations with the states. In 1777 the Continental Congress proposed a more lasting formal arrangement, the **Articles of Confederation,** which was finally adopted by all the states in 1781.

Powerful States and Weak Central Government

The states retained all the original powers they had as colonies and whatever new ones they assumed in the interval before the confederation, except for those few powers expressly delegated to the central government by the Articles. They intervened with impunity even in these latter areas, and the central government was too weak to do much about it.

The central government's responsibilities and powers were spelled out in the Articles. They may be summarized as follows:

Responsibility for relations with other nation-states. The Confederate Congress alone had the power to declare war and peace, to deal with international relations and trade, and to regulate and manage affairs with the Indians.

Responsibility for internal services that afforded the people in all the states minimum common denominators. The congress was authorized to provide a common postal system, fix standards of weights and measures, regulate the value of coinage, and arbitrate interstate disputes over lands and boundaries.

Responsibility for providing the means to operate as a government. The Articles empowered congress to equip an army and navy, borrow money, issue bills of credit, appoint army officers, and requisition the states for money, supplies, and soldiers.

At first glance, this appears to be an impressive list of powers. How do we equate them with a weak central or national government, which is the mark and intent of the confederate model? First, key powers were *not* given up by the states to the national government; second, the national government was completely dependent on voluntary state cooperation to enable it to perform its assigned responsibilities; and third, the central government lacked enforcement powers over the states.

The national government was never given that most essential power—the power to tax. Instead it was merely authorized to *request* states to provide it with funds. Two important points stand out: First, the national government could not directly interact with the people of the Republic to raise taxes. The people had no obligation to support the national government with money. In effect, the states said through the Articles of Confederation that individual Americans were first and foremost members of their states. The states as separate governments rather than the people were the primary support units for the national government. Second, the funding of the national government by the states depended entirely upon the willingness of each state to cooperate with the national government. Since a national request was not a command, the states could voluntarily comply with or ignore it. As a matter of fact, the national government was always in financial trouble because states failed to make their contributions. Without a reliable source of income, the central unit in the confederacy found its power to function seriously impaired.

The power to regulate commerce among the states was also withheld from the national government. States were free to impose taxes on commerce originating in other states. Multiple and discriminatory regulations and taxes were imposed on shipments of goods across state lines as each state jealously tried to protect its own producers and sellers. Denied the power to regulate interstate commerce, the national government could not stop such restrictive practices.

The national government was empowered to raise and equip an army, but it still had to turn to the states for troops and supplies. State governments exercised their own judgment whether or not they would meet the troop quotas "imposed" upon them by the central government.

The thirteen separate states, not the national government, were the real units of political power. The national government was dependent on the states for the key elements of political "muscle" that a government must have: money and troops. The national government could do little except request states to furnish such support, and state governments could always refuse. And instead of the Republic being one integrated economic unit, it was fragmented as the states imposed economic barriers against each other.

Ineffective Organization at the National Level

The way the national government was organized and the way it operated reflected both the traditional loyalty of many Americans to their states and their fear that a central government was inherently dangerous. First, the entire national government consisted of a one-house congress. The Articles did not provide for an independent executive to assert national leadership or follow through on what the congress did. Second, the Articles failed to authorize a national judiciary that could decide disputes among the states, between the central government and a state, or between citizens of the country. The national government was not designed to be an effective instrument of government. In contrast, each state had a governor and a judiciary in addition to a legislature.

Instead of representing the American people, the national congress was an assembly of states. As independent, jealous units of government, each state had one vote in the congress. Congressmen were chosen by their respective state legislatures rather than being elected directly by the people. Congressmen were also paid by these legislatures and, as their agents, instructed by them on how to vote.

The ability of the congress to take any significant action was severely restricted by the rule that nine out of the thirteen state delegations had to agree on any important matter. This meant that a minority (less than half) had more power than any simple majority (more than half). An extraordinary majority had to be fashioned and, since it was difficult to marshal, this severely limited the congress's ability to act.

Fundamental Change Was Almost Impossible

The Articles of Confederation required unanimous concurrence by each of the state legislatures if an amendment by the congress was to go into effect. However, jealous and suspicious units of government are rarely if ever likely to agree on major changes affecting them. Since one state could veto the affirmative action of all the other states and the congress, no amendment to the Articles was ever adopted. The unanimity rule effectively prevented any fundamental reform in the confederate system.

MODEL TWO: A FEDERAL UNITED STATES

In a free society it is very difficult to abandon one model of government for another, since different groups of people may find their first principles and self-interest at stake. Nevertheless, a group of American leaders, dissatisfied with the ineffectiveness of the national government in the Confederacy and repelled by the actions of some of the states, designed a new model at a Constitutional Convention in 1787 and "sold" it to the people in the states.

Just as new models of machinery almost invariably build on prior models, the new design of government incorporated features of the Articles of Confederation and even reflected some of the same concerns and fears. But the Constitution broke new ground and in a radical way. It represented a bold willingness to experiment with power in the interest of effective national government and to build continued experimentation into the model.

A Strong Central Government

Ironically, the **Confederate Congress** had only reluctantly consented to the Constitutional Convention on the condition that the delegates confine themselves to revising and improving the Articles. Instead, the delegates framed a new constitution that changed the basic nature of the relationship between the central government and the states as well as the people.

A comparison of the pertinent features of the alternative plans before the Convention—that of the large states (**Virginia Plan**) and that of the small states (**New Jersey Plan**)—illustrates a broad concensus (agreement) among the delegates in favor of a much stronger central government.

Alternative Plans on the Powers of the Central Government as Presented in the Constitutional Convention of 1787

Virginia Plan	New Jersey Plan
1. The national legislature could enact laws in all cases in which the states were incompetent.	1. Congress was to be given a limited power to tax as well as the power to regulate interstate commerce.
2. The national legislature could veto all state laws that were in conflict with the Constitution.	2. The treaties and acts of Congress were to become the supreme law of the land, applicable within each state and enforceable in state courts.
3. The national legislature could invoke "the force of the Union" against disobedient states.	

The Constitution that was ultimately drafted built on both plans to empower a much different congress from that of the Confederacy. The new congress had its powers expanded considerably. It was authorized to tax directly, thereby raising its revenue itself, and to regulate interstate commerce. This remedied two of the principal deficiencies of the Confederate Congress. In addition, it was empowered to raise military forces by itself. Rather than being dependent on the states for revenue and for troops, the national government was now empowered to go directly to the people for support. Americans were to be directly ruled by their national government. Even more radical was the provision for **national supremacy:** The Constitution and the laws and treaties of the national government were to be *supreme* over the laws and constitutions of the states.

In effect, the basic design was changed from one of states loosely allied together in a weak national government—a confederation—to states joined together in a union with a strong, independent national government—a federation. The states remained important units of government, but the national unit now assumed an independent power position and, in its areas of power, a superior one.

A Two-House Congress Representing States and People

In designing the new system of government, delegates from the small and the large states clashed sharply over the relative advantage of their states in the new central congress. On this issue the convention almost dissolved in failure.

The Virginia Plan. The Virginia delegates spoke for the larger, more prosperous states in proposing a two-house **(bicameral)** congress. One house was to be directly elected by popular vote of the people in the states. The other was to be chosen by the first house from a list of persons nominated by the state legislatures. The formula for representation in each house clearly favored the more populous, rich states: The number of legislators from each state was to be determined on the basis of either population or wealth.

The New Jersey Plan. The views of the smaller states were articulated in the New Jersey Plan. It called for a one-house **(unicameral)** congress in which each state was to be equally represented. Clearly this formula, a continuation of the organization and representation formula in the Confederate Congress, would have preserved for the small states the voting strength which they would not have on the basis of population or wealth.

The Connecticut (Great) Compromise.   The desire for a stronger central government, inherent in both plans, now warred with the basic suspicions and jealousies that consumed the delegates as representatives of their states. The different groups of delegates feared that their states would be at a disadvantage in having a voice in and influencing national power. Only a recognition of the overriding importance of a stronger system of national unity ultimately induced the opposing delegates to compromise.

A committee made up of representatives from each state delegation at the convention (Rhode Island never sent delegates) hammered out a third formula. Each set of contestants obtained something that it advocated, but each gave up something as well. The result was called the **Connecticut or Great Compromise** because it was the linchpin that held the Convention together.

The large states obtained the two-chamber Congress which they desired. In one chamber, the House of Representatives, states were to be represented in proportion to their respective populations, and the congressmen were to be elected directly by the people. Although the smaller states were forced to give up their demand for a unicameral congress, theirs was the form of representation that was built into the second house, the Senate. Each state was to have two votes in the Senate, which meant equal representation, and each pair was to be selected by its state legislature.

Both the controversy itself and the solution reflected the fact that the people and their leaders were still only minimally Americans. Even delegates committed to a stronger, unified system of government found that their state loyalties surfaced very quickly in any fight over power. In effect, then, our present Congress is the result of an eighteenth-century compromise, one of whose basic premises is *not* valid today. For the overwhelming majority of Americans today, primary loyalty to one's state is no longer paramount. We conceive of ourselves as Americans first.

A Strong Chief Executive

A third radical innovation was the creation of a chief executive officer, separate from the Congress, with a special branch of the national government responsible to him. No independent or powerful chief executive had been designated by the Articles of Confederation.

Both the Virginia and New Jersey plans called for a national executive, revealing the consensus among the delegates on the need for strong leadership. There was less agreement on whether the chief executive should be one person or an office shared by a number of equal political leaders, or on whether the chief executive should be chosen by Congress or some other group. The final decision was in favor of a single chief executive (a president) who was to be elected (as was a vice president) by a special group of electors, selected according to the preferences of each state legislature. In the event that these electors failed to make the choices, such responsibility was assigned to the Congress.

The president, it should be noted, was to be the chief executive of the new national government; he alone was responsible for carrying out the laws that Congress made. At the same time, he was more than an administrator of legislative policy. He was given both independent powers as well as shared powers with the Congress in determining national public policy and in selecting leaders for the executive and the judiciary. He was to be the leading actor in our relations with other countries, and he was to be the commander in chief of the armed forces. The new President of the United States emerged as a very significant political actor.

A National Judiciary

Consensus also existed among the delegates for a distinct national judiciary; both the small and large state plans called for one. Thus the Constitution specifically provided for a national Supreme Court, its method of selection, and its jurisdiction. Congress was empowered to create such other national courts as might be required.

A "Reasonable" Method for Changing the Basic Rules

You will recall that unanimity among the states was necessary for ratifying any proposed congressional amendment to the Articles of Confederation. A negative decision by any one state, or even its unwillingness to consider the proposed amendment, defeated it.

The partnership of national and state governments in changing the fundamentals was retained in the Constitution. However, the individual states were stripped of their absolute veto power. Instead of the rule of unanimity, the new ratification formula called for approval by only three-quarters of the states. Fully one-quarter could disagree and the amendment would still be adopted.

Protecting the Rights of Individuals

The Constitution, in contrast with the Articles, contained certain prohibitions against governmental abuse of human rights by both the states and the Congress. However, it made no reference to the fundamental rights many Americans felt they had fought for in their Revolution and that they considered vital to their liberty as free men—freedom of speech, press, assembly, religion, and so forth. A philosophy of fundamental rights had been articulated for them by Thomas Jefferson in the Declaration of Independence, and many of these rights had already been written into state constitutions to protect the people against their state governments.

As drafted in 1787 the Constitution was only a proposal by a national convention. To replace the Articles of Confederation, the Constitution had to be ratified by special conventions representing the people in at least nine of the thirteen states. Thus the ratification procedure in the Articles of Confederation, with its requirement of unanimous approval by the thirteen state legislatures, was bypassed.

The new design of government met with great opposition in a number of states. Some people objected to the "illegal" ratification practice. Others feared that a strong central government with power over states and individuals was a dangerous return to the tyranny of England against which they had revolted. Many opponents, and they constituted a sizable bloc, especially in key states such as Massachusetts, New York, Pennsylvania, and Virginia, argued against ratifying the Constitution on the fundamental ground that it lacked a specific guarantee of basic rights. It was pointed out that property rights had been specifically protected in the new Constitution, states being prohibited from "impairing the obligation of contract." Were human liberties deemed less important than property rights? Why not limit the power of the national government, it was argued, in favor of basic rights as had been done in many state constitutions?

In a number of key ratifying conventions, the proponents of the Constitution were forced to support the idea of amending it through the adoption of a bill of rights that would limit the national government's power. Only in that way could they swing enough votes to win the necessary majorities in favor of ratification. Without the promise that such protection would be immediately proposed by the new Congress, the Constitution would never have been approved. In that sense, the addition of these individual rights may be said to be part of the original Constitution. In 1789 the first Congress under the new system submitted such amendments to the states, which quickly ratified ten of them. Known as the **Bill of Rights,** they mark the political compromise that secured the ratification of the new design of government.

Sectional Compromises
Reflected in the Constitution

A number of features of the new Constitution reflected compromises that resolved sectional conflicts among the delegates.

The Three-Fifths Compromise.   The **Three-Fifths Compromise** bridged the difference between southerners and northerners as they tried to maneuver for a more advantageous position vis-a-vis the new central government. Southerners wanted slaves counted as equal members of their population for the purpose of determining the number of congressmen that southern states would have in the House of Representatives. Since slaves were property and could not vote, to include them in the population would have expanded the number of representatives that southern whites and the slaveholding interests had in the House. Ironically, the North also wanted slaves to be counted as equal members of the population, but only for the purpose of a capitation (head) tax that the national government was empowered to levy. Since the states were to pay this tax on the basis of their population, including the slaves as equal units of population would have increased the taxes white southerners had to pay.

The eventual compromise consisted of counting each slave as three-fifths of a person for determining both representation and head tax. On paper the South and North both gained, each receiving as well as relinquishing something it desired. But in reality the southern states were the only winners, for Congress never levied a capitation tax and the congressional strength of southern states was vastly inflated as a result of slaves being counted as part of their populations.

Limiting the slave trade.   On the issue of limiting the slave trade from Africa, sectional lines were somewhat blurred. Virginia, as part of the upper South which produced a surplus of slaves, wanted to sell them in the American market without competition from Africa. At the same time, the states of the lower South wanted the African slave trade continued because they were heavy consumers of slaves. Slaves brought directly from Africa were cheaper to buy than those raised in the United States.

The compromise consisted of permitting the slave trade from Africa to continue, but only until 1808. In the meantime, a national import tax could be imposed, not to exceed ten dollars per person imported. This compromise helped equalize competition for the American producers of slaves, and it eventually helped abolish altogether the infamous slave trade from Africa.

A tax on imports but not on exports.   Southerners, who sold their agricultural products abroad, wanted to protect exports from taxation so they could keep and expand their markets overseas. They also wanted no taxes imposed on the many products they were required to import. On the other hand, the new industries of the North wanted protection against competition from manufactured goods entering the United

States. The compromise consisted of empowering the new national government to tax imports but not exports. Representatives of both sections were satisfied that their interests were being protected. The prohibition against an export tax on American products was a form of protection or support for southerners, while a tax on foreign-made goods constituted a protection for northerners.

THE DYNAMIC PRINCIPLES OF AMERICAN GOVERNMENT

It is not sufficient to think solely of our Constitution and the system of government created by it in terms of components of government and types or arrangements of power. You must also conceptualize (think of) our system of government in terms of the dynamic principles inherent in its organization and operation. You will find none of these principles stated explicitly in the Constitution, but each is intrinsic to that document and to our system. In our next chapter we will introduce additional principles.

Federalism

In **federalism** power is divided between two independent levels of government, central and state, each of which directly rules the people. The people belong to two different components of the same unified system. Central and state governments obtain their separate powers and functions independently from a superior constitution, rather than from each other. The central government is not dependent upon the states for power. In fact, the powers of the central government, insofar as they are authorized by the Constitution, are *supreme* over those of the states. Remember the supremacy clause that was written into the Constitution and that first appeared in the plan of the small states.

Federalism also involves special sets of relations: between central and state governments; between the central government and its people; between state governments and their inhabitants; and among the states themselves.

Representative or Republican Government

Representative or republican government calls for decision-making power to be in the hands of regularly elected leaders and not in the hands of a king and his dynasty, a self-perpetuating group of nobles, wealthy people or clergy, or a dictator. In a republic, elected representatives of the citizens who have the vote serve limited terms of office, renewable upon their reelection.

This principle was *directly* embodied in the U.S. House of Representatives, whose members were to be chosen by a popular vote in the states. It was *indirectly* embodied in the U.S. Senate, whose members were to be selected by state legislators who themselves had been elected by a popular vote. It was *very indirectly* embodied in the executive; the President and Vice President were to be elected by a special set of representatives (called electors), who were chosen according to the wishes of the legislatures of the various states. The U.S. Supreme Court was the furthest removed from the principle of representative government. Its members were to be selected through joint action of the President and Senate, both indirectly chosen, and the justices served for life or good behavior rather than for limited terms of office.

Democracy, defined as popular government in which the people directly rule themselves or directly choose their chief decision makers, was *not* the principle that the framers had in mind in designing the Constitution. The overwhelming majority of the delegates who met in 1787 were suspicious of the passions of ordinary men, questioned their wisdom, and feared their economic interests. Among the four units of the central government—House, Senate, President, Supreme Court— only the first was directly chosen by the people. The others were one, two, or three steps removed from their voice and control.

The principle of republicanism was also directly embodied in a mandate placed by the Constitution on the national government: to guarantee every state a republican form of government. And it was indirectly reinforced by the prohibition against the national government's granting titles of nobility.

Separation of Powers

Just as federalism divides or distributes power between two geographical levels of government, national and state, so **separation of powers** divides or distributes power into *separate sets of hands at any one level of government.*

The framers of the Constitution were determined that, in a national government of increased power, all power would not be vested in the legislature alone. Consequently, the Congress was given legislative power, the President executive power, and the Supreme Court and other courts judicial power.

The American system reflects a fear of concentrated power; it did so in 1787 and it continues to do so today. The designers equated concentrated power with tyranny, with the government against which they had made a revolution. A concentration of power in government was considered potentially dangerous to the existence of a free republic and to the liberties of the people. Although the delegates in 1787 favored a stronger central government than that set up under the Articles of Confederation, they were nevertheless suspicious of the possible abuse of power by decision makers in the national government.

They confronted a paradox: how to reconcile the design for a more powerful central government with the apprehension that increased power automatically expands the possibility for its misuse and for the oppression of the people. Since the Constitution, as compared with the Articles of Confederation, called for a substantial expansion of national power, the dispersion of this power became a matter of major concern.

How could the advantages of power be gained and, at the same time, its abuse prevented? How could an effective national government be established without having those in power consume the republic? Separating, or dividing, power was one solution. The three major responsibilities of government—making the law, executing and enforcing the law, interpreting the law—were placed in different sets of hands, that is, different groups of political actors. Note also that the President, the Supreme Court, the House, and the Senate were authorized and empowered by the Constitution and not by each other. The designers even made certain that the political actors in each branch were chosen by separate methods and from different electoral bases. In addition, they were given different terms of office: four years for the President; two years for the House; six years for the Senate; life or good behavior for the Supreme Court. This granting of *unique powers* to each of the different branches of government and their *independence from each other*, in terms of their authority to exercise power, are critical to the principle of *separation of powers*.

Dividing power among separate sets of political leaders, with each having distinct responsibilities, would, it was hoped, prevent any person or group of people—any popular majority or minority—from having at their disposal all the powers of the central government. The designers of the Constitution were apprehensive that those holding power would and could abuse it for their group or individual self-interests. Separation of powers constituted a corrective design principle that went to the heart of this concern.

You should be aware of another representative model of government utilized by many countries that *does* concentrate power—the parliamentary model. The essential principle of **parliamentary government** is the concentration of both legislative *and* executive power in the hands of the same general set of political actors—the legislators.

Canada, our neighbor to the north, which also has a federal and representative government, is organized on the parliamentary principle of concentrated power. Its legislators choose the leaders of the executive from among themselves. This holds true both at the national level of government and in their provincial (state) governments. The executive leaders—the prime minister and his cabinet—are also legislative leaders; they set the agenda for the legislature, participate in and lead its debates, and vote on issues it confronts. As executive leaders responsible for the administration of government, they are accountable to the legislature. They may be voted out of their executive positions by the legislature if they lose the support of a majority of its members on a special vote of confidence.

It is obvious that Canadians do not share with us a fear of concentrated power. The parliamentary model was one they inherited from England, the same mother country of the American colonies, but the Canadians, unlike the Americans, did not revolt. Hence there was no reason for Canadians to reject or repudiate the parliamentary model. It was theirs originally and they feel comfortable with it. So do the people in many other countries in the world.

Checks and Balances

Another solution to the paradox of how to design machinery of government with sufficient power when power itself is distrusted and feared is the principle of **checks and balances.** It was an additional safeguard to that of the separation of powers.

Each branch of the central government was given a share in the power and responsibilities of the others. Since no branch could operate absolutely by itself, each was forced to confront the wishes, views, and powers of the others. A wise Englishman, Lord Acton, shrewdly touched on the problem of power: "Power tends to corrupt, and absolute power tends to corrupt absolutely." There was to be no president who had total and uncontrolled executive power; no congress that controlled absolutely the legislative power; no judges whose power to decide law and resolve conflict was unlimited by anyone but themselves.

Under the principle of checks and balances—each branch of government afforded a share in the power of the others—cooperation is always necessary if definitive governmental decisions are to be made, and conflict is virtually guaranteed. Both the House and the Senate must agree before the Congress can adopt legislation, authorize spending for the national government, or declare war. Since each house shares in the decisions of the other, each one can frustrate the other by refusing to give its consent. The President can veto (nullify) the laws that Congress passes, and Congress (both houses acting in unison) can, in turn, override his veto. The President can nominate individuals to be judges, military officers, and executive leaders, but the Senate can nullify his decisions if it refuses to give its consent.

When we Americans say proudly that ours, in comparison with the dictatorships of the USSR or China, is a "government of law and not of men," we are defining a **limited or constitutional government.** Yet have we not thereby proposed another paradox? Men and women make up our legislatures; they are the members of the executive as well as the judiciary at the state and national levels. They make, carry out, and interpret public laws. In that case, you might contend, we are a government of men and women after all!

But by limited government we mean that men and women who wield the powers of government are as much obligated to obey the laws as any of us. They may not disobey, ignore, or violate the law. The fact that they hold positions of authority to wield power does not exempt them from accepting the limitations inherent in our system and the rules made in the operation of that system.

National decision makers must operate in accordance with their grants of power and within the restrictions of those powers prescribed by the U.S. Constitution, the supreme law of the country. This is also true for state officials, who are in addition bound by their own state constitutions. And although both sets of officials make law—legislative, administrative, and judicial—they are as much bound by such laws as they are by the supreme law of the land. By accepting the supremacy of the law over themselves, officials acknowledge as legitimate the principle of limited or constitutional government.

This is both an ideal in our political culture and the predominant observance on the part of our officials. That the principle is not always accepted or practiced was demonstrated in a most dramatic way by the infamous Watergate scandal in Washington, D.C., from 1972 to 1974, that involved President Richard M. Nixon, his top associates in the White House, and even some of his cabinet members.

The essence of Watergate was that the President assumed he could ignore or break the law at will, that he and his associates were in fact above the law. The shock of Watergate to our political system lay in our learning that the President and his associates had become corrupted by power and that they had deliberately lied to the people and the other branches of government in order to cover up their misdeeds. Our most important national leader and his top aides had denied and violated a principle basic to the American system—the principle of limited or constitutional government. In the end freedom of the press and checks and balances, both built into the basic design of government, tripped up President Nixon and his associates and led to their downfall. The President resigned from office rather than face being impeached and convicted by the Congress. He was pardoned by his successor, but a number of his associates received prison sentences or were fined. An inevitable but unfortunate consequence of Watergate was the erosion in the invisible cement of trust and confidence that binds the people of a country to their governmental leaders.

In the long run a system such as ours survives not merely because of separation of powers and checks and balances, or even freedom of the press, but because those who offer themselves as leaders acknowledge the principle of limited or constitutional government as legitimate, necessary, and binding—in terms of their own standards and conduct. Thus the limitations prevail automatically, no matter how powerful the officials themselves become.

Concepts To Study

checks and balances	democracy	national supremacy
compromise	federalism	parliamentary government
confederation	majority	separation of powers
constitutional (limited) government	minority	unanimity

Special Terms To Review

amending process	Connecticut Compromise	ratification process
Articles of Confederation	the Constitution	representative (republican) government
bicameral legislature	Continental Congress	
Bill of Rights	New Jersey Plan	Three-Fifths Compromise
Confederate Congress	proposing process	Virginia Plan

CHAPTER 4

BUILDING CHANGE
INTO THE
BASIC DESIGN
OF GOVERNMENT

The American system of government today is a mixture of innovation and permanence: innovation, because important changes have significantly altered it since the Constitution was first conceived in 1787; permanence, because most of its original features and principles still predominate.

This chapter has two main objectives. One is to help you to understand the various mechanisms for changing the fundamentals of our system. The Constitution clearly spells out the procedures for formally amending its language. At the same time, significant changes may occur through a variety of mechanisms *outside* the constitutionally prescribed procedures. The second objective is to show you how the innovations that have emerged through these mechanisms have altered the basic design.

Change occurs for a variety of reasons and through a variety of means. Some changes are proposed to remedy obvious faults in the original design. Others are advanced to compensate for the fact that the framers of the Constitution could not, in the eighteenth century, fully anticipate the future. Each generation of Americans finds that it must reconsider the structure or principles of government to cope with its unique problems. Still other changes arise out of the bitter controversies over issues of public policy that at times divide us. Most contenders in such conflicts do no more than try to affect everyday policies of government. Others, however, are determined to rewrite or add to the basic rules, incorporating their views into the supreme law of the land.

To change is to incur risk; so is a failure to change. Unless a system is flexible enough to adapt to new conditions and new demands, the consequences for it may be disastrous. Change and risk invariably accompany each other; both are inevitable.

You may think of the Constitution as a set of fundamental rules defining the nature of the game of government and politics and naming some of the players. Ideally, everyone affected should consent to changes in the basic rules of the game, then change would not be forced on anyone against his will. From a practical point of view, such consent would virtually guarantee compliance with change. From the democratic point of view of individual freedom, self-determination, and respect for each participant, unanimous consent would be an ideal solution.

Unfortunately, the ideal of unanimity in achieving change is an illusion. The more change aims at fundamentals, the more difficult it is to attain everyone's consent. Except for the most minor issues, most proposals for change inevitably become controversial, and unanimity becomes virtually impossible to achieve.

The formal process for amending the Constitution tries to strike a rough balance between the need for practicality and the ideal of unanimity. It also requires the cooperation of the national and state levels of government that together compose our federal system. Keep these concepts in mind—a practical approach toward the ideal of unanimity and **cooperative federalism**—in examining the amending mechanisms.

The formal amending process calls for two steps: proposing and ratifying. The central government has been the key actor in proposing amendments. The states control the ratification process, although under certain centrally imposed restrictions.

Proposing an Amendment

The Constitution provides two methods for proposing an amendment, one originating in the Congress and one in the states. Only the first has ever been used. For an amendment to be officially proposed by Congress, it must be approved by a two-thirds vote in each house. Should either fail to muster this vote, an amendment is not proposed. In effect, the houses may check or balance each other. Every amendment to the U.S. Constitution thus far has been proposed in this manner.

An alternative method gives the states the initiating responsibility. Two-thirds of the states, through actions of their respective legislatures, may petition the Congress to call a Constitutional Convention in behalf of an amendment. The national legislature must then convene such a convention. The special convention proposes the amendment. So far, this proposal mechanism has never been used because no effort to persuade two-thirds of the states to petition for such congressional action has ever succeeded. Proponents of an amendment requiring the national government to operate under a balanced budget may yet accomplish this feat. During the 1978–79 congressional year, they were able to induce a large number of state legislatures to petition Congress to convene a national convention to propose this amendment.

Ratifying An Amendment

An amendment does not become a part of the Constitution until enough states have voiced their approval. Three-quarters of the states must ratify an amendment for it to go into effect.

Congress, however, determines the method of ratification: either action by state legislatures or by special state conventions. All but one of the amendments have been ratified by state legislative action. The exception was the amendment that repealed prohibition; it was the only one for which Congress authorized ratification by special conventions in each of the states.

Assessing the Amending Process

Important aspects of our political system are revealed through an examination of the amending process. Amending the Constitution is almost entirely a legislative function. Neither the President nor the national courts have any official part to play, nor do the state governors or state courts. The people as voters are also bypassed, except indirectly. The decisions are made by their regularly elected legislators or by their specially elected delegates to a national convention (never used) or state constitutional conventions (used once). In this respect the amending process exemplifies the concept of representative government.

As a mechanism for changing the fundamentals, the formal amending process tends to impede the rate of change and to require a broad-based consensus on any need for change. The obstacles facing an amendment are evident in the numbers required at each stage. Note the extraordinary majorities necessary to propose amendments: two-thirds in each house of Congress or two-thirds of the states petitioning Congress to call a national convention. Note also the extraordinary majorities required to ratify: three-quarters of all the states.

The very fact that two levels of government (state and national) must agree makes a successful completion of the process difficult. If either level does not act or concur, the amendment fails. At each level, assuming the legislatures, not the conventions, make the decisions, both houses of the required number of states and Congress must agree. Since

Congress has sometimes placed a seven-year time limit on ratification, state approval may have to occur within that limited period, otherwise the amendment fails to be ratified. Nevertheless, when the proposed Twenty-seventh Amendment calling for "equal rights" for men and women failed to win ratification within the seven-year period ending in 1979, Congress extended the deadline until June 30, 1982.

Only twenty-six amendments have been added to the United States Constitution. The first ten were immediately adopted as a package, the political bargain that went into selling the proposed Constitution. Only sixteen formal changes have been added since 1791, and two of those, the ones dealing with prohibition, cancelled each other out. The limited number of amendments is not entirely due to the difficulties inherent in the process. In our political system the ease with which change can be achieved through other mechanisms effectively reduces the pressure to use the amendment route.

Everything in the Constitution may be repealed or altered by the regular amending process *except* for changing the boundaries of a state or depriving it of equal representation in the Senate. Any amendment proposing either such action requires the consent of the state affected in addition to the mandatory two-thirds and three-quarters formula. Should that state withhold its approval, its refusal would nullify the proposed amendment even though the entire Congress and all the rest of the states agreed.

Changes Achieved through the Amending Process

How has the basic design of the American political system been altered by constitutional amendment? What changes in structure and in principles have been brought about? An examination of the twenty-six amendments to the U.S. Constitution reveals that they fall into three categories: those extending the democratic principle; those refining the federal arrangement of power; and those correcting for structural mistakes.

Extending the Democratic Principle

The original Constitution reflected its designers' preference for a representative rather than a democratic government. Yet a number of amendments have so transformed that Constitution that our political system today may accurately be designated a democratic republic.

Keep in mind some of the concepts of democratic theory that you studied in Chapter 2: the importance, dignity, and equality of the individual; control of governmental decision makers by the people through the ballot; majority rule and minority rights. Amendments that expand the system in the direction of these concepts are democratizing in effect, even if not in their original intent. After all, the end result is what counts.

Four sets of amendments built the democratic principle into the Constitution. These sets deal with: (1) individual rights protected against national power; (2) individual rights protected against state power; (3) **suffrage** (the right to vote) expanded to include all adult citizens; (4) the people's direct control extended to the election of additional decision makers.

Individual rights protected against national power.   The first ten amendments, the Bill of Rights, attest to the strong belief among Americans in the immediate postrevolutionary era that the rights of individuals were too important to be omitted from the supreme law of the land. In protecting the rights of individuals, these amendments imposed restraints on the power of the national government.

Freedom of speech, press, religion, petition, and assemblage, critical to the free formation of majorities and to the protection of minorities, are guaranteed in the First Amendment. Amendments Two through Eight address the integrity, dignity, and safety of individuals when their lives, liberties, and property are threatened by the awesome power of the national government. And the Ninth and Tenth Amendments reserve additional rights and powers to the people or the states.

Individual rights protected against state powers.   Although the nemesis of most Americans was originally the central government, it eventually became evident that to protect the rights of people states also had to be restrained by the supreme law of the land. Amendments Thirteen, Fourteen and Fifteen arose from the great moral issue of the Civil War: slavery and the need to protect the newly freed slaves from the power of hostile state governments. The impact of these amendments, however, transcended both the immediate time period and the persons who had been slaves.

The wording of these three amendments is critically important to the democratic principle in its broadest sense. They protect the rights not only of the former slaves, automatically made citizens of the United States and of their states, but the rights of *all persons*. The fact that this protection extends to persons, not just citizens, shows how wide is the sweep of these amendments.

Amendment Thirteen abolishes slavery and prohibits involuntary servitude. State laws permitting slavery as well as the private right of individuals to own other individuals are therefore forbidden by the supreme law of the land.

Amendment Fourteen protects the right to national and state citizenship of anyone born or naturalized in the United States and guarantees such persons their national rights in the states. In addition, it extends constitutional rights to all persons faced with state actions that would take from them their life, liberty, or property without due process of law. And it raises to constitutional importance the basic democratic concept of equality of individuals in its mandate that states may deprive no person of "equal protection of the law."

Amendment Fifteen, which was adopted to guarantee that the newly freed slaves would not be denied the right to vote because of race, color, or previous condition of servitude, is best mentioned in the context of an expanded suffrage.

Suffrage (right to vote) expanded to all adult Americans. A set of amendments address themselves solely to the question of voter eligibility. Although the original Constitution had left the determination of eligibility to the states, these amendments prohibit the states from denying people the right to vote on the basis of race, color, previous condition of servitude, sex, age, and money. Blacks (males) were afforded the right to vote by Amendment Fifteen; women, by Amendment Nineteen; and young adults eighteen years old and over, by Amendment Twenty-six. In 1964 Amendment Twenty-four prohibited states from imposing a special poll tax as a condition for voting in national elections or primaries. The intervention of another change mechanism, the courts or **judicial interpretation,** forbade poll taxes in state and local elections as a violation of Amendment Fourteen. No state-imposed fee may now determine who may or may not vote.

As a consequence of these amendments, the Constitution today guarantees universal adult suffrage in the United States. In terms of democratic theory adult Americans, irrespective of race, color, sex, adult age, or wealth, are now equal in their eligibility to vote for their leaders at the national, state, and local levels of government and to vote directly on policy questions in certain state and local governments.

The people's direct control (vote) extended to more decision makers. Democratic theory calls for maximizing choices individuals may make and affording them greater control over their own lives. In terms of elections, this means expanding the number of important decision makers whom people may choose.

The number of public officials chosen by the people as voters has been expanded by Amendment Seventeen, which in 1913 transferred the selection of U.S. Senators from state legislatures to the people in each state. With the passage of that amendment, the people now directly elect members to both houses of Congress.

In 1961 citizens living in the District of Columbia, a federal area governed by the Congress and not part of any state, were authorized by Amendment Twenty-three to vote for presidential electors. Thus, a group of Americans who had been disfranchised were now permitted to join their fellow Americans in choosing the President and Vice President of the United States. In 1978 Congress proposed to the states an amendment to give the District representation in both houses of Congress "as though it were a State."

One exception stands out as contrary to the democratizing amendments that have increased the number of elected national officials the people may now choose. Amendment Twenty-two limits a President to serve no more than two full terms of office and thereby reduces the options of the electorate to reelect their President more than once.

Refining the Federal Arrangement of Power

The federal principle is crucial to the Constitution; indeed, the Constitution was designed so that this principle lay at the heart of the American political system. Nevertheless, the nature of federalism has been changed through constitutional amendments.

Certain changes in federalism should already be obvious from what we have referred to as the democratizing amendments. In democratizing the American political system, limits were placed on the powers of both state and national governments, the principal components in our federal republic. The Bill of Rights was designed to limit the power of the national government in order to protect the rights of individuals. In fact, the Tenth Amendment makes clear that powers not delegated to Congress or denied to the states belong to the states or to the people.

The power of the states is limited by the other sets of democratizing amendments that deal with individual rights and the voting privilege. The national government is also restrained by the voting privilege amendments, but the impact of these amendments falls almost entirely on the states, for traditionally that level of our federal system determined qualifications for voting.

One amendment, unrelated to those democratizing the Constitution, reduces the power of the national government in favor of the states. Adopted in 1795, Amendment Eleven limits the jurisdiction of the national courts (overriding a Supreme Court decision to the contrary) so that a state may not be sued by any individual without the consent of that state. However, people may actually bring the states into court on the grounds that their national rights have been violated by an exercise of state power.

A number of amendments expand the power of the national government. None increase the powers of the states. All of the amendments that expand and protect the rights of persons against the powers of the states authorize Congress to enforce their provisions by appropriate legislation. They give the national government additional powers to restrain the states should they act in a manner contrary to the rights of individuals guaranteed by these amendments.

In addition, Amendment Sixteen (1913) frees Congress from the very restrictive taxing power that the Constitution originally granted it. Congress is empowered by this amendment to levy taxes on incomes without regard to source or population. This amendment has permitted the national government to adopt a graduated income tax and a corporate income tax. Without such an expansion of its taxing power, the national government would never have gained the tremendous resources that have enabled it to expand its role in the social, educational, and economic life of the country.

A unique power was granted both the national and state governments by one amendment, only to be withdrawn by another. The two levels of government were empowered to enforce the prohibition that Amendment Eighteen (1919) imposed on the manufacture, sale, or transportation of intoxicating liquors. This prohibition was repealed fourteen years later by Amendment Twenty-one (1933).

Correcting the Mistakes
in the Structure of the National Government

Flaws stemming from the original Constitution have necessitated changes with reference to the President, Vice President and the Congress. Amendment Twelve (1801) provides that the special presidential electors vote separately for the offices of President and Vice President. Because the original Constitution failed to specify separate ballots for these offices, the election of 1800 resulted in a stalemate in the electoral college. The Republican presidential and vice presidential candidates— Thomas Jefferson and Aaron Burr—received an equal number of votes and more than their opponents in the Federalist party. But which of the two Republican candidates was elected President? In accordance with the Constitution, the House of Representatives made the decision, choosing Jefferson. By requiring electors to vote separately for presidential and vice presidential candidates, Amendment Twelve prevents further stalemates of this kind.

Amendment Twenty (1933) advanced the date when elected officers of the national government take office. The presidential term of office now officially begins on January 20, and the new Congress takes office on January 3. Originally, the Constitution permitted a President, Vice

President, and congressmen who were defeated in the November elections to continue exercising governmental power for four additional months, into March of the next year.

Amendment Twenty-five (1967) provides a special replacement formula for the President and Vice President. The President is authorized to nominate a Vice President when that office becomes vacant. Both houses of Congress are given a voice in the nomination since the nominee must win their approval. In addition, the Vice President is authorized to take over the presidency, again only with the consent of Congress, should a President become mentally or physically incapable of fulfilling his duties. The original Constitution had not recognized such contingencies.

In 1973–74 the first part of Amendment Twenty-five was twice employed. Only a year after he had been reelected, Vice President Spiro Agnew was forced to resign, pleading no contest to charges of income tax evasion, a felony offense. The incumbent Republican President, Richard M. Nixon, immediately invoked his new power to nominate as Vice President Jerry Ford, the Republican floor leader in the House of Representatives. When President Nixon himself resigned, facing inevitable impeachment by the House of Representatives, Mr. Ford automatically became President. He then appointed Nelson Rockefeller, the former Republican governor of New York State, to fill the now vacant office of Vice President. Congress consented to both nominations.

OTHER MECHANISMS FOR CHANGING THE BASICS IN THE SYSTEM

Four major change mechanisms that enable our political system to adjust quickly to new conditions build on the *broad grants of authority* and *ambiguities* in the language of the Constitution. They are: (1) judicial interpretation; (2) congressional law making; (3) executive action; (4) state action. A fifth change mechanism is *custom and usage*, which differs significantly from the others and results from *constitutional silence* rather than language. That is, the Constitution does not speak to some important modern matters of government and politics.

Broad grants of authority and ambiguities are exemplified by such constitutional language as "the judicial Power of the United States, shall be vested in one supreme Court. . .". (Article III, Section 1). What does *judicial power* mean? What may the Court do with it? The Constitution provides no definite answer. Nor is it explicit when, after listing a number of his specific powers, it authorizes the President to exercise the "executive power" (Article II, Section 1). Does that broad phrase afford him additional unspecified powers? Although Congress is empowered by the Constitution to deal with interstate commerce, nowhere is interstate commerce defined or Congress instructed on how to deal with it. Congress is authorized to adopt laws that are "necessary and proper" in carrying out its specific powers. But *necessary and proper* is a very imprecise phrase. As we shall see in the next chapter on Federalism, almost anything can be read into it; hence its designation as the "elastic clause."

These five other mechanisms are used more frequently than the formal amending method. In addition, these mechanisms have produced equally important, if not more important, changes in American government and politics than have the constitutional amendments.

Judicial Interpretation

Early in its history, the Supreme Court so interpreted its authority as to claim the power of **judicial review** over the other branches of the national government. According to the doctrine of judicial review, the Court has the legitimate and ultimate authority to interpret the Constitution as well as to declare illegal any acts of the executive and the legislature that in its opinion violate that Constitution.

Not only was the adoption of judicial review itself a major change, but through it the Court carved out a unique and immensely powerful role for affecting change in the rest of the system. Ostensibly an equal unit with the other branches of the national government, the judiciary was now in a position to negate, approve, or modify changes in public policy that the President and Congress adopted. *The Constitution became, and remains in good part, what the judges say it means.* The Court's assertion of its preeminent position as guardian and watchdog of the Constitution, empowered to strike down what it considered unconstitutional acts, was only the first in a series of judicial decisions redefining or changing the Constitution.

Through judicial interpretation the Court has also helped democratize the Constitution. It has done this by reading some of the first ten amendments into the "due process" clause of the Fourteenth Amendment. Consequently, restrictions specifically written into the Constitution to limit the powers of the national government have been placed on the states by the Court. The vagueness of the phrases *due process* and *equal protection* has given the Court a basis for redefining the nature of federalism and for expanding the rights of individuals without additional amendments.

How judicial interpretation can change fundamentals in the state governmental structure is exemplified in the legislative apportionment controversies of the 1960s. Citizens in a number of states had appealed to the national judiciary, claiming that they were being denied fair representation in their legislatures. In some cases it was because of state legislative action or even inaction; in other cases because of state constitutional provisions. Despite many state constitutions to the contrary, the U.S. Supreme Court ordered the states to base representation in both houses of their legislatures on population and to make certain that the ratio of legislators to population was the same in every representational district. According to the Supreme Court, states that failed to establish both legislative houses on the basic principle of **one man—one vote,** or representation in proportion to population, violated the equal protection requirement of Amendment Fourteen. In effect, state constitutions were held unconstitutional according to the supreme law of the land because of the Court's interpretation of the vague phrase, *equal protection.*

Congressional Law Making

The Constitution established the bare bones or skeleton of government. Only the Supreme Court was specifically mandated for the judicial branch; all other courts were to be established by Congress. Congress created a national court system that includes three distinct layers of "judicial" courts—a large number of district and circuit courts of appeals as well as the Supreme Court. In addition, as a result of the **necessary and proper clause** and in order to carry out its other powers, Congress created special courts to deal with justice in the military and to hear appeals on such technical matters as customs, taxes, and patents. None of these courts were explicitly called for in the Constitution.

Our national executive today is characterized by a very large **bureaucracy** (those employed to carry out the laws of the United States). Yet the Constitution specifies only two executive officials, a President and Vice President. It does refer cryptically to departments and calls for an army and navy. How was the executive expanded from these two officials to the 2.5 million civilians now employed in the executive branch? By the actions of Congress.

The Departments of State (foreign relations), Treasury, Army, Navy, Justice, and Post Office were among the first to be created in accordance with the tasks assigned by the Constitution to Congress. As Congress assumed responsibility for coping with new problems, in response to public demands for help, it created additional bureaucracies to aid farmers (Department of Agriculture), businessmen (Department of Commerce), and workers (Department of Labor).

Special regulatory agencies were authorized by Congress to operate outside of the departments. These included the Interstate Commerce Commission, the Federal Trade Commission, and the Securities Exchange Commission. In recent years, to meet new conditions and challenges relating to space, Congress set up a National Space and Aeronautics Administration; to help small businessmen, a Small Business Administration; to encourage research and breakthroughs in medical discoveries, an entire cluster of National Institutes of Health.

After World War II a new Department of Defense combined the old Departments of Army and Navy with a recently created Department of the Air Force. A Department of Health, Education and Welfare (divided in 1979 into a Department of Education and a Department of Health and Human Services) was also organized. In the 1960s and 1970s, Congress authorized three additional departments—Housing and Urban Development, Transportation, and Energy—and it created special agencies, such as the Environmental Protection Agency, to cope with the new concerns of Americans.

We have at this point merely touched on the huge executive structure that Congress created. The lean executive called for in the original Constitution has grown in size and been transformed in a manner far beyond what the framers were capable of imagining in 1787. It is important to understand, however, that the enormous growth of the national executive branch and the tremendous expansion of power on the part of national bureaucracies are explained primarily by Congress's responding to new needs and new demands on the basis of the language found in the Constitution.

Executive Action

Presidents, too, have contributed to basic changes in our government. No provision of the Constitution calls for the organization of a **cabinet** to provide the President with collegial advice, to afford him aid in managing the executive more effectively, and to help him cope with the Congress. Yet starting with George Washington, all Presidents have organized their department heads into a cabinet as part of their administrations. Of late they have even provided it with a special staff.

By negotiating **executive agreements** with leaders of other countries, Presidents have circumvented the constitutional mandate that treaties with foreign nations must be submitted to the Senate for its approval. In other words, one of the traditional checks and balances is bypassed. Although the Constitution makes no mention of executive agreements, it is now a fundamental instrument of American foreign policy, accepted by the Supreme Court as well as by Congress.

Prior to the U.S. involvement in World War II, President Franklin D. Roosevelt entered into an *executive agreement* that transferred a number of American destroyers to Great Britain in exchange for the British granting us military bases along the Atlantic and in the Caribbean.

This constituted a major U.S. commitment in support of Britain's fight for existence, one which the President alone decided.

In 1945 the famous Yalta Agreement among President Franklin D. Roosevelt, British Prime Minister Winston Churchill, and Premier Joseph Stalin of the Soviet Union was also an *executive agreement.* By its terms Stalin consented to bring the Soviet Union into the war with Japan in return for an Eastern European settlement favorable to his country and its dominance in Manchuria. These three chief executives agreed to coordinate their last campaign against Nazi Germany, authorized the international conference that called for organizing the United Nations, and even agreed on some of the political arrangements for that new world government. The Yalta Agreement was never submitted to the Senate for its assessment, even though major U.S. commitments were being made.

The President's *power as commander in chief,* granted by the Constitution, has been the basis for vast extensions of executive power, far beyond that specifically called for in the Constitution. On its face, it means that the President merely heads up the military forces of the national government. But among the acts Presidents have justified under this constitutional power have been the seizure of the steel mills during a period of national emergency and the commitment of United States armed forces to military conflict. Although only Congress is constitutionally authorized to declare war, a presidential order placing U.S. troops in a military confrontation can have the effect of committing the country to a condition of war. American involvement in the Korean War and in the Vietnam War was based, in large measure, on the assertion by a number of Presidents that as commander in chief they had an inherent power to commit the U.S. armed forces into combat as well as to exercise command over them.

Presidents have also asserted an authority to invoke **executive privilege,** that is, to cloak their confidential transactions and decisions as well as themselves with immunity from congressional or judicial inquiry into executive affairs. Executive privilege is certainly not in the Constitution, but the presidential practice of claiming this authority as part of the chief executive power has helped transform it into a substantive presidential tool, one recognized by the courts.

A major issue in controversy, during the Watergate crisis in 1974, was President Nixon's adamant refusal to disclose incriminating evidence about himself and his associates, either to the national courts or the Congress, on the grounds of executive privilege. The judges refused to permit the President to withhold from the special prosecutor and the courts the famous White House tapes, recordings of his conversations with his top aides. Much of the disclosed evidence hastened both the legislative move in favor of impeaching the President and his subsequent

Does the President have to tape his conversations?

resignation to avoid that possibility. The courts, in this instance, ruled that the President was not above the law. Thus the operation of the checks-and-balances principle legitimately overrode his authority as chief executive.

State Governmental Action

To a certain extent state governments also change our basic political practices. For example, the Constitution leaves to the states the selection of electors who vote for the President and Vice President. Initially, in a number of states, the legislatures chose the electors. The people of these states had no direct voice in choosing those who selected the country's chief executive. However, states increasingly converted to the popular election, enabling the general electorate, not the state legislatures, to choose the electors. The people still do not directly elect a President. But at present, presidential electors in all the states are voted on directly by the people, which results in an extension of the democratic principle.

Custom and Usage

Certain characteristic features of the American political system have resulted from custom and usage. Although they have developed outside rather than within the Constitution, these features are integral parts of the American political system. Indeed, that system could not operate effectively without them.

Nowhere in the Constitution is any reference made to **political parties.** Yet political parties organize the electorate, afford an opportunity for individuals to compete for public office, and conduct election campaigns for leadership positions at the national and state levels. They also organize the Congress and the presidency and are relevant in the selection of judges. The same holds true with but one or two exceptions for comparable positions at the state level of government. The national government and some states even provide financial support to political parties and their candidates.

Although the Constitution is silent about political parties, ours is basically a two-party system. American government and politics cannot be understood without recognizing this fact. Most Americans identify themselves as Democrats or Republicans. Although other political parties exist in the United States and at times compete seriously with the Republicans and the Democrats, the two major parties virtually monopolize the competition.

Similarly, the vast array of **interest groups**—economic, religious, racial, ethnic—that engage in American politics are not mentioned in the Constitution. Nonetheless, together with political parties they are basic components in the American political system. Both political parties and interest groups are manifestations of the democratic spirit. They enable individuals to participate more effectively in choosing their leaders and in influencing public policies of their government.

CHANGE MECHANISMS UNIQUE
TO STATE AND LOCAL GOVERNMENT:
THE INITIATIVE AND REFERENDUM

In contrast with the national government, some of our states, counties, and cities constitutionally authorize the use of unique formal mechanisms that directly involve the people in the process of changing the fundamentals at these levels of government. Such mechanisms are the **referendum** and the **initiative.**

All state constitutions except one (Delaware) require that state constitutional amendments be voted on by the people of the state after the legislature itself has proposed them. The legislature proposes and the people, through a popular vote, decide whether or not to ratify. Since a proposed amendment is referred to the people for their decision, it is called a *referendum.* In some state and local governments, ordinary (statutory) laws that legislatures adopt may also be referred to the people for their decision. Such a referendum is initiated, or proposed, either by actions of the legislature itself or by virtue of a popular petition that prevents a law from going into effect until it has been approved in a popular vote.

In the *initiative,* constitutional amendments or regular statutory laws are proposed by some groups within the citizenry; the legislature is eliminated from the proposal stage. A minimum number of signatures from registered voters is required to place the proposal on the ballot. The vote in the popular election eliminates the legislature from the ratification stage as well. Needless to say, the referendum and especially the initiative are radical extensions of the democratic principle.

Concepts To Study

bureaucracy	democracy	one man–one vote
checks and balances	executive privilege	representative government
congressional law making	federalism	suffrage
constitutional change	judicial interpretation	unanimity
cooperative federalism	judicial review	

Special Terms To Review

amending process
cabinet
the Constitution
custom and usage
democratizing amendments
executive agreement

federal power amendments
the initiative
interest groups
necessary and proper
 (elastic) clause
political parties

presidential electors
proposing process
ratifying process
the referendum
structural
 amendments

CHAPTER 5

FEDERALISM

Federalism has always been a controversial issue in American politics. From the time it was built into the Constitution in 1787 to the present, Americans have been disagreeing over its meaning and over how it should be developed.

Some people maintain that the national government is too big, that it interferes too much in our daily lives, that it is ineffective in what it attempts to do, and that it wastes the taxpayers' dollars. They propose cutting back the national government in favor of state and local governments. These sentiments helped spur many state legislatures to petition Congress in 1978–79 for a constitutional convention to propose an amendment forcing the national government to operate within a balanced budget, in effect, to sharply restrict its activities.

Other Americans claim that many state and local governments are grossly inefficient and ineffective: unable, at times even unwilling, to provide properly for their own citizens. They argue that such governments are incapable—because of insufficient resources and very limited jurisdictional control, among other reasons—of coping with economic, social, and environmental problems that are national or sectional in scope and whose solutions require the expenditure of vast sums of money. These people call for increased national planning and spending and the adoption of national standards to govern various aspects of our lives. Many within this group contend that only the national government is capable of dealing with national economic and social problems. Without the mobilization of this government's power and resources, they say, those most disadvantaged in American society and in greatest need of help will be ignored.

Despite the heated debate that federal issues engender, both sides accept the legitimacy of strong, independent governments at both the

©1976 by Herblock in *The Washington Post*

"Ha, ha—of course I'd tell him not to bother YOU!"

state and national levels. Where they disagree is over what constitutes a proper balance among national, state, and local governments. How should one strike that balance, on what policy issues, and under what conditions? These are some of the meaningful questions that confront us in the latter part of the twentieth century.

The controversy over a proper balance was dramatically demonstrated in the 1975–76 campaign to save New York City from bankruptcy. You might reasonably ask how that city, or any city for that matter, fits into the federal formula. The Constitution deals solely with national and state governments; cities are not even mentioned. In practice, however, cities have become partners in the federal system, and without any constitutional amendment to justify that change.

In 1975 New York City had reached a point where it could not raise sufficient revenue to repay its debts and meet the costs of the services it provided. Clearly a bad risk, it was unable to borrow additional funds in the private money market. If the city could neither borrow nor generate enough money through taxes, it would go bankrupt, undermining its ability to serve its citizens.

The state of New York, itself in serious financial trouble, was unable to rescue its major city. In desperation, the state's governor and the city's mayor solicited their representatives in Congress to enlist the aid of the national government. Initially unsympathetic, Congress eventually drafted a legislative aid package. Rescuing the city provoked one of the most heated national debates of 1975. Among the adamant opponents of national aid was President Gerald R. Ford, who repeatedly threatened to veto any legislation that permitted the city to avoid bankruptcy. Finally, even he reversed himself, as private and public sentiment swung behind the city's appeals.

In an unprecedented step national, state, and city governments joined in a plan of action. New York City agreed to impose a rigid set of economies on itself to bring its operating costs under control. New York State agreed to raise money to aid the city but set up its own board of overseers who virtually took over the city's fiscal management. Congress and the President agreed on a law authorizing the secretary of the treasury to lend up to $2.3 billion a year to the city for a period of five years. In June 1976, when national officials concluded that city leaders were avoiding the tough decisions on imposing economies, the Senate Banking Committee and the secretary of the treasury demanded that the city grant no more wage increases to its employees, that it reduce their fringe benefits, and that it reexamine its policy on rent control. New York City had no alternative but to comply.

This joint package of national-state-city cooperation speaks to the new balance that is part of the dynamic federalism of the twentieth century. However, to understand **modern federalism,** you must first understand **traditional federalism.** The new federalism is based in part on the old, and both traditional and modern exist side by side and will continue to do so. Traditional federalism has been likened to a cake with two distinct layers of government, national and state, each operating basically on its own. In modern federalism not only has a local government layer been added, but the new federal cake has become a marble cake; the distinctive layers have been replaced with an intermingling of the three types of governments.

TRADITIONAL FEDERALISM

The Constitution appears to define the federal arrangement in our system in clear, precise terms. It provides for two basic federal components, a national government and state governments, each of which receives its powers directly from a superior Constitution. Thus each is independent from the other in terms of its source of power, and each deals directly with its people. The Constitution limits both sets of governments and spells out a mandatory set of minimal relations among the states as well as between state governments and the national government.

Separate National and State Powers

According to the Constitution, the national and state governments have separate sets of powers. Those belonging to the national government are delegated to it by the Constitution. Those belonging to the states are what have not been granted to the national government or denied to them. Hence we refer to two separate sets of powers: **delegated** national **powers** and **reserved** state **powers.** Nevertheless, this separation is not as specific as it appears, as we will see in our discussion of modern federalism.

In Article 1, Section 8, the Constitution prescribes the power of the national legislature to make public policy for the entire country. Such powers are listed for your convenience in Table 5–1, "Constitutional Powers Delegated to the Congress." These powers fall into two categories: *enumerated* and *implied.* Among the **enumerated** (explicitly stated) **powers** are the power to regulate interstate and foreign commerce, impose import and capitation taxes, coin money, create a military establishment, engage in war, and establish a postal service. At the same time, Congress is authorized to adopt such laws as are "necessary and proper" to carry out these powers. This authorization is called the **implied powers clause** in view of the wide range of possible implications found in the words *necessary* and *proper.* Congress is also authorized to provide for the "general welfare," another term open to varied meanings. Both fall into the category of **implied powers:** powers stated so broadly and ambiguously that almost anything can be read into them.

Although the Constitution frequently refers to the states, it never assigns them any specific powers. The original Constitution, adopted in 1787, fails to mention any state powers except to indicate what states may not do. However, the Tenth Amendment makes explicit what the drafters really intended: "The powers not delegated to the United States nor prohibited by the Constitution to the states are reserved to the States. . . ." Since we know the limited number of powers assigned the national government, the powers reserved to the states obviously encompassed a tremendous range.

What are these so-called reserved state powers? Draw your own inferences from the list of the congressional powers in Table 5–1. You

Table 5–1
Constitutional Powers Delegated to the Congress

The Congress shall have Power

To lay and collect Taxes, Duties, Imposts and Excises, to pay the Debts and provide for the common Defence and general Welfare of the United States; but all Duties, Imposts and excises shall be uniform throughout the United States;

To borrow Money on the Credit of the United States;

To regulate Commerce with foreign Nations, and among the several states, and with the Indian Tribes;

To establish an uniform Rule of Naturalization, and uniform Laws on the subject of Bankruptcies throughout the United States;

To coin Money, regulate the Value thereof, and of foreign Coin, and fix the Standard of Weights and Measures;

To provide for the Punishment of counterfeiting the Securities and current Coin of the United States;

To establish Post Offices and post Roads;

To promote the Progress of Science and useful Arts, by securing for limited Times to Authors and Inventors the exclusive Right to their respective Writings and Discoveries;

To constitute Tribunals inferior to the supreme Court;

To define and Punish Piracies and Felonies committed on the high Seas, and Offences against the Law of Nations;

To declare War, grant Letters of Marque and Reprisal, and make Rules concerning Captures on Land and Water;

To raise and support Armies, but no Appropriation of Money to that Use shall be for a longer Term than two Years;

To provide and maintain a Navy;

To make Rules for the Government and Regulation of the land and naval forces;

To provide for calling for the Militia to execute the Laws of the Union, suppress Insurrections and repel Invasions;

To provide for organizing, arming, and disciplining, the Militia, and for governing such Part of them as may be employed in the Service of the United States, reserving to the States respectively, the Appointment of the Officers, and the Authority of training the Militia according to the discipline prescribed by Congress;

To exercise exclusive Legislation in all Cases whatsoever, over such District (not exceeding ten Miles square) as may, by Cession of particular States, and the Acceptance of Congress, become the Seat of the Government of the United States, and to exercise like Authority over all Places purchased by the Consent of the Legislature of the State in which the Same shall be, for the Erection of Forts, Magazines, Arsenals, dock-Yards, and other needful Buildings;—And

To make all Laws which shall be necessary and proper for carrying into Execution the foregoing Powers, and all other Powers vested by this Constitution in the Government of the United States, or in any Department or Officer thereof.

will find few congressional powers that affect you directly. There are no references to health, safety, morals, education, marriage, divorce, gambling, land use, property, entertainment, agriculture, business, industry, or labor. The list could go on almost indefinitely. Because power over these areas of life was not delegated to the national government, presumably it belonged to the states.

For approximately the first one hundred and fifty years of our existence under the Constitution, it was generally assumed that power to make public policy in those areas properly belonged to the states and their local units, the cities or counties. These governments were more intimately involved with the daily lives of most Americans; the national government remained rather remote.

Jointly Held (Concurrent) National-State Powers

Certain powers belong to both national and state governments. These are referred to as **concurrent powers**, of which taxation is one. Note that the national government's power to tax was originally limited principally to a capitation (head) tax, never employed, and an import tax. Obviously other types of taxes were left to the states in accordance with the concept of reserved powers. When in the twentieth century a constitutional amendment empowered the central government to employ other means of taxation, the traditional power of the states to tax was left unchanged.

According to the U.S. Supreme Court, states may sometimes act in areas specifically delegated to the national government, but only under narrowly defined conditions. States and localities may make laws affecting interstate commerce, but these regulations must be reasonably related to state powers and must not place an undue burden on such commerce. For example, a state may impose speed limits and other safety restrictions on trains traveling within its boundaries, even though they are simply passing through to get to another state. And in the interest of protecting their roads, states may impose their own limits on the weight carried by trucks in interstate commerce.

Restrictions on National and State Powers

Just as the Constitution authorizes the use of state and national power, it also imposes restraints on both. The most significant restriction on their powers lies in the fact that both the state and the nation are subordinate to the U.S. Constitution, which is the supreme law of the land. In a conflict between Constitution and acts of either the national or state governments, the Constitution must always prevail. The U.S. Supreme Court acts as an umpire in the federal system, deciding disputes among states and between the national government and the states. It also decides challenges to either by individuals who claim these governments are exceeding their power or violating their constitutional restraints.

Specific prohibitions in the Constitution apply equally to state and national governments. Neither may pass a **bill of attainder** (a legislative act imposing a punishment upon an individual). Neither may pass an **ex**

post facto law (legislation retroactively making some act a crime or increasing the punishment). Both are prohibited from granting titles of nobility. In addition, judicial interpretation of the Constitution has expanded the common limits on national and state governments. By Supreme Court action, many of the prohibitions placed on the national government by the Bill of Rights have been read into those imposed on the states by the Fourteenth Amendment. Hence, both state and national governments are equally restrained in a number of areas dealing with civil liberties.

Certain prohibitions limit only the national government. Those that have not been overruled by subsequent constitutional amendments are: Except in cases of rebellion or invasion, Congress may not suspend the privilege of the writ of **habeas corpus** (the right of an individual to a judicial order removing that person from jail and compelling the executive to inform him before a court of the charges against him). Congress may not impose an export tax, give preference to ports or vessels from one state as against those from another state, or spend money from its treasury without passing a special appropriations act. Officers of the United States may not accept gifts or titles from foreign countries without congressional consent. And by defining treason, the Constitution prevents Congress from devising its own definition. In addition, portions of the Bill of Rights have been interpreted by the national courts as applying solely to the national government and not to the states.

Some prohibitions are placed only on the states. States are forbidden to make treaties, coin money, tax imports (or exports), keep troops or warships in peacetime, engage in war (unless invaded), or make compacts with other states without congressional consent. As explicit as these prohibitions are, they were drafted in the eighteenth century and remain open to interpretation and special exceptions. For instance, each state has from the beginning kept its own militia in peacetime as well as in war. In 1976 the U.S. Supreme Court overruled a 105-year decision by deciding that states and cities could tax certain imports. Additional restrictions have also been placed on the states since the Constitution was adopted. A number of amendments limit their power to decide who may vote in elections and their power to deprive individuals of life, liberty, property, or equal treatment under the law.

State-to-State Obligations

Federalism is not merely a division of powers between national and state governments or the imposition of restraints on both. One of the basic features of our model of federalism is a set of obligations among the states. The Constitution requires the states to behave in certain ways toward each other or their citizens.

Full faith and credit. Each state must afford **full faith and credit** (that is, accept as legitimate) to the civil decisions, official records, and judicial proceedings of other states. For example, a marriage certificate, adoption papers, or a divorce obtained by a person in one state must be recognized and accepted as valid in whatever state that person decides to live or travel.

Exceptions permitted by the courts do muddy the waters. Many states do not respect driver's licenses from other states, and there is some indication that states are not fully cooperating in areas of domestic relations—alimony payments, child support, and custody of children. A "quickie" divorce obtained in a state with a very limited residence period may not be accepted by the state from which the newly divorced persons came.

Although the mandate to give such full faith and credit requires each state to respect and accept the civil records of other states, its intent and effect is really to protect the rights of individuals who move from state to state. It also serves to deter individuals from changing their state residences to evade their legal responsibilities.

Extradition. **Extradition** refers to the obligation placed on a state to comply with the demand of any other state for the return of escapees from its criminal justice system. To prevent states from becoming sanctuaries for those who flee the state where they are charged with a crime, the Constitution mandates that such persons be returned on the demand of the executive authority of the state having jurisdiction over the crime. Every so often a governor will refuse to extradite (return) to another state someone who has fled after being charged with or convicted of a criminal offense. The exception is usually justified on the grounds of mercy.

Privileges and immunities. The Constitution demands that "the citizens of each state . . . be entitled to all the **privileges and immunities** of citizens in the other states." But what these privileges and immunities are is not stated by the Constitution. This is one of those vague phrases whose content has been defined entirely by the U.S. Supreme Court. In effect, it means that a state must treat citizens from the other states in the same manner as it does its own; it may not discriminate against them in the use of its basic services. Anyone in a state is entitled to use its courts, its police, its public schools, and other facilities as if that person were a citizen of the state. Nevertheless, certain exceptions have been permitted by the courts so that some services are not equally available to all. Hunting and fishing license fees and tuition for state universities may be set higher for nonresidents than for residents.

Optional Interstate Cooperation: Compacts

According to the Constitution, states may cooperate with one another in dealing with common problems. Any formal agreement or compact between or among them must receive the approval of Congress. A number of such **interstate compacts** have been concluded in the twentieth century dealing, among other things, with education, ports and transportation, crime, air pollution, and pest control.

Increasingly, individual states face problems that they cannot solve within their own boundaries. Polluted air and water, injurious pests, or crime, for example, have no respect for state lines. Therefore, cooperative arrangements to deal with these matters may be formally worked out among a set of states. The states are independent of each other and do not have to agree to the terms of a compact. None can be compelled to join.

Nation-State Obligations

The system of federalism called for in our Constitution requires only minimal relations between national and state governments. The national government owes only a few obligations to the states. It must guarantee them a republican form of government and protect them against invasion and internal violence. The national obligation to protect states from internal violence is conditional; that is, it generally depends upon a request from the proper state officials for national intervention. Presidents of the United States have, however, intervened with troops in states over the objections of their governors.

Although not exactly a national obligation, the admittance of new states to the federal union is also Congress's responsibility. In 1959, on meeting the requirements and procedures established by Congress, the territories of Hawaii and Alaska became the most recent states to join the United States.

The states have even fewer obligations to the national government. Their one responsibility is to conduct the election machinery for choosing national officers: President, Vice President, senators, and representatives.

MODERN FEDERALISM

A vast superstructure of new relationships has been erected over the basics of American federalism. In the process federalism has been transformed far beyond what the creators of the Constitution could have envisioned. The modern federalism that evolved includes a tremendous expansion in the powers of the national government and its direct, massive intervention in social and economic areas traditionally assumed to be private or belonging to the states. It calls for a bold interpretation of the Constitution by the Supreme Court. It incorporates a complex network of cooperative relations between the national and state governments, includes local government as a direct partner in a similar network and has led to the development of different types of regional governments.

Its maturity is relatively recent, it is very innovative, and it seems to reorient radically our political system; in this sense modern federalism is "revolutionary." This explains in part the intense, emotional controversies that swirl around it. Some Americans feel that the proper constitutional relationships have been subverted. Others object to portions of modern federalism because it works against their self-interests. Still others are concerned about the impact that modern federalism's expanded tax burden and large bureaucracies have on our economy and our freedom. Furthermore, a deep suspicion of all government, especially that at the national level, runs through our political culture and helps inflame controversies over federalism.

THE SUPREME COURT:
THE MAKING OF MODERN FEDERALISM

Few Americans realize that the genesis of modern federalism lies in the basics of the Constitution and derives in good part from their interpretation by the Supreme Court. The initial transformation occurred so early in our history that many people fail to make the connection between the Supreme Court's interpretation of these basics in the beginning of the nineteenth century and the new federalism in the twentieth century.

The Court as an Umpire

The Supreme Court, we have pointed out, serves as the umpire of federalism in the United States. It occupies this position as a result of its constitutional mandate to deal with conflict among states and between them and the national government. The redefining of federalism goes on continuously and almost always peacefully, and the Supreme Court plays a leading part in that peaceful redefinition. By acting as umpire it affords the contending governmental units and private groups a neutral ground for resolving their federal conflicts. That is one function of an umpire whose legitimacy to spell out the meaning of the basic rules is accepted by the contestants.

Unfortunately, some federal conflicts have been violent. We fought a bloody Civil War from 1861 to 1865 over the meaning and continuation of the federal union. In the 1950s and 1960s Supreme Court decisions actually contributed to violent confrontations. When the Court's interpretation of the Constitution voided long-standing segregation in the public schools and universities, conflict erupted. Incidents of armed confrontation occurred in Alabama, Arkansas, and Mississippi between forces of the national government and either state governments or parts of their citizenry. Resistance to national court orders for busing and integration in the Boston schools, in 1975–76, led to violent clashes among the local citizenry and between parts of that citizenry and their own city and state law officers. Although the violent and the sensational generate headlines and make television news, they are the exceptions to the rule.

Aside from providing an alternative to violence, an umpire is essential in federalism because the line dividing national and state power is very imprecise. How far may the national government go under the **necessary and proper** and **general welfare clauses** before it intrudes into areas reserved to the states? What is reserved? What is necessary and proper? What exactly is the meaning of *general welfare?* Someone must clarify these questions if nation and state are to know what they may legitimately do.

A great member of the Court, Oliver Wendell Holmes, once remarked that in preserving our constitutional system it really mattered very little whether the Court ruled on the constitutionality of congressional legislation. But it was absolutely vital that the Court have the power to assess the constitutionality of state actions. How else, one might logically ask, could the supremacy of the Constitution and the national laws made thereunder be upheld? Nevertheless, as the supreme law of the land, superior to national and state governments, the Constitution's supremacy must be protected against the claims and actions of national as well as state officials. The Supreme Court asserts this role as its special prerogative.

You might protest that as head of the judicial branch of the national government the Supreme Court constitutes a biased umpire in resolving nation-state conflicts. In practice, however, it has acted as if it were a separate unit in the entire governmental system. At times it has ruled against the claims of Congress and in favor of the states; at other times in favor of Congress. In fact, for one portion of our history the Court adopted an extremely restricted view of national power. And as recently as June 1976 it declared unconstitutional congressional legislation ordering state and local governments to adopt national minimum wage standards for their employees.

It is clear the Supreme Court serves as a practical, nonviolent, legitimate tool for deciding whether national and state governments are acting in accordance with the Constitution. It provides the American system of government with an efficient, relatively inexpensive way of resolving federal conflicts. And in so doing it serves as a catalytic agent, integrating the diverse parts of that system into a more unified whole.

Expanding National Power:
McCulloch v. Maryland and the Necessary and Proper Clause

In 1819 one of the first major decisions by the Supreme Court on federalism laid the basis for a broad interpretation of national power. In deciding a controversy between national and state governments in *McCulloch* v. *Maryland,* the Court was both unanimous in its agreement that the nation prevailed over the state and bold in its willingness to interpret basic constitutional theory for the future. The case is as much a landmark in changing the Constitution through judicial interpretation as it is a foundation for modern federalism.

What was involved in *McCulloch* v. *Maryland?* Congress had established the National Bank of the United States. The legislature of Maryland levied a substantial tax on its operation in that state, a tax which McCulloch, the cashier of its Baltimore branch, refused to pay. The case went to the Supreme Court as Maryland sought to compel the national government to comply with the law.

The controversy pitted state government against national government. That Maryland was exercising a legitimate power, the power to tax, was clear. That Congress had been given no specific grant of power by the Constitution to create a bank was also clear. However, Congress was empowered to tax as well as to coin, borrow, and appropriate money for a variety of purposes. It was also authorized to adopt laws that were necessary and proper to implement all its powers. At this point clarity took a back seat to ambiguity.

A number of issues were at stake. With regard to the Congress, did the necessary and proper clause give Congress power to establish a bank, or was the national legislature restricted to its specifically defined powers? With regard to Maryland, could a state, which legitimately had the power to tax, impose such a tax on an instrument of the national government? To refocus these questions: Was the necessary and proper clause to be read in the broadest sense of expanding the powers of the national government or in the strictest sense of its doing only what was absolutely necessary and absolutely proper? When the two constitutional levels of government conflict, which should prevail, the United States or a state?

Speaking for a unanimous Court, Chief Justice John Marshall developed the broadest construction of the Constitution in favor of the national government. The Court laid down the rule that the national government was neither confined to its explicitly stated powers nor bound by a rigid reading of necessary and proper. In carrying out the duties assigned to it, the Congress had to be afforded discretion as to the means it employed. The necessary and proper clause had to be interpreted in its broadest sense: "Let the end be legitimate, let it be within the scope of the Constitution, and all means which are appropriate, which are plainly adapted to that end, which are not prohibited, but consistent with the letter and spirit of the Constitution, are constitutional."

In effect, then, Congress could pass any law that (1) was not forbidden to it and (2) was reasonably related to carrying out the powers that had been assigned to it. The necessary and proper clause was to be interpreted very flexibly. It was almost a blank check. It meant that the Tenth Amendment, in stating that those powers not forbidden to the states or delegated to Congress belonged to the states and the people, did *not* sharply restrict national power. Congress could legislate in areas not specifically spelled out in the Constitution. This was to be done, of course, under the oversight of the Court. Could the state still exercise its legitimate power to tax the national government when the latter was acting in a constitutional manner? The Court's answer was a resounding no! The Constitution and the laws made "in Pursuance thereof. . . ." were the supreme law of the land, the Court pointed out. The power to tax also involved the power to destroy. A state law that could destroy a legitimate national activity was unconstitutional and therefore unenforceable. In effect, the Court was issuing a warning to all states. As it interpreted the Constitution, the supremacy clause (Article VI) afforded the national government protection against state action that might undermine national policies.

McCulloch v. *Maryland* defined the Constitution so as to provide the potential for extensive national action. At the same time, it guaranteed the Court a key position as umpire in determining exactly what the national government and the state governments could or could not do.

Expanding National Power:
The Interstate Commerce and the General Welfare Clauses

Both the interstate commerce and general welfare clauses of the Constitution, together with the necessary and proper clause, facilitated the growth of national power. In relying on these constitutional provisions, Congress and the Supreme Court have, especially since the 1930s, virtually revolutionized our federal system and, as a consequence, our economic and social systems as well.

The promise of additional national power inherent in the *McCulloch* v. *Maryland* decision was not systematically tapped for over a hundred years. Subsequent Supreme Courts proved less congenial to Congress's attempts at regulating the economic system under the auspices of the necessary and proper and the interstate commerce powers. In fact, for one extended period the judges interpreted the Constitution so as to prevent both the states and the national government from legislating on many economic matters. State laws were struck down as violating the liberty and due process rights of individuals under the Fourteenth Amendment; congressional laws were declared unconstitutional as invading areas reserved to the states by the Tenth Amendment.

In the midst of the Great Depression of the 1930s, a new Democratic President and a Democratic Congress drastically reoriented the focus of governmental action to Washington, D.C. Our private economic system was in a state of near collapse at the time: Factories were shut down for want of markets; farmers were unable to sell their produce; millions of workers were unemployed (an estimated 13 to 17 million in 1932–33) or forced to accept reduced pay. States, cities, and private organizations proved powerless to relieve the human suffering or to cope in economic terms with a depression that was national in scope. Under the leadership of President Franklin D. Roosevelt, Congress assumed major responsibility for reviving the economy and dealing with the human tragedy.

Initially, the Supreme Court struck down emergency legislation that sought to stimulate the economy. Regulating production in agriculture and industry was ruled an unconstitutional use of the interstate commerce power; extending financial benefits to the farmers, an improper use of the taxing power. The Supreme Court declared that the national government was illegally invading the constitutional jurisdiction of the states.

But the Court soon reversed itself and legitimated the full thrust of Roosevelt's New Deal program. National legislation affecting agriculture, labor, industry, and commerce was deemed constitutional, a necessary and proper exercise of Congress's power to regulate interstate commerce and to tax. The full sweep of Justice Marshall's approach became the law of the land. Today the national government possesses the power to regulate all aspects of our economy that directly or indirectly affect interstate commerce. It is involved in a manner and scale unprecedented in our history, except during the national emergencies of World Wars I and II.

The Court also accepted the New Deal philosophy that the national government could legitimately act under its responsibility to provide for the general welfare of the country. Article 1, Section 8, of the Constitution authorizes Congress to tax and provide for the general welfare.

General welfare is, of course, an extremely ambiguous and debatable phrase.

Under a broad interpretation of its power to tax and provide for the general welfare, the national government has entered into new and potentially unlimited areas of the private sector of our society. It directly regulates or provides financial support to millions of Americans engaged in such noneconomic activities as education, art, science, health, the environment, conservation, family planning, and abortion in the belief that these, too, are important to our general welfare. In addition, the national government has committed itself to provide social security programs for the aged, widowed, unemployed, orphans, and disabled. To raise the hundreds of billions of dollars to pay for these services and regulatory activities, the national government has expanded the range of its taxes.

Questions that address themselves to cost—the amount of the tax "bite," the desirability of different types of taxes, and who should pay them—generate controversy. So, too, does the issue of Congress's spending billions more than it raises in taxes in order to meet the social and economic needs of Americans, in addition to its spending on international and defense programs. Other controversial issues center on the degree and quality of the national government's involvement in our lives, the effectiveness of its regulations and services, and the nature of their impact upon our society.

At the same time that the national government has become increasingly involved in dealing directly with the social and economic problems of the country, it has sought to decentralize its power in many policy areas. It has turned over money, administrative responsibility, and even policy discretion to state and local governments. These two currents of change in national power, centralization and decentralization occurring simultaneously, characterize contemporary modern federalism.

COOPERATIVE FEDERALISM: DECENTRALIZATION OF BIG GOVERNMENT *Know*

Glance through the list of powers granted the national government by the Constitution. You will find virtually no reference to joint action by the different levels of the federal system and none at all concerning the policy areas in which joint action now occurs: education, pollution, crime control, recreation, slum clearance, mass transit, job training, and still others. The national government has joined with states and local governments in common efforts never contemplated by the Constitution: joint actions on policy decisions, money allocations, and administration of programs. This has helped transform the traditional federal layer cake model, to which we referred earlier, into a marble cake.

Although a radical change has occurred in nation-state-city relations, such a "revolution" has its underpinnings in traditional federal practices. Throughout our history national and state governments joined in a number of common endeavors. In 1836, for example, Congress shared its treasury surplus with the states. After the Civil War Congress offered gifts of land to the states on the condition that they establish colleges of agriculture and engineering. In the late nineteenth century, Congress offered the states money to establish agricultural experiment stations. And, in the early part of our century, states were granted funds for forestry work, highways, vocational education, and health.

The New Deal period of the 1930s marked the beginning of a "revolution" in cooperative federalism. Prior to that time cooperative federal arrangements occurred almost accidentally and sporadically; they did not reflect a decided commitment to decentralization and partnership. The sums of money and kinds of activities involved were small compared with the enormous amount of national aid and the tremendous variety of programs now available. Cooperative federalism had in the past excluded local governments; now it includes them as essential partners. Before this revolution, most Americans were untouched by cooperative federalism; today, it can and does affect almost everyone in some way.

The revolution is strikingly demonstrated in Table 5–2, "Rise in Value and Numbers of [Federal] Grants-in-Aid, 1902–1974." As early as 1932 only twelve such programs had been in existence. Under the

Table 5–2
Rise in the Value and Number
of [Federal] Grants-in- Aid, 1902–1974*

	GRANT PROGRAMS	
	Value (in thousands of dollars)	Number
1902	3,001	5
1912	5,255	7
1920	37,886	11
1925	113,746	12
1932	192,966	12
1937	2,663,828	26
1946	984,625	28
1952	2,262,912	38
1964	9,864,000	51
1967	15,240,000	379
1971	30,297,000	530
1974 (est.)	52,000,000	550

*Figures from 1967 on include local government grants.

SOURCE: Herbert Jacob and Kenneth N. Viner, eds. *Politics in the American States, A Comparative Analysis*, 3rd ed. (Boston: Little, Brown, 1976), p. 21.

political leadership of the New Deal, the number of programs jumped in five years by over 100 percent. The amount of national dollars committed to the programs rose by 1,500 percent: $192 million in 1932 to $2.6 billion in 1937. President Lyndon B. Johnson committed the nation to another advance. National aid went from $9.8 billion in 1964 to $15.2 billion in 1967, an increase of almost 60 percent. In the same period the number and variety of programs that the national government offered to states and cities multiplied greatly from 51 programs in 1964 to 379 in 1967. By 1978 national aid had jumped to an estimated $80.2 billion.

In this section you should note four major types of cooperative arrangements between the national government and state or local governments: **categorical grants-in-aid, block grants, project grants,** and **general revenue sharing.** Still other arrangements exist, such as when the national government offers to train state and local police officials at its FBI facilities or when national fingerprint banks are made available to such officials.

Categorical Grants-in-Aid

The most widely used device in cooperative federalism has been the *categorical grant-in-aid.* Such a grant transfers money from the national to the state or local levels of government on the condition that they undertake a specific, narrowly defined program (category) of activity.

State and local governments are given primary responsibility for carrying out the programs. Their officials, not the national ones, administer the programs. In almost all cases, the state and local governments must also use their own revenues to support the programs. This is called *matching.* The proportion of matching funds varies. In some programs each level of government contributes an equal share; in others the ratio may be two dollars in national money for every dollar the state or local unit is willing to invest. In building our interstate highway system, the national government contributes 90 percent, the states only 10 percent.

As independent units within the federal system, no state or local government is compelled to accept a grant. In accordance with their own priorities, they may choose among these grant programs and determine how much they will invest. Since the federal money is "free" (that is, it comes from the national government and does not have to be extracted by state or local governments from their taxpayers) national offers of grants-in-aid are difficult to turn down.

Although the grants are free and their administration decentralized, the national government does attach conditions. The money must be spent only for the purpose spelled out in the grant, and the matching formula must be met. The national government may also require that the administrators be hired on the basis of a merit system to ensure that competent personnel direct the cooperative program. After all, the national government has a responsibility to its own taxpayers to make certain their monies are not wasted. It may, in fact, penalize states or local governments that violate these conditions by withholding funds.

National conditions, national supervision, and national penalties are some of the costs that state and local governments must pay for the free money and the opportunity to provide valuable services to their citizenry. Needless to say, each grant program tends to generate its own national bureaucracy to supervise the grant and its own state or local bureaucracy to administer it. In most cases the two sets of bureaucrats cooperate with each other and conflict is rare.

Block Grants

Much less narrow in focus than categorical grants, *block grants* consolidate a number of categorical grants in a particular policy area. State and local governments are given much more discretion in deciding where

From *The Herblock Book*, Beacon Press, 1952

"In two words, yes and no."

and how to spend the money within that policy area, and they are less restricted by detailed federal rules. Thus the amount of confusion and red tape involved in negotiating with the national government for many categorical grants is appreciably reduced.

The Omnibus Crime Control and Street Act of 1968 represented the first major experiment by the national government in block grants. Rather than a number of categorical grant programs, each requiring the states to accommodate themselves to a particular policy commitment of the national government, states were offered a large undifferentiated grant in the area of crime control. How the money was to be spent, for what particular crime control measures, was left to the states. They controlled the planning, administration, and allocation of the grants. But the national government did insist that 90 percent of the funds be funnelled to local governments.

Education, manpower training, urban problems, and health are among the other policy areas in which the national government has made available block grants. Such grants represent a decision by the national government to give state and local governments greater flexibility in adjusting to specific local needs and conditions.

Project Grants *Know*

In *project grants,* the national government determines the policy area in which it wants to invest its money; local and state governments apply for aid to fund projects they design to fit their special needs. The money is not automatically granted. National administrators may reject any project they do not find meritorious. The national government may supply all the money for a project grant.

Special and General Revenue Sharing

Revenue sharing represents a national policy to transfer substantial national revenues to state and local governments with no federal restrictions on how these governments use the money. Deciding which programs to sponsor, how to allocate the funds, and how to administer the programs are left almost entirely to state and local governments. They are not required to put up matching funds. Revenue sharing is based on three premises: first, state and local governments have pressing needs but inadequate resources; second, the national government has sufficient resources that can be transferred to these federal units; and third, state and local governments know best when, where, and how to spend their money for their own needs.

Under President Richard M. Nixon's leadership, Congress passed the State and Local Assistance Act of 1972, which provided a $30.2 billion, five-year revenue sharing grant. One-third was allocated to the states in *general revenue sharing;* that is, they were free to use the money exactly as they wished except for two limitations: They were forbidden to substitute such money for state aid to local governments and they could not use this money in programs that discriminated on the basis of race, national origin, or sex. Two-thirds of the $30.2 billion was allocated to local governments in the form of *special revenue sharing.* It had to be spent for one or more special purposes: environmental protection, health, public safety, libraries, public transportation, social services for the aged and the poor, and financial administration.

By 1976, when Congress had to consider whether to renew its commitment to revenue sharing, strident controversy had arisen. Many critics argued that the results, in terms of either the quality or the kinds of services provided, did not justify transferring billions of national tax dollars to state and local governments to use at their discretion. Minority groups protested that less attention was being paid to their needs in many states and cities because of their lack of political "muscle" at these levels of the federal system. But mayors, governors, and their political allies lobbied extensively with Congress and were successful in securing a renewal of revenue sharing.

What Does the Federal Partnership Accomplish?

You may rightfully ask what the sharing of national funds with state and local governments has accomplished. Has it made our governments more or less useful for our political system? How does it affect our lives? Three characteristics stand out in any assessment of the federal partnership: It establishes common denominators of services throughout the country; it decentralizes power away from Washington, D.C., to our state and local governments; it taps the most appropriate revenue base for providing services to our people.

Creating common denominators. By offering financial aid to the other federal units, the national government has attempted to provide minimum levels of services for Americans, no matter where they live. Whatever the variations that exist among the states, because of their varying resources and their options on deciding on programs, cooperative federalism establishes a set of base lines, common denominators of governmental services. These denominators in public safety, slum clearance, job training, education, health, hospital construction, recreation, environmental protection, and welfare, to cite only a few policy areas, represent national priorities in advancing the general welfare.

Decentralization.   Cooperative federalism represents a decision on the part of the national government to use state and local governments in carrying out its priorities. Rather than centralizing in itself all responsibility for providing common services to its people, the national government relies heavily on the other federal units. It thereby avoids building an even larger national bureaucracy, which would be needed if it undertook to carry out the program itself, and it accommodates itself to the diverse wishes of the fifty states and the thousands of units of local government.

The priorities in cooperative federalism are not solely national. They also represent a series of decisions by other units in the federal system to use the national government for their own purposes. State and local officials frequently assume the initiative and induce the national government to design cooperative, financial arrangements in particular policy areas. As state and local priorities are transformed into

©1978 by Herblock in *The Washington Post*

*"However, we can spend over a billion
telling you how to flee from them."*

national priorities and vice versa, federalism becomes a dynamic inter-change between the different levels of government.

Decentralizing the administration of nationally supported programs into the hands of state and local officials helps reinvigorate their units of government as meaningful instruments for making decisions and providing services. True, national standards and regulations somewhat restrict their freedom of action. But the requirements also contribute to an upgrading of personnel and performance in the state and local bureaucracies.

Note that the availability of free categorical and block grants sometimes induces state and local governments to invest their own funds in activities that are not necessarily among their top priorities. General revenue sharing was supposed to correct for such a distortion. However, the strong commitment on the part of many national officials and private groups to specific programs and their dissatisfaction with the purposes for which general revenue funds have been used have guaranteed that categorical and block grants will continue to exist along with general revenue sharing.

Tapping the best tax sources.   National aid programs are based on the national government's access to a broader tax base than any other unit in our federal republic and on its ability to raise tremendous sums of money. Cooperative programs tap this ability of the national government to act as a revenue collector and to transfer money to states and local governments. In effect, these governments rely on Washington to raise tax revenues for them.

Many units of local and state governments have too limited a tax base to raise the necessary monies. Also, since they seek to retain or attract business and industry as a stimulus to their own economies, they are in competition with comparable units of government elsewhere. By increasing their tax rates or adopting new taxes, localities or states risk reducing their competitive advantage. The national government does not operate under such restraints.

States rely heavily on the sales tax and cities and counties on the property tax. This severely limits their ability to raise money. Taxes are more uniformly applied at the national level, and the federal tax "bite" is much deeper than that of the other governmental units. Moreover, the personal income and corporate taxes of the central government are more effective and efficient money raisers.

As a disburser of financial aid, the national government can com-pensate for the economic disparities among state and local governments. Formulas for disbursing national funds can be designed to transfer proportionately more money to the poorer units of government and to reward those making a greater effort in proportion to their resources.

REGIONAL GOVERNMENT AND FEDERALISM

Ours is a vast country with great differences among the states and local governments. They differ in climate, natural resources, economies, geography, and people. Hence, their problems differ. Those problems common to all can be approached through direct action by our common government, the United States government. Such problems can also be approached through the sharing of money and priorities among national, state, or local governments.

Some problems, however, are unique to a few states and do not exist in others. Since governmental boundaries are in most cases only artificial lines, problems often spill across them. Such problems cannot be solved individually by the states. A number of governments may need to take collective action to cope adequately with a problem that affects them all. To this end regional units of government representing a unique form of cooperative federalism have been created. They must be considered an integral element in the new federalism of the twentieth century.

Interstate Compacts

One type of regional arrangement, the *interstate compact,* is more traditional and has already been mentioned. In interstate compacts, states with a common problem may create an all-inclusive unit of government to deal with it. Although the consent of Congress is needed for the new arrangement of power, only one such agreement has ever been disapproved. The states decide on the policy area of concern, establish the administrative machinery for dealing with it, and raise the necessary funds. Over four hundred such compacts enable separate groups of states to act jointly in conservation, river development, ports and harbors, civil defense, and other policy concerns.

The Colorado River Basin Compact is one such cooperative regional arrangement. A number of semiarid far western states are vitally concerned with obtaining water from the Colorado River, which flows through all of them. On the opposite side of the continent the Port Authority of New York and New Jersey represents another cooperative arrangement. Separated by the Hudson River, New York and New Jersey must deal with an integrated urban economy whose publics cut across their state boundaries. Together, the two states have set up a common Port Authority, granting it considerable power to construct and manage port facilities, interstate bridges, tunnels, businesses, truck terminals, and airports. In the South nine states created a Southern Growth Policies Board in 1971 to help them achieve a sound and balanced growth.

Multistate-National Compacts

A second type of regional device is the *multistate-national compact.* In this a group of states and the national government join together. The powers of both levels of government are combined in a special governmental agency to cope with problems common to all the participants.

A number of states that have common problems associated with the Delaware River Basin joined with the national government to set up a commission; both the states and the national government delegated to it power for river management. Hard-core poverty is widespread in the Appalachian region. To cope with this problem twelve states stretching from the Northeast down into the South joined with the national government in the 1960s to create an Appalachian Regional Commission. This commission has the power to initiate, supervise, and coordinate economic redevelopment projects. Any action requires an affirmative vote by both a majority of the state representatives involved and the national representative; the latter can veto any proposal, as can a majority of the states on the commission.

National Regional Government

A third type of regional government involves only the national government. The Tennessee Valley Authority, created in 1936, is the sole example of this model. The TVA is a national public corporation concerned with the development of the entire Tennessee Valley and empowered with considerable authority to engage in comprehensive planning and development. Its jurisdiction crosses the boundaries of several states and its primary concerns are electric power production, flood control, and navigation improvement. It owns and operates hydroelectric plants and a major fertilizer plant; it operates an important forestry program as well as recreational and health programs. Because the TVA has collaborated closely with state and local agencies in the Tennessee Valley in planning and development work, it has also moved extensively on its own into cooperative federalism.

FEDERALISM AND CURRENT QUESTIONS

We started our discussion of federalism by indicating that it was constantly changing and controversial. Based on the traditional structure and practices of federalism in the United States, three major developments have taken place, and each has helped revolutionize federalism. One is the tremendous expansion of national power; the central government today involves itself directly and actively in the social and economic life of our society. The second development is the expansion of cooperative federalism; it has united first national and state governments and then national and local governments in shared enterprises. The third development is the growth of regional governments as a means for coping with problems that cut across the boundaries and powers of state governments.

Each of these changes in federalism generates controversy. The following questions address themselves to such controversies:

Should our national government assume more or less responsibility for dealing directly with major problems?   Many contemporary issues raise this question. We refer only to two that will remain particularly relevant for the next few years.

A determined move has been underway for some time to persuade the national government to offer national health insurance to the entire population. Aged persons are already covered for medical and hospital care under our national social insurance and our welfare systems. Should the national government move comprehensively in the area of health insurance for everyone? If it does, should it provide the insurance itself, or should it work in cooperation with private companies? How should national health care be financed: through special taxes, by increasing the social security taxes, by tapping into general tax revenues, or through a combination of the above?

In election year 1976, a number of candidates for the Democratic presidential nomination endorsed an ambitious proposal to abolish unemployment. It called for legislation to stimulate employment opportunities in the private sector, with the national government providing jobs for all who needed them if the private sector did not. Should the national government become the employer of last resort? Should it assume the responsibility for bringing unemployment down to a certain minimum?

These are very divisive issues. As we attempt to redefine the relationship between the national government, our other governments, and the rest of society, we have no objective accepted standards to help us make the decisions. Whatever the national government does, its services must be weighed against the costs to be paid and the question of who is going to pay them.

How should cooperative federalism develop?   Should we abandon categorical grants-in-aid in favor of general revenue sharing? Should we concentrate on categorical grants and block grants? Or should we settle for a mix of some kind? If so, what kind? Even if we could reach an agreement on these questions, additional questions will confront us:

How much of its revenue should the national government invest in cooperative federalism? What new areas of service or public policy should it encourage? Which old ones should it withdraw from?

Should state and local governments assume more responsibility? Perhaps if state and local governments assumed more responsibility there would be less need for the national government to intervene in our society, either directly or indirectly. What new functions should state and local governments undertake for their citizens, and how can they improve their present operations?

Comprehensive land use planning and environmental protection are two very controversial activities being urged on local and state governments. In June 1976, for example, Californians voted on an initiative proposal that would have required a two-thirds affirmative vote by their state legislature on safety standards before nuclear reactor plants could be built in that state. A bitterly fought campaign led to the initiative's resounding defeat.

Other questions address themselves to raising revenue. Should cities, counties, and states increase their taxes to meet the people's demand for new services? Or should some services be reduced so as to lighten the load on those who pay the the most taxes? Should new types of revenue-raising devices already adopted by some governments be utilized by others? For example, a number of states have legitimized lotteries or gambling casinos as a way of raising money "painlessly" for public services. Some cities have imposed their own income taxes. Or should taxes be reduced even if certain services must be curtailed? If so, which taxes and which services? In 1978 California voters drastically reduced property taxes.

Another set of questions address themselves to organization and productivity. Can state and local units organize themselves more effectively and efficiently? States and localities, not the national government, are primarily responsible for spending most of our tax dollars for public services. Their spending accounts for almost 80 percent of all non-defense government purchases of goods and services. Since state and local governments have now become "big government," it is as important for them to become more productive as it is for the national government.

Where do we go in regional government? All attempts to establish national corporations similar to the Tennessee Valley Authority in other river basins have been consistently defeated. Should the national government encourage more partnership arrangements with multistate units as a way of coping with particular regional problems? Is regionalism the most effective way to solve problems that cross the boundaries of a number of states?

You should begin thinking about these questions within the context of traditional and modern federalism. As one of the most dynamic elements in the American system of government, federalism will affect your life now and in the future. The dimensions, directions, and costs of federalism will continue to be debated in this country. Understanding the "what, how, and why" of federalism will help you make sense of the proposals for change and perhaps even help you participate meaningfully in the answers.

Concepts To Study

centralization
concurrent powers
confederation
cooperative federalism
decentralization

delegated powers
enumerated powers
federalism
implied powers
modern federalism

regional government
reserve powers
supreme law of the land
traditional federalism

Special Terms To Review

bill of attainder
block grants
categorical grants-in-aid
cities as partners in
  federalism
constitutional prohibitions
  on national powers
constitutional prohibitions
  on state powers
the Court as an umpire
ex post facto law
extradition

federal partnership
Fourteenth Amendment
full faith and credit
general revenue sharing
general welfare clause
habeas corpus
implied powers clause
interstate commerce clause
interstate compact
McCulloch v. Maryland
multistate-national
  compact

national-regional
  government
nation-state cooperation
nation-state obligations
necessary and proper clause
New Deal
privileges and immunities
project grants
special revenue sharing
state-to-state obligations
Tennessee Valley Authority
Tenth Amendment

CHAPTER 6

VOTERS
AND ELECTIONS

When we vote, each of us exercises a degree of power over our government. Each vote represents only an infinitesimally small unit of power. But enough of them added together constitute a significant concentration of power—power to select the leadership of government and, at times, to decide policy for government.

Ironically, millions of Americans do not use their power. Over 45 percent of the eligible **electorate** did not vote in the presidential election of 1976 and an even greater percentage abstained in 1978. By failing to participate, they concede to those who do vote the power to make important decisions about leadership and policy in our political system.

Who are the voters and nonvoters? What is the relationship between voter turnout and the types of elections we conduct in the United States? What proposals have been suggested to increase voter turnout and to reform elections? These questions confront you in this chapter.

VOTERS, ELECTIONS, AND DEMOCRACY

In a democracy the people have the power to select their rulers by voting in elections. The election process gives those who win the right to assume positions of power. At the same time, the election process officially decides the losers, those who may not take office or who must leave it in favor of the winners. As voters we have the power to grant or terminate the authority to rule.

Democracy would be meaningless if the individual did not have the right to choose among competing candidates for positions of governmental leadership. Note what is involved. An individual must be free to make up his or her own mind in exerting a unit of power—a vote—in determining who will be the major leaders of government. And such leaders can only obtain their public office through an open, competitive selection process.

Choosing Rulers in Nondemocratic Systems

Rulers in three-quarters of the world's governments are chosen by nondemocratic methods: violence, a decision within the military, inheritance as a member of a ruling family, or a struggle within a dictatorial political party that controls the government.

Ironically, popular elections are regularly conducted in some of these countries, and voter turnout may be extremely high. Voters in the Soviet Union, for example, participate at a rate well over 95 percent, a rate we never even approximate in our country. This nearly total turnout by the Soviet electorate and their nearly unanimous approval of their Communist party leaders actually reflect that party's monopoly of governmental power and its unwillingness to tolerate any opposition on the ballot. The voters lack any meaningful choices since there is no real competition. But not to vote might catch the attention of the authorities and invite punishment. And casting a blank ballot—in effect, a vote of disapproval—also involves risks. Because leadership selection occurs within the confines of a dictatorial party, an individual's vote is virtually meaningless. The popular elections are facades (false fronts) designed to give the population the illusion of having a real choice in selecting their leaders.

The interesting aspect of these popular elections is neither their high voter turnout nor their predetermined results. It is rather that they are held at all. That dictatorial leaders permit, indeed insist upon, such elections attests to the tremendous appeal to their people of the democratic ideal: The people should select their governmental leaders who should depend on the approval of the voters for their use of public power. These elections help the dictators hold the allegiance and obedience of their people and withstand the competitive attractiveness of the real democracies. Hence it is no coincidence that Communist dictators contend that theirs are the true democracies!

Elections in Democratic Systems

In political systems that approximate the ideal of democracy, the vote and elections are meaningful. How do elections exemplify key ingredients in the democratic formula?

Elections and self-rule.   Democracy calls for the people to rule themselves. Since it is very difficult for large numbers of people to engage in direct self-rule, the people rule themselves *indirectly* by selecting leaders to make and enforce governmental policy in their name. Modern democracies are actually democratic republics. In some instances, however, voters may participate directly in policy decisions, bypassing elected officials or even overruling them.

Public officials who depend on the approval of voters in open elections must solicit their support. They recognize that they must pay attention to the policies wanted and needed by those who vote; in the end their lifeline to political power rests on the voting power of the people.

Voting and equality.   Voters and elections illustrate still another aspect of democracy—equality. Each person participating in an election has an equal unit of voting power. The slogan "one man–one vote" may reflect a more sexist United States than we have today, but it illustrates the point. Men and women are equal in the voting booth: Each has the same unit of power.

"All" the people may vote.   Ideally, democracy calls for everyone who is affected by government to have a legitimate voice (vote) in that government. After all, if democratic government is to be, in Lincoln's words, "of the people, by the people and for the people," the people should include everyone within the political system. Yet no political system realizes this ideal. Indeed, reasonable grounds exist for not implementing it.

One measure of the degree of democracy in a political system is the extent to which we approximate that ideal. Universal adult suffrage is about as close as one can get to it.

Elections and the resolution of conflict.   All government, including the politics surrounding it, is controversial. This is especially true in a democracy where people are free to express their self-interest and to disagree with government. Because elections resolve conflict and do so peacefully, they make an important contribution to our political system. Two types of conflict—who should be the principal leaders of government and what should be official policy—are resolved by elections.

Elections permit us to decide, usually without argument and ambiguity, which candidates or which issues are the official winners. The result is determined by a numerical process, the counting of votes. It is not superior force, money, or favoritism, but the number of votes each candidate or issue receives that determines the decisions. Because votes are objective identical units that can be added, in almost all cases the winners or losers are clearly, objectively determined. This makes it easier for losers to accept the election results.

Rules for determining winners.   To require that elections be resolved by the rule of *unanimity*, all voters agreeing on a candidate or an issue, is to demand the impossible. Elections in democracies almost invariably involve conflict, which precludes unanimity.

A more workable rule for determining elections in modern democratic systems calls for a *majority vote*. You will recall that democratic government calls for majority rule. By an electoral majority, we mean that more than one-half of the voters in an election contest favor a candidate or an issue. Whichever candidate or policy issue attracts a majority wins.

A third rule, used only in **candidate elections,** calls for a *plurality vote*. When more than two competitors run for the same office, the vote may be so divided that no one receives a majority. Under the plurality rule the individual who has the most votes wins. A plurality is the highest number of votes attained by any candidate (the most votes) in the absence of a majority. The great advantage of the plurality rule is that it produces a winner almost all the time, the exception being when there is a tie.

A fourth rule for deciding elections, again applying only to candidate elections, is **proportional representation.** Under this rule, everyone's vote counts, since a number of offices are at stake in an election and they are divided up in proportion to the votes cast for different candidates or parties. In a majority or plurality election for single offices, only the votes cast for the winner count. The votes cast for the losing candidate(s) are, in effect, cancelled out. But under proportional representation, voters whose candidates do not obtain a majority or a plurality, are still able to elect some governmental officials of their own. Although proportional representation is not used in national or state elections in the United States, it is used by a few of our local units of government and by a number of other countries.

WHO MAY VOTE?

Who may vote? *How* do people become qualified to vote? These questions are decided by different levels of government in our federal system. In the original constitutional package, this decision was assigned to the states. Since 1789, however, the Constitution has increasingly reduced their discretionary power. Congress and the Supreme Court have also restricted state power, making it easier for people to vote. Today, national as well as state rules determine who may vote in elections and how they may qualify.

Democratizing the Right to Vote

Initially the U.S. Constitution made only one reference to the electorate: those people who could vote for the most numerous house of a state's legislature were eligible to vote for the U.S. House of Representatives. This meant that voting requirements for national as well as state officials were actually set by each state.

States originally limited the vote to white males, age twenty-one and over, who owned a sufficient amount of land or received a large income. Everyone else was excluded. Clearly we did not start out on a democratic basis. As democratic principles became more accepted, however, states dropped both property and income qualifications.

Black males were made eligible to vote in 1870 by the Fifteenth Amendment. This amendment forbade the states to exclude people from voting on the basis of their race, color, or previous condition of servitude. Despite this amendment, discrimination against blacks in the southern states prevented most of them from exercising their right to vote. The U.S. Supreme Court ultimately struck down most of those restrictions, enabling blacks to participate in increasing numbers. Starting in 1950, Congress itself intervened increasingly to make certain that race or color would not be used by states to disqualify voters. In 1964 the Twenty-fourth Amendment abolished **poll taxes** in state elections shortly after Congress had forbidden their use for voter qualification in national elections.

Although a few states permitted women to vote before 1920, most states excluded them. In 1920 the Nineteenth Amendment removed from the states the power to exclude people from voting because of their sex. The latest constitutional restriction on state power to determine who could vote, the Twenty-sixth Amendment (1971), ensured that individuals could not be denied the vote if they were age eighteen or older. A few states (Georgia in 1944) had lowered their voting age earlier.

We have reached a point of almost universal adult suffrage in our country. Our voting system has become democratized so that the democratic ideal—the right of all adult Americans to vote for their major officials—is now a reality.

Expanding the Power of Voters

In the process of democratizing our political system, the power of the voters was extended, allowing them to elect a larger number of officials than was originally contemplated by the U.S. Constitution. At first voters could not choose their U.S. senators; senators were elected by their state legislatures. In 1913, Amendment Seventeen transferred this election to a popular vote by the people in each state. The President and Vice President are still not elected directly by the popular vote. Rather they are chosen by presidential electors in accordance with the Constitution. But these electors, who prior to the 1850s had been selected in some states by their legislatures, are now elected directly by the popular vote in each state.

In accordance with the Constitution, the judges of the national courts are not elected by a popular vote but are chosen by the President with the consent of the Senate. However, since at present the President is much closer to the popular voter and senators are popularly elected, the judges are now selected by officials who are more responsive to the popular vote.

Legitimate Restrictions on Who May Vote

Although universal adult suffrage determines the potential electorate—all those eligible to be voters—there remain categories of people over eighteen years of age who may not vote. The states are still permitted to impose restrictions on adult suffrage.

Citizenship.   Since the 1920s, all states have required American citizenship as a condition for voting. Today this requirement excludes millions of adults who have never become citizens.

Registration.   All but a few states refuse to permit people to vote unless they are officially registered as voters before the time of election. Some states have permanent **registration**; once registered, a person remains qualified to vote unless he or she leaves the election district or fails to vote in a number of elections. Other states require periodic registration; individuals must register at regular intervals. This automatically disqualifies those who fail to renew their registration.

Registration may be made easy by allowing prospective voters to register by mail or by permitting registrars to solicit door-to-door or to set up registration booths in heavily frequented areas such as shopping centers or libraries. Registration becomes more difficult, thus reducing the number of voters, if applicants must go to a central place, such as a county court house.

States are required by the U.S. Supreme Court and Congress to allow people to register up to thirty days before an election. Even that short period restricts the number of voters, since it disqualifies those who move out of state within that period.

On the whole, voter registration is simple, quick, and easy. Nevertheless, millions of Americans do not even bother to register! They remain ineligible to vote although they meet all other requirements.

③ *Institutional incarceration.* Individuals in mental institutions and those sent to prison on felony charges are also denied the right to vote. Some states refuse to permit exfelons to vote unless their voting rights have been officially reinstated.

④ *Absentee voting.* States differ regarding their policy of permitting individuals to vote by **absentee ballot** if they are away from their voting districts on election day. Those states that set the deadline for applying for absentee ballots far ahead of the election date place additional obstacles in the path of potential voters.

ELECTIONS AND VOTER TURNOUT

The main types of elections held in the United States are candidate elections and policy issue elections. Each is conducted and paid for by the state and local governments in our federal system. Candidate elections take place for officials at all levels of our governmental system. Policy issue elections occur principally at the state and local levels of government. The type of election being conducted has a direct effect on voter turnout.

Candidate Elections

You are probably most familiar with candidate elections. The number of voters who turn out for these contests varies according to the government level and office for which candidates compete, whether the elections are partisan or nonpartisan in nature, and whether they are party elections to nominate candidates or general elections to choose public officials.

The federal system and voter turnout. In the United States we elect leaders to serve at all levels of our federal system. We elect a President and Vice President, 100 U.S. senators, 435 members of the U.S. House of Representatives, and over 500,000 state and local government officials. The governmental level of the official on whom the election centers influences voter participation significantly. The highest turnout by eligible voters is almost invariably in national elections. The next highest turnout occurs in state elections, and the lowest in elections for local officials.

A number of reasons have been advanced to explain this phenomenon. Much more dramatic issues are at the center of national politics than local politics, and national candidates spend more money on their campaigns. In addition, the media focus greater attention on national contests than on state and local elections. The caliber of the politicians may also contribute to the difference in voter turnout, the more ambitious, dynamic, successful ones tending to shoot for the highest levels of power in the federal system.

Voter participation and the separation of powers. Our governmental system establishes separate branches of government with different officials in each. These sets of officials are responsible to different electorates. Except for the national judiciary, which is appointed, elections occur for executive, legislative, and judicial officers at all levels of the U.S. federal system.

Voter participation varies with the type of office that is contested in an election. Executive elections draw a higher percentage of the eligible voters than do legislative elections. And contests for legislative seats attract a greater percentage of voters than do judicial contests.

Data for voter participation in presidential and congressional elections are presented in Table 6–1. Note the difference in numbers voting for the two types of offices. Many of those who vote for President do not even bother to vote for members to the U.S. House of Representatives who are on the same ballot. The falloff in voting is even more extreme during off-year congressional elections. Obviously, the presidency is unique. When it is at stake in elections, it significantly raises the voter turnout for all other offices as well.

Voter turnout in partisan and nonpartisan elections. Elections for national and state offices (except for the legislature of Nebraska) are **partisan elections:** Candidates run under party labels. **Nonpartisan elections,** in which candidates compete for public office without party designations on the ballots, occur almost entirely at the local levels of government. Only a minority of local governments in the United States use partisan elections.

When nominees of political parties compete, generally a higher percentage of the electorate votes than when nonpartisan candidates compete. In the absence of political party campaigns and party labels, voters find it harder to decide on candidates and local elections tend to become "issueless contests."

Table 6–1
Voter Turnout for Presidential and House of
Representatives Elections, 1960–1978 (by percentage)

	1960	1962	1964	1966	1968	1970	1972	1974	1976	1978
National vote for President	63.1		61.8		60.7		55.4		54.4	
National vote for House of Representatives	58.7	46.3	57.8	45.4	55.2	43.8	50.9	36.1	49.2	34.0 (est.)*

*Data for 1978 is an estimate by The Committee for the Study of the American Electorate, *Time Magazine* (November 20, 1978), p. 35.

SOURCE: U.S. Bureau of the Census for 1960 through 1976.

Voter turnout in primary elections and general elections. As we have used the term up to now, an election is a process by which people vote for candidates who compete for public office. These are **general elections,** open to the entire electorate. In partisan general elections, almost all candidates have originally been chosen through earlier party nominating elections called **primaries.** In *primary* (party nominating) *elections,* party members vote to select their candidates for the general elections. Only in a few states are nonmembers permitted to vote in a party's primary. A special type of party primary is the **presidential primary.** This primary either chooses delegates from state parties who will attend national presidential nominating conventions or helps determine how these state party delegates will vote at the national convention.

Nonpartisan general elections at the local government level are also preceded by nonpartisan primaries to narrow the field of candidates who will compete in the final election. Unlike partisan primaries, all eligible voters, regardless of party, may participate.

Voter turnout varies with these different types of elections. Primary elections attract only a very small percentage of those eligible to participate; general elections attract a higher percentage. Ironically, primaries were originally intended to stimulate voter participation and to democratize the candidate selection process.

Policy Issue Elections

If we conducted national referendums as do France, Switzerland, Australia, and a number of other democratic countries, Americans would be more familiar with issue or policy elections. Our policy elections are primarily held on the state or local level.

Voter turnout: policy issue versus candidate elections. Policy issue elections come closer to pure democracy than candidate elections; by voting on policy issues the voters themselves directly make governmental decisions. You might suppose that the turnout would be high. Instead, it is astonishingly low.

A number of reasons explain why fewer Americans participate in policy elections than in candidate elections. As a rule the issues tend to be unexciting, devoid of the human drama inherent in candidate contests. Moreover, although policy issues require only a simple yes or no vote, they demand a higher degree of understanding than candidate elections. Voters must make an extra effort. Party labels often simplify the choice for voters in candidate elections, and voters can identify with a person and a political party much more easily than with a proposed law. In addition, the personality of the candidates, their competition, and the activity of party organizations stimulate voting participation.

Do not conclude that all issue elections attract few voters. Those that ask the voter to decide on "liquor by the drink," "right to work" laws, gun control, legalized gambling, fluoridation of city water, or the building of nuclear power plants become supercharged with controversy. They are highly emotional issues and tend to become the focus of campaigns by opposing groups that actively publicize their side of the issue and bring out the voters.

Types of policy issue elections.   Policy issue elections break down into two different types: *referendums* and *initiatives*. Either may determine constitutional or statutory policy decisions.

Referendum policy elections allow members of the general electorate to vote on policy decisions *already made* by public officials. Legislatures may vote to refer a law that they passed to the people for their final decision. In fact, local and state legislatures may be obligated to refer certain policy issues, such as authorizing government to sell bonds or increase its indebtedness, to a popular vote. The constitutions of forty-nine states and numerous cities require their legislatures to refer all proposed constitutional amendments to a popular vote. A referendum may also start through a popular petition, signed by enough eligible voters, that stops a law from going into effect until the people have voted on it. Referendums, therefore, allow the people to become partners with their legislatures in policy making.

Initiative policy elections are proposed by some group within the public. The group develops the proposal—a law or constitutional amendment—and, by securing the signatures of enough eligible voters, places its policy issue on the ballot. Initiative policy elections bypass the legislature, governor, and even the judiciary in making policy. Policy is proposed initially by the people and voted on only by the people. Twenty-three of our states and many cities grant their citizens the right to initiate laws or constitutional amendments in this manner.

The U.S. Constitution makes no provision for popular elections on either constitutional amendments or national legislation. Congress, however, has authorized votes by special electorates on two types of policy issues, in the areas of agriculture and labor.

Farmers engaged in the cultivation of certain crops—wheat, peanuts, and cotton are among those included—are allowed to participate in government-sponsored referendums on the issue of committing themselves to restrict their acreage in return for certain government price supports. The national government starts the referendum; no popular petition method is available. Should enough farmers vote their approval, the government will offer financial support for *all* farmers producing this crop if the market price falls below a certain level. Should they reject the referendum, the government will either provide no support or a much lower level of support than if the farmers had voted their approval.

Workers who petition for union representation in their place of employment may also vote in elections conducted by the national government. The issue is whether they should be represented by a particular trade union in bargaining with management. If the majority of workers voting favor the union, it becomes their official agent.

VOTERS, NONVOTERS, AND VOTER TURNOUT

Voter turnout is *not* uniform throughout the country. Find your state's participation rate in Table 6–2 and compare it with the national percentage. The 1972 national voter turnout was 55.4 percent; it ranged from 37.9 percent in Georgia to 68.7 percent in South Dakota. In 1976 only 54.4 percent of those eligible voted for President. South Carolina had the lowest state turnout, 41.5 percent; and Minnesota had the highest, 71.6 percent.

Why do Americans in different states vote at such widely different rates in the same type of election? Students of voting behavior suggest a number of factors: level of education and income; ease of registration; degree of two-party competition. States with higher family incomes and levels of education have higher voter turnouts than states with low family incomes and educational levels. State registration laws may also affect turnout rates. So too may the degree of party competition. Southern states, therefore, may rank abnormally low in voter turnout because they rank low in education, income, and two-party competition. In both the 1972 and 1976 presidential elections, the turnout for southern states was below 50 percent. The other three regions ranked above 50 percent.

Proposals for Increasing Voter Turnout

A number of reforms have been proposed to increase the participation of Americans in their elections. They range from making registration easier to taxing those who do not vote.

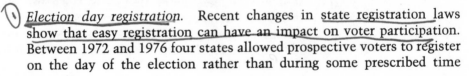

Election day registration.   Recent changes in state registration laws show that easy registration can have an impact on voter participation. Between 1972 and 1976 four states allowed prospective voters to register on the day of the election rather than during some prescribed time

Table 6–2
Percentage Voter Turnout by State,
Presidential Elections of 1976 and 1972

	NORTHEAST			SOUTH	
	1976	1972		1976	1972
Connecticut	66.5	66.3	Alabama	47.3	43.5
Delaware	58.5	62.4	Arkansas	51.1	47.9
Washington, D.C.	32.8	30.8	Florida	49.8	49.3
Maine	65.2	61.1	Georgia	43.5	37.9
Maryland	50.3	50.3	Kentucky	49.2	48.4
Massachusetts	61.0	62.0	Louisiana	50.5	44.3
New Hampshire	59.2	64.2	Mississippi	49.8	45.0
New Jersey	58.5	60.0	North Carolina	43.6	43.4
New York	50.6	56.6	Oklahoma	56.4	56.9
Pennsylvania	54.7	56.0	South Carolina	41.5	38.6
Rhode Island	63.5	62.0	Tennessee	49.9	43.6
Vermont	56.2	60.8	Texas	47.9	45.3
West Virginia	58.6	62.4	Virginia	48.1	45.5

	MIDWEST			WEST	
	1976	1972		1976	1972
Illinois	61.1	62.7	Alaska	53.5	48.2
Indiana	61.1	60.8	Arizona	47.8	50.5
Iowa	63.6	63.3	California	51.4	59.1
Kansas	59.5	59.0	Colorado	61.1	60.2
Michigan	58.3	59.5	Hawaii	48.6	50.4
Minnesota	71.6	68.4	Idaho	60.7	63.1
Missouri	58.4	57.3	Montana	63.5	67.8
Nebraska	56.2	55.9	Nevada	47.6	51.0
North Dakota	68.8	68.0	New Mexico	54.0	57.5
Ohio	55.1	57.5	Oregon	62.3	61.7
South Dakota	64.1	68.7	Utah	69.1	68.4
Wisconsin	65.5	62.0	Washington	61.3	63.8
			Wyoming	58.8	63.8

	1976	1972
Northeast	55.0	57.7
South	48.1	45.3
Midwest	60.4	60.8
West	54.4	59.7

SOURCE: U.S. Bureau of the Census.

preceding it. Table 6–3 reveals that each of these states increased its national rankings, with Maine and Wisconsin achieving the greatest advance. North Dakota is included in the Table because this state does not require those who wish to vote to register. In each of these states voter turnout increased over that in 1972, while national voter participation dropped.

Table 6–3
Voter Turnout and Ranking of Five States
That Permit Election Day Registration*

Date of Registration Change	State	Percent Turnout		Rank in Nation	
		1972	1976	1972	1976
1973	Maine	61.1	65.2	19	5
1973	Minnesota	68.4	71.6	2	1
1951	North Dakota	68.0	68.8	4	3
1975	Oregon	61.7	62.3	18	11
1975	Wisconsin	62.0	65.5	15	4

*Minnesota and Wisconsin permit registration at the polling place and ask only for proof of identity and residence. Maine and Oregon permit registration at the town hall or with the county clerk. North Dakota has no registration requirement at all.

SOURCE: *Congressional Quarterly Weekly Report,* May 14, 1977, p. 913.

President Jimmy Carter was so committed to election day registration reform that in 1977 he strongly urged Congress to adopt legislation encouraging this practice in all the states. Although his plan won initial endorsement from leaders of both major parties, Republicans quickly soured on the proposal, seeing it as aiding primarily the Democratic party. Republican opposition together with reservations raised by some state election officials, Democrats as well as Republicans, about the possibility of fraud in the election day registration plan, effectively prevented its adoption by Congress.

Government should register everyone. European democracies follow a practice of having government register everyone. Their citizens do not have to find the time or make the effort to register; all they have to do is decide whether or not to vote.

An American reform that moves away from total individual responsibility without substituting total governmental responsibility is mail registration. This method is now being tried in some states. Special registration cards are made available or are mailed to the people by the state government, which takes the initiative. The individual need only fill out and return the card.

Mail registration is still too new to demonstrate whether it increases the percentage of eligible voters and whether they turn out to cast ballots. But the result of New York State's experience in 1976 was not too encouraging. Despite the introduction of voter registration by mail, the number of registered eligibles at election time was estimated to be about 700,000 less than in 1972.

Compulsory voting: Imposing fines for not participating. At present there is no direct cost to Americans who do not vote. You might argue that nonvoters pay indirectly by permitting others to make decisions that will subsequently affect them. But indirect costs are very hard for many people to recognize.

Some democracies, the Netherlands and Australia, for example, do make it costly not to participate in elections. They impose a fine on anyone who does not vote. This may be one of the reasons why their voter turnout rate is higher than ours. Are we ready to penalize people for not voting in elections? So far, no state has adopted such a system. Would you favor it or not? Why?

Nonvoting and the Democratic System

Despite the ease, visibility, low cost, and legitimacy of voting, a large proportion of our people today are not interested in participating in elections. Almost 46 percent of eligible Americans, approximately 68.5 million, did not bother to vote for President in 1976. On the other hand, the fact that only one percentage point fewer of those eligible participated in 1976 than in 1972 may indicate a stabilization in voter turnout, in contrast with the sharp decline in voter turnout from 1960 to 1972 in presidential elections. We will have to wait for the 1980 figures to ascertain whether the decline has actually stopped or is continuing.

Although making registration procedures easier may increase voter turnout, a significant proportion of Americans will continue to ignore elections. Some are indifferent to politics, feeling that it and government are irrelevant to their lives. Some are alienated from politics, considering it a dirty business, and they want nothing to do with it. Still others recognize that politics and government are important, but believe they have no real choice. The major candidates and parties do not suit them or they believe governmental leaders will not pay attention to their needs and interests.

Can our system operate effectively when a significant proportion of our population is unwilling to participate as voters? Of course it can! It

Table 6–4
Voter Turnout in Presidential Elections, 1952–1976

	1976	1972	1968	1964	1960	1956	1952
National percentage	54.4	55.4	60.7	61.8	63.1	59.3	61.6

SOURCE: U.S. Bureau of the Census.

has, it does, and it will continue to—as long as nonvoters accept the election results. Other citizens will vote, and the elections will reflect the decisions of the majority or plurality within the electorate.

Democracy does not require all of us to participate as activists in shaping our government. What democracy does require is that we all have the power to make decisions concerning our leaders or policy issues. It requires that individuals be free to vote or to compete for office in elections without fear of governmental repression or private sanctions.

VOTERS AND NONVOTERS

Next to talking about politics, the one form of political activity in which Americans most frequently engage is voting. It requires very little effort and initiative from an individual, it costs nothing, and it is secret. The secret ballot is especially important, for it protects the participant from the risk of exposure or censure. Most other forms of political participation are more costly, in terms of time, effort, or money and require a person to be adept at interacting with others.

Some people vote because it is considered almost a "sacred" right or duty. Moreover, it has respectability, legitimacy, and visibility, advantages that other types of political involvement do not always possess. Many Americans view political party or interest group activities with skepticism and contempt as part of the "dirty" business of politics. No such stigma is attached to voting in elections.

By vividly publicizing election campaigns, the mass media make people aware of contests and their opportunity to vote. Schools and the media also stress our civic obligation to vote. In addition, political parties and a number of interest groups invest time, money, talent, and effort in bringing people to the polls to vote for their candidates or issues.

Who Votes and Who Does Not Vote?

Two weeks after a presidential election, the U. S. Bureau of the Census interviews a national sample of persons who were eligible to vote. The responses provide us with information about the voting behavior of the total voting-age population and of the various segments within it. The problem with this data is that Americans tend to exaggerate their participation. Table 6–5 enables you to compare the percentage of people who we *know* voted in the last four presidential elections with the percentage of those *reporting* they had voted. Note the disparity in each case. As long as we remain aware of and discount this exaggeration in reported voter turnout, we can use the official data to examine the

Table 6–5
*Actual vs. Reported Voter Turnout
in Presidential Elections, 1964–1976*

	1964	1968	1972	1976
Actual	61.8%	60.7%	55.4%	54.4%
Reported	69.3%	67.8%	63.0%	59.2%

SOURCE: U.S. Bureau of the Census.

differences between voters and nonvoters within various segments of the electorate.

Socioeconomic status: education, income, and occupation. Education is closely related to income and profession, and all three contribute to voter turnout. The three categories make up a way of classifying people according to what is called **socioeconomic status (SES)**. Those with higher SES (more education, higher income, and more preferred occupations) tend to see government and politics as relating more meaningfully to themselves, not as something alien and remote. They are more likely than those with low SES to feel a sense of obligation (duty) to vote, and they are inclined to be more confident about their effectiveness in politics. Not only do they involve themselves in more levels of political activity, but they expose themselves much more to the media, which increases their political consciousness and participation.

Probably the most important predictor of voter participation is a person's level of education. Note from Table 6–6 how the percentage of voter turnout increases significantly with each higher level of education. Similarly, as income level goes up, a greater percentage of Americans vote. Whereas only 20 percent of those with the highest incomes failed to vote in 1972, almost 55 percent of those earning the lowest incomes did not vote. Occupation also relates to voter turnout. Farm, blue-collar, and service workers vote at much lower rates than white-collar workers, or than farmers, who are, in effect, independent businessmen.

Age. Voting participation is also closely related to a person's age. The youngest group of eligible voters tends to participate the least; middle-age Americans, the most. Voting participation drops off among the very old, but remains higher than that of adults eighteen to twenty-four. Table 6–7 shows the proportion of each age group that reported having voted in presidential elections of 1972 and 1976.

Why are younger Americans less likely to vote? In 1976 over 60 percent of those age eighteen to twenty and over 50 percent of those age twenty-one to twenty-four reported not voting. The assumption is that

Table 6-6
Reported Voter Turnout by Education, Family Income, and Occupation, 1972 Presidential Election

Education (Years Completed)	Turnout	Income	Turnout	Occupation	Turnout
Elementary school (8)	55.2	Below $3,000	45.7	Farm laborers	42.3
High school (4)	65.4	$3,000 to $4,999	52.0	Blue-collar workers	54.2
College (4)	82.3	$5,000 to $7,499	54.1	Service workers	58.6
		$7,500 to $9,999	61.6	White-collar workers	76.4
		$10,000 to $14,999	70.5	Farmers	77.8
		$15,000 and over	79.3		

SOURCE: U.S. Bureau of the Census.

Table 6–7
Percentage of Age Groups Reporting Having Voted in
Presidential Elections, 1972 and 1976

	18–20	21–24	25–34	35–44	45–54	55–64	65–74	75 and over
1976	38.0	45.6	55.4	63.3	67.9	69.7	66.4	54.8
1972	48.3	50.7	59.7	66.3	70.9	70.7	68.1	55.6

SOURCE: U.S. Bureau of the Census.

those young adults are less concerned with politics and more preoccupied with such immediate concerns as jobs, education, dating, and sports. Perhaps because young people are more mobile, they are particularly affected by residency requirements.

Sex. Since the Constitution first prohibited states from using sex to determine who might vote, women have voted at a much lower rate than men. In more recent elections the tendency of women to be voters has increased sharply. Table 6–8 indicates that the percentage of voters among women now closely approximates that of men. It is clear that sex differences no longer explain why some Americans vote and other do not. In view of the increased education of women, their active participation in the labor force, and their greater involvement in politics, the percentage of women voting will soon equal and probably surpass that of men.

Race. Blacks have consistently voted at a much lower rate than whites even after the passage of voting rights legislation by Congress as well as decisions by the courts and actions by the U.S. Department of Justice. The lower education and income of blacks as compared to whites have continued to depress the rate of black participation in elections. Note

Table 6–8
Percentage of Females and Males Reporting Having
Voted in Presidential Elections, 1964–1976

	1976	1972	1968	1964
Males	59.6	64.1	69.8	71.9
Females	58.8	62.0	66.0	67.0
Percentile point difference	−0.8	−2.1	−3.8	−4.9

SOURCE: U.S. Bureau of the Census.

Table 6–9
Percent of Black and White Americans Reporting
Having Voted in Select Presidential Elections, 1964–1976

	1976	1972	1968	1964
Whites	60.9	64.5	69.1	70.7
Blacks	48.7	52.1	57.6	58.5
Percentile point difference	12.2	12.4	11.5	12.2

SOURCE: U.S. Bureau of the Census.

that in the last four presidential elections the difference between whites and blacks reporting having voted has remained relatively constant.

Regions. A greater percentage of southerners than nonsoutherners do not vote. The lower rate of voter turnout in the South is attributed to a number of factors: less competition between the two major parties, a higher percentage of blacks, and lower educational and income levels among members of both races. The fact that the South is more rural may contribute to its lower turnout, because higher participation rates occur in metropolitan areas and lower rates in small towns. However, as the South has begun to resemble the rest of the country, the disparity between voters in the South and the rest of the country has sharply decreased (see Table 6–10).

Profiles of the Voter and Nonvoter

From our data we can draw realistic profiles of voters and nonvoters in the United States. Look over the profiles in Table 6–11 and see to what extent they fit you and your family or friends.

A word of caution is in order. Americans who fit the voter profile

Table 6–10
Percent in South and in North and West Reporting
Having Voted in Presidential Elections, 1964–1976

	1976	1972	1968	1964
North and West	61.2	66.4	71.0	74.6
South	54.9	55.4	60.1	56.7
Percentile point difference	6.3	11.0	10.9	17.9

SOURCE: U.S. Bureau of the Census.

Table 6-11
Profiles of Voters and Nonvoters

Characteristics of Probable *Voters*	Characteristics of Probable Non-Voters
More education	Less education
Higher income	Lower income
White-collar occupation	Blue-collar, farm, and service occupation
White	Nonwhite
Middle aged	Young adult
Nonsouthern	Southerner
Urban dweller	Rural dweller
Male	Female

are *more likely* to participate in elections, but individuals sharing these characteristics also turn out to be nonvoters. Those who fit the nonvoter profile are *less likely* to participate in elections, yet many individuals who share these characteristics show up to vote.

THE ELECTORAL COLLEGE: A SPECIAL ELECTION SYSTEM

The American presidential election is unique. In all other candidate and policy elections, the people make the choice directly. However, in presidential elections, a small special group of elected officials (**presidential electors**) vote for the President and Vice President. The people only determine who these presidential electors will be. This was the election system set up by the Constitution, and it continues to remain in effect. So far, no proposal to change the electoral college system has won acceptance.

The Nature of the Electoral College

The **electoral college** is based on two principles: federalism and an indirect election by an elite group of people. Those who designed the Constitution believed in a republican form of government, not a democratic one. Because they did not trust the people, the selection of the President and Vice President (like the selection of members of the Senate and the judiciary) was not entrusted to a popular vote. Political parties, however, have introduced an element of democracy.

Federalism and the presidential election system. You will recall that the Great Compromise at the Constitutional Convention of 1787 called for a two-house Congress. In the Senate each state was to have two votes; in the House, each state's representatives were to be proportionate in number to its population. The electoral college fits this federal compromise perfectly.

Each state has as many presidential electors as it has national legislators. Look at the map of the electoral college in 1976. The number of electors in the states ranges from three to forty-five. After each national census, held at ten-year intervals, the electoral votes of some states change as they lose or gain seats in the House of Representatives. Although not a state and having no voting representative in Congress, the District of Columbia was given three electoral votes in 1961 by Amendment Twenty-three. Consequently, the presidential electors now total 538 (equal in number to the 435 members of the House of Representatives, 100 senators and 3 electors from the District of Columbia).

Note that electors are *not* members of Congress. And congressmen are *not* electors. Check the number of electors in your own state and compare it with that of the other states.

Indirect election of electors. The method for choosing presidential electors is left by the Constitution to each state legislature. Initially most state legislatures themselves chose the electors. Today, the people in each state vote for electors. In all states but one, candidates for the office of elector run at large, which means that all the voters cast their ballots for a statewide ticket of candidates. In Maine, one elector is voted on in each congressional district, and the statewide electorate chooses two at large.

Political parties and the electoral college. Those seeking the office of elector are either listed on the ballot together with the names of party candidates for whom they will presumably vote for President and Vice President or the candidates for electors are left off the ballot entirely and only the names of the different parties' candidates for President and Vice President are listed, plus the number of their electoral candidates.

Voters may think they are voting for the two candidates on a party's presidential ticket, but in reality they are voting for the unseen list of electoral candidates pledged to vote for that presidential ticket. Not only do few Americans know who these electoral candidates are, but they do not really need to know. Those responsible for selecting candidates for presidential electors, the state political parties, as a rule, nominate loyal party members who will vote for the parties' national presidential tickets.

Political parties have changed the entire nature of the electoral college. Those who designed the Constitution thought that a few prom-

Figure 6-1
1976 Electoral Votes by States

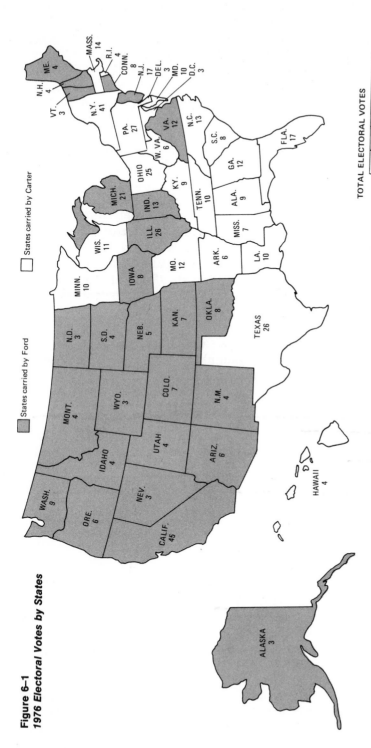

■ States carried by Ford

□ States carried by Carter

TOTAL ELECTORAL VOTES

	1960	1964	1968	1972	1976
Democrat	303	486	191	17	297
Republican	219	52	301	520	241
Others*	15	0	46	1	0

* Other electoral votes were cast as follows:
1960—Harry F. Byrd, Sr. (D., Va.) received 15 votes, including three of six of the Democratic electors in Alabama, all eight unpledged electors in Mississippi, and one of the Republican electors in Oklahoma.
1968—George C. Wallace (D., Ala.), candidate of the American Independent party, carried five states having a total of 45 electoral votes: Alabama (10), Arkansas (6), Georgia (12), Louisiana (10), and Mississippi (7). In addition, one Republican elector in North Carolina voted for Wallace.
1972—John Hospers, candidate of the Libertarian party, received one electoral vote from a Virginia Republican elector.

Note: This figure fails to indicate that in 1976 a Republican presidential elector from the state of Washington voted for Ronald Reagan.

SOURCE: *Congressional Quarterly Weekly Report,* Nov. 6, 1976, p. 3114.

inent individuals in each state would be chosen to be presidential electors. In their wisdom and on their own initiative, these electors would vote for persons they deemed best qualified to be President and Vice President. Competing political parties, appearing soon after the Constitution was adopted, quickly developed the practice of committing their electoral candidates in advance to vote for party nominees for these two executive offices.

Although presidential electors still choose the President and Vice President, they have, in effect, given up their initiative and independence. By committing their candidates for electors in advance to their candidates for President and Vice President, the political parties have made the voters the key decision makers. Since the popular electorate in each state chooses among the different sets of committed electoral candidates, one of which becomes the *electors*, the people have virtually a direct voice in making the decision on the President and Vice President. Of course, electors are still legally free to vote as they wish, and occasionally one will do so. For the most part, however, electors vote for the presidential ticket they are identified with on the ballot.

The letter of the Constitution remains the same as when it was originally drafted. But the spirit of the Constitution has been radically changed. Without any amendment, simply through custom, candidates for electors are now virtually committed to vote a party's presidential ticket in accordance with the wishes of most of the voters in a state. The popular election in each state makes the choice; in effect, the electors ratify that choice.

The role of electors. Chosen by popular vote in the November general election, the presidential electors convene in their state capitals in December to vote by secret ballot for President and Vice President. In January of the next year, the ballots are opened and counted before a joint session of both houses of Congress. The candidate with a majority of electoral votes for President wins, as does the candidate with a majority for Vice President.

Note that the electoral college can fail to choose a President and Vice President. If no candidate receives a majority of all the electoral votes—270, or one more than half of 538—or if there is a tie, the election of President must move to the House of Representatives. This has happened twice, after the elections of 1800 and 1824. If no candidate receives a majority for the vice presidency, this contest is thrown in to the Senate.

Just as the electoral college system for picking our President and Vice President is unique, so, too, is the method when the election moves into Congress. In voting for President among the top three candidates in the electoral college, the 435 members of the House do not vote as individuals. Instead, each state delegation, no matter its size, has only one vote. Whichever candidate receives a majority vote of all the state delegations (twenty-six, or one more than one-half of fifty) becomes President. This voting system is an absolute reversal of the principle on which the House of Representatives was established: greater voting representation for those states with larger populations.

In choosing a Vice President, the Senate chooses from the two candidates with the most electoral votes. Each Senator votes as an individual, and a majority of the entire Senate, or fifty-one votes, is required to elect a Vice President.

Criticism of the Electoral College

So far in this century the electoral college has always elected a President and Vice President. On the other hand, it failed twice in the nineteenth century and it only narrowly escaped a similar failure in some of the presidential elections held during the past thirty years.

From *The Herblock Book*, Beacon Press, 1952

"Don't expect me to get this real accurate, Bub."

The election may be thrown into Congress. One criticism of the electoral college is that it can break down again, throwing the election into Congress. A number of problems are associated with the House's electing a President. If a state delegation is divided equally between Democrats and Republicans, it may not be able to cast its vote and the people of its state will have no voice in the final choice. Moreover, a majority of all the state delegations in the House is necessary to elect a President, and that majority might represent the smallest states and thus a minority of the people in the country.

A majority of the state delegations in the House could be dominated by members of one party, in contrast to the electoral college where a plurality favored the presidential candidate of the opposite party. For example, if the Republicans were to win a plurality (but not a majority) of electoral votes, a Democratic-dominated House could theoretically elect a Democrat to be President.

Another problem can emerge if the choice of a President is not settled as soon as possible after an election. Congressional delay in choosing a President might very well result in confusion, loss of momentum, and uncertainty in our foreign policy. Delay can seriously affect domestic programs as well, since the Congress, the executive bureaucracy, and the people usually depend upon the President to propose ways for dealing with economic and social problems.

The electoral majority may not represent a popular majority. Another criticism of the electoral college is that it permits a person who does not win a majority of the popular vote to be chosen President. Indeed, the electoral choice for President may come into office with a plurality, or even a minority, of the votes of the people.

John Quincy Adams was chosen President by the House of Representatives in 1824, yet Andrew Jackson had the most electoral votes and the highest number of popular votes. Republican Rutherford B. Hayes became President in 1876, even though his Democratic opponent, Samuel J. Tilden, had won a majority of the popular votes. In 1888 Republican candidate Benjamin Harrison was elected President with an electoral majority, despite the fact that his Democratic opponent had won most of the popular vote.

How can a candidate win a majority of the electoral vote while receiving only a minority of the popular vote? The answer is that all electors in every state but Maine are chosen according to the **winner-take-all rule.** Because they run and are elected as a single slate, whichever set of electoral candidates in a state receives the most votes wins in that state. This means that in some highly contested states the winning electoral slate may draw only a few more popular votes than any other slate. Nevertheless, it wins all that state's electoral votes, and the popular votes cast for the losing slates do not count. This distorts the relationship between the total popular vote and the electoral vote.

To illustrate this distortion, suppose that presidential candidate X's electors won by very thin popular margins in the twelve largest states while presidential candidate Y's electors were chosen by very large majorities in the remaining thirty-eight states and the District of Columbia. Since the twelve largest states make up the overwhelming majority of the electoral college, candidate X would be chosen President with more than a majority (270) of the electoral votes. Candidate Y would lose, even though he or she had received the overwhelming majority of the popular vote in the country.

Electors remain legally free to vote as they wish.   A third criticism centers on the freedom of presidential electors to disregard the expectations of those who voted for them in the general election. As voters, we assume that Republican and Democratic electors will vote for the candidates of their respective national parties. In other words, we expect the electors to vote as we would, had we been able to vote directly for President.

But electors may legally vote as they please. The only real restraint on their voting is their sense of moral obligation to their political party and to the voters who elected them. Electors who violate such moral commitments betray their trust. Not many electors have done so, but enough have to raise questions regarding the electoral college. In each of the elections of 1960, 1968, 1972, and 1976, a Republican presidential elector refused to vote for his party's presidential ticket. One voted for a Democrat who was not even a candidate, one for a Republican who had failed to win his party's nomination, and two voted for candidates of third parties!

There is still another dimension to the free elector problem. The state party has no legal obligation to the candidates of its national party. Since each state political party picks those who compete for the office of presidential elector, it may free them from any commitment to their national party ticket. Or it may commit them to vote for another party's presidential slate. In 1948 four southern Democratic state parties committed their electoral candidates to the presidential ticket of the Dixiecrat party.

REFORMING THE PRESIDENTIAL ELECTION SYSTEM

Four principal reforms have been suggested for improving the system by which we elect our President and Vice President. These range from a most modest alteration in the electoral college to its complete abolition.

Keep the Electoral College, Remove the Electors

The most minimal reform calls for retaining the electoral college, but dispensing with the electors themselves. The people in each state would vote directly for the presidential ticket of a political party. Whichever won the most popular votes in a state would gain all its electoral votes. The electoral votes a presidential ticket received from all the states would simply be added together to determine which slate won a majority in the electoral college.

Because there would be no presidential electors to vote for President and Vice President, none could betray their trust to the electorate and to their state political parties. And no state party could use its electors to undermine the campaign of its national party ticket. Democratic President Lyndon B. Johnson and Republican President Richard M. Nixon both urged the adoption of this reform, but Congress has never seriously considered it.

Abolish the Winner-Take-All System

Another set of reforms aim at abolishing the statewide winner-take-all feature of the present system. One proposes that electors in each state be chosen in the same manner as we now elect members of Congress. One elector would be chosen in each congressional district of a state, and two would be chosen at large by the statewide electorate (as Maine does today). The other reform proposes retaining the statewide election of all presidential electors, but calls for dividing a state's electoral votes in proportion to its popular vote for the different party tickets (proportional representation). With either reform the state and the national distribution of electoral votes would more closely approximate the popular vote for the presidential tickets of the competing parties.

Critics see two dangers in these reforms. They might encourage competitive third and fourth parties, since their candidates would be guaranteed a share of the electoral vote in states where they polled a significant proportion of the popular vote. Moreover, the national electoral vote could be so divided it would prove impossible for any presidential candidate to capture the necessary electoral majority. Hence the election would more frequently be thrown into Congress.

Abolish the Electoral College

The most radical reform is to abolish the electoral college and replace it with the direct popular election of the President and Vice President. States would no longer have any weight in choosing these two officials.

The vote of the national electorate alone would determine our top executive leaders.

One objection to this reform is that minor parties might divert enough popular votes to their candidates so as to prevent any major party's presidential ticket from winning a popular majority. This problem could be resolved by permitting a presidential ticket to be chosen by a popular plurality rather than by a majority. But how much of a plurality should be required?

A direct popular-election constitutional amendment was adopted by the U.S. House of Representatives in 1969. It proposed setting the winning number of popular votes at 40 percent or more of the national total. In the event no presidential ticket received that minimum, a runoff election would take place between the two candidates with the highest number of votes. Under this amendment Congress would play no role in choosing either the President or Vice President. The Senate's refusal to approve the amendment stopped Congress from proposing it to the states.

Those criticizing the direct-election reform fear that it would destroy our traditional two-party system by fostering the growth of additional political parties. They believe that abolishing the electoral college would also weaken American federalism, since the states would cease to play any role in electing the presidential ticket.

The direct election plan is plagued with all sorts of uncertainties as to who would gain or lose by its adoption. Some fear that people in the small states would be placed at a disadvantage by this reform; others, that certain groups in the large states would lose political clout. This uncertainty has split the black leadership, organized labor, southerners, and members of both major political parties. In the face of such uncertainty for so many important political groups, the direct election plan has little chance of being passed at present.

FINANCING CANDIDATES
IN NATIONAL ELECTION CAMPAIGNS

As part of his 1977 package of reform bills dealing with elections, President Carter suggested that Congress provide subsidies for candidates campaigning for election to the House of Representatives and the Senate. "Public financing of candidates," he said in support of such subsidies, "not only minimizes even the appearance of obligations to special interest contributors, but also provides an opportunity for qualified persons who lack funds to seek public office."

The high cost of reaching the electorate to publicize candidates and induce people to vote in elections is what makes campaigns expensive.

Television and radio time, the most effective way to reach exceptionally large numbers of people, are the most expensive items. Transportation, mass mailings, telephones, headquarters, staff and advance men, plus a host of other expenses increase the cost of campaigning. Campaigning for the presidency, of course, is the most expensive. Nevertheless, candidates for the Senate in some states have had to put together campaign funds of $1 million and more. Some House races cost hundreds of thousands of dollars. Money may not assure victory, but campaigns fall apart quickly without adequate financing, and some do not even get off the ground.

The large sums of money required for campaigns have prevented many able individuals from offering themselves for public office. At the same time, high campaign costs have made candidates vulnerable to those who can offer them money. Many who offer financial help want nothing more than to participate in the excitement of a campaign or to choose an official who shares their point of view. Others, however, expect their contribution to buy them special favor or advantage. It is only natural that some candidates who win feel a sense of obligation to the big givers.

The so-called fat cats in business, labor, agriculture, and the professions, those who can spend large sums for candidates, often end up with a more influential voice in government than the ordinary voter because of their sizable contributions. Although a vote is an equalizing instrument—each of us may exercise one and only one, no matter the size of our income—the ease with which some can make large contributions severely strains the democratic concepts that all should be equal in choosing their leaders and that government should consider individuals as if they were equal.

The high cost of campaigning combined with the present method of private financing also benefit incumbent elected officials and penalize those who challenge them. Incumbents in the national Congress or the presidency have an enormous advantage in raising money because they occupy the seats of power. To give to them is to invest in proven winners, candidates who are already in positions to affect public policy. Moreover, incumbents do not have to spend as much as their opponents to achieve name recognition, and they have constant access to free publicity in the news media. Most challengers for public office are doubly handicapped in that they are less well-known than their incumbent opponents and they find it more difficult to finance their campaigns.

Private financing of campaigns also raises serious questions regarding the morality of American politics. Undoubtedly, private financing contributes to the corruption of some politicians. It helps create a political climate in which people become cynical about honesty and integrity in government. To the extent that private financing of election

ELECTION TRENDS

campaigns corrodes the trust and confidence that people have in their public officials, it undermines the strength and integrity of democratic government.

The Public Financing of Election Campaigns

The presidency was the first national office withdrawn from the private funding that previously had financed election campaigns. The Federal Elections Campaign Act of 1971 gave Americans an opportunity to check off one dollar from their federal income tax returns to support candidates in presidential elections.

The Federal Elections Campaign Act of 1974 (amended in 1976) authorized a system of public financing for presidential nominations and elections. Candidates who sought to win delegates to their parties' nominating conventions by campaigning in state presidential primaries were offered matching funds by the national government to help cover their expenses. To qualify, they first had to raise privately the sum of $5,000 in each of twenty states, and no contribution could exceed $250. This constituted a minimum total of $100,000. These provisions were designed to ensure that those running were serious candidates and were not indebted to large contributors. Moreover, the candidates were not permitted to spend more than a certain amount ($10.9 million each) if they accepted the matching funds.

When they competed for the presidency itself, both Jimmy Carter and Gerald R. Ford, the presidential candidates of the two major parties in 1976, were entirely financed by government subsidies. They were eligible for $21.8 million each. They did not have to provide any matching funds; rather, they had to agree not to accept any private donations. On the other hand, had either Ford or Carter wished to rely entirely on private funds to finance their campaigns, they had that option. It was one they both rejected.

The national campaign reform law also provided funds for presidential candidates from the minor parties. To be eligible for such financial support candidates had to secure a certain proportion (5 to 25 percent) of the votes cast in the presidential election. Since none of the minor party presidential candidates in 1976 succeeded in meeting this requirement, the government was not obligated to help them.

Now that we have experienced one presidential campaign subsidized by public funds, attention has shifted to congressional elections. Although the U.S. Senate had voted for such subsidies in 1974, a 1977 bill to finance Senate election campaigns encountered so much Republican and southern Democratic opposition that it was defeated. Nonetheless, the public financing of presidential election campaigns has established a precedent that in the long run will probably be difficult for Congress to ignore. A number of states have adopted laws that provide state funds to help finance campaigns for state elected office. In so doing, they have already recognized the importance of public funding for ensuring competitive elections and for raising the morality of elected officials.

Concepts To Study

democracy	plurality voting	separation of powers
equality	proportional representation	unanimity
federalism	republican government	winner-take-all rule
majority voting	self-rule	

Special Terms To Review

absentee voting
candidate
candidate elections
compulsory voting
elections
electoral college
electorate

general elections
initiative elections
nonpartisan elections
"one man–one vote"
partisan elections
poll taxes
presidential electors

presidential primaries
primaries (party elections)
referendum elections
registration
socioeconomic status (SES)
universal adult suffrage

CHAPTER 7

Political → reduces are choices
Parties
- group issues together

- maximize individual power

PP =
Political
Parties.
- no actual provision in ~~Cost.~~ Const.
for political parties

POLITICAL PARTIES

Had you voted in the presidential election of 1976, the chances are you would have favored either the Democratic candidate, Jimmy Carter, or the Republican, Gerald R. Ford. A little more than 50 percent of the 81.5 million people who voted chose Democratic electors; 48 percent chose Republican electors.

Depending on your state, you might have been able to vote for one of the other thirteen candidates running for President. Although none qualified in all fifty states and the District of Columbia, the following parties offered electors pledged to presidential tickets in at least two states: the American party, American Independent party, Communist party, Libertarian party, People's party, Prohibition party, Socialist party, Socialist Labor party, Socialist Workers' party, and the U.S. Labor party. In addition, three candidates competed as independents with no party backing. Together, the thirteen alternatives to the major party candidates attracted less than 2 percent of the vote.

Not only did the Democratic and Republican presidential tickets monopolize almost all the votes, but all the U.S. Senate and House of Representative contests were won by Democrats and Republicans. Virtually the same pattern characterized gubernatorial and state legislative election contests that year.

What do these results tell us about the American political party system? The major contenders for leadership in our national and state governments are members of political parties. With rare exceptions, they are the ones who win public office. Ours is essentially a **two-party system.** Above the local level of government, where nonpartisan elections prevail, competition for leadership is virtually monopolized by the Democratic and Republican parties. Measured by success in electing candidates and attracting voter support, minor parties are not significant contenders for political power. They remain on the periphery of American politics, almost totally excluded from government.

Today, the Democrats are the majority party on the national level and in most states; the Republicans are the minority party, except in a few states. For a substantial portion of our history after 1860, however, the reverse was true. The present Democratic majority developed only in the 1930s. Despite that Democratic majority, Republicans captured the presidency in 1952, 1956, 1968, and 1972. In all but one of these elections Democrats won a majority in both houses of Congress.

Our federal system is inextricably tied into our party and election systems. Presidential electors are state party candidates who have been elected to cast their state's votes in the electoral college. In addition, each state determines its own qualifications for political parties. This explains why minor parties may qualify to compete for public office in some states but not in others.

THE NATURE AND FUNCTION OF POLITICAL PARTIES

To understand the American political party system, we must first answer a number of elementary questions: What are political parties? What functions do they perform for individual Americans? What functions do they perform for the broader political system in which they operate?

What Is a Political Party?

A political party may be defined by a number of criteria: by its purpose and method; by whether it meets a state government's standards of competitiveness; and by its internal organization.

Purpose and method.   A party's *purpose* is to control the power and shape the policies of government. Its *method* is to offer in public elections, under its label, candidates for governmental leadership positions. A political party may be defined as a voluntary political organization that seeks to capture the power of government by offering its candidates in public elections for governmental office. This means that a political party must be concerned with seeking out and attracting voters if it wishes to succeed. It must subject itself to the litmus test of democracy: a public election.

Legal standards of competitiveness.   Before a party may offer its candidates to the voters, it must demonstrate by governmentally defined standards that it is a realistic competitor for public office. To secure a place on the state ballot for its candidates, a party must demonstrate to a state government, first, that it has an organization in that state and, second, that it has sufficient public support. A new party must show public support by persuading a required number of eligible voters to sign a petition in its behalf. Each state sets its own minimum. Once on the ballot, a party must continue to show that it is a realistic competitor. Unless it attracts sufficient voters to its candidates, it will be removed from the ballot by the state government. The minimum number of such voters varies in each state, but it is never more than a small percentage of the votes cast for some statewide office. A party that falls below this minimum demonstrates that it is no longer a serious contender, and it loses its privilege to offer candidates in public elections. Unless it can again qualify to use the ballot, it cannot regain its legal standing as a political party.

Organizational structure. A party may be defined as a complex political organization. In it, members and leaders play different roles. In fact, each of the major parties may be said to be composed of three different "parties": **party-in-the-electorate**, **party-in-the-organization**, and **party-in-the-government.** Each reflects a unique aspect of a political party.

While most people say they are Democrats or Republicans, they actually have a very limited relationship with their party. They are merely members of the party-in-the-electorate. They do not have to subscribe to any fixed set of beliefs, pay dues, go to party meetings, participate in their party's elections, or vote for its candidates. If you said, "I'm a good Democrat," or "I'm proud to be a Republican," in all likelihood you would be saying that you either identified with or registered as a member of the party. Of course, every party has active members who are more willing to invest time and effort in its behalf. Unlike ordinary identifiers or members, they raise money, attend party meetings, telephone people to urge them to register with their party, and solicit votes for their party's candidates.

The party-in-the-organization includes the organizational leaders at all levels of the party. Each level—precinct (the smallest party unit), ward or county, and state—is represented by its own committee and chairman. State parties, in turn, are represented in a national committee headed by a national chairman. The party-in-the-organization is responsible for keeping the party machinery operating, for activating the activists, for recruiting candidates, for helping, at times, to conduct election campaigns, and for arranging party conventions.

Those who win election to public office as party candidates become governmental leaders and make up the party-in-the-government. They have the power to make public policy and supervise its administration. The party-in-the-government is actually made up of a number of sets of parties. In Congress, for example, Democrats in the House and Senate have their own separate party organizations, each with its own leadership. These two legislative parties rarely interact as a common party unit. The same holds true for the two Republican parties in Congress. And the President and his executive leaders make up their own separate party component.

The same pattern exists in state governments, except that the executive party set is somewhat more complicated since each state elects one or more executive leaders independent of the governor. Some may be Republicans, others may be Democrats. Nevertheless, the governor is almost always the outstanding leader within the party-in-the-government at the state level, just as the President is always the outstanding leader of the party-in-the-government at the national level. Minor parties rarely have a party-in-the-government since few of their candidates are ever elected to public office.

What Functions Do Political Parties Perform?

What do parties do for the individual citizen? What contributions do they make to the operation of a democratic system?

Maximizing individual power. The power each of us can exercise over our government is limited to one vote. An isolated vote is virtually worthless in choosing our governmental leaders. But one vote is like a drop of water which, having almost no impact by itself, accumulates power when added to others. Enough drops create a river whose flow may cut through rock and transform the landscape. Enough votes added together acquire similar power to affect the political landscape.

Political parties provide individuals with a chance to increase the impact of their single votes. With a minimum of effort and cost, individuals can concentrate their votes (aggregate them) so as to elect this candidate or defeat that one. Political parties, therefore, overcome the weakness of the single vote and the weakness inherent in the dispersion of votes. They offer the voter an organized focus, a mechanism that gives an individual vote maximum impact. By offering candidates around whom voters may unite, political parties enhance the ability of the individual to play a more meaningful role in the election process.

Stimulating voter turnout. Since votes are valuable commodities, political parties must appeal to and attract the individual voter. A party that does not compete aggressively for its candidates will lose. The requirement for winning—aggregating the most votes behind their candidates—forces parties to beat their drums and bring out as many voters as they can.

Left to themselves, many Americans are politically inert. They need a stimulus to activate them to participate in elections. Political parties help overcome this inertia. For a while, at least, they make the political as visible and perhaps as interesting to potential voters as some of their other preoccupations. Candidates and their party organizations spend time, money, and effort to bring themselves to the public's attention and to involve their members as voters.

Simplifying alternatives for voters. Political parties reduce choices for voters and in doing so help make democracy work. But have we not said that democracy tries to maximize choices? How can we reconcile the two? The answer is that by simplifying alternatives, political parties make choices more meaningful for voters, thereby facilitating their participation in elections.

Consider the 1976 presidential election. For all practical purposes the choice was between Republican Gerald R. Ford and Democrat Jimmy Carter. Note that the voter had a "real" choice of only one out of two. Had you been a voter, you were spared having to decide who among the other millions of qualified Americans should be President. The Democratic and Republican parties simplified this selection process for us, the voters, by offering one candidate each for that office. Psychologically, it is much easier to choose between two candidates than among fifty or a million. Because the choice becomes more meaningful, we are more likely to participate.

Of course, the parties reduce our choice. In the November 1976 election, the voters were unable to vote for presidential electors committed to Republican Ronald Reagan, Democratic Congressman Morris K. Udall, or California Governor Edmund G. "Jerry" Brown, Jr., all of whom had offered themselves for and failed to win their parties' nominations. When choices are reduced, some of us are deprived of an opportunity to vote for the individual who really attracts us. But that is a price we pay for having parties perform the function of simplifying alternatives for the voter.

Recruiting leaders. Political parties are avenues through which ambitious Americans can aspire to win elected leadership positions in our national, state, and some of our local governments. The parties offer unique opportunities to such individuals: personal contact with the other leaders in the party and with its rank and file; exposure in political activities; experience in campaigns; and opportunity to learn the rules of politics. Whether they are already active party members or outsiders anxious to capture elected public office, these ambitious individuals must persuade a sufficient number of party members and leaders that they are potential winners. Since open leadership recruitment and selection are especially critical to democracies, parties perform an indispensable service.

Providing a psychological frame of reference.   The major political parties provide significant reference points. These enable many voters to take their bearings in elections, even those who are independents. It is true that fewer Americans follow their party labels all the way in elections nowadays. Nonetheless, even those who do not vote a straight party ticket find that party often affords them a shorthand answer to the matter of choice.

Not only is party a direction signal that helps voters choose among candidates, but it helps anchor people into a set of political beliefs. The stronger one's commitment to a party, the more that person's opinions on controversial public issues tend to differ from those of the activists and leaders in the other parties.

POLITICAL PARTIES WITHIN A POLITICAL SYSTEM

Political parties do not operate in a vacuum. The number and kinds of parties, their organization, and their ideas reflect the political system. The type of government, the particular election system, and the nature of the cleavages dividing society all help shape political parties.

At the same time, parties are themselves independent forces. That is, they affect the way the political system works, help overcome the effect of some principles of government, and even alter constitutional arrangements. Thus, parties act upon the political system even as they are shaped by it.

American Parties as Shaped by an American Environment

A number of political, social, economic, and historical conditions have helped create the type of parties that characterize the United States. From the beginning both the Constitution and the nature of conflict and agreement in our society shaped this party system. Our two-party system will be explored in this section as a case example of environmental forces shaping parties.

The Constitution

Four features of the U.S. Constitution have had a tremendous impact on our political party system: the First Amendment, the separation of powers, checks and balances, and federalism.

First Amendment.   Although the U.S. Constitution makes no reference to political parties, its guarantees of freedom of speech, press, assembly, and petition help ensure that free, competitive parties will exist. If a party is to organize and solicit financial and voter support to compete effectively for public office, it must be free from fear of governmental repression. Fortunately, party leaders who have controlled governmental power have almost always respected the constitutional rights of their opponents in competing parties to criticize, to organize, and to seek votes in an effort to replace them in public office.

Separation of powers.   At both the national and state levels of our government, separation of powers fragments the party-in-the-government. By dividing governmental power among a chief executive and distinct legislative houses, state and national constitutions foster the creation of separate and sometimes competing units within the same party. In Congress, for example, Republicans as well as Democrats have separate leaders and party organizations in both the House and Senate. And the President becomes another competing center of party organization and leadership.

Differences in the responsibilities and in the constituencies of executive and legislative officeholders introduce diverse points of view on policy issues. These different views are bound to disunite the components in the same party-in-the-government. At present, the President and a majority of the Senate and House are Democrats. Yet the President represents the entire country, the executive side of government, and many of our foreign allies. Democratic senators speak for their individual states and for their legislative branch, while Democratic representatives speak for their individual districts and for their side of the legislature. Although all are Democrats, their varying terms of office, separate organizations, and different constituencies foster differences in perspective among them that further fragment party unity.

Checks and balances.   The checks-and-balances principle compounds this fragmentation of party by causing additional conflict and tension among the separate sets of the same party-in-the-government. President, House, and Senate are empowered to say no to each other, which means they can frustrate the aims of each other. This imposes additional strains on party unity. An identical situation prevails in state government.

Federalism.   For a major part of our history the states, as independent centers of power, were more important in shaping social and economic policy than the national government. State parties were originally deeply embedded in the major decisions of our federal system and in the partisan identification of the people. Even today, when the central government has so greatly expanded its intervention in American society, ours is a party system in which state parties are more important than their national parties.

Each Republican and Democratic state party is an independent participant in its national party. State parties have their own sources of revenue and patronage (jobs and favors to allocate on a party basis), and they choose their own candidates for presidential electors, who will presumably vote for their national parties' presidential tickets. These presidential nominees are selected at national party conventions composed of their respective state parties.

In fact, the state party is the individual party member's organizational link with the national party. We register to vote as state party members, not as members of our national party. Indeed, there is no such thing as national party membership, except in name.

The Republican and Democratic parties are confederate in nature; decision-making power is highly decentralized within each. Traditionally, national party control over state parties has been limited to permitting the latter to participate in a national committee and a national nominating convention. Recently, some centralization has occurred within the Democratic party. The national party has imposed conditions on state party participation by adopting rules that expand the involvement of women, blacks, and young adults in state party affairs. Unless the state parties comply, their delegates may be challenged in the national committee and at the national convention. State Democratic parties are now obligated to commit their presidential electors to the national convention's presidential ticket. The national Democratic party has also begun to prescribe rules that state parties must follow in allocating delegates to different presidential candidates for the national party's nomination.

Absence of Fundamental Cleavages

Parties reflect the types of society in which they operate. Societies without major divisions produce major parties that more or less agree on fundamentals. Societies fragmented into distinct hostile components produce major political parties that mirror their antagonistic aims, fears, and traditions.

Religion is so divisive in some societies as to generate religious parties. This historical divisiveness continues to express itself to this day in the major Christian parties active in Germany, the Netherlands, and Italy and in India's antagonistic Hindu and Moslem parties. In some societies, _linguistic differences_ are so firmly entrenched that they, too, generate separate political parties. In Canada, for example, a pro-French speaking political party has called for Quebec's independence from Canada. _Racism and tribalism_ also produce cleavages that fracture a society. Tribal antagonisms antedate the modern black national states in Africa and shape much of their party politics. Racial antagonism between the Malays and Chinese in Malasia manifests itself in different parties and at times in bloody clashes. _Economic divisions_ that separate into antagonistic classes people who are farmers, businessmen, or workers lead to farmer parties, capitalist parties, and working-class parties. Because of this strong class identification and conflict, Socialist and Communist parties continue to attract millions to their banners in Europe, Asia, and Latin America.

These cleavages or fractures have largely been absent from our society. For this reason our major parties reflect an absence of sharp differences. Language has never been a divisive issue, because the millions of immigrants and their descendants accepted English as their operational language in our society. Tribalism has been characteristic only of the American Indian culture, but until very recently Indians did not operate within the political system.

Religion did raise some problems in the colonies and later in the republic. However, divisions between Catholics and Protestants were never so deep that each felt its best defense was to organize a separate political party. Minor protest parties concerned with religion have appeared at times but have failed to survive. During the 1960 presidential campaign the Catholic bishops in Puerto Rico, a commonwealth of the United States, helped organize a Catholic party, but it, too, ran far behind the regular parties and immediately disappeared.

Economic fractures dividing people into distinct antagonistic classes also failed to develop in the United States. Consequently, class-oriented parties never appealed to great numbers of voters. Even in the midst of our Great Depression of the 1930s, when millions were unemployed and on relief, the Socialist and Communist parties together could not attract one million votes. They have receded even further since then and today remain insignificant minor parties. Their unattractiveness to the American electorate is apparent: Five parties with _socialist, communist,_ or _labor_ in their names offered presidential tickets in 1976; combined, they polled less than 1 percent of the total popular vote.

Considering how the race issue has divided American society, political parties based on race might logically have been expected to articulate the competing interests of black and white Americans. Yet, black Americans never rallied behind separate racial parties of their own once they were freed from slavery. Until the 1930s most blacks identified with the Republican party. A Republican President, Abraham Lincoln, had issued the Emancipation Proclamation during the Civil War and a victorious national government, under the leadership of the Republican party, had pushed through the Thirteenth, Fourteenth, and Fifteenth Amendments to protect the newly freed slaves. It made sense, therefore, for black Americans, most of whom lived in a hostile South, to identify initially with that Republican party, which was also the dominant national party. Only when Democratic President Franklin D. Roosevelt and his New Deal championed the cause of the poor did most American blacks begin to support Democratic candidates.

As a result of a heritage of slavery, the Civil War, and Reconstruction, southern Democratic state parties actually tried to become white racial parties, but decisions by the U.S. Supreme Court undermined their attempts to exclude blacks. Subsequent rulings by the national Democratic party also forced the state parties to accept blacks. Then too, the votes of black southerners were becoming increasingly attractive to southern Democratic candidates who were beginning to face strong Republican party competition. These factors eventually led to the full integration of blacks in southern Democratic parties.

White, racially oriented third parties competed in the South in 1948 and in the entire country in 1968, and their presidential candidates attracted considerable voter support. However, these parties lost the elections and quickly faded into insignificance. Attempts by a few blacks to organize black parties also failed. Neither the Republican nor the Democratic party—nationally or in any of the states— is a racial party today.

The Two-Party System: A Case Example

Ours is essentially a party system in which the Democrats and Republicans alternate as the principal leading party. If one wins, the other monopolizes the opposition party position in American politics. Exceptions to this pattern are rare. Since 1860 neither of the major parties has been displaced nationally from these favorite positions. Of course, minor parties exist and in some states have at times beaten the two major parties. But minor parties remain the sideshow of American politics. Popular identification with the two major parties is weaker today than in the past, but it still includes approximately 70 percent of the American electorate (see Table 7–1). Even most independents lean either toward the Democratic or the Republican party.

The existence of a two-party system in the United States illustrates how party systems are shaped by their environment. What explains this two-party system? First, a historical pattern at the beginning of the republic helped set the dominant two-party relationship. Second, a basic commonality of views on fundamentals helped contribute to the two-party system. And finally, a winner-take-all rule for President and for governor and the single-member legislative election districts played a part.

Table 7–1
Party Identification, Presidential Election Years
1952–1976 (by percentage)

	1976	1972	1968	1964	1960	1956	1952
Democrats	48	44	46	53	47	?	41
Republicans	23	28	27	25	30	?	34
Independents	29	29	27	22	23	?	25

SOURCE: Gallup Poll survey data.

Historical patterns.   During the formative years of the new American republic, the major divisive issue centered around the adoption of the Constitution. Because this was an either-or issue, it precluded more than two sides being formed. The Federalists campaigned for the ratification of the Constitution, the Anti-Federalists opposed it. Once the Constitution was adopted the Anti-Federalists lost their rationale for existence. The Federalists continued as a party and assumed responsibility for managing the new government. A pattern of two opposing sides had emerged, even though it immediately dissolved.

This pattern reestablished itself during the administration of our first President, George Washington. His secretary of state, Thomas Jefferson, resigned from the President's cabinet to organize the Republican party. Republicans and Federalists presented candidates, fought over issues, and rallied the people behind their banners. When Jefferson was chosen President in the election of 1800, the two-party pattern became more firmly entrenched.

The Federalist party eventually disappeared and the country went through a brief period with the Republicans the only major party. Still, a two-party tradition persisted. The Republican party ultimately changed its name to the Democratic party; it was opposed first by the National Republican party and then by the Whig party. For over two decades before the Civil War, the overwhelming majority of voters divided their support between Whigs and Democrats.

Both parties split apart over slavery, another divisive issue. The Whigs were replaced by a new Republican party, whose presidential ticket first appeared in 1854 and which captured the presidency in 1860. The Democrats survived the Civil War to emerge nationally as the second major party.

From the Civil War until today, the real competition for public office nationally and in almost all the states has been essentially a two-party fight, Democrats versus Republicans. Their candidates win almost all public offices, and most of our people identify with one of these two parties. Those who do not so identify prefer, on the whole, to label themselves independents rather than to identify with any other party.

141

Is a Communist party in US.

Common basic views. The absence of major cleavages in the social, economic, and political fabric of American society undermined the rationale for an enduring system of multiple parties. Most Americans shared a common set of values: the supremacy of the Consitution; separation of church and state; civilian rule; capitalism. Almost all the millions of immigrants coming into the United States accepted these fundamentals and shared the aspirations of their fellow Americans—a chance to get ahead, obtain an education, own a farm, build a business, or work gainfully. They, too, joined in the American practice of identifying with the Democrats or the Republicans.

Both Democratic and Republican parties espoused—with different emphasis, of course— the values and aspirations central to the American culture. Parties that operated outside this framework appeared too different, radical, and threatening. As a result, they attracted few voters. When some minor parties managed to tap a favorable response in the American public, the major parties cleverly appropriated their positions. With the dominant parties espousing these new ideas, voters found little reason to support marginal parties.

The winner-take-all rule. The presidency, the most important prize in the American election system, is a single office. Only one person can win it in an election. This has made third and fourth parties less attractive. A party that wins 10 or 20 percent of the electoral college still cannot capture the presidency since a majority of electoral votes is necessary to win. To vote for electors of minor parties is, in effect, to throw away one's vote.

Presidential electors in each state are chosen by popular vote according to the winner-take-all rule. The electoral slate attracting the most votes, even by a margin of one, wins; all others lose. The same disadvantage confronts minor party candidates who run for national and state legislative or gubernatorial offices. This tends to eliminate minor parties as real competitors.

Political Parties as Shapers of the Political System

Just as political parties are influenced by the environment in which they operate, they themselves are also prime movers, independently affecting the operation of their political system.

Overcoming constitutional restraints. Political parties have blunted the effect of separation of powers by pulling together the diverse parts of government in the interest of party unity. Presidents who encounter difficulty in getting their programs through Congress can call upon their legislative party leaders for assistance. On numerous occasions, the present Democratic Speaker of the House helped persuade many Democratic congressmen to support their fellow Democrat, Jimmy Carter, and rescued a number of the President's policy proposals.

Common party identification and appeals for party support blunt the impact of the separation of powers and checks-and-balances principles. Attempts in Congress to override a President's veto almost invariably induce a majority of his party in the House and Senate to cooperate with him. In the foreign policy field as well, a President will rally most of his party's legislators behind his leadership.

The same holds true when a President nominates individuals to fill executive and judicial positions. Should opposition develop, it generally originates from members of Congress in the opposite party, who are also more willing to initiate investigations of the executive. Those of the President's party are much more reluctant to expose weaknesses in an administration of their fellow party member. Party also acts as a common denominator in state governments. A governor and members of the same party in the state legislature generally share much in common, which facilitates their working together.

Democratizing the electoral college. Political parties have changed the spirit of the electoral college while retaining the letter of the law. The intent of the framers of the Constitution was for presidential electors to make their own independent choices for President and Vice President. But with the rise of political parties, presidential electors quickly became state party representatives. The parties stripped the presidential electors of their independent roles. Although legally the electors may vote as they wish, only a very few have exercised this option. All the others vote for their national presidential tickets according to the expectations of their parties and the popular electorates that chose them.

By committing the electors in advance, the political parties virtually transformed the presidential vote into a direct popular vote. At the same time, party voting almost always guarantees that one presidential ticket will win a majority in the electoral college. If electors were to vote as free agents, they might divide their votes among so many candidates that no one would gain the necessary majority.

PARTY DIFFERENCES: DEMOCRATS AND REPUBLICANS

Most Americans identify as Democrats or Republicans. Do these partisans tend to differ in any significant way? Yes, they do. Not only do the two parties tend to differ in their social composition, but they tend to differ as well in political belief. When you examine the differences on public policy ask yourself whether you subscribe to those associated with the party of your choice.

An increasing number of Americans have recently characterized themselves as independents. Instead of identifying with either the Democratic or Republican party, they vote sometimes with one, sometimes with the other, attracted by the particular candidate rather than by the partisan label. Some Americans reject all three alternatives, and they adhere to one of our minor parties.

Social Bases for Major Party Differences

Certain groups of individuals tend to identify primarily with the Democratic party, other groups of individuals with the Republican party. Not all members of these groups so identify themselves, but a significant percentage of each do. Therefore, we can say the Democratic party is basically attractive to certain Americans, the Republican party to others.

Region. Southerners have traditionally been more Democratic than Americans in other regions. Although the South was characterized by a two-party system before the Civil War, that bitter conflict and Reconstruction eliminated the Republican party as a viable alternative for most white southerners. The Republican party was seen as a conquering military power and was associated with blacks. As a result, the South—the eleven states that seceded from the Union—became for many years a one-party Democratic region.

In the South white identification with the Democratic party has been waning, but black identification is very high. As a result Democratic party identification in that region continues to be stronger than in the three other regions of the United States. Even in 1972, a year when the

Table 7–2
Party Identification by Region, 1950s–1972 (by percentage)

| | PROPORTION OF THE ELECTORATE | | | | | | |
	Northeast 1950s–1972		Midwest 1950s–1972		South 1950s–1972		West 1950s–1972	
Democrats	35	35	41	36	67	50	47	39
Independents	28	41	26	37	16	30	26	34
Republicans	37	24	33	27	17	20	27	27

SOURCE: Kevin V. Mulcahy and Richard S. Katz, *America Votes, What You Should Know About Elections Today* (Englewood Cliffs, N.J.: Prentice-Hall, Inc., 1976), p. 40.

Republican President swept a majority of votes in every state except Massachusetts and the District of Columbia, Democratic identification in the South remained as high as 50 percent (see Table 7–2).

When we examine voting rather than party identification, however, we find that the Democratic proportion of voters in the South in recent presidential elections has at times fallen below that in the other regions (see Table 7–3). Accompanying an upsurge in southern voting for Republican presidential candidates has been a parallel rise in Republican votes and victory for Republican candidates for national, state, and local offices. A solid Democratic South no longer exists.

Religion. The party identification of Americans differs according to their religious affiliations (see Table 7–4). More Jews and Catholics identify with the Democratic party than with the Republican party. A larger percentage of Protestants identify with the Republican party than do the other two religious groups.

Not only do members of the religious groups identify differently with the two major parties, but they vote differently as well (see Table 7–5). Only once (in 1972) in the seven presidential elections in the period from 1952 to 1976 did a majority of Catholics vote for a Republican presidential candidate. Only once (in 1964) did a Protestant majority vote for the Democratic candidate for President. In each of the six elections for which we have data, a majority of Jews voted for the Democratic presidential candidates, and always by a greater percentage than Catholics and Protestants.

Obviously not all Protestants identify with or vote for Republicans; not all Catholics or Jews identify with or vote for Democrats. A significant minority in each group deviates from their co-religionists.

Race. In 1976, 78 percent of blacks in the United States identified themselves as Democrats, 7 percent as Republicans, and 15 percent as independents. In 1976, only 44 percent of the whites in the nation identified with the Democratic party; 26 percent, with the Republicans; and 30 percent, as independents.

Voting patterns in presidential elections reveal black support for Democratic candidates to be even higher than their party identification (see Table 7–6). Not once in the last seven elections, 1952 through 1976, did a majority of black voters choose the Republican presidential candidates. Only once during this period, in 1964, did a majority of white Americans vote for a Democratic presidential candidate.

Socioeconomic status. Party identification is related to the occupation, income, and education (socioeconomic status, or SES) of Americans. The higher their SES, the more likely they are to identify with Republicans.

Table 7–3
Partisan Votes By Region, Presidential Elections, 1952–1976 (by percentage)

	1952		1956		1960		1964		1968			1972		1976		
	D	R	D	R	D	R	D	R	D	R	AIP	D	R	D	R	M
East	45	55	40	60	53	47	68	32	50	43	7	42	58	51	47	1
Midwest	42	58	41	59	48	52	61	39	44	47	9	40	60	48	50	1
South	51	49	49	51	51	49	52	48	31	36	33	29	71	54	45	X
West	42	58	43	57	49	51	60	40	44	49	7	41	59	46	51	1

X = Less than one percent

D = Democratic

R = Republican

AIP = American Independent Party

M = McCarthy

SOURCE: Gallup Poll survey data.

Table 7–4
Party Identification and Religious Affiliation,
Select Presidential Election Years, 1964–1976 (by percentage)

	1964			1968			1976		
	D	R	I	D	R	I	D	R	I
Protestant	45	28	27	42	31	27	50	29	21
Catholic	54	18	28	55	18	27	62	16	22
Jewish	55	11	34	69	7	24	62	13	25

D = Democratic
R = Republican
I = Independent

SOURCE: Gallup Poll survey data.

Democratic identifiers are much more likely to be found among the less educated and in the lowest paid and less skilled occupations, those with lower SES.

Voting data confirm the relationship between SES and party. Table 7–7 shows how Americans in different educational and occupational groups voted in four presidential elections. Those with lower SES tended to favor Democrats and those with higher SES tended to favor Republicans.

In the seven presidential elections held during the period from 1952 to 1976, a majority of all occupational groups voted Democratic only once—in 1964. In all other elections the professional-business group voted by significant majorities (but by a plurality in 1968) for the Republican candidates. Except in 1972, a majority of members of labor-union families voted Democratic in all the elections.

In all these presidential elections but one (in 1964), a majority of those with college educations voted Republican. Those with a grade school education gave Democratic presidential candidates the majority of their votes in all but two elections; they defected by a thin margin (51 percent Republican, 49 percent Democratic) in 1972 and divided evenly in 1956.

Do all Americans with high SES vote Republican? No. In every election, a sizable number backed the Democratic candidate. Do all Americans with low SES vote Democratic? Again, no. A significant fraction consistently voted with the Republican party. The center of gravity of each party is different, however. Those with higher SES concentrate in the Republican party. Those with lower SES concentrate in the Democratic party. But each party cuts into the areas of principal support of the other, which blunts the differences between the two parties.

Table 7-5

Partisan Vote by Religious Affiliation, Presidential Elections, 1952–1976 (by percentage)

	1952		1956		1960		1964		1968			1972		1976		
	D	R	D	R	D	R	D	R	D	R	AIP	D	R	D	R	M
Protestants	37	63	37	63	38	62	55	45	35	49	16	30	70	46	53	X
Catholics	56	44	51	49	78	22	75	25	59	38	8	48	52	57	42	1
Jews	NA	NA	75	25	81	19	90	10	83	17	–	61	39	68	32	–

X = Less than one percent
NA = Not available

D = Democratic
R = Republican
M = McCarthy
AIP = American Independent Party

SOURCE: Gallup Poll survey data. For the Jewish vote in 1972, see NBC sample data as reported in *Congressional Quarterly Weekly Report*, Nov. 11, 1972 p. 2749; for 1976 data, CBS sample data in the *New York Times*, Nov. 4, 1976, p. 25.

Table 7–6
***Partisan Vote by Race, Presidential Elections,
1952–1976 (by percentage)***

	1952		1956		1960		1964		1968			1972		1976		
	D	R	D	R	D	R	D	R	D	R	AIP	D	R	D	R	M
Whites	43	57	41	59	49	51	59	41	38	47	15	32	68	46	52	1
Nonwhites	79	21	61	39	68	32	94	6	85	12	3	87	13	85	15	0

D = Democratic
R = Republican
M = McCarthy
AIP = American Independent Party

SOURCE: Gallup Poll survey data.

Table 7-7

Partisan Vote by Education and Occupation, Select Presidential Elections,* 1952–1976 (by percentage)

	1952		1960		1968			1976		
	D	R	D	R	D	R	AIP	D	R	M
Education										
College	34	66	39	61	37	54	9	42	52	2
High School	45	55	52	48	42	43	15	54	46	X
Grade School	52	48	55	45	52	33	15	58	41	1
Occupation										
Profession & Business	36	64	42	58	34	56	10	42	56	1
Farmer	33	67	48	52	29	51	20	NA	NA	
White Collar	40	60	48	52	41	47	12	50	48	2
Manual Worker	55	45	60	40	50	35	15	58	41	1
Member of Labor Union Family	61	39	65	35	56	29	15	63	36	1

*Republicans won in half of these elections (1952 and 1968); Democrats, in the other half (1960 and 1976).

X = Less than one percent
NA = Not available

D = Democratic
R = Republican
M = McCarthy
AIP = American Independent Party

SOURCE: Gallup Poll survey data.

Age. Older Americans are more likely to be Republicans; younger Americans, Democrats. Table 7–8 indicates that voters below the age of thirty tend to support the Democratic party more than those forty-nine years of age and older.

Sex. Sex related differences seem to have the least effect on individuals supporting the two major parties. As Table 7–9 reveals, the partisan voting difference between men and women is a minor one. At times a greater percentage of women than men have voted for the Democratic presidential candidates; at other times the reverse has been true.

Population concentration. Although we present no data for party identification by population concentration, a distinct pattern of voting in presidential elections is discernible. Large metropolitan centers tend to be more heavily Democratic than Republican; small towns and rural America tend to be more heavily Republican.

Typical party profiles. If we drew a partisan profile based on voting in the 1976 presidential election, certain individuals would more likely be Democrats; others, Republicans.

Democrats Are More Likely To Be	**Republicans Are More Likely To Be**
Southerners	Nonsoutherners
Blacks	Whites
Jews and Catholics	Protestants
Younger Voters	Older Voters
Grade and High School Educated	College Educated
Union Laborers	Professional and Business
Urbanites	Small Town and Rural
Men	Women

Table 7–8
Partisan Vote by Age, Select Presidential Elections,
1952–1976 (by percentage)

	1952		1960		1968			1976		
	D	R	D	R	D	R	AIP	D	R	M
Under 30	51	49	54	46	47	38	15	53	45	1
30–49	47	53	54	46	44	41	15	48	49	2
Over 49	39	61	46	54	41	47	12	52	48	X

X = Less than one percent

D = Democratic
R = Republican
M = McCarthy
W = Wallace
AIP = American Independent Party
SOURCE: Gallup Poll survey data.

Table 7–9
Partisan Vote by Sex, Select Presidential Elections,
1952–1976 (by percentage)

	1952		1960		1968			1972		1976		
	D	R	D	R	D	R	AIP	D	R	D	R	M
Men	47	53	52	48	41	43	16	37	63	53	45	1
Women	42	58	49	51	45	43	12	38	62	48	51	X

X = Less than one percent

D = Democratic
R = Republican
M = McCarthy
AIP = American Independent Party

SOURCE: Gallup Poll survey data.

In any particular presidential year, the Voter Party Profile may be somewhat different, but it has been relatively accurate for the past twenty-four years. Do you fit it? If not, how do you explain your deviation?

Party Differences on Policy Issues

Both major parties support the fundamentals of our political, social, and economic system. They accept the Constitution and its principles as well as the legitimate role of the Supreme Court as the interpreter of that Constitution. Neither favors socializing the economy or completely withdrawing governmental control over business, labor, or the environment.

Significant differences between the two exist, but within a democratic, capitalistic framework. These differences do not reflect the viewpoints of every Democrat and Republican. However, it should not surprise you that the party with strong union member support (Democratic) should favor social and economic policies espoused by labor unions, or that the party most closely associated with business and professional people (Republican) should support tax and regulatory policies favoring their interests.

Party differences as expressed by party identifiers. One way to illustrate partisan differences is to compare those who identify as "strong" Republicans with those who identify as "strong" Democrats on policy-oriented questions. The more intensely a person identifies as a Democrat or Republican, the more that individual should identify with that party's central position on issues.

152

Questions concerning the role of the national government in socio-economic affairs and on foreign aid were asked of national samples of our population in each presidential year during the period from 1956 to 1972. The percentages cited in Table 7–10 are those *favoring* more governmental involvement.

Democratic majorities favored national aid for education, a progressive tax on income, national programs for medical care, job guarantees, and fair employment almost consistently in the sixteen-year period covered by the polls. In almost all cases, only a minority of "strong" Republicans favored such policy stands. The division among strong partisans within the parties-in-the-electorate is indeed striking.

Party differences among elected officials. The behavior of members of the party-in-the-government furnishes us additional evidence on policy differences between the parties. One way to test for such differences is to look at ratings of congressional voting by four interest groups.

Americans for Constitutional Action (ACA) is an avowed conservative group that favors reducing the role of government in society as well as cutting expenditures for social programs. The U.S. Chamber of Commerce, a business group, is also interested in reducing the involvement of government in the economy and in removing governmental regulations from business as well as reducing the tax burden on business.

Americans for Democratic Action (ADA) is an avowed liberal organization committed to government's improving the condition of the poor, the disadvantaged, and the minorities. The Committee on Political Education (COPE) is the political arm of the AFL–CIO, the principal

Table 7–10
Republican and Democratic Identifiers Favoring More
National Government Action, 1956–1972 (by percentage)

	Issue	1956	1960	1964	1968	1972
Strong Democrats	Education-Taxation	80.0	66.8	51.0	53.6	52.6
Strong Republicans		67.7	44.5	15.5	12.0	39.8
Strong Democrats	Medical Care	74.2	74.5	78.2	81.3	67.4
Strong Republicans		45.5	54.2	23.6	42.7	40.9
Strong Democrats	Job Guarantees	75.6	71.2	52.6	53.1	62.6
Strong Republicans		51.5	52.7	16.1	25.4	20.5
Strong Democrats	Fair Employment	73.3	63.0	56.3	61.9	64.9
Strong Republicans		66.8	65.9	20.6	31.3	39.4
Strong Democrats	School Integration	38.7	39.8	53.7	58.9	55.3
Strong Republicans		38.8	41.5	34.8	31.5	34.8
Strong Democrats	Foreign Aid	49.5	51.4	64.7	51.3	38.9
Strong Republicans		51.4	61.5	49.7	41.8	47.8

SOURCE: Gerald Pomper, *Voters' Choice, Varieties of American Electoral Behavior* (New York: Dodd, Mead, 1975), p. 168.

spokesman for union labor. It is primarily concerned with legislation to increase jobs, expand unemployment compensation, improve the social security system, and enhance the right of unions to strike and to bargain collectively.

ACA and the U.S. Chamber of Commerce reflect a conservative-business point of view; ADA and COPE, a liberal-labor point of view. Each judges congressmen according to its own list of key votes. Tables 7–11, 7–12, and 7–13 document their ratings of votes by party leaders and members in the House of Representatives and in the Senate in 1976. The Democratic leaders and members were rated high by the liberal-labor groups and low by the conservative-business groups. Conversely, Republican leaders and members were rated high by the conservative-business groups and low by the liberal-labor groups. Some Republicans were rated high by the liberal-labor scale, and some Democrats were rated high by the conservative-business scale; neither party is homogeneous.

The evidence from the party-in-the-electorate and the party-in-the-government (Congress) reinforce each other. Just as both major parties

Table 7–11

Interest-Group Ratings of Votes by Congressional Party Leaders, 94th Congress, 2nd Session, 1976 (by percentage)

LIBERAL-LABOR GROUPS		PARTY LEADERS	CONSERVATIVE-BUSINESS GROUPS	
ADA	COPE		U.S. Chamber of Commerce	ACA
		Senate		
75	75	Democratic Floor Leader	0	13
45	79	Democratic Whip	22	31
45	73	Chairman, Democratic Conference	0	0
40	53	Republican Floor Leader	33	20
10	19	Republican Whip	78	80
0	6	Chairman, Republican Conference	83	100
5	10	Secretary, Republican Conference	67	100
5	11	Chairman, Republican Policy Committee	100	92
		House of Representatives		
60	87	Democratic Floor Leader	13	8
30	86	Democratic Whip	50	19
90	87	Democratic Assistant Whip	13	0
0	9	Republican Floor Leader	100	67
5	9	Republican Whip	94	81
50	28	Chairman, Republican Conference	54	29
0	0	Chairman, Republican Policy Committee	100	100

SOURCE: Adapted from data in *Congressional Quarterly Weekly Report,* Feb. 5, 1977, pp. 216, 220–222. The highest support score is 100, the lowest is 0.

Table 7–12
Rating of Democratic and Republican Senators By Four
Interest Groups, 1976 (by percentage)

		ADA		COPE		U.S. CHAMBER OF COMMERCE		ACA	
		D	R	D	R	D	R	D	R
High	100%	2	0	2	0	0	16	0	22
	70% and higher	38	14	75	14	7	49	8	57
Low	Less than 30%	18	68	7	60	82	30	74	27
	Zero	5	16	0	0	61	5	23	5

D = Democratic
R = Republican

SOURCE: Adapted from data in *Congressional Quarterly Weekly Report,* Feb. 5, 1977, p. 222.

Table 7–13
Interest-Group Ratings of Votes of Democratic and
Republican Members, U.S. House of Representatives, 1976 (by percentage)

		ADA		COPE		U.S. CHAMBER OF COMMERCE		ACA	
		D	R	D	R	D	R	D	R
High	100%	2	0	0	0	0.7	9	0.7	4
	70% & higher	42	0.7	69	3	10	63	12	63
Low	Less than 30%	22	83	9	75	62	7	67	11
	Zero	2	22	0	0.7	11	0.7	14	0

D = Democratic
R = Republican

SOURCE: Adapted from data in *Congressional Quarterly Weekly Report,* Feb. 5, 1977, pp. 220–221.

have different social bases in the population, so too do they have different policy orientations. Party does make a difference in the United States.

INDEPENDENTS AND THE PARTY SYSTEM

Many Americans refuse to identify with either major party. They prefer to refer to themselves as independents. What is their percentage in the electorate and what do we know about independents as distinct from those who identify as partisans?

Percentage of Independents

Examine Table 7–14. You will note that the proportion of adult Americans identifying as Democrats has remained relatively constant in the period from 1960 to 1976. Those identifying as Republicans declined sharply, from 34 percent in 1952 to 23 percent in 1976. For a long period until 1968, the percentage of independents remained relatively constant, but in 1968 their percentage began to rise, and now more Americans identify as independents than as Republicans. The percentage of independents in presidential election years has risen only very slightly in the total period from 1952 to 1976 and seems to have stabilized in the last two presidential election years.

Does the increase in independents foretell an electorate in which as much as one-half or more repudiate any identification with the major parties? Although the 1972 and 1976 data suggest that this is unlikely, two elections do not prove a trend. On the other hand, the period from 1966 to 1974, in which independent identification increased to approximately 30 percent of the electorate, was characterized by the country's involvement in the increasingly unpopular Vietnam War and the Watergate scandals of the Nixon administration. An increase in the general distrust of government and of politicians fostered a disillusionment with

Table 7–14
Party Identification, Presidential Elections, 1952–1976 (by percentage)

	1952	1956	1960	1964	1968	1972	1976
Democrats	41	NA	47	53	46	44	48
Republicans	34	NA	30	25	27	28	23
Independents	25	NA	23	22	27	29	29

NA-Not available

SOURCE: Gallup Poll survey data.

both parties. At the same time, approximately ten million young people, age eighteen to twenty-one, became eligible to join the electorate. Many were disenchanted with government and politics, and identifying as independents was a way of registering their disapproval. Should trust in our government and its partisan leaders increase in the future, the percentage of independents will probably not resume its former rate of expansion.

Who Are the Independents? *Youngest most education*

Independents are concentrated among the youngest members of the electorate and among those with the most education. Aside from their youth and education, are independents any different from partisan Americans? Yes and no. Compared with those who identify strongly as Democrats and Republicans, independents do not vote consistently for one party. In 1976 over 70 percent reported having voted in prior elections for presidential candidates of both parties. Over 65 percent of the "strong" Democrats and "strong" Republicans reported having always voted for the same party. Independents, moreover, are not as interested in candidate campaigns as are strong party partisans.

Among the independents those who lean toward one of the major parties are also very different from those who feel close to neither. The "leaners" are more likely to be interested in campaigns and to vote. In this respect, they approximate the interest and participation levels of the weak Democratic and Republican identifiers. Those least interested in campaigns and least likely to vote are the pure independents.

Republicans, Independents, and the Future

The Republican party seems to have become a permanent minority among party identifiers, fewer in number than Democrats or independents. Does this mean that it will vanish? Not at all. The party is still a very vigorous competitor for votes. Republican President Richard M. Nixon was overwhelmingly reelected in 1972. And Republican President Gerald R. Ford, who lost to Democrat Jimmy Carter in 1976, attracted 48.5 percent of the popular vote—38,531,000—at a time when Republican identifiers had dropped to a low of 23 percent.

The Republican party remains the main competitor to the Democratic party in all the states and, as such, its candidates are the inevitable recipients of anti-Democratic votes. Witness the increase in Republican representation in Congress, in state legislatures, and among governors as a result of the 1978 election. It may be a sign of the times, however, that one Republican state party changed its name in 1976 to the Independent-Republicans of Minnesota. Republican candidates must cut deeply into the ranks of independent voters if they are to win public office as Republicans.

MINOR POLITICAL PARTIES

While Democrats and Republicans monopolize the real competition for votes and public office, minor parties do exist on the fringes of politics. We have already tried to explain the reasons for their marginality: an absence of any fundamental cleavage in American society; the tradition of two-party competition; and the winner-take-all rule determining the outcome of elections. Thus minor parties are basically dead-end streets in the political landscape; they lead nowhere.

Through the years some new third parties have seriously challenged the major parties. The Republican party succeeded in replacing the Whigs as the second major party, but no other minor party has managed to duplicate that feat. Nor has any succeeded in establishing itself as a winner in national politics over any period of time. A few have temporarily captured the enthusiasm of large numbers of voters and have even elected state legislators, governors, and members of Congress. Some have swept millions of Americans into their ranks, even winning electoral votes. In the end they have disappeared as serious competitors from the national political scene. The most significant of these minor parties that have competed for the presidency in the period from 1880 to 1976 are listed in Figure 7–1.

In two states, Wisconsin and Minnesota, minor state parties persisted as successful competitors for longer than usual in the American system. Eventually, the Progressive party of Wisconsin was driven out of the competition in the face of traditional Republican-Democratic rivalry, and the Farmer-Labor party of Minnesota merged with the state Democratic party.

Today, only New York State has minor parties—the Liberal and Conservative parties— that occasionally elect candidates to office. Most frequently the Liberal party wins largely because it endorses Democratic candidates, the Conservative party, by endorsing Republican candidates. Just once has the Conservative party captured a state-wide office. This occurred in 1970 when the Democratic and Republican candidates so split the vote that the Conservative party candidate for U.S. Senate from New York won with a slim plurality. Its candidate was defeated by a Democrat in the 1976 elections.

Figure 7–1
Significant Minor Parties, 1880–1976*

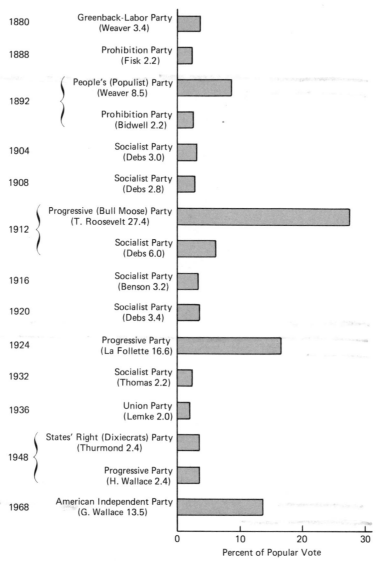

*Includes only those minor parties that polled 2 percent or more of the popular vote. In 1972 and 1976 no minor party received 2 percent.

SOURCE: Neal R. Peirce, *The People's President* (New York: Simon and Schuster, 1968), pp. 305–307. Reprinted by permission of Simon and Schuster; Donald B. Cole, *Handbook of American History* (New York: Harcourt Brace Jovanovich, 1968), pp. 304–305; *Politics in America,* 4th Edition (Washington, D.C.: Congressional Quarterly, 1971), p. 91.

Minor parties are not all alike. There are three principal types: splinter parties, crisis parties, and "cause" parties.

Splinter parties. A **splinter party** emerges out of a serious division within a major party. A faction that decides it cannot compromise any longer on policy or leadership within the party splits off to form its own party.

In the early twentieth century, two major splinter parties broke away from the Republican party. Former Republican President Teddy Roosevelt led dissenting liberal Republicans in 1912 into a Progressive party. Republican U.S. Senator Robert LaFollette led another revolt of Republican liberals to create the Progressive party of 1924. In recent times the major splits have occurred within the Democratic party. A southern conservative faction in 1948 split off to create the Dixiecrat or States' Rights party, and a liberal element split off to form the Progressive party. And in 1968 Democratic Governor George C. Wallace of Alabama pulled many disgruntled Democrats into an American Independent party.

Crisis parties. A second type of minor party (**crisis parties**) arises in response to a drastic deterioration (a crisis) in social or economic conditions. In the early nineteenth century, faced with a depression and competition for jobs from waves of Irish immigrants, many Protestants reacted by organizing a nativist party, the Know-Nothing party. When farmers and small-town people in the West and South suffered severe economic losses, one response was to organize farmer parties. The Greenback party of the 1880s and the Populist party of the 1890s expressed the deep resentment harbored by farmers against railroads, warehouses, and Wall Street—the bankers and capitalists of the East.

"Cause" parties. A third type of minor party (**"cause" parties**) develops around a special cause. A group within the country that is committed to a particular set of values and a unique solution to society's problems may field its own party. For example, the Prohibition party, recently renamed the Statesman party, is committed to the abolition of the sale of alcoholic beverages. The Socialist, Communist and Labor parties are "cause" parties that believe they have the ideal solution to the basic socioeconomic problems of the United States. In New York State, the Liberal and Conservative parties are, in effect, also "cause" parties, as is the new Right to Life party, which opposes abortion.

Spoilers
Source of policy issues
Safety valves

If they rarely win office and if most find it impossible to attract enough voters to remain on the ballot over any period of time, what impact do minor parties have on our political system? At times, they have none at all. At other times, their impact has been considerable.

First, minor parties can function as *spoilers* for one of the major parties. By pulling a significant number of votes away from a candidate of one major party, they may enable the other major party candidate to win. The election of Democrat Woodrow Wilson to the presidency in 1912 was a result of the Republican party's splitting into two competing parties. The Progressive party candidate pulled sufficient votes away from the Republican ticket in enough states to allow Wilson to win a majority of the electoral college.

Second, minor parties provide a *source of policy issues* for the major parties. When they attract significant popular support, minor parties demonstrate that their policy positions are tapping public discontent. Major party politicians, who are constantly searching for votes, frequently adopt such minor party policy positions as their own. Thus, some of the policy proposals offered by the Populist and Socialist parties at the turn of this century were transformed into law after Democratic politicians incorporated them into their own platforms.

Third, minor parties serve as safety valves. They help vent the frustration that inevitably builds up in a political system. By focusing the anger, resentment, and hatred of discontented people into party politics, minor parties deflect these dangerous feelings into a safe, ineffective form of political expression. Safe, because such feelings are expressed in campaigning and in voting rather than in violence. Ineffective, because minor parties are the dead ends of American politics; their candidates rarely if ever win office.

NOMINATING PRESIDENTIAL AND VICE-PRESIDENTIAL CANDIDATES

Our definition of parties stressed their offering candidates in elections for public office. Obviously, the most important public office in the United States is the presidency. In selecting their candidate for this office, both major political parties employ a mix of state party primaries and state party conventions to choose delegates to a national convention.

Although the U.S. Constitution refers to elections, it is silent about the nomination of candidates. Political parties fill this void. Our major parties nominate their presidential tickets at national conventions made up of their state parties' delegates. Such conventions have been the characteristic method for nominating candidates only since the 1830s when they replaced the existing nominating mechanism called "King Caucus". Under "King Caucus," all the congressmen of one party met together (caucused) to decide on a presidential ticket.

Choosing Convention Delegates

Delegates selected to a major party's national convention represent all fifty state parties plus party members who live in the District of Columbia and overseas. Democratic and Republican parties from Puerto Rico, the Virgin Islands, Guam, and the Panama Canal Zone also send delegates. In 1976 the Democratic party for the first time recognized the party faithful in Europe by allocating some delegates to them.

Allocation of votes.   Today the number of delegate votes allocated to each state party by its national committee represents a two-part formula: The Democrats use the state's population and the popular votes cast for the party's last three presidential candidates; the Republicans use the number of House and Senate seats in the state plus the record of voter support for the party's gubernatorial and national candidates.

The Democratic national party has been using its control over state party participation in the national convention to impose standards on its state parties. In sending delegates, state Democratic parties now are obligated to commit their presidential electors to the convention's ticket, under the name and emblem of the state party. More recently, the national committee has adopted rules governing the composition of the state parties' delegations to the national conventions. In 1972 each state party was required to choose a delegation composed of women, non-whites and young people in proportion to their percentages within the population of the state. The "quota" rule was abandoned in 1976 in favor of a requirement that state parties demonstrate a *good faith* effort to involve these groups in the delegate selection process. Although the percentage of delegates from the three categories declined, it still remained considerably above the 1968 proportions (see Table 7–15). The 1980 national convention rules call for each state party to make a good faith effort to send an equal number of men and women delegates.

Table 7–15
Social Composition of Democratic National Conventions, 1968, 1972, and 1976 (by percentage)

	1968	1972	1976
Women	13	38	34
Nonwhites	5.5	15	9
Young Adults	4	21	14.8

SOURCE: *The Party Reformed, Final Report of the Commission on Party Structure and Delegate Selection* (Washington, D.C.: Democratic National Committee, July 7, 1972), pp. 7–9; *The New York Times*, July 12, 1976, p. C5.

Choosing party delegates. The methods for choosing delegates vary with different state laws. The two principal methods are party conventions and party primaries. With thirty states using primaries in 1976, the overwhelming majority of delegates were selected by this method.

The state party convention method is the most standardized. It involves a series of indirect elections, beginning with meetings of party members at the precinct level. Delegates are elected to county conventions and ultimately to state conventions that pick the national delegates. Sometimes the county delegates convene at congressional district conventions to choose some of the national delegates, the remainder being chosen at a state convention.

Presidential primaries vary. The simplest form is one in which party members in a state may vote directly for one among competing slates of delegates to the national convention, each committed to a different presidential aspirant. Another type is a preferential primary; party members vote separately for delegates and for presidential candidates. The delegates may or may not be bound to vote in accordance with the preference expressed in the primary. A state party may combine the convention and primary methods, selecting delegates at congressional district conventions and at a state convention, but committing them to vote at the national convention for presidential candidates in proportion to the popular vote for these candidates in the party's primary.

Democratic national party rules have now begun to affect the delegate selection process itself. In 1976, for the first time the national party rejected the winner-take-all principle in the state parties' selection of national delegates. Each state party had to allocate delegates to those presidential candidates who competed for support in the state in proportion to the strength of their supporters within that party.

Candidate strategies and the delegate selection process. Candidates for the presidential nomination may choose one of a number of strategies to win. One strategy—involving high risk but low financial cost—is to avoid the delegate selection process altogether. Such a strategy is based upon the assumption that the convention will deadlock. Should no one receive a majority of votes, delegates might turn to a party leader who had avoided the bruising battles for delegates in the state primaries and conventions. Although there is some evidence that Adlai E. Stevenson followed this strategy in 1960, and Hubert H. Humphrey in 1976, neither was nominated. It is a high-risk strategy, for no major party convention has deadlocked since 1924!

A radically different strategy, carrying with it different kinds of high risks, calls for the candidate to enter all or almost all the state primaries and conventions in search of delegates. This strategy gives the candidate an opportunity to demonstrate he is a winner, but it requires his constant involvement in delegate contests, the setting up of an elaborate political organization, and the raising of large sums of money to finance the campaign. A small army of volunteers can substitute for some of these expensive resources.

The campaign of a winner in the state primaries and conventions tends to pick up momentum; that of a loser tends to decelerate very rapidly. Thus this strategy is risky, because a candidate who stumbles in the early primaries is easily labeled a loser by the media. Even the candidate who consistently wins second or third place is frequently labeled a "no win" candidate by the mass media. On the other hand, this strategy produces delegates and very favorable publicity for those who lead the other candidates in delegate selection battles.

In the 1976 campaign for the Democratic presidential nomination, Jimmy Carter started out immediately with a "victory" in the Iowa precinct elections for party delegates, who eventually chose the Iowa delegates to the national convention. He did not win all these delegates, but he won the most and his win was unexpected. Since Carter's initial problem was lack of recognition, "Jimmy Who?" being the question most frequently asked, this success earned him national publicity. In subsequent primaries his opponents split the votes among themselves, allowing him to come in first. Even when he did not emerge as the frontrunner in some of the primaries, Carter's image as "Number One" undermined the campaigns of his opponents and helped gain him the necessary delegates.

A candidate who is not expected to win easily can afford to lose a number of contests, especially close races against a highly favored opponent. But eventually the candidate must demonstrate an ability to win; consistent defeat, no matter how close, spells the end. Although Ronald Reagan, the former governor of California, lost the initial Republican contests to President Gerald R. Ford, the favored candidate, Reagan's subsequent victories in southern primaries turned the race around so that he entered the national convention as a very serious threat to the President.

A more moderate strategy is for a candidate to run only in a select number of convention and primary contests. This strategy permits the candidate to campaign only in those states where conditions are more likely to prove favorable and to avoid those that look too risky. Such a strategy makes less of a demand on accumulating enormous sums of money or building an extensive campaign organization, but it too involves certain risks. If too few contests are entered, the candidate comes to the national convention with insufficient delegates to have a chance to win. Defeat in specially chosen primaries can prove even more disastrous because the candidate loses in an area of supposed strength.

An incumbent President who seeks renomination changes the nature of the game by forestalling the candidacy of others within his party or by destroying their chances for victory at the national convention. No matter how unpopular he may be, an incumbent President can almost always win his party's nomination. Republican President Herbert Hoover was renominated by his party in 1932, even though the country was in the depths of a depression and there was widespread discontent with his performance. Democratic President Harry S Truman won his nomination in 1948, despite his unpopularity in the country and in his own party. Although Democratic President Lyndon B. Johnson withdrew from the 1968 nomination race after almost losing the New Hampshire primary to Senator Eugene J. McCarthy of Minnesota, in all probability he could have forced through his own nomination.

Financing Nominating Campaigns

Until the 1976 nominating conventions, candidates who campaigned for delegates had to raise their own finances. For those pursuing an aggressive strategy, the costs were high. Republican Richard Nixon's winning effort in 1968 cost approximately $10 million. In capturing the 1972 Democratic nomination, U.S. Senator George S. McGovern of South Dakota spent $12 million. Those who cannot raise such sums either do not offer themselves as candidates, drop out of the race, or have difficulty mounting an effective campaign.

With the enactment of its Federal Election Campaign Act of 1974, the national government undertook to help finance the campaigns of candidates for the presidential nomination. The purpose of the law was to make candidates much less dependent on private contributions, to help them run competitive campaigns, and to restrict drastically the amount any one contributor could offer a candidate. Prior to the 1976 campaign, a few private individuals donated hundreds of thousands of dollars to their favorite candidates.

To defray part of the cost of campaigning for the nomination, the national government now matches dollar for dollar the amount an *eligible candidate* raises up to approximately $5.5 million. To qualify for this support, a candidate must agree that his total expenditures in the nominating campaign will not exceed a certain maximum—approximately $13 million in 1976, and a candidate must first raise $5,000 in each of twenty states, a total of $100,000. Those who cannot generate this minimal amount of private money are assumed not to be serious contenders, and they receive no matching grants. The election law also limits the maximum individual contribution to $1,000 per candidate, or a total of $25,000 to all candidates and committees. Clearly, this law has drastically curtailed the importance of large individual contributors in presidential nominating politics.

NATIONAL CONVENTIONS MAKE KEY DECISIONS

Choosing a presidential candidate is the principal decision facing a national convention. But the delegates must also make other critical decisions regarding their organization, the selection of a vice-presidential candidate and the adoption of a platform. The latter two, especially, are crucial to the national convention's functioning as a mechanism for unifying its state parties for the upcoming general election campaign.

Organizing the Convention

In organizing a convention, decisions must be made involving credentials, officers, committees, and rules.

Credentials. One of the first important decisions for the delegates is to decide on an official slate of delegates from each state. This item is transformed from a routine matter to a critical one when competing sets of delegates claim to represent the same state parties, or when delegates are challenged as not coming in good faith as loyal party members.

In 1952 the Eisenhower forces at the Republican National Convention won the presidential nomination on the basis of a fight they raised over contested delegates. Two sets of delegates came from a number of southern states, each asserting it represented the Republican party of that state. One set favored General Dwight D. Eisenhower and the other, Ohio's Senator Robert E. Taft. After a bitter debate in the convention, the Eisenhower forces captured most of the contested seats. With Taft having sustained a serious loss of delegate strength, Eisenhower's managers were able to win his nomination.

Officers, committees, and rules.   A decision on the convention's officers as well as the composition of its committees comes initially from the national committee. These decisions must be officially accepted by the delegates before they become binding. Controversy may flare up if candidates consider it to their tactical advantage to challenge the choice of the presiding officers, the assigning of delegates to any of the four committees—credentials, rules, organization, and platform—or the adoption of special rules governing the behavior of the delegates.

Choosing a Presidential Candidate

Each state party delegation caucuses together and sits on the convention floor under its state party banner. Although the total state party vote is announced to the convention by the spokespersons for the state party delegations, each delegate casts an individual vote for a presidential candidate.

No "unit" rule.   Since 1968 state party delegations in Democratic National Conventions may no longer vote as a unit. The **unit rule** permitted a majority in a delegation to cast the entire delegation's votes, preventing a minority from having its votes counted. Republicans have never allowed the use of the unit rule.

A majority nomination.   Until 1936 Democrats operated under a two-thirds rule for presidential nominations. To win, a candidate needed two-thirds of the convention's votes. A sizable minority of the delegates could prevent a candidate, even one with a majority, from winning the convention unless that candidate successfully bargained with them. Democratic conventions were more susceptible to deadlock under the two-thirds rule than today when a simple majority ensures the nomination. In the 1924 national convention, for example, the delegates balloted 103 times before nominating a candidate. Neither of the two leading candidates could win the two-thirds majority, and neither would withdraw in favor of the other. The convention finally had to turn to someone else to break the deadlock.

Contemporary conventions of both parties have invariably nominated a presidential candidate on the first ballot. The winner comes into the convention with a majority of delegates already committed as a result of primary and convention contests, or the leading candidate is sufficiently ahead of anyone else so that he is able to pick up the extra votes to reach a majority.

Political "qualifications" of candidates.   Certain traditional assumptions about the political qualifications of potential winners have now been undermined. Since governors and military heroes have in the past predominated as winners, it was assumed until 1960 that a candidate from Congress had little or no chance of being nominated. In 1960, however, Senator John F. Kennedy, of Massachusetts, won the Democratic nomination. Subsequently, Senator Barry Goldwater, of Arizona, won the Republican nomination in 1964 and Senator George McGovern, of South Dakota, the Democratic nomination in 1972.

Another invalid assumption is that to be nominated a candidate must come from a populous state. A populous state sends a large delegation to conventions and, if its candidate is nominated, the state will presumably guarantee him a sizable bloc of electoral votes in the general election. Nonetheless, the Republicans nominated someone from Kansas in 1936 and someone from Arizona in 1964. The Democratic nominees in 1972 and 1976 were from South Dakota and Georgia. None of the four ranks among the ten most populous states.

The assumption that a southern politician could not be nominated for the presidency was valid from the time of the Civil War until 1976. The nomination of Lyndon B. Johnson, from Texas, in 1964 did not contradict this "rule" because he was already President, having moved up from the vice presidency when President Kennedy was assassinated.

The first southerner since the Civil War to win the presidential nomination of a major political party on his own credentials was Jimmy Carter of Georgia in 1976. With his successful election, southern leaders should now find it easier to offer themselves as realistic candidates for the nomination.

Another longtime assumption of politics was that a Catholic could not be nominated. New York Governor Al Smith, who won the Democratic nomination in 1928, was the first Catholic ever nominated for President by a major party. However, he lost the election, in part, because of his religion. Not until 1960 was another Catholic nominated for the presidency. Although his Catholic religion did indeed become a heated issue and cost him votes, Senator John F. Kennedy won the Democratic nomination and the presidential election. The Catholic issue no longer seems relevant to presidential politics. It was not even raised when Senator Edmund S. Muskie of Maine campaigned for the Democratic presidential nomination in 1972 or when California Governor Jerry Brown (both Catholics) ran for the Democratic nomination in 1976. Nor did the Catholic issue surface when a draft-Kennedy movement was started to win the 1980 nomination for Senator Edward M. Kennedy of Massachusetts.

Although public opinion polls indicate a willingness on the part of a majority of Americans to vote for a woman, a black, or a Jew for President, the major political parties have still not demonstrated a willingness to test this sentiment. In all probability a political leader from any of these three groups stands a better chance of winning the vice-presidential nomination before one is ever considered for the top of the ticket.

The Vice-Presidential Nomination

Another decision facing party delegates at their national convention is the nomination of a vice-presidential candidate. No politician seriously campaigns for the vice-presidential nomination before the national convention. The selection has almost invariably been made by the presidential nominee and ratified by the convention.

What does a presidential nominee look for in choosing a vice-presidential candidate? Almost always it is someone who will balance the ticket, add unity in the party, and reinforce its chances for winning in the November election. The second position may be offered to a defeated candidate for the presidential nomination or to someone who is more attractive to certain key elements in the party coalition than is the presidential nominee. Sometimes the candidate is chosen for regional balance, matching a northerner with a southerner or a westerner with an easterner. A presidential candidate who chooses someone who does not unite the party magnifies the risks facing his ticket in the general election.

Jimmy Carter, who ran an anti-Washington campaign, chose as his vice-presidential candidate U.S. Senator Walter F. Mondale of Minnesota, an experienced Washington politician. Mondale also represented the Midwest, as distinct from the South, and he had congressional, as distinct from gubernatorial, experience. His strong liberal-labor connections made the ticket more attractive to urban labor Democrats suspicious of a southern peanut farmer. Republican Gerald R. Ford's choice was designed to placate the followers of Ronald Reagan, who were bitter that their candidate had lost the presidential nomination.

Adopting a Party Platform

At each national convention, a platform committee presents to the delegates a set of policy proposals it hopes the party will adopt. Should the proposed platform engender bitter division, such conflict could be terribly damaging. It could fragment the party when unity is essential to ensure success in the election campaign. Most party leaders deplore and fear such conflict. Hence their eagerness to paper over differences by designing compromises.

Sometimes neither side is willing to compromise on some emotional issue. In 1924 the Democrats clashed bitterly in their national convention over a resolution specifically condemning the Ku Klux Klan.

The motion was eventually defeated by a single vote, 542 and 3/20 to 541 and 3/20. This divisiveness helped contribute to the defeat of the presidential ticket in the general election. In 1948 the Democratic National Convention was caught up in a fight over a resolution from the floor of the convention to strengthen the platform's position on civil rights. With its adoption, half the Alabama delegation and the entire Mississippi delegation walked out. They subsequently joined with other discontented southern Democrats in organizing a third party with its own presidential ticket.

Defeat of a motion to condemn extremism, presented by moderates at the 1964 Republican National Convention, left many Republicans feeling that the nominee and his majority were insensitive to their concerns and therefore undeserving of their support during the election campaign. And in 1968 an extremely divided Democratic convention split even further apart as a result of its debate and vote over a resolution condemning the country's involvement in the Vietnam War. Some Democrats were so dismayed by the defeat of the motion that they refused to campaign for the election of their party's presidential candidate.

Most of the time, however, party leaders attempt to compromise so the major factions in their party will be able to accept the platform. They know a united party has a much better chance of waging a successful fight for the presidency than one in which a major group is alienated by the decisions of the national convention.

Even though a party platform may serve to unify a party, it does not necessarily commit the presidential candidate to all of its policy proposals. Candidates have felt free to repudiate or ignore those parts they disagreed with or those they judged would lose them votes.

NATIONAL CONVENTIONS AND THE ELECTION

The Republican and Democratic conventions provide the nation with the main sets of contenders for the top executive offices of the United States. Ideally, the major national party conventions also pull together their respective state parties, unifying them behind their presidential tickets.

The Convention Begins the Election Campaign

The national convention actually begins the election campaign. An extremely dramatic event, the convention captures the attention of millions of Americans, exposing them to the party and its leaders.

Nowadays, television and radio bring the excitement of national conventions directly into the homes of America. The acceptance speeches of the nominees become their first major campaign addresses to their parties and to the general electorate. In essence, then, the conventions are both the end products of an internal leadership fight within the parties themselves and the beginning of the competitive national election campaign.

Public Financing for Conventions

In 1976, as a result of the Federal Election Campaign Act of 1974, the Republican and Democratic national conventions were for the first time financed by the national government. According to that law, a national committee of a major party (one whose candidate had secured at least 25 percent of the national popular votes in the previous presidential election) is eligible for $2.2 million to finance its national convention. The national committee must agree not to spend any additional money for the convention and not to use any of the national government's money to support a particular candidate.

Minority parties that qualify are also provided financial support for their national conventions, although they are given a lesser amount than the major parties. A minor party is defined as one whose presidential candidate in the previous general election received from 5 to 25 percent of the vote. If its candidate received less than 5 percent of the vote, the party would not be eligible for any public financial assistance in holding its national convention.

No minor party polled 5 percent of the popular vote in 1972, and so none was eligible for public financial aid for its conventions in 1976. Moreover, since all the minor parties together in 1976 did not approximate 5 percent of the popular vote, they will be denied public funds for their national conventions in 1980. In effect, the new national financing law further embeds the two major parties in the American political system and handicaps minor parties in offering candidates for President on a competitive basis.

Concepts To Study

capitalism	federalism	two-party system
checks and balances	freedom/liberty	winner-take-all principle
democracy	separation of powers	

Special Terms To Review

"cause" parties
crisis parties
electoral college
independents
interest groups
major parties
minor parties

national conventions
national parties
nonpartisan elections
party-in-the-electorate
party-in-the-government
party-in-the-organization
party platform

political party
presidential electors
socioeconomic status (SES)
splinter parties
state parties
two-thirds rule
unit rule

Some very politically involved - some aren't usually not political private individuals in common goal interest groups in (Senate.) govt. aren't allowed

10/20

INTEREST GROUPS AND POLITICS

Thousands of interest groups are active in our political system. Most interact directly with government, hoping to use its power to gain their objectives. Others try to influence it indirectly by participating in political parties and in candidate elections. Still others bypass government completely, campaigning in policy issue elections. A few groups resort to all of these strategies.

An interest group can be defined as a set of individuals who on the basis of shared attitudes make claims upon others in society. In this chapter we will be concerned with those interest groups that seek to advance or defend their objectives through political means. Traditionally, people have formed groups along economic, religious, social, or racial lines to express those common interests that differentiated them in some way from their fellow Americans.

As new issues and problems arise in American society, different individuals become sufficiently concerned to unite to articulate their common interests in the political arena. Or groups that are already organized for some nonpolitical purpose shift their attention to political activity, either to compensate for their incapacity to achieve their goals elsewhere or to resist the intervention of government into the affairs of their members.

What are some of the groups that have emerged very recently on the American political scene? The demand for the equal status for women in our society has stimulated the organization of such groups as the National Organization for Women, the National Women's Political Caucus, and the Women's Lobby. In turn, the women's movement has helped generate a special consciousness on the part of divorced men and homosexuals. Fathers for Equal Rights and United Father's Coalition for Fair Divorce and Alimony Laws are new groups formed by divorced men to fight for changes in child custody practices and alimony payments. Homosexuals have united in numerous groups as part of a "gay" liberation movement to campaign publicly for the abolition of social, economic, and political discrimination directed against them.

A large number of vociferous, contending groups have formed around the abortion issue. The National Right to Life Committee serves as an umbrella (coordinating) organization for the many new interest groups that oppose the legalization and availability of abortion. The National Abortion Rights Action League and the Religious Coalition for Abortion Rights are two groups that favor women's access to and government support for abortions.

Many Americans have joined together to work for the protection of our environment. Environmental Action, Friends of the Earth, Environmental Defense Fund, and Save the Whales are only a few of these newly created groups. A widespread network of consumer interest groups spearheaded by Ralph Nader, "Mr. Consumer" himself, now operates at all levels of politics. These groups call for governmental protection against businesses, industries, and professionals who exploit consumers through excessive prices, harmful ingredients, shoddy products and sloppy services.

More traditional interest groups have also been active in most of these areas of concern: the League of Women Voters in women's rights; Planned Parenthood Federation in population control; the Sierra Club and the National Wildlife Federation in environmental concerns; the Consumer Federation of America in the consumer field. The newer groups, however, have attracted numerous additional Americans to the political arena, have sharpened the cutting edge of agitation, and have expanded the conflict over the goals and intervention of government in our society.

INTEREST GROUPS AND DEMOCRACY

Underlying the political involvement of interest groups are the dynamic quality of modern society and the democratic nature of our political system. An increasingly complex and interdependent society leads more and more people to feel a need to defend or advance their interests through group action. The very powerlessness of the individual endows the organized interest group approach to government and politics with great attraction. And the power of government to intervene in social and economic matters acts as a magnet, drawing individuals and groups into the political sphere. In a democratic system this tremendous concentration of power is always available to those individuals and groups that can mobilize sufficient resources. In this respect a democratic political system encourages the emergence and operation of interest groups.

Interest Groups Help Make Democracy Work

Democracy calls for government of the people, by the people, and for the people. Interest groups help bring this about. They give people a more effective voice in their government and make government more responsive to the people. In fact, interest groups provide individuals with a special representation that parallels the more general public representation provided by political parties and their elected officials.

Democracy calls for freedom of speech, press, assemblage, and petition for groups as well as for individuals. The First and Fourteenth Amendments, which guarantee these rights, constitutionally protect the right of interest groups to exist and to operate freely. By enhancing the ability of individuals to express and make effective their choices on public policy, interest groups help us realize democratic values of individual diversity and freedom of choice.

Interest Groups Maximize the Power of the Individual

You have learned that the adult citizen has a single unit of power, a vote. By itself a single vote has very little impact but, united with others and focused behind a common objective, individual votes acquire significant political power. Interest groups, like political parties, give individuals a meaningful way to maximize their power. In mobilizing many individuals and their resources on behalf of political positions, interest groups can overcome the relative powerlessness and inertia of the single individual.

Considerable time, money, effort, and organization—resources which few of us possess—are necessary to qualify an initiative or referendum issue for the ballot because this always requires thousands of signatures (over 300,000 to qualify a policy issue for the 1978 elections in California). Whereas single individuals are virtually powerless, interest groups can marshal these vital resources. They can tap the individual resources of their members and allies, and their officers can concentrate their energies on organizing the campaign for signatures. An interest group can also mount the necessary campaign to shape public opinion and bring out the voters. As a member of an interest group, a person becomes part of a collective effort whose potential strength far exceeds that of the single individual.

Interest groups magnify the voice of an individual in the public arena. There is an old saying in politics: "The squeaky wheel gets greased." But the world of politics is a noisy one, and the single voice tends to be drowned out or to have little or no impact even if it is heard. Interest groups can significantly raise the level of "noise" by involving hundreds and thousands of individuals, and they can effectively focus this noise so that public officials cannot avoid becoming aware and attentive.

Although individuals may invest little money in their interest groups, the small contributions added together may be sufficient to buy the services of research experts and to employ skilled spokespersons to work in the legislative, executive, or judicial arenas. In mobilizing the limited resources of separate individuals behind staffs of technical and political specialists who can express their interests, organized groups provide single individuals with tremendous benefits at little personal cost.

Leaders of interest groups do more than articulate the views of their members. They serve as recognized contact points for governmental officials and leaders of other interest groups. When those who exercise public power want to know a group's position on a given issue, they can readily seek out its official representative. Interest group leaders also make it easier for governmental decision makers to bargain with a group. A few people, meeting face-to-face around a table, can more easily determine where they agree or disagree and how they can reconcile their differences. In addition, leaders of interest groups are in a position to fashion alliances with other organized groups, thereby increasing their own groups' chances for realizing their policy goals.

Who Belongs to Interest Groups?

With so many groups catering to the diverse interests of people in our society, you might think almost every individual belonged to at least one such group. Organizing a new group is relatively easy and the costs to individuals tend to be relatively low. But despite these features which facilitate group involvement, a large segment of our population does not belong to any interest group. This means that many Americans do not have their own interest groups representing them in the political world. As a consequence they and their interests are often ignored or disregarded in the making of public policy.

What is true about participation in parties and elections is also true about interest group involvement, another form of political participation: Those who have better educations and incomes participate much more than those who do not. In other words, the interest group world reflects a bias in favor of those with greater resources and skills. Of course, the monetary cost of interest group membership is always greater than that involved in voting or in party membership, which cost nothing. Interest groups do generally require financial support from their members. Irrespective of its monetary costs, interest group involvement seems to be associated with an individual's degree of confidence and competence in politics. The poor, having the least education, the lowest income, and the least desirable work or no work at all, exhibit the least confidence and competence in politics. Consequently, they are the least involved as voters and as members of interest groups. Therefore, their interests are not well-represented in the struggle to use the power of government.

This is not to say that no group speaks directly for the poor and the least educated. However, those that do tend to be poorly organized and underfinanced, and they have very small memberships. Fortunately, the concerns of a number of established, well-organized groups overlap or coincide with those of the poor. Thus, when the AFL-CIO and the National Council of Churches push for full employment, improved health services, more educational opportunities, and better housing facilities, they also represent the interests of the disadvantaged. Nevertheless, inasmuch as almost all of these groups have their own memberships and interests, their leaders must concentrate primarily on advancing their own causes. In a possible conflict between their interests and those of the very poor, the latter are bound to be more easily sacrificed.

CHARACTERISTICS OF INTEREST GROUPS

Certain characteristics distinguish interest groups from each other: their degree of involvement in politics; whether they are intrinsically political or private; whether they are special or public interest groups; whether they have narrow or broad objectives; whether they represent public governments or private sectors of our society; whether they are composed of individuals, single organizational units, or a number of such units.

Degree of Political Involvement

Some interest groups are never politically active; they prefer to advance the common interests of their members solely through private action. Others may enter the political arena for a single issue and then withdraw. Still others may move in and out as their interests demand. And some are constantly immersed in political action.

A church, for example, primarily serves the religious needs of its members. But should the state legislature consider legalizing gambling or levying a tax on church-owned property, that church might try to persuade the legislature to reject these proposals. Once the issue was resolved, the church might withdraw to its traditional concerns. It would become involved in politics only intermittently, in response to governmental actions that cut across its concerns. A business might become involved in an issue election if its interests were threatened, or it might protest to an executive agency that had changed the administrative rules affecting its industry. Normally, the same businesspeople might spend most or all of their time in the private economic sector.

However, interest groups in ever increasing numbers are becoming continuously involved with influencing governmental decisions. Because government action is so closely tied to the availability of jobs and the economic health of the country, such interest groups as the AFL-CIO and the U.S. Chamber of Commerce employ large, full-time staffs to monitor and try to influence government officials. Labor and business groups are also becoming increasingly involved in election campaigns to choose public officials and to decide directly on public issues. Groups find that they have too much to lose or gain not to spend part of their resources in constantly guarding their interests in executive, legislative, judicial, and election decisions.

Interest groups can interact with any or all parts of government. Some groups interact with that part of the executive bureaucracy whose rules affect their members. Others feel that their interests must be protected in the legislative, judicial, and the executive centers of decision making. Some interest groups concentrate only on the local level of government; others on the state level. Still others concern themselves solely with national politics. An increasing number, however, find that they must be active at all levels of the federal system if they are to protect their interests.

Basic Focus: Political or Private

Interest groups may be distinguished by their fundamental orientation: political or private. Most are privately oriented: Their existence and interests are inherently nonpolitical and predate their involvement in politics. For example, the National Rifle Association has an essentially private focus, the ownership and use of guns for sport. The AFL-CIO is a labor union organization; the American Dental Association, a professional organization; and the National Audubon Society, an organization of bird enthusiasts. Government and politics became important to these organizations only when their interests were threatened or when they saw in government a better way of advancing these interests. The major economic, social, professional, and religious groups in the United States fall into this category.

A smaller number of groups operating in our society are solely political. Such ideological groups as the Americans for Democratic Action or Americans for Constitutional Action were established to advance their respective liberal and conservative views on politics. Common Cause addresses itself to improving the quality and operation of government, and the American Civil Liberties Union fights in behalf of civil liberties. Their purpose and focus are political, as are those of most consumer and environmental groups.

Special Interests or Public Interests

Most groups are **special-interest groups.** They advocate governmental action that directly benefits their members. Both the U.S. Chamber of Commerce and the National Association of Manufacturers support legislation and decisions by public officials that favor members of the business community. The AFL-CIO advocates governmental policies beneficial to union labor, whereas the National Grange and the American Farm Bureau Federation advocate those that advance the interests of farmers. At times, these interest groups may join legislative, executive, or judicial battles for public policies not directly benefiting their members. That is when they begin to approximate **public-interest groups.**

Not just economic groups fall into the special-interest group category. The National Association for the Advancement of Colored People is a racial group concerned with advancing the civil rights of blacks and improving their economic well being. The National Rifle Association centers its political efforts almost entirely on guaranteeing its members (and others who own or use guns) the unrestricted ownership and peaceful use of such guns. The National Organization for Women (NOW) concentrates on enhancing the rights and opportunities of women, and the National Council of Senior Citizens concentrates on the interests of the aged.

A public interest group, on the other hand, seeks to protect and improve the quality of society or the political system for all, not just for its members. Its members may benefit from stronger consumer guarantees on goods and services, cleaner air and water, the protection of civil rights, more honest and capable politicians, whatever. But the advantages accrue primarily to the *public as a whole.* This does not mean public interest groups encounter no opposition. Some group's special interest almost always conflicts with the general interest being advanced by public interest groups. Moreover, what the general interest is at any one time in American society is itself an issue of controversy.

Environmental groups pushing for clean air and water may conflict sharply with industries that refuse to invest in expensive antipollution

From *The Herblock Gallery* (Simon & Schuster, 1968)

"There's getting to be a lot of dangerous talk about the public interest."

equipment or with city officials who are reluctant to raise taxes to pay for improved sewage treatment plants. Members of the Wilderness Society, Sierra Club, or Wildlife Federation repeatedly clash with mining and lumber companies and with sheep and cattle ranchers who claim they will be denied important economic benefits should government declare land a wilderness area. The general interest in clean air and water and in preserving our natural resources may, in fact, clash with the general interest in employment opportunities and fighting inflation.

Narrow or Broad Group Objectives

Most politically involved interest groups concern themselves with narrowly defined governmental policy. Right to Life groups seek to prevent abortions; the National Coalition to Ban Handguns seeks to prevent the sale and ownership of handguns. Group Against Smokers' Pollution (GASP) and Action On Smoking and Health (ASH) lobby for laws to prevent smoking in public places, and Save the Whales concerns itself with protecting whales from extermination by commercial fishermen. Each of these groups, like the overwhelming majority of economic interest groups, concentrates on a narrow sector of public policy.

A small number of interest groups concern themselves with a much wider arc of public policy. Special interest economic groups, such as the National Association of Manufacturers, the U.S. Chamber of Commerce, the AFL-CIO, and the American Farm Bureau Federation, as well as such public-interest groups as Common Cause, involve themselves in a much broader approach to public policy. These interest groups may be concerned with any or all aspects of economic policy: deregulating the price of oil, instituting wage and price controls, balancing the budget, increasing taxes. They may also intervene in such noneconomic issues as federal aid for education, civil rights, campaign finance reform, and protecting the environment.

Governments as Interest Groups

Public governments also participate as interest groups. Certain governments in our federal system, those that share unique concerns and must rely on another level of government for necessary resources or rules to operate effectively, organize their own interest groups. The U.S. Conference of Mayors represents the chief executives of the large cities who have to interact with national and state governments. Smaller cities and towns, whose interests often differ from those of the large metropolises, are represented by the National League of Cities.

Foreign governments, too, act as interest groups. When necessary, their diplomats may try to influence congressmen and members of the national executive, or the foreign governments may employ special agents (lobbyists) for this purpose. In recent years, the governments of France and England successfully conducted major campaigns to convince both the national government and New York City government to allow their supersonic airplane, the Concorde, to land at JFK International Airport. Through campaign contributions and other gifts, South Korea attempted to influence American congressmen to oppose both a reduction of economic aid and a pullout of U.S. troops from that country. France, England, and South Korea are not the only foreign governments that have sought to influence public policy decisions in the United States. Their efforts merely generated more publicity than those of other governments.

Group Size and Structure

Interest groups come in all sizes and shapes. Most depend on voluntary memberships; a few do not. Some include only a few individuals; others have thousands or even millions of members. The American Legion, a veterans' group, has approximately 2.7 million members; the Veterans of Foreign Wars, 1.8 million.

Some interest groups are self-contained economic, social, or governmental units. Others are huge federations of such units. Still others are narrowly based federations, such as those representing business firms in a single industry or farmers producing a particular crop. U.S. Steel and Exxon, for example, two giant corporations, are as much interest groups when they interact with government as are the enormous federation of manufacturers (NAM), in which they may be members, or the special steel or oil producers' associations to which they also belong. Individual unions, such as the United Automobile Workers, Teamsters' Union, and Carpenters' Union, act as separate interest groups, as does the AFL–CIO, to which some of them belong. Even though a city, state or county belongs to a national association of similar governments, it may feel it must pursue, by itself, its own unique interests with other levels of government.

Whom Interest Groups Represent

A warning to help you avoid an easy mistake. Never confuse people who share a distinct characteristic with an interest group. Labor or business, agriculture, women, blacks, or Jews are not interest groups. Conversely, never conclude that an organized group is necessarily identical with that general part of the population it claims to represent.

Note, for example, the difference between veterans and veterans' interest groups. Veterans are individuals who share the common characteristic of having served in the armed forces. They are *not* an interest group. Only if they interact in some organized manner on the basis of their common identification as veterans are they a veterans' interest group.

The overwhelming majority of veterans do not belong to any veterans' group. The two largest veterans' interest groups, the American Legion and the Veterans of Foreign Wars may claim to speak for the American veterans, but most veterans are probably indifferent to their policy positions. Moreover, other veterans' groups, such as the American Veterans Committee, may present government officials with views on policy issues that oppose those of the major organizations.

Competing interest groups frequently claim to speak for the same general category of people. The American Bar Association and the National Lawyers Guild both maintain that they represent the legal profession, but they often take opposite sides on issues. The U.S. Chamber of Commerce, the National Association of Manufacturers, the Committee for Economic Development, and the Business Roundtable all claim to speak for the general business community whereas in fact they represent different business groups. The AFL-CIO purports to represent the interests of labor, but some unions do not belong to that federation, and most of the national labor force belongs to no union.

Although some interest groups claim to speak for a general group, many just speak for specialized subcategories within that general group. For example, the American Farm Bureau Federation, the National Grange, the Farmers' Organization of America, and the Farmers' Union all claim to represent the farmer. Those farmers who cultivate specific crops, however, have their own associations to speak for their unique interest, whether it be tobacco, rice, cotton, corn, wheat, or soybeans. Some farmers have organized their own special cooperatives and federations of cooperatives. Who then speaks for the farmer? They all do. But they speak with different voices and quite frequently for different sets of agricultural interests.

FEATURES OF AMERICAN GOVERNMENT: ADVANTAGES AND DISADVANTAGES FOR INTEREST GROUPS

Three features of our governmental system are particularly important for interest groups: federalism, separation of powers, and checks and balances. They are important because they provide a large number of access points to groups seeking to influence government. All three allow interest groups to shift their focus of attention should they be frustrated or defeated at any one level or in any single branch of government. These features can also make it more difficult for some interest groups to affect public policy. Some groups may only have to secure the consent of each of the branches of government at any one level; others may have to concern themselves with all three levels—national, state, and local—to guarantee that public policy coincides with their interests.

Federalism

Federalism sets up a system of levels of government, each with independent powers to make binding, authoritative decisions. This system affords interest groups a variety of access points to power. Many interest groups can resolve their problems at the state and local levels since these governments possess the resources and authority to meet their special needs. Other interest groups must focus political action at the national level. Still others find they must operate at all three levels of the federal system. Indeed, cooperative federalism—involving the national government in joint ventures with cities, counties or states—has stimulated many groups to operate throughout this entire range of governments to affect the nature of policy decisions, the amount and allocation of money, and the administration of programs.

Federalism allows some interest groups time to refine their issues and to develop the essential political skills at the governmental level where they have their greatest strength before they compete at other levels of the political system. The Anti-Saloon League illustrates the point. This interest group, which was primarily responsible for the adoption of the Prohibition Amendment to the U.S. Constitution, benefited greatly from its experience competing at the state level of government before the national amendment battle. By winning in state legislatures, by helping its supporters gain public office, and by defeating its opponents, it significantly impressed many politicians. It also was able to organize in various parts of the country so that when it launched its national campaign for the Prohibition Amendment, it was in an advantageous position.

On the other hand, federalism may work to the disadvantage of a group if it is forced into the national policy-making level before it has marshalled sufficient strength to be effective there. The Townsend Movement, the popular name for an old-age pension group prominent in the 1930s and 1940s, was prematurely compelled to battle for its policy proposal in Congress. Its leaders had accumulated no political experience in campaign politics or in working with legislators and had not had time to develop a carefully drafted bill. Moreover, its membership base was confined principally to the far western states, which severely limited its ability to influence more than a few legislators. As you would expect, it was decisively defeated.

Separation of Powers and Checks and Balances

The division of national and state governments into executive, legislative and judicial branches further encourages interest group activity. Each branch opens up another set of access points for influencing public policy. Interest groups can move freely from one branch to another in their quest to shape policy. Each branch of government, moreover, has many subdivisions. These serve as additional cracks in the structure of government through which interest groups can gain entrance to the decision-making process.

Because of the checks-and-balances principle, many interest groups find they must be able to operate in all three branches. Since each branch shares in the power of the others, each can modify or cancel what the others do. If interest groups were to direct their efforts at only one branch, the advantage gained there might be cancelled in another.

Since officials in the different branches and their subdivisions also compete with each other for money, jurisdiction, and authority, the officials themselves solicit interest group involvement. Our political system encourages a circular arrangement: Interest groups seek to influence units of government while these units reach out for interest group support to enhance their own positions. Indeed, any one policy fight may find some interest groups, executive agencies, and legislators competing against other interest groups, executive agencies, and legislators.

INTEREST GROUP RESOURCES

Interest groups differ in the resources they bring into the political arena. What resources help ensure a group's success in politics?

Money

Groups with large sums of money have a decided advantage. This is not because the overwhelming majority of candidates, voters, and public officials are open to bribery; they are not. The overwhelming majority of interest groups do not resort to such tactics. But money can easily be converted into other resources that can legitimately influence the decisions of public officials. Money buys expensive TV and radio time and space in newspapers and magazines. It buys expertise in subject matter areas, in publicity, in governmental relations. Money is exceptionally valuable in helping candidates win primary and general elections and in mounting referendum or initiative campaigns. Money is *not* all-important, but it can either limit or expand the strategies and tactics available to the group.

Membership

A large membership is another valuable resource. First of all, an interest group capable of speaking for a large percentage of those it claims to represent will find greater acceptance by governmental officials who view it as a legitimate representative of that public. Second, a mass membership can give an interest group access to a greater number of officials and, by mobilizing its membership, it can raise the consciousness of public officials about the group's proposals and strength. Third, a large membership may become a valuable resource—votes, money, and workers in candidate and issue elections.

Status or Respectability

The degree of status (respect and esteem) afforded an interest group by others will enhance or detract from its efforts. Groups with high status encounter less opposition and are treated more considerately by officials and members of the public than low status groups.

When certain groups in the 1970s tried to persuade state legislators to legalize the use of laetrile (an extract from apricot pits) as a treatment for cancer, its rejection as a legitimate treatment by the American Medical Association, a high status organization, seriously thwarted these efforts. From the time homosexuals first became active in politics during the 1970s, their groups have faced a serious problem of respectability. A widespread belief that homosexuality is immoral and abnormal has hampered their efforts to secure local laws banning private social and economic discrimination and, at the same time, has made it easy for groups opposing homosexuals to defeat them in issue elections.

Leadership

A skilled, able leadership is an especially valuable resource. Leaders who unify their groups are more likely to have cohesive support when they approach public officials. And leaders who understand the political environment and know how to operate within political institutions improve their chances to be effective. Conversely, leaders who cause dissension within their interest groups damage them politically, as do leaders who are ill-prepared and clumsy in representing their groups.

Dr. Francis E. Townsend, the head of a national old-age pension group, was so autocratic that his leadership caused endless dissension and splits among its members. Dissident Townsend leaders formed opposing pension groups that challenged the claims of his group to speak for the aged. And financial contributions to the Townsend organization dropped off just when they were most needed, during periods of intense political campaigning. When legislators in Congress felt particularly threatened by the Townsendites in primary and general elections one year, they were able to capitalize upon Dr. Townsend's behavior by authorizing a special committee to investigate charges that the pension leader ruled in an arbitrary manner and personally profited from his leadership. This adverse publicity materially reduced the Townsend threat to Congress.

The strategy and tactics of interest groups in politics vary with the resources and aims of the group. For example, the National Association for the Advancement of Colored People (NAACP) turned to the national judiciary to secure its policy goals because it lacked significant resources needed to approach other centers of power. For many years it had virtually no influence in the state and national legislatures, and it could not generate enough votes in elections to affect the decisions of elected public officials. In the national courts, however, the only resource necessary was expertise, a resource the NAACP was able to mobilize. Moreover, access to the courts was relatively easy. The NAACP was able to make considerable progress in behalf of blacks in the courts before civil rights groups found the allies, status, and votes to operate successfully in American legislatures and with executive officials.

Lobbying the Legislature

Interest groups try to influence the legislature because it is the basic governmental institution for making public policy regarding economic and social aspects of life. Legislatures adopt laws, propose or ratify constitutional amendments, and have tremendous power over executive officials—their budget, their authority to operate, their very structure and discretion. Legislative action can often overrule or redirect judicial decisions. In essence, a legislature represents a tremendous concentration of power that can be put to use for or against the interests of an organized group. Lobbyists—those employed to speak for interest groups in contacting and influencing government—endeavor to penetrate the legislature to advance the positions of their employers.

What do interest group lobbyists want and need from legislators? First of all, lobbyists want and need *access*, an opportunity to present the case for the groups they represent. These lobbyists seek as allies legislators who are friendly to the policy goals of their groups. Second, lobbyists want to be permitted to share the making of public policy: They want to be consulted on legislation affecting the interests of their groups and to have a voice in the substantive compromises essential to moving legislation along and in the tactics and strategy that must be fashioned. Third, they want to be furnished information on what is happening in the legislature and to be given advice on whom to see and when to do so. Lobbyists want to know who the undecided legislators are so they or their allies can try to influence them, and they want to know who their legislative opponents are so they can monitor their strategy and tactics or ascertain how to counter their actions. Lobbyists

© 1978 by Herblock in *The Washington Post*

"He's quite independent—of political leadership, that is."

also want legislators to speak in their behalf to their colleagues, since the legislators influence each other on how to vote. They want legislators to intervene for the interest group with officials in the executive side of government. Finally, of course, lobbyists want legislators to vote for their proposals.

Most legislators permit and sometimes even encourage lobbyists to present their case. As elected representatives of the people, legislators recognize that lobbyists also represent people, special groups of people who have interests of their own and therefore a right to be heard in their behalf.

Legislators frequently need help in the substance and politics of policy making. Lobbyists are often specialists in certain policy areas, or they have recourse to such specialists. They can assist legislators with much needed expertise in designing and assessing public policy. Lobbyists can often aid legislators in the politics of legislation by helping them round up votes and by advising them on strategy and tactics. Through their interest group membership, lobbyists can stimulate letters, telephone calls, telegrams and visits from live constituents—grass-roots pressure—in behalf of or in opposition to policy proposals. Indeed, legislators frequently call on lobbyists to generate a public outcry on some issue so as to make a significant impression on other legislators. Furthermore, to the extent interest groups help friendly legislators receive key committee assignments or provide them with the proper staff to become more influential in policy making, the interests of both legislators and lobbyists coincide.

Although both legislators and lobbyists need each other in many ways, the lobbyists are the most vulnerable in this relationship, for if legislators cut them off from access or assistance, their value to their interest groups will be drastically curtailed. This means lobbyists must be careful to play by the rules of the game established by the legislators. They must always be candid with legislators, ready to explain the problems and pitfalls their proposals may pose for these officials. Lobbyists must not pressure legislators into acting in ways that are politically dangerous to their reelection chances or that embarrass them within the legislature. And they must respect confidential information. Only if lobbyists are accepted and respected by the legislators, especially the key ones for particular policy areas, will the lobbyists be in a position to become influential in behalf of their interest groups.

Lobbyists employ direct and indirect tactics to advance their objectives. **Direct lobbying** involves the lobbyists personally with the legislators: servicing their needs, consulting with them, or trying to persuade them. In **indirect lobbying**, the lobbyists use other political actors to influence legislators. These individuals may have more status and expertise than the lobbyists, better access to legislators, or more influence with them. "It is a waste of my time to go up on the Hill (Congress) and lobby myself," reported a lobbyist for the U.S. Chamber of Commerce in 1970. "I'm much more effective if I pull together fifty businessmen and let them do it." Lobbyists can also marshal the interest group's membership to contact their legislators by phone, wire, or letter. Legislators are particularly sensitive to an aroused public opinion.

Lobbying the Executive

The enormous power exercised by officials in the executive branch also attracts the intervention of interest groups. Congress and state legislatures depend on their chief executives to propose the most important items on their policy agendas. With the exception of the North Carolina governor, all the national and state executives have the power to veto legislation. In addition, they are empowered to make appointments to judicial and executive leadership positions.

Both the President and the governors serve as the principal budgetary officers for their governments. They and their staffs fashion an executive budget (a plan of expenditures) and then propose it to the legislature for adoption or modification. Once the budget is approved by the legislature, the chief executive is politically responsible for supervising the spending.

Finally, executive officials are authorized to administer the law. They are charged with putting into effect the services and regulations mandated by their legislatures. The spirit and tempo of administration is largely set by executive officials, who are often delegated considerable discretionary rule-making power by their legislatures.

Interest groups therefore try to interact with and influence executive officials. Their lobbyists may try to shape those budget items submitted to the chief executive by subordinates; they may attempt to influence the proposals the chief executive recommends to the legislature: the budget, the authorization of policy, the nominations of executive and judicial leaders. Interest groups may also cooperate with executive officials in joint campaigns for these objectives within the legislature. And since interest groups are vitally concerned with the administration of government as it affects their members and their goals, they try to affect the spirit, tempo, and rules by which government is carried to the people.

The more specialized the interest group and the more narrow its policy objective, the more it confines itself to a single department or even a subunit within a department. Interest groups concerned with more general policy find they must interact with the chief executive and with the leadership of various departments.

The executive branch of government is not unified or tightly controlled by the President or governor. Because it is fragmented, interest groups can penetrate executive government at numerous points and can even play one part against another.

One division in the executive is between partisan and bureaucratic officials. **Partisan executives** are either elected or appointed by elected officials to lead the executive system. Usually members of the political party of the chief executive, they are short-term officials who assume responsibility for administering the executive departments in the name of their chief executive.

Because the chief executive is the most remote and responsible official, access to him is the most limited. Few interest groups have enough influence to intervene at this point. The immediate staff assistants to the chief executive, however, are much more available and serve as key access points to this officer. Executive department heads and their staffs may also be influenced to bring matters to the attention of the chief executive. In addition, department heads make important decisions about the administration of their parts of government. Department leaders often develop a loyalty to the interests of their particular departments, a loyalty that sometimes brings them in conflict with other departments or with their chief executive over policy and administration. Interest groups shrewdly try to take advantage of these differences.

Bureaucratic executives in the national government and in most state governments are career officials. Their tenure generally does not depend on their partisan superiors; they serve either Democratic or Republican masters. As long-term administrators of government, their interests may not even coincide with those of their partisan leaders.

Responsible for the day-to-day administration of the executive branch, bureaucrats develop long-term relationships with those interest groups concerned with their special units of administration and areas of policy. When a bureau head, legislative committee, and interest group that are all concerned with the same policy objectives over a long time combine forces, they may prove more influential than any partisan leaders or even the chief executive. For example, the U.S. Corps of Engineers, in alliance with certain congressional committees and allied interest groups, for years was able to frustrate presidential decisions in its policy areas.

The **independent regulatory agencies,** another division within the national executive system, are also critical to certain interest groups. Although their leaders are appointed by the President, the heads of the national regulatory agencies are semiindependent. In addition, these agencies have been delegated a combination of executive, legislative, and judicial powers.

Each regulatory agency has been given supervision over some special area of economic life. Traditionally, these independent regulatory agencies have attracted the special interest groups associated with the parts of the economic system regulated by the agencies. Railroad and truckers' groups represent their interests before the Interstate Commerce Commission (ICC), which determines their rates and the degree of competition in the field. Television, radio, and telephone companies concern themselves with the leadership, rules, and regulations of the Federal Communications Commission (FCC), just as stock exchanges, stockbrokers, and the companies that issue stocks and bonds for sale to the public concern themselves with the Securities and Exchange Commission (SEC). Those who study our national regulatory agencies have long criticized them for their tendency to be "captured" by the very groups they were supposed to regulate.

What do interest groups want from executive actors? They want exactly the same things they seek from legislators. They want access and an opportunity to be heard when decisions are being made about public policy that concern them. They want to be in a position where they can propose rules and advise on changes in administrative regulations. They also want a voice in appointments to those parts of the executive system relating to themselves. In effect, interest groups want to be partners in the administration of the executive system.

Ideally, an interest group would like an agency devoted to its special concerns created within the executive branch. This would place the interest group in a particularly advantageous position, for the executive officials would be authorized to support its objectives. Small business interest groups succeeded in persuading Congress to establish just such an executive agency, the Small Business Administration, to aid small businesses. But consumer groups have thus far been unsuccessful in inducing Congress to set up a special agency to advance consumer interests.

Executive officials themselves use interest groups to gain their own ends. Both partisan and bureaucratic officials are highly vulnerable in the legislature and need allies. They depend on the legislature's approval for their financial support and their authority to act. Because their requests may become controversial and may be challenged by rival executive units, hostile legislators, or other interest groups, they seek out friendly interest groups to generate support in the legislature.

Early in 1977 officials in the Carter Administration realized they had no real base of public support for their treaties that transferred the Panama Canal to the control of the Republic of Panama. Moreover, a vocal, well-organized opposition was engaged in mobilizing public opinion and Senate votes against the treaties, and the treaties were likely to be rejected in the Senate. President Carter endeavored to enlist the support of interest groups in behalf of the Senate's ratification of his treaties. His initial request for such support from major veterans' groups fell on deaf ears. He was more successful in enlisting public endorsement of the treaties from the leadership of the AFL-CIO. Ultimately, the White House itself helped organize a unique interest group that included former Republican and Democratic secretaries of state, politicians, business leaders, and former military leaders.

Since bureaucratic and partisan officials often conflict over policy and administration within the executive branch, those who feel most vulnerable may call on their interest group allies to help them resolve such differences in their favor. When the secretary of labor in the Johnson Administration attempted to fire his under secretary, the latter called on and was aided by his close allies in the AFL-CIO. The influence of these labor unions with the President was instrumental in protecting his position.

Executive officials also use interest groups to help them carry out their administrative responsibilities more effectively. In certain instances, interest groups can alert officials to problems with their clientele. Or they can suggest alternative approaches on policy and administration. In addition, interest groups can explain executive policies and administration to their members, which helps minimize confusion and conflict and may lead to better cooperation with the executive unit.

Influencing the Judiciary (Courts)

Interest groups come to the courts for the same reasons they involve themselves with the legislature and the executive: The judiciary constitutes a power center in government. It can interpret the national and state constitutions. It can declare unconstitutional the laws or actions of the legislature and the executive. It can interpret the statutes (laws) of legislators and the rules of the executives. It can order executives and legislators at all levels of government in our federal system to behave in certain ways. The judiciary can also order private individuals, businesses, and groups to alter their behavior, and it can impose punishments if they do not comply.

Interest groups without access to the legislature or the executive may more easily find access to the power of the judiciary. In addition, those interest groups put at a disadvantage by legislative decisions or administrative rulings may challenge them in the courts to have them modified or reversed. Groups that win in the legislature and the executive may be forced by their opponents to defend their gains in the courts.

The courts are accessible to all, but the kind of lobbying that prevails in the legislature and the executive is not permitted in the judicial system. Judges are supposed to remain neutral, above the struggle among groups, and they are supposed to make their decisions without favoritism. Thus flooding a court with thousands of letters, an acceptable tactic in trying to influence legislative or executive decisions, is considered inappropriate behavior. Lobbying individual judges is against the rules of the judicial system; so too is offering campaign contributions to judges while they are deliberating on a case.

How then do interest groups try to use the power of the courts in their behalf? They litigate cases. They request the right to participate in cases as "friends of the court." They attempt indirectly to influence judicial thinking through the legal journals which judges read. And they may intervene in the politics of judicial appointments in the executive and legislative systems.

In litigating cases, interest groups come to court as immediate parties to cases in conflict. They may challenge government orders, demand that the courts either order a public government or private enterprise to take certain action or forbid them to act in a certain manner, or they may sue other interests groups. Or government itself may sue interest groups in court.

Interest groups may appeal for permission to intervene in a case as a "**friend of the court**" (**amicus curiae**). When this occurs the interest group is not an immediate party to the case in conflict. But, believing it has a stake in the outcome of the case, it may petition for the right to be heard on the grounds that the issues involved transcend the immediate parties in conflict and are critical to the interests of the group. As a "friend of the court," an interest group asks to file a legal brief arguing its position and advising the judges how to decide.

An interest group has an advantage in appearing as a "friend of the court": it makes its appeal in the context of helping the court reach its decision. The interest group offers its expertise on complex public policy issues to aid the judges in reaching an intelligent decision. Like legislators and executives, judges recognize the complexity of issues in the cases before them and tend to be receptive to such offers of help. Judges also acknowledge the legitimacy of a group's petition to be heard in a case if the decision will have an important bearing on the interests of the group. Judges, like legislators and executives, recognize the right of groups to speak in the name of their particular publics on the shaping of public policy. And like executives and legislators, judges may cut off access. But since judges are supposed to be neutral and fair, their decision to permit or refuse a group's petition to intervene as a "friend of the court" hangs on one question alone: whether they believe the interest of the group is sufficiently relevant to the issues involved.

Interest groups may resort to three other tactics for influencing the courts. One, used successfully in the past by the NAACP, is to try to stimulate the publication of articles in law school journals that suggest a particular way of looking at or resolving issues. Since judges and their legal assistants read these journals, they may be induced to accept the views expressed in the articles. Another tactic is to influence executive and/or legislative action on the appointment of judges. A more direct tactic is to institute class action suits: the interest group helps individuals bring cases before the court in the name of an entire "class" of similar individuals. A favorable decision extends far beyond the individual immediately involved in the case to include everyone fitting into that class of individuals.

Some interest groups concentrate entirely on the courts in their effort to shape public policy. Others, willing to intervene in all three branches of government to influence public policy, have organized special auxiliaries for court action so that they can attract tax-deductible contributions. Contributions to interest groups that lobby cannot be deducted by the donor, whereas contributions to their legal defense funds can. Groups such as the Sierra Club, interested in protecting the environment, and the NAACP, concerned with the rights of blacks, have set up special legal defense funds. These legal auxiliaries devote themselves entirely to court action while their parent interest groups engage in lobbying with executive and legislative officials.

Working through Political Parties

It is relatively easy for an interest group to lobby friendly officials in the executive and legislative branches. It is difficult, if not impossible, to lobby its enemies. An increasing number of interest groups have concluded that they can more effectively influence government if they help elect friends to serve as legislators and executive officials and defeat those public leaders who are their enemies.

In pursuing a strategy of electing friends and defeating enemies, interest groups may participate in party nomination contests and in general elections where opposing party candidates run for public office. Interest groups may try to shape the platforms of the parties to include their own points of view or negate those of their opponents. And interest groups may try to build themselves into a party-in-the-organization— their members becoming party leaders responsible for conducting internal party affairs. This puts these interest groups in a position to affect both the nomination of party leaders and the party's position on public policy.

Attractions of a party-oriented strategy. When a group helps a politician capture a major party nomination, its candidate becomes one of the two real contenders for that public office. A party candidate who wins the election as a result of this support becomes a public official and is inclined to cooperate when the group's lobbyist solicits his or her support.

A group that can demonstrate its ability to help elect public officials acquires an influence far greater than the sum of its victorious candidates. Officials who are neutral on the group's policy concerns may deem it wise to reconsider their position in view of this proven strength. Moreover, by defeating hostile incumbents, the interest group eliminates from government those who are unreceptive to its claims and it sends a message to other public officials to recalculate both the strength of the interest group and the advisability of opposing its policies.

Interest groups can also benefit by trying to influence the party-in-the-organization. Some groups send representatives to state and national party conventions where they lobby to have their policy positions included in a party's platform. Executive leaders, who must propose policy recommendations to legislatures, frequently recommend items built into their **party platforms.** Having its positions included in such platforms improves a group's chances for its proposals to become part of the official policies of a chief executive.

Few interest groups have become so closely woven into a major political party's leadership structure as the AFL-CIO has in the Democratic party. Not many have its tremendous mass base, its concentration of members in key areas, and its hierarchy of organizers who can shift their union organizing skills to party work. In certain states labor unions have for years controlled many Democratic precinct organizations. Many labor unions encourage their members to run as delegates to their Democratic state party conventions and to the Democratic National Convention. Consequently, labor union leaders have played a major role in choosing candidates in some state Democratic parties and at times have influenced decisions on presidential and vice presidential candidates of the national Democratic party. American business groups have, on the whole, not been successful in inducing their management officials to become active in the organization of either the Republican or the Democratic party.

Risks of a party-oriented strategy. Many interest groups do not involve themselves in party and candidate election politics. Although the advantages are many, the risks are high. Most interest groups are likely to have some members in both major parties. If their group supports candidates of one party, those who identify themselves with the other party may be antagonized. An interest group that involves itself in party politics runs the risk of losing the support and allegiance of members who feel their financial contributions to the group are being used to help the party of their opponents.

In the 1930s the Townsend leadership bitterly split its old-age pension group by supporting the Republican and third-party candidates for President. Financial support from the membership declined, many members withdrew from the interest group, and numerous Townsend clubs broke away to organize rival old-age pension organizations. True, few interest groups are as drastically affected by their leader's strategy as was the Townsend Movement, but it is a risk all face. In any case, many interest groups prefer to avoid completely any party-oriented strategy.

Another risk in party-oriented politics stems from the possibility that those the group supports will lose the elections. If this occurs, their lobbyists will find themselves confronting indifferent or hostile public officials whom their interests groups had tried to defeat. An interest group may also overestimate the commitment of those candidates it endorses and supports. The pledge given by the candidate may be so general as to be meaningless once a candidate is elected. Still another risk arises: an interest group can become too closely identified with one political party. When this happens, its allied party leaders may feel they can take the group's support for granted and ignore it when making critical decisions on nominations, appointments, and policy. Where else can such an interest group go in party politics? The other major party may be bitterly opposed to its policies, and a minor party simply is not a practical alternative. In their alliance with the Democratic party, labor union leaders have intermittently complained that they have trapped themselves by becoming too closely tied to that party.

Interest group resources needed by parties and candidates. To compete effectively, political parties and their candidates need money, organization, and votes. Interest groups can contribute money directly to the parties and the candidates to spend as they see fit; they can provide all kinds of auxiliary help; they can encourage their members to vote in the elections. The only candidates now forbidden by law to accept money from any private source are presidential nominees who have agreed to rely on financing from the national government.

Contributing directly to candidates. For years two types of interest groups, unions and corporations, have been forbidden by law to donate money to candidates campaigning for national office. Unions were the first to discover a loophole for circumventing this prohibition. The law forbade tapping union treasuries, which were supplied by compulsory dues; therefore, they ingeniously asked their members to contribute voluntarily to special **political action committees** (**PACs**). With these voluntary contributions, the AFL-CIO's Committee on Political Education (COPE) not only gives financial contributions directly to the candidates it endorses, but it actively campaigns to bring labor union members and their families to the polls in behalf of those candidates. A number of individual unions within the AFL-CIO sponsor their own PACs, as do unions that do not belong to that labor federation.

Although corporations appeared to be complying with the law forbidding them to donate money to parties and candidates, a number of them were actually contributing corporate funds, a practice they covered up by illegal bookeeping techniques. The Watergate scandal, which brought down the Nixon White House, exposed the extent to which some corporations had secretly been violating the law for years.

The president of Gulf Oil Corporation, for example, pleaded guilty to illegally contributing $100,000 in corporate funds to President Nixon's 1972 reelection campaign. In filing its financial statements with the Securities and Exchange Commission, Gulf Oil had falsified the data, hiding a secret $10 million corporate fund used for illegal political contributions between 1960 and 1974. Sixteen major American corporations negotiated guilty pleas with the Watergate special prosecutor for having knowingly violated the national law prohibiting corporate contributions to candidates. A few unions have also been charged with violating the law against giving funds raised by compulsory union dues to political candidates. For the most part, however, unions have relied upon voluntary contributions from their members to political action committees.

American corporations are now setting up their own political action committees to collect voluntary contributions from corporate executives, employees, and stockholders. Through such committees, corporations can legally distribute financial support directly to candidates. During the 1976 election campaign 450 corporate PACs contributed $4.8 million to candidates, with most of the money going to those competing for seats in Congress.

Political action committees have been set up by a great variety of interest groups. Some environmental groups have organized the League of Conservation Voters as their campaign arm for political action. Both the American Medical Association and the National Education Association have their own national PACs and have encouraged their state affiliates to establish their own. These are only a few of the hundreds of interest groups that have created PACs, which permit them to use voluntary contributions from their members to help finance candidates for public office. In January 1979 the Federal Election Commission revealed that a total of 1,360 PACs gave $32 million to candidates for Congress between January 1, 1977, and October 23, 1978.

Before the 1974 Federal Election Campaign Act, interest groups and individuals could contribute as much as they could raise to candidates for national office. The new law places a $10,000 limit on the amount of contributions a PAC may give to any candidate for the House, the Senate, or the presidency. No individual may contribute more than $1,000 to any such candidate. As campaigning becomes ever more costly, a limit of $10,000 automatically depreciates the impact any one interest group can have on the political future of nationally elected officials or their challengers in elections. But, to the extent that such contributions help reelect incumbents or elect their challengers, groups that can raise the money for campaign contributions will have an advantage in policy making over groups that cannot.

Contributing indirectly to candidates. Interest groups themselves may now spend money to campaign for candidates without depending on voluntary contributions. The 1974 Federal Election Campaign Act permits unions, corporations, and other associations to use their _own_ funds to campaign _among their members_. Labor unions may now use union dues to communicate with their members in behalf of candidates

Ed Vallman, *The Hartford Times* (1975)

"Well, since you asked me, Bob. I voted for heavier trucks because they deliver more."

the unions support. They may send letters, newspapers, and literature, use the telephone to contact union families, and engage in door-to-door canvassing. Similarly, corporations may now use corporate funds to campaign among their stockholders and their managers in behalf of candidates whom the corporate leadership support. Note, they may not use these funds to contribute directly to candidates, but they may spend the money on their own parallel campaigns among their members.

In 1976 organized labor took full advantage of this new opportunity. It invested millions of dollars of membership dues to persuade union members and their families to vote for the Democratic candidate for President, who had been endorsed by the executive council of the AFL-CIO. Only a handful of corporations exercised their legal right to use corporate funds to campaign among their executives and stockholders in behalf of the Republican presidential ticket. Although the chairman of American Business Volunteers for Ford wrote to the presidents of one thousand of the largest corporations urging them to take such action, only a half-dozen corporations notified him they had sent out communications in support of the Republican national ticket.

Providing other aid to candidates. Interest groups may provide valuable nonmonetary aid for their candidates' campaigns. A number of interest groups publicly endorse candidates for office, the assumption being that the membership will follow the endorsements of their leaders.

Some interest groups may offer candidates the use of their facilities or equipment: helicopters, automobiles, typewriters. Groups may even offer the services of political experts. In 1976 the National Committee for an Effective Congress, a liberal-oriented interest group, offered those candidates whom it endorsed the services of campaign experts on polling, voter turnout, publicity, and campaign organization at or without cost.

Engaging in Policy Elections

In 1976 voters in forty-one states had the option of voting yes or no on 330 ballot issues. Most of the issues were not particularly notable. Voters in Maine and Michigan, however, decided on the very controversial issue of mandatory deposits for nondisposable bottles, an issue that pitted environmentalists and consumer groups against business and labor groups. Voters in Massachusetts turned down, by a two to one vote, an initiative proposal to control handguns. And, in six states—Arizona, Colorado, Montana, Ohio, Oregon, and Washington—voters rejected by overwhelming majorities initiative proposals supported by environmentalists to regulate the growth of nuclear power plants.

Legalizing gambling to add revenues to state treasuries confronted the electorate in a number of states. New Jersey voters supported a constitutional amendment to establish a gambling casino in Atlantic City. New York City voters approved "Las Vegas" nights for churches and other charitable organizations. And a majority of voters in Colorado and Vermont supported state lotteries. On the other hand, California voters rejected a proposal to legalize greyhound racing, and Delaware voters turned down a proposal to legalize slot machines.

Initiative proposals allow interest groups to place a proposed law or constitutional amendment on a state or city ballot simply by gathering enough signatures from registered voters. Referendums allow interest groups to prevent laws passed by a state or local government from going into effect until the voters themselves decide upon them. Again, a predetermined number of signatures must be collected. Referendums may also be offered to the voters by state or local legislatures without interest group intervention. In all states but one, constitutional amendments must be referred to the voters at an issue election.

Advantages of a policy-election strategy.   Policy issue elections through referendums or initiatives afford interest groups an advantageous strategy to pursue at the state and local levels of government. Interest groups can avoid the normal complexity of legislative, executive, and party politics and can capitalize on their own resources.

All that is needed to qualify an initiative or referendum issue is a sufficient number of signatures on a petition. Groups that have a mass base from which to solicit the necessary signatures or that have or can raise the money to employ special canvassers have little trouble qualifying.

An initiative or referendum startegy allows the interest group to avoid a battle in the legislature and with elected or bureaucratic executives. The group may be weak in these centers of power, or if influential, it may have to compete with other groups for attention and support. By going directly to the people for a policy decision, the group bypasses the many possible veto points in the legislative and executive branches that raise the risks and the price of pushing through public policy. Moreover, in pursuing this strategy the interest group can present its proposal to the electorate in exactly the form it wishes.

Political parties tend to avoid entanglement in such ballot issues, seeing them as too dangerous for their candidates. Consequently, interest group proposals on the ballot are rarely opposed by the major parties, and a group is not forced to risk combat with a party or worry about losing the support of its own members or the general public because of their party identification.

One additional advantage accrues to interest groups using an initiative or referendum strategy. Because many voters are unfamiliar with or disinterested in the particular policy issue, a major portion of the electorate is likely to abstain from voting on the referendum or initiative measure. This allows the interest group members and their allies to poll a larger percentage of the votes on the issue.

Disadvantages in a policy-election strategy. Obviously groups with neither the membership base nor the money to obtain sufficient signatures to qualify their proposals are at a disadvantage. So, too, are those groups that cannot raise the finances required to campaign for a controversial proposal. The Sierra Club, an environmental group, charged the public utility companies and their allies with spending $6 million in 1976 to defeat initiative proposals regulating and limiting nuclear reactors in six states. Unable to match this sum, the proponents were at a great disadvantage in the propaganda war of influencing potential voters. People vs. Handguns, the name of the interest group leading the losing fight to control handguns in Massachusetts in 1976, maintained it was outspent by at least ten to one by its opponents, the gun manufacturers, the National Rifle Association, and others. Money alone did not necessarily defeat these two exceptionally controversial proposals. However, money helped buy TV and radio time, newspaper advertising, and telephone messages. It helped pay for individuals who canvassed the public and tried to bring out the voters on one side or another.

Although political parties do not usually contest interest groups on issue elections, other interest groups may take up the battle. Therefore, whether a group is fighting an election campaign for or against an issue on the ballot, it must organize and act as if it were a political party, at least for that one issue. Victory is as uncertain in controversial issue elections as in competitive two-party elections. In the end, it comes down to which interest group can attract the most voters to its side.

An interest group faces serious risk if it loses badly in an issue election. When it subsequently engages in lobbying, the group may find legislators and executives rejecting its claims on the grounds that it has been repudiated by the voting public. As public servants, why should they go counter to the public's will? In addition, public officials may discount the ability of the interest group to help or hurt them in future elections.

Influencing Public Opinion

One of the most difficult and uncertain strategies pursued by interest groups is the shaping of general public opinion for the long run. The purpose of this strategy is to ensure that executive and legislative decision makers will operate in a political climate favorable to the policy orientation of the interest group. However, since so many diverse forces shape the political attitudes of people and condition the political culture within which politicians operate, such a strategy may easily prove ineffective.

Nevertheless, a number of interest groups do work through the mass media and even through the schools, if they can, either to reinforce those values in our culture that support their claims or to undermine attitudes and values detrimental to the groups' appeals. Business interest groups have been especially active in trying to shape long-range attitudes. For years they have disseminated the message that what was good for business was good for the people of the United States.

Obviously, those interest groups whose policy claims conflict with key elements in the American culture face difficulties in shaping public opinion. Women's liberation groups and gun-control groups must still fight deeply suspicious and hostile cultural attitudes. And labor unions confront similar problems in shaping public opinion in the South.

Even those groups whose interests reflect the dominant values and attitudes in our culture never know for certain whether their propaganda makes any impression on the attitudes of the general public. They may find that time and events have eroded their wide appeal to traditional values, thereby reducing their ability to be politically effective. The medical profession, for example, has discovered it no longer occupies that high-prestige position traditionally accorded it in American society.

© 1978 by Herblock in *The Washington Post*

"You think it'll sell?"

As a result, the AMA 's efforts to push through its political policies have been constrained by a public opinion less sympathetic to it than in the past.

Some groups proposing change that may seem unpopular at the moment may discover that in time perceptible shifts in public opinion occur which improve their chances. Environmental groups have benefited from such a shift. However, economic recessions and inflation in the last half of the 1970s have made public opinion once more less hospitable to the sacrifices required for environmental action.

Interest groups that feel they are being completely ignored in the political system tend to pursue a short-run strategy. They want to produce an immediate effect on public opinion and governmental decision makers. Such groups may organize public demonstrations to capture the attention of the general public and officialdom. Sometimes they resort to the nonviolent breaking of laws or even to violence.

Such a strategy can occasionally prove successful. At the beginning of our entrance into World War II, the very threat of a massive march by blacks upon the national capital to protest racial discrimination in employment induced President Franklin D. Roosevelt to establish by executive order a Fair Employment Practices Commission. Black civil rights groups in the 1960s successfully used demonstrations in the streets, economic boycotts, and nonviolent confrontations with authorities to generate public sympathy and support. When interest groups representing the handicapped concluded in 1977 that the U.S. Department of Health, Education and Welfare was dragging its feet in devising rules to protect their rights, thousands of crippled, blind, and otherwise disabled Americans demonstrated in Washington, D.C., and elsewhere, even occupying governmental offices. New rules were very quickly designed and implemented.

Public demonstrations, nonviolent confrontations with the law, and the use of violence are clearly very risky tactics. They are more likely to prove counterproductive, arousing public anger and official resentment, if only because they appear threatening and violate the general assumption that individuals and groups will play by the established rules of the game. Hence, they are more the tactics of marginal, desperate groups than those in the mainstream of American politics.

Concepts To Study

checks and balances	federalism	representation
cooperative federalism	maximizing individual	separation of powers
democracy	power	

Special Terms To Review

access	independent regulatory	political action
amicus curiae (friend of the	agencies	committees
court)	initiative election	public interest groups
bureaucratic executives	interest groups	referendum election
government as an interest	lobbying: direct and	special interest groups
group	indirect	
grass-roots lobbying	partisan executives	

THE CONGRESS

In December 1977 the U.S. House of Representatives and the Senate resolved a five-month dispute over using federal money to finance abortions. Although conflict between the legislative chambers over public policy is not rare, compromising their differences seldom takes this long. So intense were the feelings of the majority in each chamber that bridging their differences proved almost impossible. Held hostage to the resolution of this issue was a $60.1 billion **appropriations bill** for the operation of two executive departments, that of Labor and of Health, Education and Welfare (HEW).

Earlier in the year the U.S. Supreme Court had ruled that the Constitution did not require government to finance abortions. A woman had a constitutional right to abort, but government had no constitutional obligation to finance abortions for those who could not afford them. Antiabortion groups seized upon that decision to help persuade a majority of House members to attach an antiabortion amendment to the bill funding the two executive departments for the next fiscal year. This amendment forbade government financing of abortions. The Senate adopted a less restrictive amendment, which permitted abortions in certain circumstances to be financed by Medicaid (the national government's health program for the poor).

The agreement reached by a joint committee of the House and Senate constituted a retreat from both positions. It permitted Medicaid-financed abortions only for victims of rape or incest and for physically ill women. This proposal easily won approval in the Senate. Antiabortionists in the House put up a bitter fight, but they were defeated 181 to 167. Although both Republican and Democratic party leaders in the House had urged their members to approve the compromise, each party split, 148 Democrats and 33 Republicans voting for and 85 Democrats and 82 Republicans voting against.

Once the Senate and House agreed on an identical bill—the $60.1 billion appropriation plus the abortion compromise—Congress had officially acted. Its policy proposal was then signed into law by the President. This law called for the secretary of health, education and welfare to issue directives for implementing the abortion provisions. When these rules were announced in January 1978, they reflected the liberal spirit of the compromise. Undaunted, the antiabortionists promised to continue their fight in Congress.

The abortion controversy was only one incident in the ninety-fifth Congress, which in 1977–78 considered numerous controversial issues: tax reform and tax reductions; an energy policy; labor reforms; Panama Canal treaties; military aid to Mideastern countries, and others. However, both the fight between House and Senate and their abortion compromise illustrate some of the major characteristics of Congress.

1. *Congress is made up of two independent chambers, the House of Representatives and the Senate.* Each must agree with the other if Congress is to make policy and appropriate money. Congress, therefore, embodies within itself the constitutional checks-and-balances principle that the Constitution imposes on relations among the three branches of the national government.

2. *Since Congress deals with controversial issues, compromise is one of its unofficial operating rules.* Only by both chambers retreating from their original positions and agreeing to a mutually acceptable policy on abortions could Congress have passed the bill. If legislators are unwilling to compromise, Congress often cannot pass legislation.

3. *Congress conducts most of its work through committees.* When the House and Senate reach different conclusions on a complex matter of public policy, they set up a **conference committee** representing both chambers and assign it responsibility for resolving their differences. Each delegation on this committee invariably includes members of the House and Senate **standing committees** that had originally recommended the legislation. If a proposal is to be sent by the conference committee to the two chambers, each delegation must agree to it by a majority vote.

4. *The President is a partner with Congress in the making of laws.* By approving or rejecting the policy proposals of Congress, the President shares in its legislative powers. Affirmative action on his part is much more typical than disapproval.

5. *Political parties can play a significant role in congressional decision making.* Support by both the Democratic and Republican leaders in the House had helped win the adoption of the abortion compromise. Yet more than 70 percent of the Republicans and approximately 36 percent of the Democrats voted against the wishes of their leaders. Party leaders obviously cannot control the behavior of their

followers. The vote also indicated that at times the two parties differ in their approach to public policy. A majority of Democrats voted in favor of the compromise; a majority of Republicans opposed it.

6. *Interest groups often play an important role in congressional politics.* Right-to-life groups in the congressional districts had mounted an aggressive campaign to pressure House members into voting for the strictest ban on funding abortions. A representative of the National Committee for a Human Life Amendment, an interest group funded by the U.S. Catholic Conference (representing the nation's Roman Catholic bishops), worked closely with the eleven House members on the conference committee.

7. *Congress legislates national policy and finances the operation of the executive branch.* The national executive could not operate without financial support, which only Congress can provide. What the executive branch does—its services and regulations—is largely determined by congressional decision making. The two executive departments were dependent on congressional funding to continue their operations.

8. *Congress may decide national policy, but executive officials often have tremendous discretion in shaping it.* Legislators often find it difficult to agree on every detail of policy, or they may decide that it is unwise to do so. Therefore, Congress frequently designs its laws so that executive officials have considerable discretion in implementing them. HEW Secretary Joseph Califano was authorized to draw up rules for carrying out the intent of the legislature.

9. *A congressional-presidential decision on public policy is not necessarily final.* The issue may be reopened in the Congress itself, if not elsewhere. Since Congress annually decides what the national government will do, the amount of money to support its activities, and what restrictions to impose on it, the fight over financing abortions can arise anew each year. In fact, as soon as the Congress had adopted the compromise, both the proponents and opponents turned to the executive to try to influence the rules implementing the policy. Within a year, the opponents in the House once again wrote restrictions on funding abortions into other bills. The fight had begun all over again!

FUNCTIONS OF CONGRESS

The Constitution assigns Congress four broad types of responsibilities: making laws for the nation; selecting and removing executive and judicial leaders as well as resolving disputes over executive leadership; representing the people in the decision-making processes of government; and overseeing the executive branch. In carrying out these functions, Congress serves as a conflict-resolving institution for our society.

The Constitution specifically designates Congress the law-making branch of the national government. So it is. But it is not the only branch to make rules and regulations that are official and binding. The executive and judicial branches also make law, but making rules and regulations are incidental to their other major functions. Not so the Congress. Law making is its principal responsibility.

The constitutional mandate of Congress to legislate, as interpreted by the Supreme Court, is so broad that Congress may make laws in almost every area of life. Its list of legislative powers, which includes the necessary and proper clause and the clause authorizing it to tax and spend for the general welfare, permit our national legislature to deal with a great variety of social and economic problems in our society. As a consequence, Congress attracts the intervention of the President and units of the executive system, the courts, individual citizens, and all sorts of interest groups, including cities, counties, states, and foreign countries.

Not only does Congress design general laws for the country, but it also adopts special legislation to aid a particular governmental unit, an individual, or an economic enterprise that appeals to it for help. For example, Congress granted loans to New York City to rescue it from bankruptcy and to Lockheed Aircraft Corporation to keep it solvent. This type of law making is very different from social security legislation, which taxes millions of employers and employees to protect them and their families from loss of income due to old age, disability, retirement, or death. Both types, referred to as statutory legislation, can be passed by simple majorities in the two houses and involve the President as a partner in law making.

Two other types of law making are unique: constitutional amendments and **treaties.** Amendments propose changes in the Constitution itself. They must be approved by a two-thirds vote in the House and Senate. The President has no formal role in changing the Constitution; instead the states become the partners of Congress.

Treaties with foreign nations have their own special conditions. Initially, they are negotiated by the executive branch. The President submits a treaty to the Senate at his discretion, but its approval is necessary for the treaty to become law. The President initiates; the Senate reacts. Note that the Senate alone—the House is excluded from this process—votes on a treaty and that its adoption demands more than a simple majority, a two-thirds vote.

It should now be clear to you that in *none* of its law-making activities—statutory, constitutional, or treaty—is Congress autonomous. In each instance, the national legislature cannot make the decision alone.

©1976 by Herblock in *The Washington Post*

"Here's the way it reads now: A treaty amendment guaranteeing U.S. Senators the right to continue on-the-spot investigations in Panama during the winter months . . ."

Leadership Selection and Removal

Congress has a major voice in the selection of national executive and judicial leaders. It may itself remove them from office. And it is authorized to resolve a clash between the Vice President and the President over the issue of the President's capacity to carry out the duties of the office.

Selecting executive and judicial officials. Senior executive leaders are nominated by the President and, with a few exceptions, must win Senate approval. The Senate must approve the heads of the executive departments and agencies, the heads of the independent regulatory agencies, the top diplomatic representatives of the United States to other countries, and all the officers of the military. Similarly, all national judges, including members of the U.S. Supreme Court, must be confirmed by the Senate after the President has nominated them.

Although the overwhelming majority of these nominations encounter little or no opposition, enough candidates have been rejected to forewarn the chief executive of the independence and power of the Senate. In recent times two of President Nixon's nominees for the Supreme Court were denied confirmation, and President Carter's original nominee for CIA director encountered so much opposition in the Senate that he withdrew his name before any vote.

Congress may itself choose a President or Vice President. Should no presidential candidate win a majority of electoral votes, the House picks the President from among the three with the largest number of electoral votes. Should no vice-presidential candidate receive a majority of electoral votes for Vice President, the Senate is authorized to choose from between the two with the most electoral votes.

Since 1965 congressional approval must be obtained to fill a vacancy in the Vice President's position. Until that time there was no constitutional device for replacing a Vice President who had resigned, died, or been impeached. The Twenty-fifth Amendment (1967) authorizes the President to nominate a Vice President when a vacancy occurs and requires a majority vote in both chambers of Congress to confirm the nominee.

In 1973 Vice President Spiro Agnew resigned and pleaded "no contest" in the courts to charges of criminal conduct. President Nixon nominated the Republican floor leader of the House of Representatives, Gerald R. Ford, to be Vice President, and Congress readily confirmed him. Within two years, Nixon himself resigned in the face of charges of criminal behavior. Having moved up to become President, Ford now nominated Nelson Rockefeller, the Republican Governor of New York, to be Vice President. A Democratic Congress again confirmed this choice.

Congress is also empowered by the Constitution to adopt a plan of replacement should both the office of President and Vice President be vacant at the same time. Its present plan calls for the Speaker of the House to assume the presidency in such circumstances, followed in order by the president *pro tem* of the Senate (an honorific office only), the secretary of state, and most of the heads of the executive departments.

Removing executive and judicial leaders. The Constitution authorizes Congress to remove executive and judicial leaders who commit treason, high crimes, and misdemeanors. The House impeaches; that is, it brings the official charge of misconduct. The Senate sits as a court, determining whether the official is guilty or innocent. In effect, the House prosecutes and the Senate judges. Although **impeachment** requires only a majority vote in the House, a two-thirds vote is necessary for the Senate to convict. Congress may not impose any punishment after such a conviction, but the Constitution calls for the automatic removal of the individual from office and disqualifies that individual from again holding any national office.

Few executive or judicial officials have ever been impeached or convicted by Congress. Of the twelve who were impeached, only four were convicted and removed from office. Only one President was ever impeached: Andrew Johnson in 1868. The Senate failed by a margin of one vote to declare him guilty. President Nixon, however, resigned his position in 1974 after members of Congress from his own party warned him he would be both impeached and convicted. Impeachment proceedings had progressed to the point where the House Judiciary Committee had voted in favor of charges against the President.

Resolving a leadership conflict between the President and Vice President. Suppose a President became mentally ill or suffered a serious illness? Unless the President voluntarily resigned or temporarily turned over his responsibilities to his Vice President, the national government and the country would suffer a fundamental crisis in leadership. The original Constitution made no provision for such situations. In this century President Woodrow Wilson suffered a serious stroke but remained President, despite the fact that he was severely disabled. President Franklin D. Roosevelt also persisted in office until his death in 1945, although his health and mental alertness had significantly deteriorated. And President Dwight D. Eisenhower was twice incapacitated by serious illnesses while he occupied the presidency. In none of these instances did a Vice President attempt to assume the leadership of the executive branch.

To correct for this flaw in our political system, the Twenty-fifth Amendment (1965) now gives the Vice President the initial authority to propose a change in top leadership. It also gives Congress the ultimate authority to decide, if the two top executive officials disagree, on the capability of the President to function as the national leader. Should a Vice President, together with a majority of the principal officials of the executive departments (the cabinet) or such a group as Congress may provide, inform the Congress in writing that a President is unable to discharge the duties of his office, the Vice President immediately assumes the powers of Acting President. A President may, however, reassume the presidency by sending a written notification to the Congress declaring his capability.

Suppose, however, the Vice President disagrees and again notifies the Congress that the President is incapable of performing his duties? At this point we have a constitutional crisis. The President's claim that he is capable confronts the Vice President's challenge that the President is incapable of leading the country. Only Congress is authorized to resolve this dilemma. If Congress determines by a two-thirds vote of both chambers that the President is unable to function in office, the Vice President continues as Acting President. Clearly a failure to marshal such a majority in either house means the President prevails. So far, no Vice President has ever invoked the amendment to challenge a President's capacity to perform the presidential duties.

Representation

As representatives, all members of Congress share four characteristics in common: First, they are chosen from within distinct geographical constituencies: 435 in the House; 150 in the Senate. Second, to attain their positions, each must win a popular election in his or her particular **constituency,** although senators may be appointed by the governors of their states for unfinished terms if vacancies occur. Third, to remain in Congress, they must win reelection, because their terms of office are limited to two years in the House and six in the Senate. Fourth, within their chambers, each representative has an equal vote.

Congress is designed to bring the voices of people from different parts of the country, as expressed through their elected representatives, into the decisions of the national government. And it is designed to make these representatives especially sensitive to the particular interests of their constituencies.

One dimension of the representation function concerns the continuation and update of the constituency requirements of the Constitution. Congress must regularly comply with the constitutional requirements that it represent states equally in the Senate and in accordance with their population in the House. Every ten years, after a national census, representation (seats) in the House must be reapportioned (reallocated) among the states.

Another dimension of the representation function concerns the attitudes and behavior of members of Congress with regard to their constituents. Legislators have a number of representational roles they may play in serving as links between the interests of their constituents and the decision-making process in Congress. They also act as service representatives, helping their constituents interact with the executive branch. Moreover, constituency representation is sufficiently important so that it affects other aspects of the legislators' behavior.

Complying with the constitutional requirements of representation.   The Senate presents no problem in meeting the constitutional requirement of representation. Each state must have two senators; no more, no less. The people in each state are equally represented in the Senate, regardless of the population distribution revealed by the census every ten years. On this matter the Constitution is unequivocal. It also provides that no state may have its Senate representation changed without its own consent.

As each state was admitted into the United States, it was assigned two seats in the Senate. Thus the Senate has grown from its original twenty-six members to one hundred, two for each of our fifty states. In 1978 the Congress proposed to the states a constitutional amendment whereby the District of Columbia would be allowed two senators and one representative *as if it were a state.* Should three-quarters of the states ratify this amendment, the Senate would increase to 102 and the House would temporarily increase to 436.

The House of Representatives, on the other hand, regularly poses a problem in constitutional representation. Every ten years, after each census, the units of representation (House seats) must be redistributed (reapportioned) among the states in proportion to their population. Although the Constitution does not specify its size, since 1912 the House has limited itself to 435 members. Its size increased temporarily to 437 when Alaska and Hawaii became states and then almost immediately reverted to 435.

Reapportionment—redistributing units of House representation to states in accordance with their population and a base figure of 435—can become a very controversial issue. No one wants to be a loser, neither the states involved nor the particular legislators whose constituencies are cut out from beneath them. But with the House size restricted to 435, some states are bound to lose representation if they lose population or if their population does not increase as much as that of some other states. Other states will gain representation, and still others will undergo no change in their number of House seats. After the 1920 census, the House became so embattled over the issue that it failed in its constitutional obligation to reapportion. To avoid future failures or the nasty fights that inevitably arise over reapportionment, the House has authorized the Bureau of the Census and the President to propose the new apportionment of representatives. These executive officials recommend the apportionment plan to the House, which now accepts it as a matter of course and relays it to the states.

The main problems in complying with the constitutional mandate on representation occur in the states. State legislatures must design new districts if a state gains representation or eliminate existing districts if representation is lost. Even when the number of districts remains unchanged, state legislatures are obligated to draw congressional district lines which ensure that each House member from a state represents an equal number of people. The Supreme Court has ruled that the principle of one man–one vote requires all congressional districts within a state to contain the same number of people; equal numbers of people must have equal units of representation.

Until the Supreme Court proclaimed in a 1964 decision that the one man–one vote principle determined representation, many state legislatures designed, or permitted, their congressional districts to be disproportionate in representation. This deprived some people of their proportionate amount of representation and gave other people excess representation. In 1960, for example, 802,994 people in Michigan's Sixteenth Congressional District were represented by one member of the House, while 177,431 people in the state's Twelfth Congressional District were also represented by one member.

Some state legislatures deliberately drew district lines that created unequal congressional districts, giving one party a decided advantage. Drawing constituency lines that favor the representation of one group of people over another group of people is called **gerrymandering.** Other state legislatures refused to redraw lines, despite a substantial shift in population from rural to urban and suburban areas. As a result, rural and small-town people retained disproportionately more representation in the House of Representatives than people in more populated urban and suburban areas. Deliberately not changing legislative district boundaries or units of representation per district, even though districts become disproportionate in population and hence favor one political party or group of people over another, is called **silent gerrymandering.**

Table 9–1 illustrates the impact of the Supreme Court's 1964 ruling that congressional districts in each state be as equal in population as possible. The 1962 figures reflect both types of gerrymandering and favor rural Americans. The 1966 data reveal the states beginning to comply with the Supreme Court's mandate; 27 states with 258 congressional districts had redistricted within two years of that decision. The 1974 data constitute the first redistricting to represent accurately the urban, suburban, and rural divisions of our population.

Table 9–1
Number of Metropolitan and Urban Districts in the
U.S. House of Representatives, 1962, 1966, and 1974

	1962	1966	1974
Metropolitan (urban and suburban)	254	264	305
Rural	181	171	130
Total	435	435	435

SOURCE: Richard Lehne, "Suburban Foundations of the New Congress," *Annals of the American Academy of Political and Social Sciences,* Vol. 422 (Nov. 1975), p. 143.

Representational roles of legislators. Once the constitutional requirements of representation are met, there still remains the practical question: How should a member of Congress represent his or her constituents? One answer is for the representative to mirror their views. This is called a **delegate role.** Its rationale is that since the people of the constituency chose the legislator, that official should accurately reflect and articulate their views.

An alternative response is for the legislator personally to decide what is in the best interest of the constituency, irrespective of the views of the constituents. This is called a **trustee role.** The rationale for a trustee's role is more complex than that for a delegate's role. It is that the constituents may not know their best interests or they may be divided on any one issue. A trustee-oriented legislator also justifies an independent judgment on issues by asserting the primacy of private conscience as well as the advantage of inside, expert knowledge.

Still a third approach to representation is to combine the two roles in what is called a **politico role:** The legislator acts as a trustee on some issues and as a delegate on others. Where the legislator believes the constituency to be wrong, too divided, too uninterested, or even ignorant of its own self-interest, that official operates as a trustee. Where the legislator decides the constituency is united on an issue, the issue is too controversial to take a position other than that of the constituency, or the issue does not merit any particular concern, that official mirrors the wishes of the constituency.

More legislators favor the politico role than the other two, according to a study of House members (see Table 9–2). Constituents, on the other hand, prefer their congressional representatives to be delegates. A 1977 Louis Harris public opinion poll found that the public preferred House members to vote in accordance with the majority views of their congressional districts, even when a district's views conflicted with the personal

Table 9–2
*Distribution of Representational Styles among
87 Members of the House of Representatives, 1963–64*

Representational Roles	Percent
Delegate	23
Trustee	28
Politico	46
Undetermined	3
Total	100%

SOURCE: Roger H. Davidson, *The Role of the Congressman* (New York: Pegasus, 1969), p. 117.

conscience of the representative or with that legislator's perception of the national interest.

Service: representing the constituency in the executive branch. In addition to considering legislation, members of Congress intervene in the executive branch on behalf of their constituents. With the national government becoming ever more complex and intervening increasingly in their lives, more and more constituents turn to their legislative representatives for help in dealing with executive agencies and departments.

What kinds of service representation do constituents ask from their legislators? Veterans may request assistance in locating their records or in obtaining pensions or educational benefits from the Veterans Administration. Parents may want special leave for children who are serving in the armed forces. Businessmen or farmers may ask for help in calling the attention of bureaucrats to their special needs when such officials draft executive rules or implement laws. Or these constituents may want help in securing contracts with executive departments. Widows and widowers, dependent children, the disabled, or retired people may need help in dealing with officials from the Department of Health, Education and Welfare. Some constituents may want assistance in obtaining jobs with the national government. Cities, counties, or states may want their legislators to aid them in securing grants from the executive departments.

Legislators willingly act as spokesmen and allies for their constituents. Whatever services they provide enhance their political standing and their reelection chances in their constituencies. Moreover, many legislators recognize that the size, complexity, and impersonality of the executive bureaucracy often confuse and disturb constituents. Individuals may need help in cutting through executive red tape and delay and help in understanding and dealing with detailed rules. The legislators claim they have the necessary clout to obtain results, since bureaucrats and partisan executive leaders are dependent upon them for their policy authorizations and appropriations. Consequently, members of Congress organize their offices and allocate most of their staff around the function of representing their constituents within the executive. Members of Congress also assert that they, themselves, benefit as a result of their service representation with the executive because it enables them to learn more about the operation of the executive branch they are supposed to supervise.

Representation and other legislative behavior. Representation of constituency has such a high priority among most legislators that it affects their decisions and behavior in many ways. We will discuss only three: committee assignments, informal blocs, and office resources.

Committees that consider legislation are the most important, official, decision-making centers within Congress. Virtually all legislators are assigned to one or more committees. Some committees are more suited than others for advancing special constituency needs, and so some legislators seek assignments to these committees: Rural members of Congress, for example, tend to want seats on the agricultural committees; those who represent urban areas tend to select committees dealing with labor, education, and welfare.

To better serve the interests of their constituents, some legislators have organized informal coalitions on the basis of common constituencies. Thus, representatives from steel producing districts have recently joined together as a steel caucus in the House. Such representational blocs cut across party and state lines. Similarly, all the members of a state's delegation in the House may meet regularly to represent the interests of their state within the Congress and the executive branch.

To further aid legislators in representing their constituencies (and in winning constituency support), the House and Senate allocate to their members resources that help keep them in continuous contact with their constituents. Legislators are permitted a specified number of free round trips to their constituencies. All are allowed to use the mails free of charge (the franking privilege) to communicate with their constituents. Most legislators send special newsletters to inform their constituents about their activities and to keep their names and faces constantly before their constituents. In addition, members of Congress are authorized to open offices in their constituencies so their people will have easier access to them.

Executive Oversight (Supervision)

Supervising the executive branch is another major function of Congress. In part, **executive oversight** stems from the checks and balances built into the relations between the two branches by the Constitution. Executive oversight also reflects the attitudes of members of Congress toward the executive branch and the fact that legislators find such activity satisfying and rewarding. For a variety of reasons, therefore, Congress has organized itself to engage in executive oversight.

Three legislative attitudes stand out in the congressional approach to executive oversight. One is a *lack of trust* that the executive will always comply with the policy decisions Congress adopts. Supervising executive officials to ensure that they do not ignore or change the thrust of the laws Congress adopts is especially essential when Congress passes legislation that leaves considerable discretion to executive officials. Members of Congress share the attitude that executive officials may *abuse their power.* Some executives may attempt to enrich themselves or their friends; others may satisfy their egos at the expense of the ordinary citizen. Congress also feels that executive officials *operate more responsibly* when someone with outside authority is looking over their shoulders.

Members of Congress, therefore, intervene in executive affairs to ensure that executives are honest, effective, and efficient and that they comply with legislative intent. And, because it is empowered to grant or deny executive requests for authority and money, Congress occupies a unique position for engaging in such oversight. Executive officials are fully aware of this fact of life and feel very vulnerable to expressions of congressional displeasure.

It would be unrealistic to ignore another reason why Congress engages in executive oversight: It works to the advantage of Congress. A natural rivalry and suspicion exists between legislative and executive officials. Executive oversight caters to the psychological advantage of legislators in their dealings with executives. Oversight can also generate favorable publicity for the legislators and unfavorable publicity for the executive. Members of Congress can thereby impress their constituents with the good job they are doing in exposing any wrongdoing in the executive branch.

To engage in executive oversight, each house has established a Committee on Governmental Operations (renamed Governmental Affairs in the Senate in 1977). Their primary responsibility is to investigate the operation of the executive branch. The Appropriations committees, which are responsible for recommending to their chambers the amounts of money executive departments and agencies may spend, have also taken it upon themselves to examine executive efficiency and effectiveness. And almost all of the other standing committees into which the House and Senate are organized also engage in executive oversight, but they scrutinize only the particular parts of the executive within their jurisdiction.

From time to time special investigating committees are set up by the House and Senate to cut across any cozy arrangements that may have developed between the standing committees and executive units. **Special, or select, committees** are more likely to investigate executive officials with vigor and determination. These committees are also established to investigate executive action that lies outside the jurisdiction of any one committee or that is so "politically hot" that special personnel from Congress must be recruited to undertake the task.

The special Senate committee that investigated the Watergate scandal in 1973–74 dealt with one such hot issue. Its investigation reached into the White House and touched on the conduct of the President himself. In the 1970s both the House and Senate set up special committees on intelligence to investigate the activities of the CIA and FBI, when evidence surfaced that these agencies had at times abused the civil rights of Americans and that the standing committees had failed to provide proper oversight.

Congress also has a special staff agency of its own to engage in executive oversight. The General Accounting Office (GAO) was first set up in the early 1920s to check on the legality of public fund expenditures by executives. It also makes recommendations for greater efficiency and economy in the executive branch. Lately it has been increasingly used to conduct special inquiries into the executive branch.

Concepts To Study

checks and balances	law making	majority
compromise	leadership selection and	representation
executive oversight	removal	separation of powers

Special Terms To Review

conference committee	informal coalition	special, or select, committee
constituency	interest groups	standing committee
constitutional legislation	one man–one vote	state delegation
delegate role	political parties	statutory legislation
electoral college	politico role	treaties
franking privilege	reapportionment	trustee role
general accounting office	redistricting	Twenty-fifth Amendment
gerrymander	service representation	
impeachment	silent gerrymander	

know now mode up

CHAPTER 10

CONGRESS:
Leadership
and Organization

Sizes influence

committe system   10/27

Leadership and organization in Congress are extremely fragmented. Power to make most legislative decisions is divided initially between the House and Senate and then, within both, into the hands of different committees. There is no single leader or even set of leaders, but rather diffuse sets of leaders. None wield sufficient power to move the decision-making process along by themselves or to pull it together so that public policy is considered in a comprehensive manner.

Congress, moreover, is made up of representatives from diverse geographical constituencies who feel they must articulate and defend their unique interests. While this representation coincides with concepts of democracy and republican government, it adds to the public's image of a Congress pulled in countless directions and embroiled in conflicts of narrow, selfish interests to the neglect of the general interest.

Little wonder then that Congress is not very highly rated by the American public. In a 1977 public opinion poll only 22 percent of the public gave Congress a favorable rating; 64 percent gave it an unfavorable rating. Our business-scientific oriented society puts a great premium on efficiency, unity, action, and dispatch. On the whole, Congress violates all of these values, except in time of extreme emergency.

A DIVIDED CONGRESS: SENATE AND HOUSE

The Constitution places "all legislative Powers" in Congress and divides it into a House and a Senate. By defining these powers, the terms of office of the two sets of legislators, their eligible ages, and their constituencies as well as their presiding officers, the Constitution guarantees that the House and Senate will be very dissimilar.

223

Powers

Almost all power to legislate public policy is shared equally by both the House and Senate. Should either refuse to act, the other is powerless. The House may check the Senate; the Senate may check the House. Unless both agree, no legislation is adopted.

Each also possesses unique powers it alone may exercise. Only the Senate may vote on treaties and approve or reject presidential nominations of appointed executive and judicial officials. It sits as a trial court when the House impeaches a governmental official. Should the electoral college fail to produce a Vice President, the Senate is responsible for making the choice.

The House has fewer unique powers. It elects a President, should the electors fail to do so, and it initiates impeachments. But the House last chose a President in 1824, and impeachments are rare in our history. By custom, appropriation legislation starts in the House, and according to the Constitution, the House alone initiates tax legislation. In both cases, however, the Senate becomes an equal partner in shaping and passing such legislation.

Constituencies, Terms of Office, and Age

Statewide constituencies and longer terms of office give the Senate greater prestige than the House and lead to different types of chambers. Almost all House members come from smaller, more narrowly defined constituencies than do senators. The average population of a congressional district in the United States is now approximately 450,000 people. Senators represent entire states—proud, semiindependent components of our federal system—which are almost invariably larger in size and more diverse in composition than congressional districts. Since they have to represent and balance a greater number of conflicting points of view than do most House members, senators are aided by much larger staffs.

The two sets of legislators also differ because of their terms of office. Six-year terms afford senators more secure positions for taking the long-range view on issues. The horizons of House members are inevitably limited by their two-year terms. Because they must begin preparing for their next election within a year of taking office, they cannot avoid weighing policy issues in terms of any possible impact on their impending renomination and election campaigns. For the major part of their terms, senators are much freer than House members from the constraints that facing an election tends to impose on a legislator.

A minimum entrance age of twenty-five years for the House and thirty years for the Senate is mandated by the Constitution. The House membership therefore tends to be somewhat younger than that of the Senate.

25 yrs. House
30 yrs. Senate

The Influence of Size

Today the House is made up of 435 representatives from the states plus three nonvoting representatives, one each from Puerto Rico, Washington, D.C., and the Virgin Islands. With one hundred members, the Senate is less than one-fourth the size of the House.

The Senate's small size has encouraged an informal, more intimate relationship among its members in considering their business. With just two Senators from each state, the members have insisted on wide discretion to articulate the views of their states. They have also been tolerant of their colleagues' tendency to speak on topics not germane to the immediate business before the Senate.

A unique characteristic of the Senate is its rule of *unlimited debate*. A senator may speak for as long as that legislator can stand and talk. As a result, debate has tended to be more extensive and profound in the Senate than in the House. Debate is generally terminated only after all who wish to speak have been satisfied that they have had an adequate opportunity to do so. Imagine what this would do to the House with its 435 members.

The importance assigned to each senator and their equal representation of semi-sovereign states has led them to rely upon a unique device for closing debate—*unanimous consent*. Not everyone must agree to close debate, but no one must object: One senator can veto a motion to terminate debate.

The rules of unlimited debate and **unanimous consent** have permitted individual senators to prevent the Senate from voting on a legislative proposal, in other words, to **filibuster.** To filibuster is to control the floor (and the right to speak) by speaking long enough to deny to the Senate the opportunity to vote. The purpose of a filibuster is to force a bill's proponents to withdraw the bill from consideration—in effect, to abandon efforts to secure the bill's passage. It is used only to kill extremely controversial legislation. Generally, those who filibuster know they will lose if the bill comes up for a vote. Therefore, they jam up the Senate's business to block that vote from taking place.

Only as late as 1917 did the Senate adopt a device—called **cloture**—for cutting off a filibuster. To initiate cloture, sixteen senators must first file a petition in favor of taking a vote to cut off debate. At the end of two additional days of debate, the Senate must vote on whether its members wish to shut off debate on the bill and bring it to a vote.

Originally, cloture could be adopted only if two-thirds of the senators present voted in its favor. Few filibusters were cut off under this rule, for it required sixty-seven votes, assuming all senators showed up to vote. In 1975 the number required to impose cloture was reduced to three-fifths of the entire Senate, or sixty votes. Even this number continues to present obstacles for senators determined to force the end of a filibuster.

The size of the present House prevents it from tolerating unlimited debate. All bills are considered under very limited time rules, which severely restrict the freedom of its members on the floor. Consequently, when the House debates and votes on controversial legislation, it moves with much greater dispatch than the Senate.

Presiding Officers of House and Senate

Even the constitutional officers of the House and Senate are different. One is a member of the Congress; the other is not. **The Speaker,** who presides over the House, is an elected member. The U.S. Vice President, who presides over the Senate, is not a senator but represents the executive branch. One is picked by the legislators to preside, the other is not. The Speaker is chosen by a vote in the House in a contest with the leader of the minority party. The electoral college chooses the Vice President, who automatically becomes the Senate's presiding officer, as specified in the Constitution. One is a legislative party leader, the other is not. The Speaker is always a member and the chosen leader of the majority party in the House. In contrast, the Vice President, a member of the President's party, may share the same party as the Senate's minority party members.

The two officers differ also in their power, influence, and prestige. The Constitution authorizes the Vice President to preside and cast a vote only to break a tie. Otherwise, that official may neither vote nor speak on any question before the Senate, except to respond to a question of parliamentary rules. Since the Vice President is a member of the executive branch, senators have refused to authorize the Vice President to play any significant role. Informally, a Vice President may be active behind the scenes but principally as an extension of the President's leadership. Vice Presidents Hubert H. Humphrey (1965–1968) and Walter F. "Fritz" Mondale (1977–) served as agents for their Presidents, mobilizing legislative support for their programs.

The unwillingness of Senate Democrats in 1961 to accept Vice President Lyndon B. Johnson as chairman of their caucus illustrates the disinclination of senators to accept the Vice President as a party leader. Johnson had been a Democratic senator since 1949, deputy Democratic party leader in the Senate since 1951, and Democratic floor leader there since 1953. In 1960 Senator Johnson was elected Vice President on the Democratic party ticket. A proposal to elect him chairman of the **Democratic Caucus** (the meeting of all the Democrats in the Senate) encountered such opposition among his former colleagues, as violating the constitutional separation of powers, that his nomination was quickly withdrawn.

The Speaker of the House, on the other hand, is the most important member of that chamber. His preeminence as its leader stems from his being both the constitutional presiding officer and the official leader of the majority party in the House.

Few formal powers belong to the Speaker as the constitutional presiding officer. Whoever occupies that position rules on motions from the floor of the House and recognizes members who wish to address the House. His rulings on parliamentary motions, which can be crucial to the strategy and tactics centering on legislation, are rarely overridden. The Speaker is empowered to appoint members to certain types of committees (special and conference) and to refer bills to the standing committees. As a member of the House, the Speaker may participate in the debate and may vote as any other legislator, although he tends to vote only to break a tie.

At one time Speakers represented the greatest concentration of power in the Congress. They could appoint the members as well as the chairmen to all House legislative committees; they could recognize or refuse to recognize at will members who wanted to speak on the floor. They interpreted House rules according to their leadership interests and those of their political party. They recognized only such motions as coincided with their purposes. They served as a member and chairman of the important scheduling committee of the House, the Committee on Rules.

A revolt in the House in 1910–11 against the arbitrary actions of its Speaker stripped from that office almost all the power to appoint the chairmen and members of the House standing committees and to serve as a member and chairman of the Rules Committee. The Speaker's power to recognize (or to refuse to recognize) members was also sharply curtailed. Since that "revolt," power in the House has been highly fragmented. It is now divided among a large number of its official and unofficial leaders.

Ironically, the Speaker's present influence as a leader has come about precisely because of this very fragmentation. Someone must serve as coordinator of policy and process in the House. Additional influence stems from the fact that the Speaker is also leader of the majority party.

As both presiding officer and head of the majority party, the Speaker is in a strategic position to know what is happening in the House, to help his party, and to bargain with the opposite party's leadership. At the center of a vast communications network, the Speaker is in touch with all the fragments of power. Moreover, both parties have allowed their Speakers to have a voice in party decisions assigning members to House committees.

HOUSE AND SENATE COMMITTEES

Committees of the House and Senate consider legislative proposals, undertake investigations, engage in executive oversight, and screen executive and judicial appointments. They are the principal work units of Congress. With few exceptions, the House and Senate debate and act only on their recommendations. The importance of the committee system encourages legislators to make their mark within the House and Senate as committee specialists. Committees also provide a set of leadership positions for members of both parties.

Kinds of Committees

The Congress makes use of different kinds of committees. The two principal ones are standing and special, or select, committees. When members from both houses serve on the same committee, it is a joint committee.

Standing committees. Standing committees dominate the decision-making process of Congress. They are the only "permanent" committees; once established they continue to exist without need for any further special authorization. They are virtually the only ones that can report legislation to their respective chambers. Each committee has its own area of jurisdiction. Bills go first to those standing committees whose jurisdiction covers their subject matter. Here is where the bills will be studied or ignored, killed or amended. Although approximately twenty thousand bills are introduced during both sessions of a two-year Congress, relatively few bills are recommended by the committees to their parent chambers.

Standing committees tremendously reduce the workload of Congress. By bringing together small groups of legislators in committees to concentrate on different policy matters, both chambers are able to handle expeditiously a heavy load of legislative proposals. Since they eliminate most of the policy proposals introduced in the Congress, the committees enable the House and Senate to concentrate their attention on a limited number of bills. And because they recognize that their committee specialists have made critical decisions for them, the other legislators tend to follow their lead.

Deference by the House and Senate to their committees is attested to by the fact that, although mechanisms exist for overriding the committees, members rarely withdraw for their own consideration a bill that a committee refuses to report. A petition to discharge a bill from a committee in the House requires 218 signatures—over half the entire membership—before the House can even vote on whether to do so. Between 1947 and 1973 only nine bills were discharged in this manner and passed. Although the House permits other motions to remove bills from committees, they too are difficult to invoke.

Overruling a committee is easier in the Senate. Any senator may move to discharge a bill from a committee, and a majority vote of those present accomplishes that objective. However, the rule of unlimited debate permits the use of filibusters against discharge motions. This is one reason why few senators attempt such a tactic. From 1789 to 1966 only fourteen discharge motions were filed, resulting in six bills being discharged, only one of which ever became law.

Two other devices for circumventing committees reduce the attractiveness of the Senate's discharge rule. A legislator may offer any amendment to a bill before the Senate. Since the Senate does not operate, as does the House, under strict rules of germaneness (that one item must be relevant to another), a bill bottled up in committee may be proposed as an amendment to a totally unrelated bill being considered by the Senate. A committee may also be bypassed when a bill comes to the Senate from the House. The Senate may decide to deal with the bill itself without first referring it to a committee, or the Senators may vote to send it to a committee but with binding instructions to report it within a few days. The Civil Rights Acts of 1957 and 1964, which originated in the House, were passed in the Senate by completely bypassing its hostile Judiciary Committee. And in 1960 a civil rights bill from the House was sent to that committee with orders to report it out within five days. These are extreme measures that are rarely invoked, for the preference of senators, like that of their colleagues in the House, is to defer to the wishes of their committees.

Standing committees are not absolutely permanent; existing ones may be terminated and new ones authorized. The standing committees in 1977–78 are listed in Table 10–1. Note that they break down into different types. Some are housekeeping committees (Rules and Administration in the Senate; House Administration in the House). Some are money committees (Finance, Appropriations, and Budget in the Senate; Ways and Means, Appropriations, and Budget in the House). Others are

Table 10–1
Standing Committees, U.S. Congress, 1977–1978

House of Representatives	Senate
Agriculture	Agriculture, Nutrition and Forestry
Appropriations	Appropriations
Armed Services	Armed Services
Banking and Finance	Banking, Housing and Urban Affairs
Budget	Budget
District of Columbia	Commerce, Science and Transportation
Education and Labor	Energy and Natural Resources
Government Operations	Environment and Public Works
House Administration	Finance
Interior and Insular Affairs	Foreign Relations
International Relations	Governmental Affairs
Interstate and Foreign Commerce	Human Resources
Judiciary	Judiciary
Merchant Marine and Fisheries	Rules and Administration
Post Office and Civil Service	Veterans Affairs
Public Works and Transportation	
Rules	
Science and Technology	
Small Business	
Standards of Official Conduct	
Veterans Affairs	
Ways and Means	

exclusively oversight committees (Government Operations in the House; Governmental Affairs in the Senate). One is a scheduling or leadership committee (Rules in the House). And one is an ethics committee (Standards of Official Conduct in the House; the Senate ethics committee is not a standing committee). The remainder deal with distinct areas of public policy.

Select, or special, committees. Special, or select, committees are temporary committees established to study or investigate specific matters. They may be concerned with some facet of executive government, an interest group, or a special problem or policy area. Recent examples would be the House Select Committees on Aging and on Assassinations and the Senate Select Committees on Intelligence and on Indian Affairs. Special committees automatically terminate at the end of a two-year Congress, unless they complete their work earlier. To be revived, they must have their authority renewed. A very few are given authority to report legislation; most, however, are not.

Joint committees. **Joint committees** include members of both houses. Since 1946 only one was ever authorized to propose legislation, the standing Joint Committee on Atomic Energy, but it was abolished in

1977. Although none of the other joint committees may legislate, a few do important work. The Joint Committee on the Economic Report, for example, analyzes for Congress the President's annual Economic Message.

One type of joint committee is very important—the conference committee, whose function is to resolve major differences between the House and Senate over legislation. A new conference committee is created each time both chambers pass similar bills, which must be reconciled through negotiation. Unless an identical bill is passed by both chambers, Congress cannot adopt legislation. Conference committees are also important because their recommendations are not subject to amendment. They must be accepted, if at all, in their entirety by each house. In rare cases a conference committee may go beyond the matter of reconciling House-Senate differences and itself write new legislative provisions. Members of conference committees are always bipartisan and are drawn from the standing committees that first recommended the legislation.

Committee Composition

The makeup of the committees in Congress is determined by two factors: political party and the preferences of the legislators.

Parties and committees.   Almost all committees reflect the proportion of Democratic and Republican legislators in the House and Senate. The majority party, therefore, dominates the committee system, except for the House and Senate ethics committees whose memberships are divided equally between the two parties.

Not only do the parties determine the ratio of majority to minority seats on the committees, they also assign the legislators to particular committees. All four party organizations (two in the House, two in the Senate) share common rules regarding individual assignments: Newly elected members must request their parties to assign them to the committees they prefer. Reelected incumbents who wish to change committees must also request their parties to reassign them. Thus both sets of legislators are at the mercy of their parties, which may comply with or ignore such requests. The requests of reelected legislators to continue serving on their former committees are always respected, except when the party ratio in the House or Senate changes because of the previous election. When this occurs some reelected incumbents— those with the least seniority or tenure on the committees—may have to vacate their old committees so the new ratio of majority to minority party members prevails. They, too, must request reassignment.

Each legislative party has its own committee for assigning its members to the official committees of the House and Senate. The Republican Committee on Committees in the House is composed of the most senior Republican from each state delegation; each committee member casts as many votes as the number of Republicans on his/her delegation. Since 1975 House Democratic assignments have been made by a Steering and Policy Committee. It is composed of elected and appointed Democratic leaders plus other party representatives, and it is chaired by the Democratic Speaker. The assignments made by the two party committees must be ratified by the full meetings of their legislative parties before they are officially adopted by the House.

In the Senate, the Democratic floor leader appoints a party steering committee to assign Democrats to legislative committees; the chairman of the Republican Conference (all Republican senators meeting together) appoints a committee on committees to assign their party members. Both parties invariably accept their committees' assignments, and once the Senate approves them they become official.

Individual members and committee assignments. Assignment to a committee is critical to a legislator's career. Specialization in an area of public policy is one accepted informal rule for earning the respect of one's colleagues. Specialization on a committee also affords a member a basis for influencing executive as well as legislative policy. Frequently committee assignments prove important to legislators in servicing the needs of their constituents. Whereas senators may belong to three committees, most House members serve on a single committee.

Committees are not all equal in prestige and potential influence. Some are more desirable than others. The fact that only so many "good" committee slots are available makes for keen competition at times and enhances the power of those party leaders distributing committee assignments. It also influences the behavior of members, who know they are dependent on those leaders for "good" assignments.

The Senate itself makes a distinction among its committees, calling the more important ones *major* committees, the less important ones *minor* committees. Thirteen of its standing committees are designated *major* committees. In 1977 the Senate began limiting each of its members to two major committees and one minor committee. Since the 1950s both political parties have followed the practice of affording all freshmen senators at least one major committee.

The House divides its committees into three categories: exclusive, semiexclusive, and nonexclusive. Members assigned to an exclusive committee—Rules (scheduling bills), Ways and Means (taxes), and Appropriations (spending)—may not serve on any other committee. These are considered the most important and busiest committees. An assignment to one of the ten semiexclusive committees means a member may serve also on one or two nonexclusive committees. Nonexclusive committees are clearly the least desirable. Members may belong to two or three in this category.

As members acquire seniority (length of continuous service), many move to the more desirable committees. In the House the most attractive committees (those that members are least willing to transfer from and most anxious to join) are the three exclusive ones plus International Relations and Armed Services. Among the least attractive committees have been District of Columbia, Merchant Marine and Fisheries, Post Office and Civil Service, and Veterans Affairs. In the Senate, the most attractive committees have been Foreign Relations, Finance (taxes), Appropriations (spending), Armed Services, and Judiciary. The new Budget committees in Congress appear to be prestigious and attractive; the committees on ethics are not.

Legislators apparently link their search for "good" committee assignments with their personal aspirations. Such committees as Agriculture, Interior, and Public Works are particularly attractive to service-oriented members of Congress. Members more interested in shaping public policy are attracted to committees such as Education and Labor (Human Resources in the Senate) and International Relations (Foreign Relations in the Senate). Those concerned with increasing their influence among their colleagues in the House and Senate find the taxing and spending committees as well as the House Rules Committee most appropriate.

Committee Leaders

Two sets of key leaders in the House and Senate are the committee chairmen and the subcommittee chairmen; they are always members of the majority party. Their importance as leaders is recognized by the other legislators, by executive officials, and by the lobbyists who interact with their committees.

A parallel set of leaders are the ranking (or senior) minority party members of the committees. Although by no means comparable in power to the chairmen, the ranking minority members are influential among their party colleagues on the committees and on the floor of the House and Senate.

Selecting committee leaders.   Chairmen and ranking minority members were formerly selected (for approximately a hundred years in the Senate and for most of this century in the House) by strict observance of the rule of **seniority.** The individual with the longest continuous service, or seniority, on the majority party side of the committee became chairman. The most senior person on the minority party side became the ranking minority member. Never an official rule of the Senate or House, but one followed by both parties in each, seniority was automatic. Committee members moved up to a position of chairman, or ranking minority member, simply by continuing to be reelected and by outlasting the other members of their party on the committee. When the majority and minority parties reversed positions in the House or Senate, and therefore on the committees, the previous ranking minority members became the chairmen and the former chairmen became the ranking minority members.

Seniority, because it was automatic and inviolate, bolstered the influence base of the formal committee leaders. Official committee leadership positions did not depend on the wishes of the other committee members or on the good relations of the chairmen and ranking minority members with their parties. These leaders retained their positions, no matter how they voted or behaved, until they left their committees. Their influence was reinforced because committee members recognized that they had to deal with these leaders for as long as the leaders continued to be reelected. Only on rare occasions were chairmen in the twentieth century stripped of their leadership positions.

Seniority has now been officially weakened. In the early 1970s House Republicans changed their rules to allow all Republicans in the House (the Republican conference) to vote by secret ballot on the nominations for their ranking minority members (Republicans were in the minority) made by their Committee on Committees. House Democrats also modified their rules to permit their general party membership (the Democratic Caucus) to vote secretly on the nominations for chairmen made by their committee on committees. In 1975 they voted to deprive three individuals of their chairmanships.

In the Senate, Republicans have adopted a different device for replacing the automatic seniority rule. They now allow their party members on each standing committee to elect their own committee leader. The choice remains subject to ratification by the Republican conference. In 1975 the Senate Democratic Caucus changed its rules to provide for a secret election of chairmen by the entire Democratic membership.

Seniority is no longer the automatic road to committee leadership. This does not mean that seniority is not the most important element in choosing such leaders. Virtually all those serving today are still the most senior members on their committees. The reforms do mean, however, that chairmen and ranking minority members may no longer feel free to abuse their power or deviate too far from the policy concerns of their party colleagues without worrying about losing their leadership positions.

Official committee leaders: power and influence.   Chairmen have traditionally exercised broad powers. They had power to call meetings of their committees, to set the agendas, to appoint and dismiss committee staff, and to participate as voting, ex-officio members (by virtue of their chairmanship) on all their subcommittees. They determined the order in which bills would be considered. They decided whether to hold public hearings and which witnesses would appear, and they controlled the time devoted to the questioning of witnesses. They created subcommittees, determining their jurisdictions and appointing their chairmen and the majority party members. Most of these powers still belong to the chairman today.

When bills come up for consideration on the floor of the House and Senate, chairmen normally act as their managers during debate or appoint someone else to this important position. Chairmen also lead the conference committee delegations from their chambers and help select the other conferees. The powers of these chairmen remain formidable, even though some pertaining to committee procedures have lately been taken away or restricted by committee rules, by action taken by their chambers and by party decisions.

The influence of the chairmen with their colleagues and in their respective chambers rests as much on their personal skills as on their formal powers. Those who become especially knowledgeable about their committees' subject matter are recognized as experts by their colleagues, by interest group lobbyists, and by executive officials, who tend to rely on these chairmen and come to them for help. In addition, those chairmen who are solicitous of the needs and ambitions of their committee members are better able to secure their cooperation. As a result of the powers they have and the support they can provide, chairmen become the center of committee communications networks. Benefiting from inside information, they are in a position to convey accurate information to both those in and out of Congress who are interested in the policy and politics of their committees.

If they have the political skill, personality, and subject matter expertise, the ranking minority party members on the committees can also have a decided impact upon their committees' deliberations. They bargain with the chairmen over policy and procedure and mobilize their party members to support these positions. Ranking minority members have some voice in the scheduling of hearings and in the appointment of minority members to special and *ad hoc* subcommittees. They also control the professional staff assigned to the committees' minority members.

Subcommittee chairmen and ranking minority leaders.   A proliferation of subcommittees has had the effect of reducing the power of the standing committees and their chairmen and ranking minority members.

As standing committees set up more subcommittees, they expand the number of formal committee leaders in the Congress and increase the opportunity for more legislators to gain expertise on policy issues. Many standing committees have adopted rules that now require all bills to be referred first to their appropriate subcommittees. This further reduces the power of the full committee leaders.

The House of Representatives has gone the furthest in strengthening its subcommittees by adopting a "Subcommittee Bill of Rights" that strips from the standing committee chairmen some of their traditional power over subcommittees. Committee members of the majority party now vote on who their subcommittee chairmen will be. The Senate has restricted the number of subcommittee chairmanships that any of its full committee chairmen may hold. As a result, almost every member of the majority party has at least one subcommittee chairmanship.

CONGRESS AND POLITICAL PARTIES

Each chamber of Congress contains two parallel systems, an official one and a partisan one. Officially, the House is presided over by its Speaker, the Senate by the Vice President, and both chambers are organized into committees with their own leaders. At the same time, Democratic and Republican organizations exist, with their own House and Senate leaders, that shape the committee systems. All members belong to one of these party organizations. Even the present independent senator from Virginia helps the Democrats organize the Senate and obtains his committee assignments from them.

Legislative political parties try to overcome the fragmentation that characterizes the official decision-making system. The majority party helps set the agenda in each chamber and imposes priorities in determining how legislative items from the official committees will be considered. Each party also tries to affect the attitudes and behavior of its members.

Legislative Parties and Congressional Presiding Officers

Because Vice Presidents represent the executive party in the government, they have not been allowed to serve as leaders of their legislative parties. House Speakers, however, are clearly legislative party leaders.

Both Republican and Democratic parties in the House compete to elect their most important party leader as Speaker. This officer is therefore both the most significant leader of the majority party and the official leader of the House. As a party leader, the Speaker tries to unify his party and advance its program. If President and Speaker share the same party identification, the Speaker participates in the President's legislative leadership meetings and endeavors to assist him.

Individual members of the majority party see the Speaker as one of their most important sources for information, advice, and assistance. Because he is in a position to do favors for them and serves as their elected party leader, the rank and file in the party are disposed to cooperate with him. This enhances the Speaker's influence, permitting him to ask members to abstain from certain votes, to vote in favor of or against particular pieces of legislation, to delay or offer motions, and so forth.

Both the Republican and Democratic parties have enhanced the influence of their Speakers by allowing them a major voice in the assignment of their members to the legislative committees. In the process Speakers have been able to reorient certain committees so they were more disposed to the public policy views favored by the Speakers. In 1975 House Democrats formally expanded their Speaker's powers within their party, making him chairman and the dominant member of a new party unit, the Steering and Policy Committee, which recommends the assignment of Democratic members and chairmen to the standing committees. In addition, the Democratic party empowered its Speaker to recommend to it those who should serve on the House Rules Committee.

Party Floor Leaders and Whips

In the House the defeated candidate for Speaker becomes the floor leader of the minority party. The majority party votes separately for its floor leader, who serves as a lieutenant to the Speaker. Each floor leader assumes responsibility for unifying party members behind the party's position and for directing party strategy and tactics on the floor of the House. The one who shares a common party affiliation with the President also participates in the President's legislative leadership conference and helps advance his program.

In the Senate the absence of anyone comparable to a Speaker permits the **majority floor leader** to act as his party's primary leader; the **minority floor leader** fills the same role for the opposite party. The floor leader sharing the party affiliation of the President is invited to leadership meetings at the White House and tries to help the President in the Senate. Both sets of floor leaders participate in their parties' committees on committees.

Senate and House floor leaders are aided by assistant leaders called **whips.** The problems of communicating with their members in a chamber as large as the House has induced its party leaders to establish deputy and even regional whips who act as links between the senior party leaders and party members. Whips pass on information and instructions to the party rank and file, and they carry information back to their superiors. When votes on bills or amendments are pending on the floor, the whips may be asked to canvass (poll) the members of the party to ascertain their feelings and intentions. The whips are also responsible for ensuring the presence of their party members for key votes and for lining up votes behind positions their leaders and party take on important legislation.

Scheduling House and Senate Business

The majority floor leaders (and the Speaker in the House) are responsible for scheduling legislation for debate and a vote after the standing committees have reported their bills. It is the prerogative of the leader of the majority party to set each week's agenda for the House and Senate. Nevertheless, both House and Senate majority party leaders are limited in their discretion to determine the conditions of the debate on bills, the kinds of amendments that will be offered, and the votes that will be taken.

In the Senate almost all important bills are considered under what are called *unanimous consent agreements*. Most are easily arranged, for the informal rules of the Senate demand that senators make an effort to accommodate each other and their leaders. Complex agreements must often be negotiated by the majority leader with the minority leader and senators from both parties before a controversial bill is considered. Spelling out the length of debate, at times the amendments to be offered, and the date for a final vote require delicate, extensive negotiations. If one senator declines to agree, the Senate is prevented from adopting the unanimous consent agreement. The majority floor leader is, therefore, vulnerable to those members of the Senate who are concerned with the bill.

On extremely controversial issues, some senators may refuse to accept a unanimous consent agreement closing debate and permitting votes. Opposed to the bill, they may try to filibuster it to death. Proponents of the bill and the majority leader may then try to override the opposition by the device of keeping the Senate in continuous day and night sessions in an attempt to break the stamina of the obstructionists. An alternate strategy is to file a cloture petition and try to muster the sixty votes needed to permit a vote to be held on the bill itself.

In the House the majority leader and the Speaker share with a bipartisan standing committee responsibility for scheduling important legislation. For a controversial bill to come to the floor of the House, the Committee on Rules must first recommend a rule determining the length of debate, who will control debate time, and whether amendments may be offered. Virtually every important proposal recommended by a standing committee comes to the House through Rules. Only appropriation (spending) and revenue (tax) bills are exempt, but they tend to be so complex that the committees recommending them almost invariably turn to the Rules Committee for a special rule. If Rules refuses to give a bill a rule, the bill has almost no chance to be considered by the House. Mechanisms exist for bypassing or overruling this committee, but they are difficult to invoke and seldom employed.

Although the majority party maintains a two to one ratio on this important committee, such a partisan advantage has not guaranteed that the committee will recommend to the House a rule in accordance with the wishes of the majority party leaders. In the 1970s, therefore, the Democratic party, the majority party in the House, asserted some degree of control over its members on the Rules Committee. The Democratic chairman of that committee is no longer automatically determined by seniority, but is voted into office by the party's caucus, upon a recommendation of the party's Steering and Policy Committee, which the Democratic Speaker chairs. And the Democratic Speaker has been especially empowered by his party to recommend which of its members should serve on Rules. This has given the Speaker considerable leverage in dealing with the committee's majority party members. Whether this will subordinate the Rules Committee to full domination by the majority leadership is still to be ascertained. These reforms have helped, however, reduce the independence of this committee and bring it more in line as a leadership tool of the Speaker and majority leader.

Party Caucuses (Democratic) and Conferences (Republican)

All Democrats in the House belong to the Democratic Caucus; all Republicans to the Republican Conference. The same holds true for party members in the Senate. *Caucus* and *conference* are simply different names for a general party meeting where the members of a particular party transact party business.

One function of the caucus/conference is to select party leaders. After their committees on committees have made their recommendations, the caucus/conference in both chambers make the final party determination on the assignment of members to the standing committees. At present, House and Senate Democratic caucuses also vote on who will chair these standing committees. The House Democratic

Caucus now also votes on the chairmen of the Appropriations subcommittees. Since it is in the minority at present, the House Republican Conference votes on who will be the ranking minority members of the standing committees. The Senate Republican Conference has delegated this authority to its party members on each committee.

The general meetings of the parties also consider legislative policy matters. Members are not obligated to vote in the House or Senate in accordance with any party position, although at various times in the past Democratic members were bound to vote according to the decisions of their caucus. Today the most important function performed by the caucus/conference on legislative policy is to afford party leaders and members an opportunity to discuss important policy issues before they come up for a vote in their chambers. The debates and votes in these general party meetings result in establishing a party position.

In the 1970s the House Democratic Caucus began to assert its authority over Democrats on the standing committees by voting to instruct them on how to act. On one occasion, the caucus voted to instruct Democrats on the Rules Committee to delay approving for House consideration a bill on committee reforms. On another occasion, it instructed these Democrats to grant a rule for a tax bill that allowed the House to vote on an amendment cutting the oil depletion allowance. It also voted to instruct Democrats on the International Relations Committee to prepare and report a bill setting a date for ending American military involvement in Indochina. So far Democrats on the committees have followed the instructions of their party caucus.

Legislative Parties and Votes on Issues

Rarely do all members of one party oppose all members of the other party on a legislative issue. American parties are not that homogeneous. On some issues a majority from both parties vote together in agreement; on other issues a majority of Democrats oppose a majority of Republicans. Interest-group ratings of Democratic and Republican legislators demonstrate (see pp. 154–55) that the Democratic leaders and their rank and file differ from the Republican leaders and their rank and file in their votes on key bills before the House and Senate. But the degree of internal party unity in such interparty competition reflects more the common viewpoints and similarity of constituent interests among the members of the same party than any exercise of power by party leaders.

With very little disciplinary power at their command to unite their rank and file, party leaders tend to rely more on personal relations, persuasion, favors they can do for party members, and assistance they can provide them in the passage of legislation. For the most part, individual legislators want to vote and cooperate with their party; indeed, they feel uncomfortable when they cannot do so. These feelings make it easier for party leaders to make certain demands on them. Yet, these leaders know that at some point some of their party members will refuse to cooperate because of personal conviction, the nature of their constituencies, their commitments to interest groups, or bargains they have made with other legislators.

With party unity frequently an uncertain condition in Congress, leaders must work carefully at fashioning coalitions to win. These coalitions are ad hoc (temporary) and must constantly be refashioned as the House and Senate move from issue to issue. Sometimes party leaders can find enough votes within their own party. At other times, they must secure support from members of the opposite party to accumulate the necessary votes.

Presidential intervention in congressional affairs frequently stimulates the parties to achieve a greater degree of internal unity in opposing each other. Legislation high on a President's agenda, the President's executive and judicial nominations, and foreign affairs issues have a cohesive effect on the members of the President's legislative party. So, too, do investigations into the executive branch conducted by members of the opposite party and votes on presidential vetoes.

Reelection of Party Members to Congress

The four legislative parties in Congress are also involved in the reelection campaigns of their members and in helping new party candidates win election. Each party has established its own congressional campaign committee, which raises money and disburses it to its party's congressional candidates.

INFORMAL GROUPS
AND CONGRESSIONAL DECISION MAKING

Other sets of legislative groups, in addition to party and legislative committees, structure the organization of Congress and affect its behavior. These groups are not official units of Congress.

One of the most significant sets of such groups are the state delegations. Republican and Democratic legislators from the same states interact to support their states' interests in congressional and executive decision making and to help their members advance their careers within the committee system. Some state delegations are highly organized and meet regularly; others are more informal.

Other congressional groups have organized for a variety of reasons. Almost all have emerged in the House, the much larger chamber, where the individual member is less important than in the Senate and where the rules are more rigid. Some employ their own staff. Race and sex have been the basis for two such groups. The Black Caucus includes all the black legislators in the House. The Women's Caucus includes all the women members in the House and has extended an invitation to women in the Senate when they have appeared in that body.

Another set of House groups comprise members from special economic and geographic constituencies. The Rural Caucus is a loosely organized group of approximately one hundred members who feel their unity works to the advantage of their rural constituents in bargaining within Congress. A more recent, even larger group is the Northeast-Midwest Economic Advancement Coalition, representing constituencies with high unemployment, a large number of depressed cities, and declining populations. In the middle 1970s a Blue Collar Caucus, a Steel Caucus, and a Suburban Caucus were formed.

Whatever the nature of these legislative blocs, they seem to reflect their members' feeling that they must rely on more than political party or state delegations to protect the interests of their constituents. These special groups often cut across party lines and are somewhat similar to the outside interest groups in that both meet special representational needs. However, within the House, special legislative groups have also been organized along ideological-party lines: a liberal Democratic Study Group; a conservative Democratic Research Organization; a moderate Republican Wednesday Club and a conservative Republican Study Committee.

In contrast with the House of Representatives, few such informal groups have been organized in the Senate. The small size of the Senate, the intense individualism of its members, their extremely busy schedules, the burden of representing states as their constituencies, and the availability of committee and subcommittee chairmanships to almost all members of the majority party (ranking minority member positions for the minority party) may make it unnecessary to organize special informal groups. In the 1950s, when Republican Dwight D. Eisenhower was President, liberal Democratic senators together with a few liberal Republicans organized a Liberal Caucus, but it did not survive past the Kennedy presidency. Since 1974, however, a number of conservative Republican senators have been working together on a systematic basis. Calling themselves the Steering Committee, they meet regularly, trade information, plan strategy on upcoming Senate issues, and finance a small staff of their own.

Concepts To Study

democracy   organization   republican government
leadership   representation

Special Terms To Review

cloture
committee chairmen
Committee on (House)
  Rules
conference committees
congressional campaign
  committees
constituency
Democratic Caucus
Democratic Steering and
  Policy Committee
discharge petition
electoral college

filibuster
germaneness rule
House revolt
  of 1910–11
informal legislative
  groups
joint committees
majority floor leader
majority party
minority floor leader
minority party
ranking minority
  members

Republican Committee
  on Committees
Republican Conference
select or special
  committees
seniority rule
Speaker of the House
standing committees
state delegations
subcommittees
unanimous consent
unlimited debate
whips

243

11/3

CONGRESS
PASSES A LAW

When Congress passes a law, the process can involve virtually all the actors and types of organizations we have discussed. In this chapter we will explore how Congress develops a particular policy proposal and enacts it into law, and we will examine the criticism of Congress as a law-making body.

You will recall that Congress adopts three kinds of laws: statutory, constitutional, and treaty. Our concern here is with statutory law; the other types occur very infrequently and either exclude the President (constitutional amendments) or the House (treaties) from the formal legislative process. The process and politics of adopting statutory laws involve House, Senate, and President. But others may also play a part: bureaucrats, interest groups, constituencies, political parties outside the government, and the press.

A LAW TO SUPPORT
A MANNED SPACE EXPLORATION TO MARS

Let us move an imaginary statutory policy through the congressional process. It proposes that the national government support a manned space exploration to Mars. To achieve this purpose, it empowers the National Space and Aeronautics Administration (NASA) to work up the proper space technology and plan and carry out the flight. NASA is authorized to spend $10 billion to pay for this project.

STEP 1: Introducing a Bill

Our law must start out initially as a formal written proposal called a bill. The idea itself or the entire bill may come from outside the Congress and often does. It may have originally been conceived and written by bureaucrats in NASA who asked a particular legislator to introduce it. Or a legislator may have thought up the proposal and requested help from experts in the executive branch in determining whether it was a sound idea. It may have come to the Congress from the President as part of his legislative program. Or it may have been proposed by an interest group or a coalition of groups—scientists, engineers, and manufacturers in space technology—which approached NASA or a legislator on behalf of the idea. Whatever its origins, only a member of Congress may introduce a bill.

STEP 2: Referring the Bill to a Standing Committee

Assume that similar bills are introduced in the House and the Senate (of course, it could just as well start in one chamber). Each bill is given a number: H.R. 2000 and S. 1000. These numbers simply indicate the numerical order in which bills have been introduced in the House and Senate. The presiding officers of the two chambers than refer the bills to their appropriate committees. The subject matter of our bills clearly dictate their being sent to the committees with jurisdiction over space exploration, the Space and Technology Committee of the House and the Commerce, Science and Transportation Committee of the Senate.

Of course, not all bills are as easy to categorize as ours. Some bills cut across the jurisdiction of a number of committees, which may complicate their committee assignment. In that case, each of the appropriate committees may have to consider the part that falls within its jurisdiction. Sometimes a bill may be logically sent to either of two committees. Discretion lies in the hands of the presiding officers of the House and Senate. Their decisions may determine whether the bill is referred to a hostile or a friendly committee.

STEP 3: Committee Consideration

H.R. 2000 and S. 1000 are now at a very crucial point. Should either of the two committees refuse to consider its bill, its chances of moving to Step 4 and possible enactment will drop close to zero. In fact, most bills are never considered by their committees; they die there. According to unofficial norms or rules of the House and the Senate, the decisions of committee specialists should be respected by the other members, who in turn expect similar deference to the decisions of their own committees. Although there are official rules for prying bills loose from hostile or indifferent committees, they are infrequently employed because they violate that congressional norm.

Should the two committees agree to consider the bills, they may do so or they may assign them to their appropriate subcommittees to be studied. Remember, most committees are organized into subcommittees, each dealing with a different part of the policy jurisdiction covered by its full committee. A favorable recommendation by a subcommittee is likely to lead to a favorable report by the full committee.

A decision to consider the bill could lead the committees to hold public hearings on H. R. 2000 and S. 1000. Given the present uncertainties inherent in manned space exploration, the legislators might want to examine the question of its feasibility with experts on the subject. And, given the tremendous sums required by the project, the legislators might want to study its anticipated cost. In all likelihood the proposed spending of billions of dollars on a major space exploration would draw into the hearings a variety of contending interest groups as well as spokesmen from NASA and the President.

After conducting open hearings in which both opponents and proponents can present their cases, committees decide on the bills. Recently, both houses have ordered their committees to hold all such decision-making meetings in public. Only by a majority vote of its members may a committee meet in closed session.

What now are the options of the committees? The members may decide to recommend the original Mars manned space-probe bills to their parent chambers. Or the committees may amend the bills, altering them to their members' satisfaction, and then recommend them. The committees may even refer the bills to their parent chambers without a recommendation, but such action is rare since it is resented by the rest of the legislators. By forwarding bills without offering any recommendation, the committees would be abandoning their responsibility for making the key decisions about which bills should be killed and which should be considered further. The Senate and the House would be left floundering without guidance from their policy experts. A final option is for a majority on a committee to kill the bill by voting against recommending it. In the case of our proposal for a manned space flight to Mars, each committee has attached its amendments and recommended the revised bill to respective chamber.

STEP 4: Scheduling Legislation for Action by the House and Senate

Before the House or Senate may debate and vote on our bills, they must be scheduled for such consideration. Each chamber has its own special procedures, and in both the majority party leadership plays a major role.

The House of Representatives. As each bill comes out of a committee, it is placed on a calendar in the order it is reported. H.R. 2000 is placed on the "House calendar" on which all public nonmoney bills are listed. There are other calendars that come up for consideration by the House

[handwritten notes:] put on Calendar

[handwritten notes:] under control of speaker on floor
no bill will be discussed w/o first
going through Rules committee

on regularly scheduled days each month, but they are inappropriate: a discharge calendar for discharge petitions; consent and private calendars for bills that are basically noncontroversial or for private individuals.

The most important, controversial legislation in placed either on the House calendar, as our bill is, or on the Union calendar, which is for tax revenue and expenditure bills, obviously inappropriate for our bill. Normally, the powerful Rules Committee determines whether bills from these two calendars get to the floor and how they will be considered. It is possible to bypass this committee, but these alternatives for bringing a bill to the House raise special difficulties of their own and are therefore rarely used.

The chairman of the Space and Technology Committee that originally recommended our bill must request the Rules Committee to propose a special rule for it. Members of the Rules Committee have a number of options. They may refuse to hold hearings or may actually vote against giving a rule to allow the bill to go to the floor of the House. Either action has the effect of killing our bill's chances or of compelling the chairman of Space and Technology to venture the difficult, alternative routes for forcing bills to the floor. On the other hand, the legislators on Rules may grant a rule on the bill, or they may bargain, offering a rule in return for substantive changes in the bill.

Should the Rules Committee recommend a rule for H.R. 2000, it may propose an **open** or a closed **rule.** The first permits the House to consider amendments, thus opening our bill up to further substantive changes. A **closed rule** imposes a ban on amendments, forcing the House to accept or reject the bill as recommended by the original committee. A modified closed rule permits only certain amendments. In its rule, the Rules Committee also specifies the amount of time permitted for debate in the House. The majority of its rules allow four hours or less for general debate on bills.

Like all standing committees, Rules can only propose recommendations. The House itself must vote on whether to accept the rules. Only on rare occasions has the House rejected a proposed rule.

Once the House has adopted a rule, the next decision concerns the particular day on which the bill will be considered. The majority party leadership has the discretion to make this decision. Timing can be critical to the success of the bill. If the bill has developed insufficient support, the Speaker and majority leader will delay the debate until they have mustered enough votes to improve its chances. At this point the political skill of the majority party leadership and the effectiveness of their whip system become especially important.

Let us assume that our bill, H.R. 2000, has been granted an open rule, that the House has voted to operate under the conditions of the rule, and that the majority party leadership has scheduled H.R. 2000 for

House Calendar
non money bills

Union Calendar
tax bills

House consideration. It is now ready to go to Step 5, the floor of the House.

The Senate. Scheduling consideration of our bill, S. 1000, by the Senate is both more simple and yet somewhat more tricky than in the House. There are only two calendars in the Senate: an executive one for nominations and treaties and a calendar of business for all other bills, such as ours. The majority leader becomes the most important decision maker at this stage, since the Senate Rules Committee has no authority over scheduling legislation.

The decision to schedule S. 1000 becomes tricky because the majority leader must obtain permission from the rest of the Senate to bring up the bill. How bills will be considered and what arrangements will prevail for the debate, amendments, and final vote are almost always accomplished through unanimous consent agreements. The majority leader and the bill's key proponents must work out an agreement with the minority party and the opposition to S. 1000. On those few issues to which they are unalterably opposed, some legislators will refuse to agree to a rule permitting debate and a vote. When this occurs, the majority leader must decide whether to schedule the bill in the face of a threatened filibuster.

Assume S. 1000 has been scheduled by the majority leader for debate. Although opposition to it has materialized, no senators feel their first principles or the interest of their constituencies demand they prevent the Senate from voting on the bill. As opponents, they will try to modify or even kill the bill, but they defer to the traditional norm of the Senate and agree to permit a vote on S. 1000.

STEP 5: Floor Action in the House and Senate

The House and Senate differ also on how each considers important pieces of legislation. The House operates under much more rigid rules of procedure than the Senate.

House considerations. Our bill, H.R. 2000, will first be considered by the House itself *sitting as a committee.* Then the House will reconvene as a House to adopt or defeat our bill. This is the special procedure called for by the rules of the Rules Committee.

Special advantages accrue to the House when it transforms itself into the **Committee of the Whole House.** As such, it can conduct business with only 100 members present. This smaller number is relatively easy to attract to a debate, and those not interested in the details of the bill are free to engage in business elsewhere.

The types of votes permitted in the Committee of the Whole expedite matters. A *voice vote* involves a collective expression of yeas and nays with the presiding officer determining which wins. Members rise to be counted in a *standing vote*. In a *teller vote*, first the proponents and then the opponents are counted as they walk en masse down the center aisle of the House. All three types of votes can be taken quickly. Until recently, none recorded how a particular member had voted. However, the House has changed its rules, permitting a teller vote that publicly commits individual members.

Since H.R. 2000 has been granted an open rule, the bill will be considered in two stages: general debate and a consideration of amendments. Each has special advantages. General debate is always restricted to a very short period, which allows the Committee of the Whole to proceed with dispatch. Time is divided equally between proponents and opponents, guaranteeing each side an equal chance to make its case. The chairman and ranking minority member of the committee initially recommending the bill are usually given control over the proponents' and opponents' time. They, in turn, allocate units of this time to those who wish to argue pro and con. Under the open rule, when the allotted time for general debate has expired, amendments to H.R. 2000 are in order under a five-minute rule. Any member may offer an amendment, but no one may speak to it for more than five minutes. When all who wish have spoken, the amendment is put to a vote. In this way many members may deal with many amendments without consuming much time.

After having voted on the amendments the Committee of the Whole House dissolves itself. The Speaker and the majority leader now take over and determine when the bill comes before the House. Its members must reconvene as a House to consider the bill, for no committee has the authority to adopt legislation. The necessary quorum reverts to 218, and roll call or record votes are now permitted on H.R. 2000. However, the special rule adopted earlier by the House is binding all the way through the final stages of procedure on the bill.

The rule on H.R. 2000 may permit additional amendments to be offered in the House or it may limit all motions to two. One is always authorized: a motion "to recommit", or send the bill back to its original committee. It is an indication of disapproval. Almost always the success of this motion signifies that the bill has no future and for all practical purposes is dead. Should the recommittal motion on H.R. 2000 fail, the last motion in order is to adopt the bill.

Roll call or record votes are almost always used for these last two motions. Until very recently, a roll call vote required individual members to respond orally yea or nay as their names were called in alphabetical order. Their names and votes were then recorded in the *Congressional Record*, the daily transcript of business that transpires on the floor of the House and Senate. The House now uses electronic voting machines.

Assuming H.R. 2000 has been amended, a recommittal motion has failed, and a majority has voted to adopt it, our bill has completed one-half of its congressional procedure. The Senate must adopt an identical bill for Congress to have enacted a law.

The Senate considers S. 1000.   Senators usually proceed at a more leisurely pace than do members of the House. When the majority party leader, in consultation with the minority party leader, considers that the general debate has proceeded long enough, amendments are called up under the unanimous consent agreement. A motion to recommit precedes the move to adopt the bill. The Senate uses voice, standing, or roll call votes.

If a simple majority of those voting favors the bill, S. 1000 has passed the Senate. This could have occurred before the House passed H.R. 2000, afterwards, or simultaneously. What is critical is whether the two bills are identical. If they are, Congress has enacted legislation and it is moved on to the President (Step 8). If they are not identical, Congress has not adopted legislation and two additional steps must be taken before Congress must turn to the President. Our bills are different because of amendments attached to them in the House and Senate.

STEP 6: A Conference Committee   *allowed to come up with a whole new bill then back to House & senate*

For our manned space exploration to be approved by Congress, H.R. 2000 and S. 1000 must be reconciled so they are identical. On minor differences, one house might easily agree to adopt the language of the other. Should a large number of differences emerge or should the differences reflect substantive disagreements between the two chambers, careful and hard bargaining may become necessary to reconcile the two bills. For this purpose, the Senate and House are too large, too busy, and too cumbersome.

The House and Senate resolve such differences by falling back on a familiar mechanism, another committee. Each house sends a delegation to serve on a conference committee. If the conference committee cannot reach a compromise on our two bills, the committee dissolves and another may be established. If a proposal acceptable to both sets of delegates cannot be agreed upon, the bills are dead. Let us assume that a majority of each delegation has agreed to reconcile the differences and that identical bills authorizing the manned space probe are brought back to the House and Senate.

STEP 7: House and Senate Adopt Identical Bills

The House and Senate make the final decision on the conference's version of the bills. Should either chamber refuse to adopt the recommendation of the conference committee, our policy proposal would be dead. Should one of them propose new changes, the other house would have to agree. If not, a new conference committee would have to be established. Only when both the House and Senate vote for the same bill has Congress adopted the legislation.

STEP 8: The President as a Partner in the Legislative Process

Our Constitution gives the President significant legislative power. All statutory legislation enacted by Congress must come to the President for a decision. If the President signs Congress's proposal or if he takes no action within ten days after receiving it while Congress is still in session, the legislation becomes law. But if Congress adjourns within the ten-day period after the President has received the bill, the President can kill it simply by not signing it. This is called a **pocket veto.** No subsequent action by Congress is possible since it has adjourned. Should the Congress be in session, the President may officially reject (**veto**) it.

If a President formally vetoes the bill, he must return it to Congress for reconsideration. Let us consider, simply to examine the process, what Congress can do if its proposal is returned to it. Step 9 follows only in such circumstances.

STEP 9: Congress May Override a Veto

If Congress is still in session, it has the power to override the President's veto and enact into law its legislation. However, this action requires extraordinary majorities in both the House and Senate.

Like all statutory legislative proposals, H.R. 2000 and S. 1000 needed only a simple majority of the votes cast in the House and Senate to be adopted. The conference committee's bill also could be adopted by simple majorities. But a presidential veto can only be overridden by two-thirds of those voting in both houses. If the proponents fail to muster such a two-thirds majority in each chamber, the veto prevails and the bill is dead.

Clearly the Constitution gives the President a tremendous advantage. Accumulating a two-thirds majority to override a veto of a controversial proposal is very difficult. Presidents are, therefore, much more successful in killing the policy proposals of Congress than Congress is in overriding presidential vetoes.

252

→ When crisis arise arises difficult to get congress to move

Fortunately, the President was favorably disposed to our legislation and agreed to its becoming the law of the land. Can we sit back and congratulate ourselves? No, now we must start the process through Congress all over again!

Starting Over, Steps 1 through 8 or 9

"This does not make sense," you might exclaim. "Why start all over again? After all, a manned space flight to Mars has been officially approved by the Congress and President as official public policy. Shouldn't NASA start to work on the project?"

The answer to these questions is that our legislation has only *authorized* NASA to spend the money for our space project. Next the money itself must be *appropriated* by Congress. Congress and the President must decide whether to provide the necessary funds and how much. This requires additional legislation, meaning we have to begin all over again, except this time we start with a different set of committees.

What you are being asked to understand is that a policy decision that involves the expenditure of money must successfully complete the congressional-presidential circuit twice: first, as an **authorization bill** to *authorize* both the policy itself and the amount involved; second, as an appropriation bill to *appropriate* the exact amount that may be spent. Our recently enacted manned space exploration law is worthless unless money is actually appropriated for its implementation. This double circuit process applies only to legislation involving the expenditure of money.

Why is the bill sent to a different set of committees this time? It is because the Appropriations Committee in each house has jurisdiction over money bills. Although there are ways of allowing the executive to spend money by bypassing these committees, Congress's preference is to take the appropriations route. The original committees with jurisdiction over space legislation were concerned with the substance of policy; the Appropriations committees are not supposed to legislate on the substantive features of the proposal (although they do so at times), but rather to recommend the amount of money that may be spent. By custom, such legislation starts in the House. Its Appropriations Committee is unlikely to refuse to fund our program, for Congress has already approved it. However, it may make cuts in the total amount NASA may spend, or it may reduce funds for different parts of the program. Of course, it could, and in our case does, recommend the entire authorized amount.

For appropriation legislation to become law, it must pass through every stage required of authorization legislation. Should the appropriation legislation become law, Congress and the President will have

increase speed of action

considered the entire proposal twice: once on its substantive merits and once to appropriate money for carrying out the proposal.

Our legislative proposal for a manned space exploration of Mars has now been authorized and appropriated. At this point the principal decision shifts from the Congress to the executive branch. But although NASA assumes responsibility for the project, Congress may still intervene. In pursuing its oversight function, its committees may monitor the executive to make certain the money is being spent wisely and in accordance with the intent of the law.

SOME CURRENT CRITICISM OF CONGRESS

Congress has come under serious attack from many sides and for a variety of reasons. Critics of Congress have raised a number of charges.

Congress Responds Too Slowly to the Problems of the Country

It takes too much time to decide upon public policies. It procrastinates. Sometimes it does nothing when immediate responses are called for.

Congress Is Handicapped by Its Own Organization

There are too many veto points all along the circuits in which policy is supposed to be made. To pass through any one step of the legislative process guarantees nothing except that new battles must be fought all over again at the next step. And at any one step policy may be completely stopped.

Congress Relies Too Much on Compromise

Not the best, but the possible is the axiom characterizing legislative policy making. Policy is compromised all along the way. In the end, much of what Congress adopts reflects a hodgepodge of the different points of view necessary to win votes. The integrity and effectiveness of public policy making is therefore weakened.

Congress Is Unable to Approach Problems Comprehensively

Congress lacks a central focus. Yet the policy problems confronting it are increasingly complex and highly interrelated. Policy integration is virtually impossible, given the two independent chambers, their jealousy toward each other, and their handling policy by assigning it to commit-

limit external income

tees, which divide into subcommittees. Each of these components is independent, considers public policy from its own limited point of view, and fights to protect its turf and powers. The political parties have failed to serve as policy initiating and integrating mechanisms: Their leaders are too weak and too divided; their rank and file, too independent and too irresponsible.

The Narrow and Local Prevail over the General Interest

Primarily responsible to their local constituents, legislators tend to see policy from a narrow, parochial perspective. The general interest is frequently not the sum total of the various constituency interests that permit the forming of legislative majorities. The general interest of the country too often disappears amidst the conflict of constituencies, committees, parties, and the self-interest of individual legislators.

Interest Groups Are Too Influential

The traditional, wealthier, better organized interest groups have an excessive impact on public policy. Legislators develop friendly relations with such groups, which have the resources and know-how to intervene effectively in legislative decision making. Policy is too often stopped or shaped by interest groups pushing their own selfish goals, irrespective of the public interest. The unorganized and poorly organized groups in American society lose out in the process.

Congress Has Low Ethical Standards

As leaders of our political system, members of Congress should be models of political honesty and responsibility. Too frequently, however, they pursue their own self-aggrandizement or tolerate unethical behavior on the part of their colleagues. Some accept bribes or solicit them in return for their votes or help on issues. Some support policy issues or intervene in executive affairs to advance their own financial interests as lawyers, businessmen, or farmers. Some become beholden to interest groups that help finance their campaigns or their travel and entertainment expenses.

Congress Has Abdicated Its Responsibility to the Executive

Laws are often drafted in such broad terms, with executive officials authorized to fill in the details, that these officials replace the legislators as policy makers. Moreover, Congress has given up its constitutional

©1978 by Herblock in *The Washington Post*

"When do you think the trashmen will get here?
It's really piling up."

authority over certain areas of public policy. It has authorized the President to commit our armed forces to conflict overseas on his own initiative, whereas the Constitution makes Congress responsible for declaring war. Congress has also authorized the President to impound (refuse to spend) money that has already been authorized and appropriated. In effect, this gives the President another veto over Congress, one not provided by the Constitution.

Congress Intervenes Too Much in Executive Affairs

A contrary criticism is that Congress undermines executive leadership by intervening unnecessarily in executive affairs. Legislative investigations often immobilize executive officials for long periods of time. In pursuing constituent interests, Congress often distorts and renders ineffective the fair implementation of the law and increases the costs of government. Legislative prohibitions against presidential action in foreign affairs handicap the President in dealing with our allies and work against the best interests of the United States.

RECENT REFORMS

In the 1970s Congress adopted a number of reforms. They address some of the criticism levied against Congress and mark a significant step in improving the operation and ethics of our national legislature.

Reducing Procrastination and Increasing Accountability

The installation of electronic voting machines has enabled the House to reduce considerably the time spent on roll call votes. And with individual votes now recorded in some teller votes, House members may no longer keep all their votes in the Committee of the Whole secret from constituents, interest groups, and the press. By authorizing radio and television coverage of its proceedings, the House has opened itself to greater public scrutiny.

In the Senate, the cloture rule has been made somewhat easier to impose. Filibusters are still used successfully, but cloture is invoked more often than in the past. The Senate has also moved to require more germaneness from members in their consideration of issues.

Ethical Standards

Both chambers have set up committees to deal with the ethics of their members. The legislators have now voted to disclose to these committees and to the public their outside incomes. Members of Congress have recently raised their salaries from $44,600 to $57,500 a year; they also agreed at that time to limit the outside income they could earn (excluding interest and dividends) to 15 percent of their congressional salaries. One purpose of this limitation is to reduce their reliance on interest groups. Another is to reduce the possible conflict of interest legislators might face in voting on bills that could affect their own professional or business incomes. Unfortunately for Congress's ethical posture, the Senate in 1979 voted a four-year postponement of its rule to limit the amount of outside income senators may add to their legislative salaries. Senators may therefore collect up to $25,000 in speaking fees rather than the $8,625 that represented 15 percent of their salaries.

Congress has already taken action against some of its members for unethical behavior. In 1976 the House publicly reprimanded one of its committee leaders, Democrat Robert L. F. Sikes of Florida, for unethical conduct. The next year a caucus of Sikes' Democratic colleagues stripped him of his chairmanship of the military construction appropriations subcommittee. In 1977–78 the House Committee on Standards of Official Conduct investigated charges that former as well as incumbent representatives had been involved in a Korean influence-buying scandal. A number were either indicted or convicted in the courts; some were publicly reprimanded in the House. The Senate ethics committee investigated two of its members, Republican Edward W. Brooke of Massachusetts, in 1978, and Democrat Herman E. Talmadge of Georgia, in 1979, to ascertain whether they had violated financial reporting rules or otherwise engaged in improper conduct that might reflect upon the Senate. In 1979 Pennsylvania Democrat Daniel J. Flood, under indictment for bribery, and Michigan Democrat Charles C. Diggs, Jr., convicted of criminal offenses, voluntarily gave up their subcommittee chairmanships rather than risk sanctions by their colleagues in the House. Subsequently the House officially censured Diggs for his misconduct and the Senate officially denounced Talmadge for reprehensible behavior.

A More Comprehensive Approach to Making Public Policy

Congress has taken some steps to overcome the fragmentation, duplication, and lack of centralization that characterize its approach to public policy. It has now made a decided effort to approach planning the national budget from a comprehensive, integrated point of view.

In the early 1920s Congress assigned responsibility for planning an annual budget to the President. Each year Congress considered the President's budget, but in piecemeal fashion, examining each item apart from the others. Beginning in 1974 Congress accepted responsibility for coordinating its spending and taxing legislation in accordance with a comprehensive budget plan of its own. Standing budget committees were established for this purpose, and a staff agency, the Congressional Budget Office, was set up to help them.

After a President submits his annual executive budget to Congress, the budget committee in each house works out a tentative congressional budget with target goals for expenditures and taxes. A common resolution to that effect must then be adopted by both chambers by May of each year. The other standing committees are required to use these target goals as guides in considering authorization and appropriation legislation. In September the budget committees propose a final, or ceiling, resolution, which takes into account any changes Congress may have made in expenditures or revenues since setting its target goals.

Each chamber must adopt its own budget plan, and the two must be reconciled in a conference committee if they differ.

In the 1970s both the House and Senate considered plans to set up a more rational committee system by reducing the number of their committees and giving single committees jurisdiction over public policy that had been divided among a number of them. The Senate was able to reduce the number of its standing and special committees and to realign their jurisdiction so that there was less policy overlap among them. For example, it centralized responsibility for energy policy in one committee, Energy and Resources.

The House of Representatives was much less successful in reorganizing its committees. Therefore, to overcome the dispersion of authority to deal with certain complex policy issues among a number of its standing committees, the Speaker began experimenting with ad hoc coordinating committees. At the Speaker's instigation, the House set up an Ad Hoc Select Energy Committee. Not only was it a temporary committee and therefore not a threat to the standing committees, but each relevant standing committee was given membership on it. This allowed the different committees to bring their special expertise to bear on the problem of devising energy legislation within the confine of a common committee. This device worked effectively for the energy legislation the House finally adopted.

Reasserting Authority in Policy Making

Congress has not fully abdicated to the executive its responsibility and power for shaping public policy. *As long as it has the will and the determination to do so,* Congress can exercise its independent judgment and power and at the same time take advantage of executive initiative and dispatch. One device for doing so is called the legislative veto. In exercising a **legislative veto** over executive policy making, Congress permits executive officials to make the initial decisions, but reserves to itself the authority to cancel them.

Having authorized the President on his own initiative to commit U.S. troops abroad in armed combat in the War Powers Act of 1973, Congress still reserves to itself the power to terminate such a decision within sixty days of its inception or to extend the time for presidentially-ordered armed involvement for another thirty days. Congress can cancel the action initiated by the President by adopting a concurrent resolution by a simple majority vote in each house within this time period, one that the President may not veto. At the end of the sixty- or ninety-day period of discretion given to the President, if Congress does nothing, it has reversed his decision and the troops must be withdrawn.

Note the simplicity of this legislative veto: Congress may cancel the decision by a vote anytime within sixty days. At the end of the sixty day time period—or one legislatively extended by thirty more days—congressional inaction becomes a veto.

Congress has also limited executive initiative in policy making by authorizing a legislative veto over the President's impoundment of expenditures. In 1974 Congress empowered the President to refuse to spend money approved through authorization and appropriation legislation but reserved to itself the authority to override the President. As in the case of his committing armed forces in conflicts overseas, the President must immediately notify Congress of an impoundment. Either legislative chamber can, within sixty days, disapprove a presidential decision to *delay* the spending of money, thereby compelling the President to spend it. Any presidential decision to completely *cancel* the expenditure must be approved within sixty days by both the Senate and House. Should either chamber withhold its approval, this negates (vetoes) the President's action. In effect, the final decision rests with the legislature.

Congress has empowered the President to reorganize executive agencies and departments by an executive order. But Congress may vote to cancel any such reorganization. Congress has also authorized the President, on his own initiative, to provide weapons to foreign countries, but with the proviso that such executive decisions must be brought to the attention of Congress for its final decision. A simple majority vote by both houses rejecting such aid is necessary to overrule the President.

Some of these executive policy decisions must be overruled by both the Senate and the House; some can be overruled by only one of the two chambers. Over two hundred national laws now in force include a provision for a one-house veto. Nearly one hundred were enacted since 1970, testifying to the determination of Congress in recent times to assert its authority in policy making.

Making Committee Leadership More Responsible and Available

In the 1970s the political parties in the House and Senate seriously weakened the seniority rule. This rule had permitted some committee chairmen to continue in positions of power, even when they had lost much of their drive, energy, and intellectual faculties or had behaved in an autocratic and irresponsible manner. Party control was reasserted, and prospective chairmen and ranking minority members are now voted into office. The House Democratic Caucus, in secret ballot in 1975, actually removed three chairmen of standing committees, refusing them the committee leadership that once would have been theirs automatically. One was replaced by a Democrat who was *not* next in line in the committee majority according to seniority; in other words, seniority was completely bypassed. Chairmen are now on notice that their behavior can cost them their official committee leadership positions.

Many committees have adopted special rules empowering a majority of their members to overrule an arbitrary chairman and to take control over the procedures of the committee. Moreover, the multitude of subcommittees has decentralized committee leadership, opening up a large number of leadership slots for other legislators and further reducing the power of the committee chairmen. Ironically, this has tended to blunt another set of reforms that focus on allowing the House and Senate to take more comprehensive approaches to problems.

Other Reforms

Limits have now been imposed on the congressional use of the franking (free mail) privilege. This reform prevents members of Congress from abusing this constituent-oriented device during election campaigns to the disadvantage of their opponents. Another reform, strengthening the staffs of individual members, has improved the ability of legislators to cope with the tremendously complex problems facing them. Minority party members on committees also have been granted additional staff with which to challenge the majority party contingent. And a new House staff agency, the Office of Technology Assessment, now helps legislators understand and deal with policy matters relating to modern technology.

CONGRESS AND THE FUTURE

Some of the criticism that has been leveled against Congress is warranted; some is not. Certain aspects of congressional behavior are intrinsic to Congress. Unless we transform radically our Constitution or our political party and election systems, not much can be changed. Little can be done in response to criticism that focuses on slowness, inaction, or compromise. A Congress in which each chamber is independent and yet dependent on the other, whose members represent different types of constituencies and are jealous of their separate institutional prerogatives, cannot lead to anything but slowness, occasional inaction, and frequent compromise. The independence of the standing committees means that they operate at their own pace. Legislators who are divided into separate, opposing parties are bound to delay and frustrate each other's plans. The fact that there are separate House and Senate parties with their own sets of leaders reduces the ability of a majority party to act as a unifier in Congress.

Slowness, inaction, and compromise may actually represent worthwhile features of Congress. They prevent the legislature from being stampeded by a forceful President or an insistent interest group. They allow legislators time to think through the implications of policy initiatives. Given the diversity of interest groups, constituencies, and points of view in this vast country, compromise may often be the only way legislators can reconcile basic differences over what should be done. The national interest is not as easy to define as the critics would have us believe. In fact, to compromise may be in the national interest, especially if it moves necessary reforms a step closer to reality and if it enables contending groups to feel the political system is still open and responsive to them. Of course, slowness, inaction, and compromise have their price, sometimes a very high price. But there would also be a high price if Congress were to downgrade bargaining and compromise and speed up policy making.

A number of reforms have already been put into effect to help correct weaknesses in the way Congress goes about its business. Other reforms will be proposed in the future to improve the process, organization, and output of Congress as well as the ethical standards of its members. It must be understood, however, that all reform is difficult to achieve. Reforms require legislators to abandon their traditional attitudes and practices for new, untried ones that may cause still other problems. Reform is also bound to affect adversely the power positions of certain legislators and their allied interest groups. Thus reforms inevitably generate considerable opposition when proposed and, even if they are not defeated, take considerable time to win adoption. Frequently they must be extensively compromised to win the necessary support for their adoption.

As a reaction to the Johnson and Nixon presidencies, a momentum developed, both within and outside Congress, to give Congress a more independent voice in policy making and a greater check on presidential power. By the time of President Carter's administration, a partial reaction had set in. Many critics argued that Congress had become too independent, that it was gutting presidential leadership, and that its intervention in executive affairs undermined the President's initiatives. Just as Congress will continue to be a center of influence over policy, so will conflict continue over the proper role of Congress in our political system and over the nature of reforms that the national legislature should undertake.

Concepts To Study

national interest

Special Terms To Review

appropriation bills
authorization bills
Budget committees
Budget message
bureaucrats
calendars
closed rule
cloture
committee chairman
Committee of the Whole House
conference committee
Congressional Budget Office
congressional norms

constituencies
Democratic Caucus
filibuster
five-minute rule
franking privilege
germaneness
House Rules Committee
legislative veto
motion to recommit
open rule
party floor leaders
pocket veto
power to impound

quorum
roll call (record) vote
seniority rule
standing vote
statutory law
teller vote
unanimous consent
veto
voice vote
War Powers Act of 1973

Committee Chairmen in Congress
- time limit
- veto

reforms - weakness in seniority rule — voted on
- over rule chairmen (Chairmen in power committee can take secret vote to override)
- increase in a number of sub committees

263

CHAPTER 12

11\3

THE PRESIDENT:
A Unique Leader

The office of President is the preeminent position in the American political system for asserting national leadership. Although not all Presidents live up to its full potential, others stretch it to its outer limits. Presidential leadership, however, is not dependent merely on particular incumbents. Its bedrock lies in the responsibilities and powers assigned the office by the Constitution. With the Constitution as their base, decisions by Congress and the Supreme Court have greatly expanded the leadership potential of the presidency. In addition, the expectations of the American people and their other leaders, as well as the leaders of foreign countries, contribute to that potential. All expect the President to assert leadership.

The ability of the President to tap this potential for leadership will vary with the conditions facing the country. Crises focus the attention of people and their leaders on the need for unity, initiative, and sacrifice. More than any other leader or institution in the United States, the President is admirably suited to respond to such a challenge. In the absence of a national crisis or confronted with a lack of consensus regarding one, the President's ability to lead diminishes considerably.

The President's power to make binding decisions for the country is greatest in foreign affairs–national security matters. His authority is strengthened by the fact that Americans and their leaders tend to defer to the President's initiative and judgment in these areas. In resolving domestic issues, however, presidential power is much more limited, and other leaders feel equally if not better qualified to supply solutions. Moreover, the public itself tends to be both personally concerned and much more divided over domestic issues.

The ability of a President to function as the country's leader in these policy areas also depends on the willingness of other officials to

Tony Auth, *The Philadelphia Inquirer*

cooperate with him. Our governmental system is one of separation of powers, checks and balances, and federalism, all of which make it difficult for a President to be an effective leader. Members of Congress, judges, governors, state legislators, and mayors, all of whom have independent powers of their own, may refuse to comply with presidential leadership. With their own political interests to protect and their own perceptions of what is important and necessary, they may feel compelled to challenge and try to defeat the President.

The President faces other constraints inherent in a democratic political system. The general public may not respond to his appeals and interest groups may reject his proposals in favor of their own. The mass media, which is free to criticize a President, may focus the public's attention on the mistakes and scandals that may arise in his administration. Members of the opposition political party often attempt to frustrate the President's policies and are joined, at times, by members of the President's own party. Even executive subordinates of the President may ignore or thwart his proposals. Outside the United States, our allies may prove reluctant to accept the President's initiatives. Often, there is little the President can do to *compel* any of these groups or individuals to accept his leadership.

Since so few are obligated to follow his leadership or to share his perception of what needs to be done, the President must be a superb politician to succeed as a leader. Presidential leadership becomes equivalent, therefore, to an ability to persuade, to evoke loyalty, and to bargain. The President must take advantage of the fact that others need the decisions and resources he controls and he must take advantage of their willingness to bargain or trade with him. Presidential leadership depends also on his ability to convince the people that the sacrifices required by his programs are vital both to themselves and to the nation.

This means that the President must be able to articulate his view of the public interest in a way that enables enough people to identify with it.

Consequently, Presidents cannot depend solely on constitutional and legislative powers to be effective leaders. They must be popular advocates and consummate politicians, marshalling behind them coalitions from among the different interest groups and the general public, building majorities for their programs in Congress, and rallying officials in the executive branch.

UNIQUE CHARACTERISTICS OF THE PRESIDENCY _Know_

Any discussion of presidential uniqueness must start with an understanding that the President has much in common with many leaders in the American political system: The President is an *elected politician*. Those who win the presidency must first have demonstrated success in the internal politics of their parties and then have appealed to sufficient voters in a general election. Incumbents must renavigate the party–popular election–electoral college route to continue in office.

On the other hand, certain political and structural features of the position of President accent its uniqueness and make it synonymous with national leadership. These are the nature of the election constituency, the perquisites and term of office, and the unity of the incumbent and the institution.

A National Election Constituency _NATIONAL Basis, limit on # of terms_

The President is the only elected leader of the entire nation, the Vice President being merely a stand-in. The contest for the presidency is a national one, taking place in the fifty states and the District of Columbia. All members of the electorate have an opportunity to vote for presidential electors.

The presidency is therefore filled by someone whose constituency is the nation and whose concern must transcend the interests of any state or region. The nature of the problems that come from that kind of constituency and the horizons that determine the vision of a President are very different from those of the elected officials in the national legislature. Members of Congress are elected in very circumscribed constituencies; they cannot afford too often to lift their horizons beyond them. Even problems coming to individual House or Senate members are limited by the size and relative simplicity of their election constituencies.

The President is elected for a four-year term and may only be reelected once. For over a hundred and fifty years a two-term tradition prevailed. President Franklin D. Roosevelt broke that tradition by being elected to a third and fourth term. This induced Congress and the states to adopt the Twenty-second Amendment (1951), which prevents a President from being elected to more than two terms. Neither House members, who are elected for two-year terms, nor Senators, who are elected for six-year terms, are limited by the Constitution in the number of terms they may serve.

The President has almost four years to make a reputation as a leader before coming back to the people for reelection. If he has served two terms, a President becomes a lame duck in the eighth year, with all the disadvantages of a leader compelled to step down while members of Congress and the courts continue to serve.

The perquisites of the office also attest to the uniqueness and the importance of the President's filling a leadership position. A President is housed, paid, and guarded in a manner unequalled by other American officials.

The White House is both the home and working quarters of the President and his family. It is also a symbol of presidential leadership for the nation. Aside from the Vice President, who only in the 1970s was provided with a special residence, the national government makes no provision for the personal housing of its other leaders.

The large amount of money paid the President emphasizes his preeminence as a leader. He receives an annual salary of $200,000 plus an expense allowance of $50,000 (both taxable) for official duties. In addition, he is given a nontaxable $100,000 yearly allowance for transportation and entertainment. On leaving office, he receives a lifetime pension of $60,000 a year, free office space, free mailing privileges, and up to $90,000 a year for office help. Upon his death, a President's widow receives an annual pension of $20,000.

Compare these salaries and financial benefits with those of other national government leaders. The Vice President receives an annual salary of $75,000 plus a taxable expense allowance of $10,000. Members of the Supreme Court are paid $72,000 a year; the Chief Justice, $75,000. Salaries of the heads of the executive departments are $66,000 a year. Members of Congress are paid $57,500 a year; the Speaker of the House, $75,000. Their incomes are all taxable and they must contribute to their own pension funds. Since it is Congress that determines these perquisites, the generous financial support afforded the President testifies to the legislative branch's recognition that the President is, indeed, the preeminent national leader.

As a primary leader of the country, the President is also given special protection. The main mission of the Secret Service is to protect that one official. Throughout our history Presidents, more than any other governmental leaders, have been the target of assassins. The Vice President is also provided Secret Service protection, as are certain officials in the President's Cabinet, but not members of Congress or the Supreme Court.

The President Is a Single Person

In no other part of the national government do the institution and the person so closely merge as in the presidency and the President. The President is and can only be a single individual, which automatically enhances the leadership potential of the presidency.

A single individual can more easily make a decision than can a multimember institution such as the House, Senate, or Supreme Court. Hence *decisiveness* characterizes the presidency. A single individual can more easily act on the basis of that decision. Thus *action* is a key characteristic of the presidency. *Dispatch*, or speed, in responding to problems and emergencies is more characteristic of the presidency than of Congress or the courts. Unlike the latter two, the President, as a single individual, can express a single point of view or insist on one point of view among his subordinates. *Unity* of purpose and expression is therefore a special leadership advantage of the President. As a single individual, a President can come to a decision and act upon it without publicly engaging in debate and controversy. This means that a President has all the advantages of *secrecy* in examining facts and alternatives in reaching a decision. A unique combination of decisiveness, action, dispatch, unity, and secrecy contributes to the leadership potential of the office of President.

All Presidents come under attack at one time or another for failing to exploit those structural features contributing to leadership. Especially during his first two years in office, President Carter was sharply criticized by members of his own party in Congress and by the press for his lack of decisiveness on some issues, for his inability to put together a unified program in urban affairs and in the area of health insurance, for his willingness to compromise on some issues and not on others, and for his toleration of the advocacy of different views on foreign policy by his secretary of state and his national security adviser. However, his establishing full-scale relations with the People's Republic of China and his initiative in persuading the leaders of Egypt and Israel to agree upon a peace treaty show a President exploiting magnificently the full potential for leadership in his office.

As Act secretly when dealing with
people a decision

A single individual representing the presidency enhances its capacity for leadership in still another way. People can more easily identify with their President as a leader since only one person embodies the institution, in contrast with a multimember Congress and Supreme Court. Individual Americans can also identify with the President as a fellow human being. They can take delight in his performance as he dodges some questions at news conferences and responds with humor to others. These are human traits that no multimember governmental institution can project to us.

The prestigious White House is also a home in which the President and his family live. People can identify with home and family. Presidents entertain, hold meetings, and have weddings in the White House. They, or members of their immediate families, go on vacations, attend school and church, become ill, or die. People observe these events through the media and share in the joys and sorrows of the President. In fact, for many Americans this identification starts in early childhood. It is this official who first enters their political consciousness; they initially associate country and government with the presidency, not with complex institutions such as Congress or the courts.

As a single leader, moreover, the President can easily appeal to the people for support, speaking directly to them at mass meetings, talking to them in their homes over television and radio, shaking their hands in personal appearances. Can you visualize Congress trying to address the American public in their homes in this manner? Who can speak for Congress: the House? the Senate? which individual? which party? which committee? The judicial branch operates under similar handicaps. Only the President can authoritatively speak for the presidency in approaching the people.

The fact that the President is a single individual who differs in unique ways from congress and the courts just begins to explain the extraordinary leadership potential invested in the office. These unique characteristics merely facilitate an exercise of leadership mandated by the Constitution, the Congress, the courts, and the political party–election system.

ORGANIZING THE PRESIDENCY

The presidency is more than the President, but it is less than the executive branch. No modern President can conduct the presidency by himself. It is not that the responsibility of leadership is too great, but that so much is demanded from a President, as you will learn in the next chapter. Every President today is served by an elaborate network of advisers and aides. The modern presidency extends far beyond the

[handwritten margin note: must be approved by senate + Pres not closes to him]

President to include key personal staff in the White House, units somewhat further removed but still within the Executive Office of the President, and the top leadership of the departments and the major executive agencies. Collectively they are referred to as the President's *administration*, which may include the Vice President as a significant participant.

[handwritten note: White house staff - not approved by senate, press closes to him usually selected for political reasons]

The Vice President

Although the Vice President has certain constitutional responsibilities—principally that of presiding over the Senate and being available to fill the presidency should the office become vacant—it is as an instrument of presidential leadership that the modern Vice President plays any sort of meaningful role. The President is the one who decides whether a Vice President will be an integral member of his leadership team or whether the Vice President will simply twiddle his thumbs presiding over the Senate.

Many Presidents in the past preferred to ignore their Vice Presidents. As presidential candidates they selected their running mates for reasons concerned with capturing the nomination, uniting their party, or winning the general election. Rarely if ever were vice-presidential candidates picked because they were personally and politically close to the presidential candidates. A great psychological and political distance therefore often separated a President from his Vice President. A built-in antipathy and jealously also tended to develop between their staffs. Those serving the President were inclined to see the Vice President as a potential rival or embarrassment to their own superior. Because of this attitude toward Vice Presidents, most officials occupying this position have been isolated from any real involvement in executive policies and politics.

Since Franklin D. Roosevelt, modern Presidents have increasingly involved their Vice Presidents in presidential affairs. Some Vice Presidents have been assigned responsibility for carrying out certain executive policies—civil rights in the case of Hubert H. Humphrey, and intergovernmental reorganization in the case of Nelson Rockefeller. Some have been sent abroad to represent their Presidents on strictly ceremonial missions; a few have been given more important diplomatic missions. Presidents have employed Vice Presidents as their emissaries to the Senate, not just as communication links but as active lobbyists who helped marshal majorities in behalf of presidential programs. In addition, Vice Presidents have represented Presidents before select publics in the United States in an effort to build popular support for their Presidents' programs.

President Carter has used his Vice President in a more active, creative way than any previous President. Not only has Vice President Walter F. "Fritz" Mondale engaged in all of the activities other Vice Presidents have had assigned to them, but he has been a senior, personal adviser to the President and an intimate participant in the shaping of foreign and domestic policy in the White House. The closeness of Carter and Mondale and the willingness of the President to rely upon the latter for leadership and trouble-shooting illustrate the opportunities for the Vice President when he is included as an integral part of the presidency.

The White House Staff   *not Congressional approval*

Key members of the White House staff comprise the day-to-day working aides and advisers to the President. They tend to be among the President's most intimate confidants, and all serve as his instruments. None are constitutional officials, and few are specifically authorized by Congress. Instead, they are appointed by the President without Senate consideration and serve at the President's pleasure.

To a certain extent their responsibilities are already structured or institutionalized by the needs of modern Presidents. A typical President today appoints a press secretary, an appointments secretary, a national security adviser, a military aide, a legal counselor, a legislative liaison officer, and others. Each has a special set of responsibilities for helping the President with different aspects of his job, and each may have a staff of his own. In addition, Presidents select aides to help them write speeches and to develop, coordinate, and implement policy within the executive branch. They also appoint assistants to work with interest groups and with state political parties.

Increasingly, White House aides have been recruited from among the campaign staffs of presidential nominees. As members of the winning team that fought the nomination and election battles, they dominate the team that assumes control of the presidency. Not only are they likely to be known and personally trusted by the President, but they see their primary mission as that of protecting and advancing his leadership. Aside from the usual drive of personal ambition on their part and the rivalry that often breaks out among them for status in the White House, they have only one constituent—the President.

A few within the White House staff have more authority than the others. They tend to be the intimate advisers to the President. The President consults with them and depends on their advice; they above all others have ready access to him. Of course, Presidents also reach outside the White House for some of their closest advisers. They may seek these advisers from within the executive branch or from outside it and government altogether. President Kennedy was very close to one of his brothers, who served as his attorney general (head of the Department of Justice). A member of the U. S. Supreme Court, Justice Abe Fortas, acted as one of President Lyndon B. Johnson's key advisers. President Carter regularly turns for advice to an Atlanta lawyer who had been close to the President when the latter had served as governor of Georgia.

President Carter has distinguished himself from other Presidents by including his wife as a full member of the White House team. Personally and politically closer to the President than any one else, she is highly respected by his other senior aides for her political judgment and for her influence on the President. He apparently consults her and relies on her political assessments. She attends cabinet meetings, has served as an advocate in certain policy areas, and has been sent by the President to represent him and the nation to certain foreign countries. Only one other President, Franklin D. Roosevelt, used his wife as extensively as a political aide.

The Executive Office of the President

A number of agencies designed to help the President carry out his leadership responsibilities make up what is called the Executive Office of the President. Most were created by Congress; some by the President. Unlike personnel in the White House, most of the leaders of these agencies must be approved by the Senate after they have been nominated by the President. Many are appointed for their expertise in certain policy areas, and some of these officials have major responsibilities of their own, other than those assigned them by the President. As a result, they tend not to be as close—physically, emotionally, or politically—to the President as his staff aides in the White House. Nevertheless, these agencies afford the President, as national leader, an immediate, expert backup staff for making critical decisions. Reference to four of these agencies will illustrate the range of assistance they provide the President.

The Office of Management and Budget (OMB), created originally by Congress in 1921, is responsible for helping the President develop the executive budget he must transmit annually to Congress. It serves also as the President's staff for overseeing the implementation of that budget within the executive branch once Congress approves it. In addition, the OMB acts as a coordinating agency for the President, resolving differences among departments and agencies and making certain their legislative proposals do not conflict with those of the President. Its director works closely with the President and participates in policy meetings at the senior level of the Administration. Its staff is professional, not partisan, and is prepared to work with both Republican and Democratic masters.

The Council of Economic Advisors, authorized in 1946 by Congress, is responsible for helping the President assemble his annual Economic Report to Congress. Its chairman acts as the principal economic adviser to the President, participates in policy determinations at the top level of the President's administration, and represents the President on economic matters before Congress and to the people.

The National Security Council (NSC) differs considerably from the other two. Created in 1947 by Congress, its job is to help the President coordinate foreign, economic, and military policies pertaining to the national security of the country. Its membership core, as prescribed by Congress, is made up of the Vice President, the secretary of defense, and the secretary of state. Other executive officials, chosen by the President, also serve as members of the NSC. The President's personal assistant for national security affairs serves as its executive secretary and coordinates the work of its special staff. The authority of the NSC is limited to making recommendations to the President. Each President shapes its structure and adapts its procedures to suit his personal style.

The Domestic Policy Staff was created by a presidential executive order in 1977. It is designed to facilitate contributions by cabinet members and other presidential advisers to the development of domestic policy in the White House. It is headed by the President's personal assistant for domestic affairs.

A President may bypass these agencies, ignore their advice, or adopt their recommendations and transform them into his own policy decisions. Ultimately, major leadership decisions are the responsibility of the President.

Executive Departments and Agencies

The heads of the executive departments and agencies also serve as members of the President's team. Appointed by the President, but subject to confirmation by the Senate, they are directly responsible to him for managing their bureaucracies and carrying out programs of the national government. As the President's senior executive managers, they are an integral part of his administration. They are expected to act as advisers to the President and to serve as his agents, helping shape congressional decisions and public opinion. These senior executive managers are usually members or leaders of the President's political party.

Collectively, the heads of the thirteen executive departments, plus other executive officials designated by the President, make up the cabinet of the President. The Vice President may also be invited to participate as a member of the cabinet. Before the elaborate staffing of the modern presidency in this century, Presidents had no Executive Office to help them, and the White House staff was very small. The cabinet comprised the official advisory group with which Presidents consulted.

Cabinets operate at the discretion of the President. A President may convene his cabinet for the discussion of policy and strategy, or he may completely ignore it. Votes are seldom taken at cabinet meetings, since the President is the superior of all its members, and their votes are not binding upon him. Moreover, the heads of the departments tend not to be chosen because of any close, confidential relationship with the President, but rather because they are political leaders with governmental experience—governors, members of Congress, mayors—outstanding business and labor leaders, or leaders in their professions. They are often selected for geographic, religious, political party, and ethnic representativeness.

The cabinet is also weakened as a tool for the President because these departmental leaders tend to develop loyalties to their own executive units as well as to the President. In addition, department heads may not necessarily be interested in each other's policy concerns. Only the President pulls them together as a cabinet, *if* this suits his operating style.

The heads of the executive departments are more likely to act as presidential advisers and share in the designing of his strategy and tactics as individuals or in small groups rather than collectively as a cabinet. Like all other members of the President's team, they are expected to accept presidential leadership decisions without any public expression of disagreement. President Carter's first secretary of health, education, and welfare, for example, strongly opposed, within the administration, the creation of a separate Department of Education. Once the President had made his decision, however, the head of HEW withdrew his opposition.

These executive leaders usually lobby Congress only for their own departmental policy proposals. But when the President feels it vital to his program, they become part of an administration team in Congress. The White House then coordinates their efforts in behalf of presidentially endorsed legislation. Virtually the entire Carter cabinet was utilized in this manner in White House lobbying for the Panama Canal treaties and for the President's civil service reform bill in 1978.

In addition to these departmental leaders, the President may also call on a number of other executive leaders of agencies for their advice as experts. For example, the director of the Central Intelligence Agency, who has been assigned responsibility for coordinating for the President all foreign intelligence information from the various intelligence-gathering agencies, keeps him informed about foreign intelligence and participates in the President's National Security Council. For military advice the President may turn to the chairman of the Joint Chiefs of Staff and to the Joint Chiefs, themselves. Neither the CIA director nor the Joint Chiefs is utilized by the White House as a lobbyist for its general legislative program in Congress.

Concepts To Study

checks and balances	federalism	politician
democracy	leadership	separation of powers

Special Terms To Review

cabinet	Executive Office of the President	Office of Management and Budget
Central Intelligence Agency	heads of departments	two-term tradition
constituency	Joint Chiefs of Staff	White House staff
Council of Economic Advisers	lame duck	
Domestic Policy Staff	National Security Council	

CHAPTER 13

THE PRESIDENT:
Leadership Roles

Know roles & Characteristics

One way to understand presidential leadership is to examine its component **roles.** These roles are sets of behavior patterns defined for anyone occupying the presidency by the Constitution, Congress, and the courts; the expectations of those interacting with the President and looking to that official for leadership; and the expectations of incumbent Presidents, themselves.

The Constitution explicitly mandates two leadership roles: chief executive and commander in chief. Four others—chief of state, legislative leader, manager of the economy, and head of foreign affairs—stem from constitutional grants of power and responsibilities, from legislative and judicial decisions, or from both, as well as from the expectations of other political leaders and the people. A seventh role—party leader—has its source in the national party of the President. And an eighth—shaper of public opinion—is based on the others as well as on the semipopular election of the President and the identification of the people with the office and the incumbent.

CHIEF EXECUTIVE

Article II of the Constitution begins with a sweeping grant of power: "The executive Power shall be vested in the President of the United States of America." And it commands the President to "take Care that the Laws be faithfully executed." The President is clearly the chief executive of the national government. But this does not mean that the executive branch operates entirely in response to his leadership.

The executive branch is a highly divided, unwieldly organization of many different units, some of which are very independent of the President's authority. Only a minute group among the over two million civilian employees and over two million military personnel who make up the executive branch feel any strong personal commitment to a President. A President must therefore devote considerable thought, energy, and time to managing the executive branch and to energizing its members to accept new initiatives and follow presidential guidelines. Because the President's control over the executive branch is limited by Congress, by the courts, and at times by interest groups, his executive leadership also depends upon his ability to influence nonexecutive officials and groups.

Selecting and Firing Executive Officials

One method for imposing presidential leadership is by exercising the chief executive's power to appoint and dismiss executive officials. By selecting those who share his views and feel obligated to him for their leadership positions and by discharging those who refuse to cooperate or who undermine his policies, a President can exert some control over key managers of the executive branch.

Absolute authority to hire and fire covers only those few people employed as immediate personal aides to the President in the White House. The President shares the power to select other advisers and the senior leaders of the departments and executive agencies with the Senate. However, he has unrestrained power to remove these officials at will, according to the Supreme Court. They continue to serve only at his pleasure.

Leaders of the so-called independent regulatory agencies in the executive branch are somewhat further removed from the President's control. He exercises only limited appointment and removal powers over these executive officials. First of all, they serve for fixed terms, many longer than that of the chief executive. Hence a newly elected President finds he has inherited some senior regulatory leaders appointed by previous Presidents; these leaders may share his predecessor's policy objectives, not his. Second, even if he does appoint, with the consent of the Senate, his choices to fill vacancies on the regulatory commissions, the President's power to dismiss these leaders is very restricted.

The Supreme Court has held that a President may not fire a member of an independent agency simply because the member belongs to a different party or because the President disagrees with his policy decisions or considers the agency leader personally objectionable. He may fire such an executive official only in accordance with the congressional laws establishing their agencies. Consequently, these officials need not be concerned with presidential wishes or fear presidential power unless their terms lapse and they seek reappointment.

The President has absolutely no hiring or firing control over the millions of civil service employees who work in the executive branch. They are hired through an impartial, nonpartisan system. And they may be dismissed only for insubordination, for inability to perform their work, or for a number of other reasons defined by civil service regulations. Almost all military personnel are also shielded from the President's appointing and dismissing powers.

Designing and Controlling the Executive Budget

Probably the strongest instrument of presidential leadership over the policies and operation of executive units lies in the President's control over their budgets. Proposing to Congress a budget for each executive unit for the upcoming fiscal year is entirely a presidential responsibility. The departments and agencies must fit their budget requests within the president's guidelines. Depending on his priorities, he can agree to their requests, reject their appeals for more money, or cut back their operating revenues. This control over money requests by executive units, for inclusion in the President's budget, becomes an important control over policy direction.

To help him present a comprehensive budget for the executive branch to Congress—the total budget is now over half a trillion dollars—the President relies upon a special staff agency, the Office of Management and Budget (OMB). It reviews all proposals for the President's budget within overall spending guidelines decided on by the President. The OMB requires each department and agency to justify its requests for money, thereby providing this presidential agency with a critical insight into their operations. Senior executive leaders may appeal its decisions to the President.

A President's budget is only a recommendation to Congress. Congress determines the amount of money the different units in the executive branch may spend. Hence, those subordinate executive officials who are extremely dissatisfied with what the President has proposed for their units may informally contact their allies in Congress and among the interest groups in an attempt to reverse these presidential budgetary decisions. To the extent that his decisions may be challenged and overruled in Congress, the President does not fully control the financing of the executive branch.

Once the budget is adopted into law, however, the President continues to exert control over executive expenditures, for his OMB exercises general supervision over spending by the departments and agencies. In addition, Presidents may impound (refuse to spend) funds that Congress has appropriated. Impoundment decisions afford the chief executive an additional control mechanism over executive units, although Congress may still overrule him.

Relying upon Senior Executive Managers

The major part of the executive branch—thirteen departments and certain agencies—is directly responsible, through subordinate executive managers, to the President for policy determination and implementation. Their legislative proposals to Congress must first clear the President's OMB. It acts as his legislative clearinghouse, making certain that the bills advocated by these departments and agencies conform with the President's own legislative program. OMB also helps the President resolve interdepartmental differences over policy and administration.

No President has a consuming interest in all these departments and agencies or in everything they do. Nor does a President have the time or the mechanisms for monitoring them all. He relies on the senior leaders of these departments and agencies to act as his managers. A President assumes that they will carry out the law and manage their executive units in accordance with, or not in opposition to, presidential guidelines and instructions. Remember that all or most of them share a common party identification with their President, and that he appoints them (with the consent of the Senate) and dismisses them at will.

Nonetheless, Presidents cannot always rely on their partisan executive managers to implement White House policy directives. Although they are agents of the President, they are also spokesmen for their own executive departments and agencies. Moreover, in carrying out the responsibilities that Congress has assigned to their executive units, they must relate to constituencies other than the White House—their clientele, special interest groups, and particular congressional committees. This special identification of the President's senior executive managers with their own departments and agencies and with their other constituencies often brings them into conflict with the White House leadership.

The senior leaders of the independent regulatory agencies, such as the Interstate Commerce Commission, the Federal Trade Commission, and the Federal Communications Commission, tend to manage their own agencies with little deference to presidential wishes. Congress deliberately created them as semiexecutive, semijudicial, and semilegislative units, outside the executive departments and *free from direct policy and management control* by the President. Most of these special executive units are headed up by a commission, a number of equal leaders, and by law are bipartisan in membership.

One of the important independent agencies, whose policies often conflict sharply with those of Presidents, is the Federal Reserve Board.

Set up by Congress in 1913 to regulate the financial activities of the nation's banks, its policies affect the entire economy. Its actions can expand or contract the money supply of the country and increase or lower interest rates, thereby determining the availability of credit in the economy. Serving fourteen-year terms, the seven members on the board of governors of the Federal Reserve system are virtually beyond the control of any chief executive.

The President appoints the chairman of the board (to a four-year term), but even this may not give him much leverage in influencing its policies. Federal Reserve Board chairmen have at times strongly and publicly opposed the economic policies proposed by Presidents, and boards have been willing to take positions that have clashed with presidential initiatives. True, both the board and its chairmen as well as Presidents and their secretaries of the treasury tend to cooperate to avoid imposing contradictory policies upon the economy, but it is a cooperation among equals.

Controlling the Bureaucracy as it Implements the Law

The executive branch also divides along another dimension that causes problems for presidential leadership. Beneath the partisan leaders of the departments and agencies are the career civil servants. They commonly are referred to as bureaucrats—nonpartisan, permanent executive employees chosen mainly through merit examinations. You will remember our discussion of bureaucrats as part of the unique executive subsystems that interact with interest groups for their mutual advantage. We have also referred to the special relations between the different committees of Congress and the different units of the bureaucracy. In the executive branch, it is the bureaucracy that drafts many of the rules and regulations implementing congressional legislation, and its members administer the services and regulations of the national government.

The Constitution may make the President responsible for "faithfully executing the law," but it is in fact the bureaucracy that does the day-to-day "executing." This makes the President very vulnerable to bureaucratic performance. If career officials are incompetent, they can defeat the President's efforts to run the executive branch effectively and efficiently. If they are corrupt, they not only cheat the taxpayer but detract from the leadership image of the President. If they distort the law or administer it at a pace or in a spirit that conflicts with that of the President, they can undermine his leadership. By the same token, if they resist the orders of a President who wants to misuse government for his own personal or partisan aggrandizement, bureaucrats can also defend the integrity of the executive branch.

Although normally not concerned with the day-to-day activities of bureaucrats, Presidents occasionally find it necessary to intervene in their affairs. A chief executive may want some part of the bureaucracy to move faster or slower. He may want it to give special consideration or favors to a member of Congress or a constituent. He may want bureaucratic officials to write a different set of rules than the ones they feel are called for by the law. Or a President may want these officials to reorient their approach to carrying out the law so that it better reflects special White House priorities. By delaying, compromising, complaining to Congress, or refusing to comply with these requests, bureaucrats can obstruct and weaken a President's leadership.

A common set of complaints heard in the Kennedy, Johnson, Nixon, and Ford administrations was that the bureaucracy was reluctant to try new ways of doing things, that it moved too slowly in response to orders and overtures from the partisan executive leadership, and that it obstructed presidential directions at times. Presidents have complained

Copyright © 1977 by Herblock in *The Washington Post*

"And, in this corner, the undefeated champ—"

that they must do battle with their own bureaucracies, that bureaucrats far down the executive ladder have successfully defeated their attempts at leadership. As a result, modern Presidents have increasingly become concerned with how to control these career officials. In 1978 Congress adopted some of President Carter's proposals for exerting such control. Partisan executive managers were given more discretion to fire bureaucrats for incompetency, and they were also authorized to transfer senior bureaucrats among the various departments as well as to offer them significant merit increases for superior performance.

Restructuring the Executive Branch

Presidents have attempted to exercise more effective management by reorganizing departments and agencies. A President, however, is dependent on the willingness of Congress to cooperate with any reorganization plan he proposes.

A President may organize his personal staff as he wishes. If he wants to create or reorganize executive units below the level of the White House, he must either request Congress to make the changes, or he must initiate the reorganization and subject it to a legislative vote. In the first option, a President must persuade Congress to enact his reorganization plan into law. In the second, he must persuade it not to reject the plan that he proposes to initiate.

Asking Congress for legislation authorizing a specific executive reorganization can prove to be a very unpredictable exercise in presidential leadership. In 1977–78 President Carter, together with consumer interest groups and some business and labor groups, attempted to secure the adoption of a bill creating a powerful Consumer Protection Agency. Even after he cut back considerably on the powers of the proposed agency in a desperate effort to attract votes, the bill failed to win congressional approval. The U. S. Chamber of Commerce, the National Association of Manufacturers, and the Business Roundtable, three major national business groups, marshalled such widespread opposition throughout the country that all the efforts of the President and his allies to have Congress create an independent consumers' agency failed.

A second reorganization strategy is for a President himself to initiate the reorganization. In the 1930s Congress began permitting Presidents to assume the initiative in executive reorganizations by passing laws authorizing the chief executive to propose specific reorganization plans. Each proposal had to be submitted to Congress, which had sixty days in which to consider it. In the absence of a vote rejecting it in either the House or Senate during that period, the reorganization plan went into effect. Congress has continued to authorize Presidents to

"Help! I'm in danger of being run down!"

utilize the presidential reorganization–congressional veto strategy, although since 1964 Presidents have been prohibited from creating cabinet-level departments by this method.

Most such presidential reorganization plans have been allowed to go into effect. Between 1946 and 1973, for example, five Presidents proposed a total of ninety-nine reorganization plans, only twenty-two of which Congress rejected. In 1977, at President Carter's request, Congress extended for a three-year period the chief executive's authority to reorganize the executive branch in this manner.

Executive Privilege: Protecting Executive Leadership

Starting with George Washington, Presidents have advanced the doctrine of executive privilege to protect their leadership decisions within the executive branch against scrutiny by Congress and even the courts.

Under this doctrine, Presidents have not only withheld from Congress the documentation of certain executive decisions, but they have at times refused to permit their senior aides to testify before congressional committees. Such a privilege of immunity, Presidents have contended, is implied in the constitutional language that vests in them executive power. Hence, the separation of powers protects decision making at the top level of the executive branch from legislative and judicial examination.

Executive privilege is justified on two utilitarian grounds. Certain sensitive, top-level decisions, especially but not solely pertaining to military, diplomatic, and national security matters, are so critical to the interests of the country or the constitutional exercise of power by a President as to obligate him to shield them from scrutiny by Congress or the judiciary. In addition, Presidents require frank and freely given advice on controversial matters from their aides. To guarantee the continued availability of such advice, the confidentiality of their relations with their top advisers must be protected.

President Richard Nixon's administration made especially exaggerated claims in the name of executive privilege. At one point, his attorney general asserted that *every* executive communication and *every* executive employee was covered by executive privilege! President Nixon contended that former as well as present members of the White House staff were equally immune to congressional inquiry under the doctrine of executive privilege. Nixon's attempts to withhold knowledge of conversations between himself and his aides in the White House brought him into direct conflict with Congress, with a special prosecutor established to investigate charges of misconduct in the White House and with the courts. His continued refusal to release tapes of these conversations helped destroy his support within the country and Congress. The eventual publication of material from some the the tapes that the courts compelled him to give up contributed directly to his downfall as President.

Is executive privilege constitutional? Yes, said a unanimous U.S. Supreme Court in 1974 in an opinion explicitly recognizing the "constitutional underpinnings" of executive privilege. May the President invoke executive privilege at will? No, responded the Court. When the claims of executive privilege are unrelated to military, diplomatic, and national security matters, executive privilege must defer to the needs for evidence in criminal cases before the courts. In other words, fair administration of justice in a criminal trial *overrides* the constitutional authority of a President to guard the confidentiality of executive material unrelated to military, diplomatic, and national security matters.

The Court did not deal in this case with the authority of Congress to override a President's claim to executive privilege. This issue is still unresolved. If executive decision making relevant to military, diplomatic, and national security matters may legitimately be protected by executive privilege against judicial inquiry, may it also be withheld from Congress? Until the Court decides otherwise in some future case, Presidents will certainly continue to invoke executive privilege, in these and other policy areas, against congressional attempts to penetrate decision making at the top of the executive branch.

COMMANDER IN CHIEF

not allowed to declare wars

The Constitution designates the President commander in chief of the country's military forces. At the same time, the designers of the Constitution separated the policy-making power of committing the country to war from the executive power to carry on a war. Congress alone is empowered to declare war—that is, to make the fundamental policy decision; the President is merely given chief command over the armed forces.

In practice, however, Presidents have virtually assumed Congress's policy responsibility for determining whether the United States should engage in armed conflict with other countries. By ordering, as commander in chief, the armed forces to engage in such conflict, Presidents have used their military leadership position to make fundamental political decisions.

U.S. military conflict in Vietnam and Korea were only the most recent of a number of wars the United States waged that were not initiated by Congress. They were presidentially authorized wars, examples of the leadership potential inherent in the commander-in-chief role. In each conflict, the United States committed hundreds of thousands of troops and suffered heavy casualties. Although Congress did not officially declare war, at no time did it ever vote to disengage the United States from these wars. Instead, it appropriated billions of dollars to allow the executive branch to continue the armed conflict.

In the early 1970s, as the Vietnam War became increasingly unpopular, Congress finally began to assert itself, limiting the President's discretion. It forbade the President to bomb Cambodia as part of his strategy for winning in Vietnam. It also adopted a law that authorized Congress to cancel war-making decisions by Presidents. Although the *know* → War Powers Act of 1973 explicitly authorized the President to commit the armed services to conflict, it also authorized Congress to veto such action.

As commander in chief, the President acts as the supreme military leader. If he wishes, a President can take personal command of the forces in the field. He can make both strategic as well as tactical decisions that can have tremendous consequences for the conduct of hostilities and for the country's foreign policy. In World War II, for example, President Franklin D. Roosevelt decided that defeating Nazi Germany and its allies in Europe had the highest priority. Only then would the military concentrate on the Pacific area of conflict against Japan. President Harry S Truman made the awesome decision to drop the atomic bombs on Hiroshima and Nagasaki, which almost immediately induced the Japanese to surrender. To force the removal of long-range Russian missiles from Cuba, President Kennedy imposed a naval blockade around that Caribbean island. This led to a dramatic confrontation with the USSR.

Presidential leadership over the military forces extends to the selection and dismissal of their commanders. President Abraham Lincoln chose and discharged a number of generals before picking General U.S. Grant to lead the Union forces. President Truman fired General Douglas MacArthur from his position as commander of U.S. and U.N. troops in Korea for publicly disagreeing with the President's policies. For the same reason, President Carter relieved a major general from his command of the American forces in South Korea.

As commander in chief, the President may use the military to defend the country on his own initiative if it is attacked. In 1861, faced with a confederate attack on U.S. forts in southern states and the impending breakup of the Union, President Lincoln actually usurped some of the constitutional power of Congress in order to preserve the country. A quickly convened Congress ratified (legitimated) his actions. The modern President is the only person empowered to command the use of nuclear weapons.

Presidents may also deploy troops to resolve internal crises within the United States. President Eisenhower employed troops to enforce the desegregation of Central High School in Little Rock, Arkansas, and President Kennedy dispatched soldiers to put down violence associated with the desegregation of the University of Mississippi, two actions that testify to the leadership Presidents may assume in coping with major internal disorders.

Aside from its War Powers Act, Congress can limit the President as commander in chief through its authorization and appropriation powers. Presidents and Congress have clashed over authorizing and funding particular weapons systems, extending the military draft, and defining the role and strength of particular branches of the armed services. President Carter was opposed by the Air Force and its congressional supporters who wanted to build a new supersonic bomber and by the Navy and its congressional supporters who wanted more nuclear-powered aircraft carriers. Although the President prevailed in both these instances, such battles are not easily, or even always, won by the commander in chief.

© 1978 by Herblock in *The Washington Post*

"Damn pentagon pantywaists—they're just small-time spenders."

The courts, too, can constrain the leadership exercised by the President under the auspices of his commander-in-chief role. In order to avert a crippling stike during the Korean War, President Truman seized the steel mills from their private owners under his constitutional authority as commander in chief. In response to a challenge by the steel mill owners, a majority on the U.S. Supreme Court overruled the President and ordered him to return the mills.

HEAD OF FOREIGN AFFAIRS   *Speaks for entire nation*

As the recognized leader of the country in the field of foreign affairs, the President has enormous freedom of action in making foreign policy. In most of our relations with other countries, the voice of the President is, in fact, the voice of the United States.

Congress does, of course, participate in shaping foreign policy. The Constitution requires presidential treaties with other countries to come to the Senate for its approval, and both the House and Senate must appropriate funds if a President's foreign policy involves the spending of money. On the whole, however, Congress and the people tend to be much more concerned with domestic rather than foreign affairs. Moreover, Congress recognizes the importance of a single, authoritative voice speaking for the United States in the world arena, a function it is unable to perform. Congress also tends to defer to the President's unique access to information about international events. The need for secrecy and dispatch in this policy area further inhibits Congress from interfering in the President's conduct of foreign affairs.

Congress limits on policies

Shaping Foreign Policy

From a strategic point of view, as well as on a day-to-day basis, the President dominates the foreign policy making process. It is the President who establishes the main directions of American foreign policy and undertakes the policy initiatives to carry them out. For example, President Franklin D. Roosevelt decided that this country should normalize relations with the Union of Soviet Socialist Republics, and Presidents Nixon and Carter committed the United States to official relations with the People's Republic of China. Negotiation with the Soviet Union on strategic arms limitation agreements (SALT) has been pursued by a number of our recent Presidents, including President Carter. President Carter has also undertaken to shore up the NATO alliance, to improve U.S. relations with Mexico, to speak up for human rights in other countries, and to arrange a peace treaty between Egypt and Israel.

Almost all these foreign policy positions were taken at the initiative of the President; in pursuing them he placed his leadership reputation on the line. Congress may have been consulted; some legislators certainly spoke up. But the decisions were those of the President.

Official Link with the Rest of the World

The President is the chief diplomat for the country. He has virtually a free hand in choosing his principal diplomatic agents, the secretary of state and the American ambassadors to foreign countries and to the United Nations. His appointees must win approval in the Senate, but the legislators are disposed to follow the President's leadership in this respect. Once appointed, these agents are extensions of the President and, as such, speak for the country. The foreign policy positions he develops are automatically those they expound.

The leaders of other countries communicate directly with the President and his secretary of state as well as with the President's diplomatic representatives in their countries. The ambassadors from these countries present their credentials to the President as the legitimate representative of the United States. When necessary, they meet with the President or his secretary of state to convey the opinions and decisions of their countries' leaders.

The President also has the authority to cut off both linkages—that of the United States to a foreign country and that of the foreign country to the United States. He may recall the United States ambassador from a country, and he may demand that the diplomatic representative of that country in the United States leave this country.

Center of American International Information Networks

The President's foreign policy leadership is greatly enhanced by his unique access to information about the affairs, intentions, and potentials of other countries. A variety of networks service the intelligence needs of the President as leader of the country's foreign policy.

Day-to-day diplomatic intelligence flows either through the State Department or directly from American ambassadors to the President. The State Department engages in researching and assessing foreign data as well as in recommending and implementing foreign policy. The military services have their own attaches stationed in American embassies all over the world who feed information back to the Defense Department and, eventually, to the President. Futhermore, the Central Intelligence Agency, the government's civilian foreign espionage agency, collects information through its agents in other countries and digests and analyzes this data. Its director, a presidential appointee, also briefs and advises the President.

Restraints on the President's Leadership in Foreign Policy

Congress is the principal domestic constraint on presidential leadership in foreign policy. The Senate has power over treaties and both the House and Senate control the authorization of foreign aid programs and the appropriation of money to carry them out. Foreign policy initiatives that include the expenditure of money make the President vulnerable to the wishes of Congress.

Treaties with foreign countries often represent important policy commitments by the United States. It is the President who decides whether to seek a treaty and who is responsible for working out its terms with leaders of the other country (or countries). Only after the treaty is drawn up must a President come to the Senate for its approval. In the Senate a two-thirds majority of those voting must favor the treaty or else it fails. This means that only one-third plus one of those senators voting can block the treaty.

Impressed with how vulnerable they were to their congressional partners, Presidents have sometimes avoided making treaties in the face of Senate disapproval, have modified them to meet Senate objections, or have engaged in extensive national campaigning to induce the Senate to vote favorably for their treaties. After a strenuously fought campaign for public and Senate support in 1977–78, President Carter won approval for two treaties that turned the Panama Canal over to the Republic of Panama and guaranteed an American military presence there until the year 2000. To secure the necessary two-thirds support, the President had to agree to compromises in the treaties that satisfied the objections of certain senators. Even with these compromises the treaties barely won the required votes.

Presidents can avoid a confrontation with the Senate over treaties by resorting to what are called *executive agreements.* These are understandings negotiated between the heads of countries. Most executive agreements are administrative arrangements that do not represent major policy decisions. Sometimes, however, executive agreements do have tremendous policy implications. In 1940, when Canada was at war with Germany and the United States was still neutral, President Franklin D. Roosevelt negotiated an executive agreement with the Canadian Prime Minister to establish a joint defense board. Before Pearl Harbor in 1941, the President traded fifty American destroyers to Great Britain in return for American military bases extending from Canada into the Caribbean and South America. Neither agreement was ever referred to the Senate.

Should a President's foreign policy initiative or treaty call for the spending of money, the consent of both the House and Senate is required. No money may be spent by the President unless Congress first authorizes and then appropriates the necessary funds. A presidential policy to supply other countries with military or economic assistance must therefore also become congressional policy. The legislators may give the President, with some deletion or addition, the authority and sums he requests, or they may reject his proposal altogether.

Congress has developed three additional options in responding to presidential proposals for foreign aid. It can adopt the President's policy, but forbid him to assist a particular country. In the aftermath of the 1974 Turkish invasion of Cyprus, Congress imposed an embargo on American arms sales to Turkey. When it subsequently became apparent that this action had failed to compel Turkey to make concessions on Cyprus and that Turkey was appraising its relations with the Soviet

Union, the President was able to persuade Congress to repeal its embargo.

A congressional option that affords the President more discretion is exemplified by laws forbidding aid to specific countries but authorizing the President, under certain conditions, to overrule Congress. Amendments in 1976 to the Foreign Assistance Act forbid economic aid to such African countries as Angola, Mozambique, Tanzania, and Zambia, unless the President determines that such assistance would "further the foreign policy interests of the United States" and so informs Congress.

Still another option stresses presidential leadership initiatives but reserves a veto to Congress. The 1976 Arms Export Control Act gives *Know* Congress the authority to disapprove major arms sales to countries decided upon by the President. Such presidential policy proposals must be brought to Congress. Only a vigorous lobbying campaign by President Carter prevented the imposition of a congressional veto on a package sale of military aircraft to Egypt, Saudi Arabia, and Israel. Since both houses had to disapprove in order to exercise the congressional veto, victory for the President's foreign policy in the Senate meant victory in Congress.

Presidents have complained that such congressional restrictions rob the White House of the flexibility it needs to accommodate American foreign policy to the complex, rapidly shifting developments in the world. Members of Congress recognize this dilemma, but they maintain

Chief diplomat ⇒ Can recieve people

Paul Conrad. Reprinted by permission

"One at a time, dammit, one at a time!"

that, if they are to have any significant voice in foreign policy, such legislative controls are absolutely necessary.

Domestic constraints on the President's leadership in foreign affairs are also found outside of Congress. The State Department, the special executive unit responsible for assessing and carrying out foreign policy, has sometimes refused to move in the direction and with the speed and spirit Presidents have deemed necessary. In addition, a number of interest groups lobby in Congress and try to shape public opinion on foreign policy issues. Sometimes their goals are identical with those of the President, but at other times they contradict presidential policies, bringing these interest groups into conflict with the President.

In the international arena, the allies of the United States may also operate to constrain the President. Their security interests do not always coincide with the foreign policies he advocates. Or they may view particular international issues from a very different perspective than that taken by the President. To the extent that a President must compromise with them in behalf of a common policy or that they refuse to follow his lead, the President's leadership in shaping foreign policy is limited.

International opponents of the United States also limit the President's leadership. In negotiating with the leaders of the USSR and the People's Republic of China, the President often has to compromise and adjust to their demands. Their foreign policies frequently challenge and undermine those of the President in different parts of the world. In fact, the foreign policy initiatives of these opponents often place the President in a position of reacting to their leadership rather than asserting his own.

CHIEF OF STATE

A chief of state symbolizes the governmental system of a country and its people. Whoever is chief of state stands as a unifying symbol over and above the normal conflict of politics. Many other political systems have chiefs of state who are separate officials from their partisan executive leaders; in contrast, the American presidency combines the chief-of-state role with the other more controversial leadership roles.

A chief-of-state role is basically a ceremonial one with which Americans can identify regardless of political party, interest group, race, sex, religion, or region. When the President throws out the first ball of the professional baseball season, the President is acting as chief of state, symbolically lending the dignity of the nation to the national sport. The same principle applies when a President initiates the March of Dimes or other campaigns to raise money to fight certain diseases. On these occasions, the President symbolically acts for all Americans and the campaigns thereby become national American undertakings.

One set of powers associated with the chief-of-state role enhances the image of the President as a magnanimous leader. Representing the nation as a whole, the President is empowered by the Constitution to dispense mercy by granting pardons "for offenses against the United States except in cases of impeachment." A President may grant full pardons, commute (reduce) sentences, or delay the executions of individuals who violate national laws. A President may also grant amnesty—pardon entire groups of people, en masse. None of these acts may be overridden by Congress.

The latest, most dramatic example of the exercise of the pardoning power was President Gerald R. Ford's pardon of former President Richard M. Nixon in 1974, after Nixon resigned the presidency rather than face impeachment charges. Although Nixon had not been convicted of any crimes, this pardon absolved him fully of any criminal charges that might have been brought against him because of his conduct in office. An example of amnesty was President Abraham Lincoln's Proclamation of Pardon and Reconstruction in 1863, which pardoned most secessionists, provided they swore an oath of allegiance to the United States and accepted the laws and proclamations abolishing slavery. In the 1970s Presidents Ford and Carter both offered amnesty to Vietnam draft evaders.

In pursuing his other leadership roles, the President benefits greatly from the opportunity to be chief of state. As the symbol of the nation, he evokes from Americans feelings of respect, reverence, and unity. By capitalizing on this reservoir of good will and solidarity, a President is enhanced in his ability to fill his other roles, all of which involve him in conflict.

SHAPER OF PUBLIC OPINION

polls - public opinion

The President is also a moral leader who helps shape public opinion in the country. President Theodore Roosevelt once characterized the presidency as a "bully pulpit," a strategic and visible position from which to offer moral leadership to the people. Presidents must, in fact, be teachers, helping the people understand and accept the sacrifices that have to be made for the good of the country. A President must also help people raise their vision, and he must articulate for them the ideals and aspirations of the nation.

Presidents are not always able to rally public opinion behind what they feel is crucial for the country. For example, President Carter's television address to the nation appealing to Americans to consider the energy crisis the "moral equivalent of war" failed to inspire in the people a sense of great crisis and a willingness to sacrifice. Nevertheless, a President must try to rally the nation, for with a supportive public behind him, his ability to act as a leader on controversial issues is greatly enhanced.

Panama Canal

PARTY LEADER → not much power

A President is the leader of one of the major political parties. This position affords him opportunities for bridging the separation of powers, for blunting the checks and balances in the national government, and for surmounting the divisions inherent in federalism. Members of Congress and many governors who share his party affiliation recognize that he is their national party leader. A President may not always succeed in securing their cooperation, but their common party identification is an important link in his calling on them for support. To capitalize on his party leader role so as to help him carry out his other leadership roles, a President must work at cultivating his party and strengthening his position within it.

Having previously ignored many established party figures, President Carter set out in 1978 to mend his fences in the Democratic party. State party leaders had complained that they had no meaningful access to the White House and that they were being bypassed in the selection of patronage appointments. The hostile atmosphere that developed threatened to weaken the campaign of Democratic candidates in the 1978 elections and to hurt the President's chances for being renominated by his party in 1980. This antagonism toward the President from within his own party was illustrated in comments to the press by an aide to a Democratic congressional leader in 1977: "The President seems to forget that it was the Democratic Party that won the election for him, and that party feels that it has a right to share in organizing the government."

The Carter White House actively sought to improve its strained relations with the Democratic National Committee and the state parties. In January 1978, for the first time since January 1977 when the President was inaugurated, the full Democratic National Committee (360 members) was invited to the White House for a candlelight and champagne reception with President and Mrs. Carter. In addition, the President and his senior staff organized a series of breakfast meetings in the White House with groups of state party chairmen.

A special office for political coordination was established in the White House to coordinate political activities (including patronage appointments) with the rest of the Democratic party. President Carter and Vice President Mondale promised to participate more actively in party affairs in the future. According to one presidential aide, these new efforts represented "a recognition that we didn't handle our contacts with the party as well as we should have last year." The President personally apologized to the members of his party's national committee for having neglected to support it, and he assured them that he needed them. He called for their help to ensure "that a wall is not built between me and the country."

⟶ *Propose budget, lightening rod for criticizim + praise*

The modern President has become the principal economic leader in the country. By making the President responsible for designing a comprehensive executive budget, Congress placed the President in a unique position to shape the course of the economic system. The present budget for goods and services to the governments and people of the country exceeds half a trillion dollars. In proposing a budget to Congress, the President must consider its possible impact upon the economy and whether a deficit or surplus is desirable for coping with the country's economic problems. He must determine whether the economy requires tax and spending policies to depress or to accelerate economic activity.

Know — Congress also officially committed the national government to preserve the health of the economic system by enacting the Employment Act of 1946, which calls for the President to assess the state of the national economy and to propose measures to ensure employment and prosperity. The President, moreover, appoints the chairman of the Federal Reserve Board and tries to work closely with that agency to determine both the supply of money and the availability of credit in the country. Both Congress and the people expect the President to provide economic leadership. When the economy falters, they blame him; when it revives or prospers, they praise him.

As an economic leader the President acts under enormous constraints. Congress must be induced to give its consent to taxing and spending legislation and to legislation regulating the private economic sector. It can reject the President's proposals or reshape them as it wishes. Within the executive branch, the President is also not in full control of the policy-making machinery as it affects the economic system. The independent, economic-oriented regulatory agencies cooperate with the President in economic planning and action only if their perception of the economy and the measures for dealing with it coincide with his.

Within the private sector, a President has very little power to affect economic decisions. A President can reason, plead, or threaten. But without congressional authorization, he cannot order business, industry, farmers, labor unions, or the professions to control prices, wages or salaries, to produce more, or to improve the quality of their services. Sometimes presidential appeals do have an effect. When some major steel producers announced their intention to raise prices in 1962, President Kennedy's tough personal and public appeals to the other steel companies induced them not to follow suit, and the price leaders in the industry retreated. "Jawboning," the President's public and private exhortations to private economic decision makers, is not always that effective. To combat inflation in 1978, President Carter twice asked

Also congresse limits

business and labor leaders to voluntarily restrict wage and price increases in accordance with his proposed guidelines. While business leaders tended to respond favorably, labor leaders were divided.

The President is also constrained in his economic leadership by the decisions of political leaders in countries whose economies interact significantly with that of the United States. President Carter was only partially successful in persuading the Japanese leaders to voluntarily curb their exports to the United States and to increase their imports from this country. The determination of the new leaders in Iran in 1979 to curtail their production of oil and the decision of OPEC, the world oil cartel, to raise the price of crude oil, hit the United States particularly hard, at a time when the President was trying to cope with the problem of rising inflation.

CHIEF LEGISLATOR → *must address Congress 3 times a yr.*

Panama Canal

The Constitution gives the President a share in the legislature's powers (a veto over congressional bills) and mandates that he annually send to Congress his assessment of the State of the Union. In effect, this lays the basis for the President's role as chief legislator. Congress also expects him to take on this role, despite the ambivalence of the legislators themselves toward presidential leadership. As members of an independent branch of government—elected by the people and empowered by the Constitution—they feel that legislating for the country is basically their prerogative and that the President is an outsider. Yet they also want and expect the President to present Congress with a program of legislative action and to intervene in its behalf.

Not just the Constitution and Congress, but the thrust of their other roles compels Presidents to offer legislative leadership. As party leaders who competed for their parties' nomination and then the popular votes in the general election, Presidents have had to articulate a program of national action, much of which can only be realized through congressional action. Presidents *must* also intervene in Congress to carry out their responsibilities as chief executive, commander in chief, foreign policy head, and leader of the economy.

A President who fails to provide Congress with policy direction, neglects the politics of fashioning majorities, avoids key decisions on timing or compromise, or is indifferent to the needs and desires of individual legislators can dangerously undermine his ability to be the national leader his roles demand. Failure to achieve success in the Congress weakens a President in the eyes of the people. In turn, a low rating in the public opinion polls can adversely affect his leadership in

Congress. When his public prestige is high, legislators are more likely to accept presidential guidelines; when it is low, they are more inclined to ignore or oppose his leadership.

Formal Tools for Leading Congress

Presidents have a number of formal tools for carrying out their legislative leadership role. Some are mandatory; they must be employed. Others are optional; they depend on the political judgment and skill of the President. Some are constitutional in origin, although the Constitution does not call for a President to be the chief legislator. Others are congressional in origin, reflecting the disposition of Congress to turn to the President for policy guidance. All enhance the potential of the President to be the chief leader of Congress.

Presidential messages to Congress. Both the Constitution and Congress call upon the President to address the Congress on certain topics of national importance. Presidents have no choice; they must comply. The nature of these messages reveals that both the Constitution and Congress intend Presidents to offer legislative leadership.

Each January the President must deliver three messages to Congress. His State of the Union Message, the only one mandated by the Constitution, indicates to Congress (and today via radio and television to the American people) the President's assessment of the general situation of the nation. This message points up the problems facing the country and indicates in general terms how the President feels we should respond.

Congress itself asked for regular policy guidance from the President when it adopted the Budget Act of 1921. Each year the President is required to recommend to the legislature a budget, an expenditure plan for the entire national government. Thus Congress has placed the President in the position of offering it leadership through a comprehensive plan of action for government stated in monetary terms. A presidential message explains the budget and urges its adoption.

Congress may cut, add, ignore, or rearrange what the President proposes. But its policy considerations are conducted within the framework of the President's plan. In effect, the legislators have said to the President: "We cannot put together a comprehensive expenditure plan of our own. Please help us. Tell us what to do." Even now that Congress has begun to develop its own comprehensive budget program, it still waits for the President's budget proposal before beginning to work on its own.

Congress once more turned to the President for leadership in the Employment Act of 1946. It requires him to submit each year an Economic Report. In the message accompanying this report on the state of the economy, the President makes recommendations to Congress for protecting and improving the economic health of the country.

In these three messages, the President spells out to Congress and the people what he expects the national government to do. On the basis of these leadership guidelines, the President and the executive departments draft their own bills and submit them to Congress to be transformed into law. Since presidential requests to key legislators to introduce these bills are rarely rejected, the key policy bills of the President become the key items on the agenda of Congress. The major policy matters that face the Congress are, therefore, primarily determined by the President. Congress wants and expects such leadership.

The Constitution also authorizes the President to send messages to Congress any time the President wants to call its attention to some matter. When the President sends individual bills to the Congress, they are accompanied by these presidential messages, which explain why the President is proposing the legislation and what it will accomplish. Presidential messages catch the attention of the national media as well as Congress, which helps embellish the President's image as a legislative leader.

The veto.   After Congress adopts a bill, the legislation must come to the President for his decision. The President has a ten-day period, excluding Sundays, to decide whether to agree to the legislation or reject it. His signing the bill transforms it into law. It also automatically becomes law if he takes no action on it within the ten-day period while Congress is still in session.

Should he oppose the bill, the President has two options: a *veto* or a *pocket veto*. A veto is a formal rejection by the President. Should the legislature be in session in the ten-day period after he receives the bill, the vetoed bill must be returned to Congress for reconsideration. Congress is constitutionally empowered to override his veto. But because of the two-thirds majorities needed in both houses to override a veto, most presidential vetoes prevail. In essence, Presidents can effectively stop most congressional policy making if they strongly disagree with it.

Should Congress have adjourned during the ten-day period after it has sent the legislation to the White House, the President's refusal to sign automatically kills the bill. This is called a *pocket veto*. In effect, he puts the bill into his pocket and forgets about it, for with Congress not in session, there is no legislature to consider his action. Since Congress has no opportunity to override the President's decision, a pocket veto is absolute in its effect.

A veto is primarily a tool allowing a President to react to Congress's initiative. However, the very *threat* of a presidential veto can be used to deter or even shape legislation. In the face of a President's warning that he will exercise his veto, legislators may conclude that it would be futile to proceed with their bill, or they may alter it to coincide more closely with his wishes.

Convening and dissolving Congress.   Presidents are empowered by the Constitution to convene Congress into a special session. Rarely do Presidents take advantage of this power any more, since Congress has taken to remaining in regular session a major part of each year. Moreover, a specially convened Congress need not accept the agenda proposed for it by the President.

No President has ever dissolved a Congress. The Constitution authorizes a President to do so *only* if the two houses cannot agree on an adjournment date. But Congress has never failed to do so. It is even doubtful whether a President would presume to dissolve such a Congress, for his action might readily be misconstrued by the media, the people, and the Congress as arbitrary executive interference in congressional affairs.

Informal Tools for Leading Congress   *pork barreling ⟹ money going to State*

If the President wishes, he can employ a wide range of informal devices to induce Congress to take the policy positions he deems proper. Some of these devices are, in fact, more effective than the formal ones. All, however, depend upon the political will, astuteness, and skill of the President and his executive associates.

Personally participating in congressional politics.   Presidents may personally take their case to Congress in a variety of ways. These range from addressing a joint session of Congress to meeting with individual legislators.

Normally, Presidents send most of their formal messages to Congress. But when they feel it necessary to dramatize their case, they may address in person joint sessions of the two houses. Such appearances take on the character of major national events, since presidential speeches are now carried by television and radio to the general public. Only a few such direct appeals to Congress are undertaken each year; otherwise, they would lose their impact.

Campaigns to enact presidentially proposed legislation almost always require detailed and selective contact with members of Congress.

A President must narrow his attention to smaller and smaller groups of key legislators, eventually to those few who are undecided or listed as opposed, but who may be turned around by special appeals.

Large numbers of legislators may be invited to the White House by the President to meet with him and his top aides. Sometimes these invitations are strictly social occasions—a formal dinner, dance, or concert—and are intended simply to generate good will, on which the President may later capitalize. At other times, he may invite smaller groups to a briefing at the White House, where the President and his aides present facts and arguments to justify their case. The honor of being invited to these more intimate gatherings is supplemented by the direct appeal made by the President and his aides and by the opportunity afforded the legislators to question them. Such meetings are clearly more focused than the purely social gatherings and are intended to generate support for specific presidential positions.

In 1977, anxious to circumvent the chairman of the House Government Operations Committee, who opposed recommending a renewal of the President's authority to reorganize the executive branch, President Carter invited members of that committee to a series of meetings in the White House. "It's the thing that the President does best," said one of the participants to the press. "He takes a small group of people and strokes us. At the end of the meeting, I don't think there was anyone in that room who wasn't for him." The chairman of the committee acknowledged ruefully that his opposition to the reorganization proposals had been effectively undermined by the President. "He's romancing them, and they're easily got," he exclaimed in disgust. Of course, not all such presidential meetings with committee members conclude that favorably for a President.

A President may also appeal to members of Congress on a one-to-one basis. He may call the legislator on the phone or invite a particular House or Senate member to the White House for a personal talk in order to make his case. President Carter, for example, strongly committed himself to helping New York City obtain long-term aid from Congress. In the Senate, the chairman of the relevant standing committee opposed such long-term aid. To swing the uncommitted members of that committee, the President, as well as his secretary of the treasury, personally telephoned these senators. When the committee voted, it approved the bill by a margin of one vote.

As *the* national leader of his political party, a President makes special claims on the legislative members of that party. Regularly, sometimes weekly, Presidents meet with their legislative party leaders to discuss the agenda of the two chambers and the state of the President's legislation and to coordinate strategy and tactics. The President seeks to enlist them as key members of his own team. His legislative party leaders normally offer advice and try to assist the President in their respective houses.

Inducements to individual legislators.   Presidents can only try to influence legislators to support their positions. They have no authority to command obedience or power to enforce compliance. However, they do have a number of incentives they can offer legislators to secure cooperation.

As a rule, Presidents and their aides try to persuade legislators on the merits of their case. Although this method may succeed with some legislators on particular issues, merit alone may not suffice to persuade those who are indifferent to the President's proposal, whose constituencies are unaffected by it, or who may be exposed to political risk by voting their support. And obviously, opponents are rarely affected by this approach.

As an inducement for winning support from legislators, Presidents have attractive incentives that benefit both the legislators and their constituencies. Because they exercise considerable discretion over the allocation of executive resources, Presidents can locate special projects (dams and laboratories, for example), and they can award contracts to businesses and industries in the legislators' constituencies. They can also promise jobs for favored constituents. Legislators are keenly aware that executive leaders can delay or withhold these benefits, or even transfer them elsewhere if they so desire.

For legislators interested in advancing their own bills, Presidents can offer different sorts of incentives. For example, the President can induce other legislators to offer their support. Or presidential opposition to bills can be withdrawn or presidential support announced. A President is an imposing legislative ally, one whom House members and senators prefer to have on their side. A President who opposes their bills can prove to be a formidable opponent.

A President may also offer campaign services to members of his legislative party. As a newsworthy figure, his presence in a legislator's campaign can rally the party faithful and attract considerable publicity for the candidate. A President can sometimes help a legislator raise campaign funds. Of course, a President whose popularity is low finds that his campaign offers do not appeal to most legislators. As another incentive, Presidents often transform the act of signing bills into a media-covered public ceremony. An invitation to the White House lawn for the ceremony and press coverage affords the key supporters of the legislation additional honor and valuable publicity.

Using executive officials and interest groups to influence Congress.   No President has the time, energy, or inclination to devote himself entirely to his legislative leadership role. He must attend to his other roles, and those of foreign affairs leader and chief executive are exceptionally demanding. Moreover, Presidents cannot effectively carry out their congressional leadership role by themselves. They must rely on other executive officials and interest groups to help campaign for presidential programs within Congress.

Recent Presidents have built up special legislative liaison staffs in the White House to keep in touch with Congress. These aides act as both intelligence agents and advocates for the President; in effect, they are presidential lobbyists. Other senior White House assistants are also used occasionally as lobbyists. In addition, the heads of the executive departments and agencies and their legislative liaison staffs are occasionally asked to lobby for presidential policy goals in Congress.

Presidents also reach out to interest groups for help with Congress. Those whose policy positions coincide with the legislative goals of Presidents are brought in as allies to campaign for congressional votes. With their own lobbying staffs and special access to the legislators as well as to their home constituencies, these groups can help in legislative campaigns. They furnish intelligence on what legislators are thinking, what they intend to do, the compromises and amendments that can be worked out, and the shifts in position of individual legislators. Their lobbyists can be used to garner votes, and the leaders of interest groups themselves can mobilize their membership to express public opinion in behalf of presidential objectives.

Appealing directly to the people.   By appealing directly to the people, Presidents try to generate constituent support, to which legislators are sensitive. The television and radio networks almost invariably accord the President free time to address the nation. A national presidential address is a dramatic event. It preempts most of the originally scheduled programs and it not only captures the attention of millions of Americans but also receives widespread press coverage. Hence its attractiveness to Presidents who hope to motivate Americans to communicate support for presidential proposals to their legislators.

Presidents also make personal appearances in various parts of the country to enlist the support of the people. Sometimes select groups of people are brought to the White House so the President and his senior aides can try to convince them of the merits of the President's legislation. The purpose for employing these approaches to the public remains the same in each case: to build a rapport between the people and their President and to sell them on the merits of the President's proposals; to motivate them to communicate their support to their legislators; and to stimulate them to urge others to contact members of Congress in behalf of presidential goals.

An Example of Successful Use of Presidential Tools: The Panama Canal Treaties

Senate adoption of the Panama Canal treaties in 1978 reflected a superbly orchestrated congressional campaign by the Carter White House. It illustrated perfectly how a President can lead Congress when he and his aides play their political cards correctly. Securing the Senate's approval of the treaties posed an extremely difficult problem for the President. The United States was voluntarily giving up an invaluable strategic asset and receiving little in return. The treaties called for the American government to transfer ownership and control of the Canal to the Panamanian government and for United States troops to be withdrawn from the Canal Zone by the year 2000.

The treaties generated an emotional, well-organized opposition on the part of conservative senators (and House members) from both major parties. An aggressive public relations campaign was mounted by conservative interest groups to make certain public opinion overwhelmingly opposed the treaties and constituent feelings were forcefully expressed to senators. Initially, public opinion polls indicated that opponents outnumbered proponents. Moreover, the opponents had a great advantage in the Senate itself. They did not need to convince a majority of senators to oppose the treaties. Because treaties must be approved by two-thirds of those voting, opponents needed only one-third plus one to beat the President.

The White House not only faced the difficult task of generating favorable public opinion, but it also had to put together a super majority in the Senate. So controversial were the treaties that the White House had to assume the entire membership would vote. Therefore, its bottom line was sixty-seven senators. Since some Democratic senators were obviously defecting, the Democratic President had to win over senators from the opposition party. Fortunately, former Republican Presidents had favored negotiating a Panama Canal treaty, and the last Republican President, Gerald R. Ford, supported his Democratic successor.

The Carter administration pursued a sophisticated, multilevel approach to win over the general public and the Senate. An all-out effort was made to mobilize specific publics in behalf of the treaties and to shape a favorable response among the general public. From August 1977 through January 1978, for example, nineteen meetings with different sets of public opinion leaders were held at the White House. Some 1500 bankers, businessmen, editors, labor leaders, religious leaders, and others were personally briefed by the President and his top diplomatic and military aides. These public opinion leaders were asked to join the President in this campaign, to speak up for the treaties in their communities, and to use the mass media to stimulate people to communicate their support for the treaties to their senators.

The White House also concentrated on fifteen states in which one or both senators remained undecided. Administration spokesmen made over six hundred appearances in these states in an effort to help shape public opinion. Large town meetings were staged in a number of cities with the cooperation of the Foreign Policy Association, a prominent, respectable private group. The President addressed these meetings from the White House over a special telephone hookup and the secretary of state appeared at several of them. Not only did the Administration help its allies organize a special interest group of their own to work for the treaties, but the President made personal appeals to a number of established interest groups for their support. And, before the Senate voted, the President delivered a special television address to the nation, appealing for the understanding and support of the people. As a result of all these efforts, public opinion shifted. Public opinion polls before the key vote in the Senate revealed that more Americans now favored the treaties than opposed them.

The President's principal lobbyist in Congress, plus the lobbyist representing the State Department, coordinated the campaign within the Senate itself. Senators who were committed to the treaties were assisted with facts and arguments for the Senate debate. Uncommitted senators became the chief targets of the White House. During the final days of the debate on the first of the two treaties, the Vice President met almost daily with senators who were listed as undecided and with opponents whose votes the administration believed it could change. The President telephoned individual senators and held a series of meetings with uncommitted senators a week before the vote. He not only spoke in favor of the treaties but, like a good politician, asked how he could be helpful to the senators: what legislation did they want and what projects were they seeking for their states; if they were Democrats up for reelection, he asked how he best could help in their campaigns.

Approximately two weeks before the vote, the White House reversed itself and supported a plan to buy $250 million worth of copper for the country's strategic stockpile. The uncommitted Democratic senator from Arizona, a copper mining state, had requested such a reversal. A week before the vote, the White House quietly dropped its opposition to a $23 billion emergency farm bill, conforming with the wishes of an uncommitted southern senator whose vote it was seeking. One high administration official was reported to have exclaimed: "I hope the Panamanians will get as much out of these treaties as some United States Senators." To win the last crucial votes, the administration also agreed to a reinterpretation of the treaties so as to satisfy the Democratic senator from Arizona. The final vote on the initial treaty justified all the efforts of the Carter administration. The President and his associates won by a margin of two votes.

Obstacles to Presidential Leadership in Congress

Presidents face a variety of special obstacles in their attempts to lead Congress. These impediments arise from conditions outside the Congress, the two-party system within the national legislature, the ability and style of the President himself, and the independent leadership systems in the Congress.

The absence of a recognized crisis. One type of obstacle is the absence of a feeling of crisis on the part of the people and Congress when the President calls for new directions. A crisis acts as a solvent, dissolving much resistance to change and therefore to new presidential initiatives.

Compare Franklin D. Roosevelt's leadership during the initial one hundred days of his administration with Jimmy Carter's initial year or so. Roosevelt came into office in 1933 when the country was already in the depths of a catastrophic depression. Business and agriculture were in a state of collapse, approximately one-third the work force was unemployed, and millions of Americans were frightened or had lost hope. In this environment, virtually every piece of legislation proposed by President Roosevelt, no matter how novel, was eagerly passed by Congress in his first one hundred days.

In 1977–78 President Carter's attempts to lead Congress to adopt a comprehensive energy policy ran head-on into the disbelief that the country really faced a crisis of overwhelming proportions. Through the mass media he warned that the energy crisis confronted the country with the moral equivalent of a war and that it demanded immediate legislative action. But he convinced neither the general public nor Congress. As a result, Congress took almost two years to respond to the President's proposals, and he barely won a very watered-down version of what he requested.

Legislative party opposition. A President who faces a Congress in which the opposing party has a majority can encounter considerable problems as a chief legislator. In such a case, the Speaker and the majority leader in each house have no party obligation to cooperate with the President. Indeed, they may decide that it is to their party's advantage to oppose major portions of his program and to embarrass him by investigating the executive branch. A Republican-controlled Congress aggressively fought the domestic programs Democratic President Harry S Truman advanced in 1947–48. A searching investigation of Republican President Richard M. Nixon was conducted by a Democratic-controlled Senate through its Watergate Committee, and as a consequence a Democratic-dominated House Judiciary Committee voted to impeach him. It is questionable whether a Congress controlled by the President's party would have so aggressively pursued the Watergate scandal involving the President, his White House, and his campaign organization.

Legislative members of the President's own party may also oppose his leadership. A number of Democratic senators adamantly opposed President Carter's Panama Canal treaties, his energy legislation, and his proposal that Congress combine military aid to Israel, Egypt, and Saudi Arabia in one package. When the Democratic President vetoed a public works bill in 1978, over strong objections by his party leaders in Congress, the Democratic majority leaders of the Senate and the House as well as the Democratic Speaker led the fight to override the President. The President won this fight in the House, thereby killing the bill, but the majority of his fellow Democrats had joined their legislative party leaders in voting to override his veto.

The President himself may be a major obstacle. A major impediment to effective presidential leadership in Congress may be the President himself. An innovative President is tempted to overload the congressional agenda. Since the machinery of Congress is designed to move slowly, except in emergencies, committees often cannot cope with a large number of presidential proposals. In addition, his party leaders in Congress may find themselves without presidential guidance in determining which items, among the many on the President's agenda, have priority status: which is he willing to sacrifice and which is his "must" legislation.

Underlying this confusion and concern with priorities often lies another problem. Each major innovation offered by the President inevitably results in a bruising political battle. To the dismay of a President's party leaders in Congress, these fights tend to split their own legislative party and prove perilous for their members. Supporting a President's position on a very controversial bill may hurt these legislators in their constituencies and threaten their relations with their allied interest groups.

In his first year in office President Carter presented Congress with a long list of controversial proposals, all of which he insisted had to be adopted: a national energy plan; major tax reform; revision of the Civil Service system; overhaul of the welfare system; abandonment of the B-1 bomber; Panama Canal treaties; voter registration reform; and many more. By the end of that first year, he had won only a few. The Democratic Speaker of the House repeatedly warned the President that he was pushing too much onto Congress and that he had to establish his priorities. Major battles over some of these issues generated hostility and bewilderment on the part of many Democrats and some committees could not cope with all the legislation the President wanted them to process.

As a consequence, the reputation of President Carter as chief legislator suffered. By the end of the first year, his Vice President conceded that a presidentially imposed overload had resulted in an adverse effect on both the bills the President wanted and on the relations between Congress and the President: " . . . we found out in this first year . . . that one must be careful not to overcrowd the institution and try to solve too much too rapidly."

Another major mistake a President can make is to be insensitive to the political needs of individual legislators: to fail to consult with them, to propose actions that threaten their constituencies, to ignore their personal political problems. One of President Carter's first moves in Congress absolutely infuriated many legislators from water-hungry western states. Without first consulting the legislators whose districts and states were affected, the President publicly warned that he would kill a number of major irrigation and flood control projects that Congress had already authorized. Almost all the members of Congress affected by his decision saw his action as a deliberate slap in their face and as one that threatened them politically in their constituencies.

Despite the President's public avowals that he would never yield, a number of these projects were restored by Congress, and the President finally settled for only one-half of his original goal. Not only did the fight leave many Democratic legislators suspicious of their own President and his legislative party leaders split, but the President's retreat convinced many in Congress that he was weak and could be beaten by a determined opposition. The Senate Democratic floor leader actually wrote to the President warning him not to make major decisions without first consulting Congress.

Obviously referring to the costly price the President had paid in Congress, the Vice President announced in December 1977 that the President's new approach in 1978 would include more advance consultation with congressional leaders. The White House, he promised, would lean toward "precooking" its legislative proposals rather than developing them in secrecy. In December 1977 one of the President's closest political confidants, his wife, conceded in a national television interview that the President's most important mistake of the year was "not consulting in the very beginning with Congress as much as he could have."

Resentment by Democratic legislators over what they saw as indifference on the part of the Carter administration to their personal political needs led to a series of defections among them on some of his bills. In 1978 over one hundred Democrats in the House shocked the White House by defecting on its consumer protection bill. Their votes, together with those of the Republicans, were enough to defeat the bill. A week later, at an emotional meeting of twenty-six Democratic whips, many said they saw little reason to support an administration that had been indifferent to their needs. "The President has no money in the bank up here," declared a regional whip who had sponsored the bill.

Later that year, as a way of relaying their resentment to the White House, a number of Democrats—most of whom were ordinarily administration supporters—again defected on a bill which the administration wanted and helped defeat it. One of these Democrats pointed out that they had found an occasion "to send them [the White House] a bit of a message."

The Democratic whip in the House met with the President to help him fully understand the complaints of his party's legislators. Among the complaints were these: The administration had failed to consult them on appointments in their own districts; their recommendations on grants and contracts were ignored by his executive leaders; executive departments did not notify legislators when awards were made in their districts, which prevented them from benefiting politically from the announcements; and their telephone calls to administration officials were not being returned. "Democrats here want the President to be sensitive to their concerns as he wants them to be sensitive to his concerns," the Democratic whip reported to the press. "We've got to communicate the sense that we're all on the same team."

The independence of official and party leaders of Congress. The fact that the President has no voice in or control over the organization of decision-making systems in the House and Senate presents him with still another major obstacle in trying to lead Congress. His party leaders are chosen within their legislative parties; therefore, they are independent leaders in their own right. A President must negotiate with them; he cannot order them to comply with his leadership decisions. Since the committee and subcommittee leaders are also chosen independently of the President, they too are free to cooperate or oppose his leadership as they wish.

PRESIDENTIAL DILEMMAS

Modern Presidents confront a number of dilemmas which are inherent in their office. Each arises out of the leadership potential that characterizes the presidency. And each complicates a President's problems as a leader.

Americans expect a great deal more from Presidents than they can perform. In part, Presidents are themselves to blame for this since, as presidential candidates, they tend to make extravagant campaign promises. And, in part, the people are themselves to blame. They tend to expect results merely because Presidents announce a policy or call for action. The power potential of Presidents to shape foreign and domestic policy does not always coincide with these high expectation levels.

Demands for leadership are constantly being made upon the President by Congress, his political party, our allies, various interest groups, the press, the general public, and parts of the executive branch. However, his power to make binding authoritative decisions that others must obey is very limited. The President is constrained by the Constitution, the independent powers of Congress and the courts, the massiveness, inertia and resistance of the executive bureaucracy, and the independence of the regulatory commissions. The absence of central discipline and cohesion within the President's own political party and the influence of a variety of interest groups impose additional restraints upon presidential leadership. So, too, does the independence of decision makers in the private, domestic economy and of the leaders of foreign countries.

As a leader, the President initiates and implements policy decisions that major segments of the public inevitably find objectionable. The President's proposals to Congress, his handling of foreign policy, his calls for the nation to pursue moral goals, his use of troops, and his management of the executive branch and of the economy are all bound to arouse the opposition of some parts of the population. They disagree over the wisdom of his policy decisions or feel their own self-interest to be adversely affected.

President Carter's civil service reforms angered the major veterans' interest groups as well as the federal employees' unions, which complained that the interests of veterans and civil servants were being subverted. His call for Senate approval of the Panama Canal treaties led conservative groups and others within the general population to accuse the President of unnecessarily bartering away American national security, prestige, and territory. The President's support for the sale of sophisticated fighter-bomber planes to Saudi Arabia antagonized a major part of the American Jewish community, just as his call for Congress to remove restrictions on the sale of arms to Turkey antagonized Greek-Americans. Appeals by President Carter for voluntary restraint in wage and salary increases irritated many union leaders and members, and presidential support for an independent consumer protection agency antagonized many business groups.

Leadership calls for hard decisions and for innovative policy recommendations and actions. Some are bound to be unpopular with some groups within the American public and therefore stimulate active opposition to presidential leadership.

In contrast with the separation of powers and checks and balances principles, the modern presidency represents a tremendous concentration of power. This new concentration of power clashes sharply with the traditional American notion that power should be divided and checked because it is essentially dangerous.

In the last fifty years the challenges confronting the United States—domestic, international, and economic—have accented the leadership roles of the President. Congress has officially transferred to the President authority to involve the country in armed conflict and to impound funds already authorized and appropriated. It has called upon the President to design the budget and help manage the economy. It has empowered the President to reorganize the executive branch. And it has increasingly expanded the discretionary power of the President and his subordinates to "make" law.

In the face of constantly recurring emergencies and demands for action, Presidents have responded by tapping their potential for leadership. They have been willing to make decisions, to act swiftly, to intervene directly, and to try to mobilize other centers of power in the political system. The temptation always exists for Presidents to push their power beyond its outer limits. The resignation of Richard M. Nixon in 1974 resulted from a popular and governmental revulsion against his blatant abuse of power. But even out of office, Mr. Nixon continued to insist that whatever a President deems appropriate for the country is, in effect, legal and proper; that official restraints imposed by Congress and the courts and unofficial restraints contained in the normal rules of the game of politics do not apply to Presidents.

Traditionally negative American attitudes toward their national government conflict with the tremendous expansion of its power, which is most easily identified with the President. American culture reflects a profound suspicion of government, especially at the national level. To many in our society, government is at best a necessary "evil" but an "evil" nonetheless. The national, or federal, government is viewed much more suspiciously than are state and local governments, which in the popular culture are identified as "closer to the people" and therefore less of a threat.

A tremendous growth has occurred in the national government during the last fifty years, although recently state and local governments have been growing at a faster rate. This expansion in the federal government, its enormous costs, and its increasing involvement in the private sector of society are still a cause of culture shock to many within the American political system. Because of the nature of our political system, the executive branch, headed by the President, epitomizes these changes more than does Congress or the judiciary.

The President, who is responsible for carrying out the national laws in the land, must implement the policies Congress adopts. When the national courts decide on policy, the national executive, presided over by the President, enforces that policy. Finally, the President heads up the departments and agencies whose millions of bureaucrats serve and regulate their fellow Americans in a manner unprecedented in the country's history. Under the President's overall direction and authority, they collect and spend the hundreds of billions of dollars used by the national government. Little wonder, therefore, that antipathy toward big government, big budgets, big deficits, a big national debt, big bureaucracies, and big taxes at the national level focuses on the President.

Americans expect their Presidents to be statesmen, above politics. But Presidents must be politicians, immersed in politics. In a culture that looks down upon politicians, the President must be a superb politician to succeed as a leader. A parallel dilemma for the President lies in the contradiction between expectations that the President represent all the people and the fact that every President is the primary leader of a major political party, therefore a politician.

Americans may want their Presidents to be above politics, but Presidents can rarely afford this luxury. To fill most of their leadership roles, Presidents must be involved in the pull and tug of politics. No President has enough independent power, in dealing with our allies, Congress, and the executive branch, or in shaping economic policies, to succeed simply on the basis of authority or command. This holds true for his relations with his own party as well as with the opposition party and with interest groups and the public at large. A President must be skilled at politics and prepared to negotiate, mediate, and compromise. He must know how and with whom to bargain, what to trade, and how to affect the decisions and actions of others by employing a variety of tools and appeals. To take politics out of the presidency is as impossible and absurd as taking the presidency out of politics.

In essence, we have returned to the basic points with which we started our examination of the presidency. The President is esentially a national leader: the outstanding leader of the national government and the country. Although Americans expect a President to be above politics, the combination of demands on the office of the President, the responsibilities assigned to it, and the constraints on the powers of the President require a President to be a skillful politician if he is to be an effective national leader.

Concepts To Study

checks and balances	**roles**
federalism	**separation of powers**

Special Terms To Review

amnesty
appropriation legislation
authorization legislation
bureaucrats
Central Intelligence Agency
chief executive
chief legislator
chief of state
commander in chief
departmental managers

Employment Act of 1946
executive agreements
executive budget
executive privilege
Federal Reserve Board
head of foreign affairs
independent regulatory
   agencies
interest groups
legislative liaison staff

manager of the economy
Office of Management and
   Budget
pardoning power
party leader
shaper of public opinion
State of the Union Message
treaties
War Powers Act of 1973

CHAPTER 14

12/1

THE JUDICIARY

Article III of the United States Constitution establishes a Supreme Court and empowers Congress to create **inferior courts.** The judiciary constitutes one of the equal branches of the national government, but compared with the President and Congress the judiciary is the least developed in the Constitution. Nowhere does the supreme law of the land designate the specific powers of the courts, except to say they are invested with the "judicial Power" and will decide cases and controversies between certain participants. Among the three branches, the judiciary is the one furthest removed from control by the general electorate, the one that least embodies the democratic and republican principles that characterize our political system.

Is the national judiciary, therefore, the least significant, the least powerful of the three branches? On the contrary, in some respects it is superior to the other two parts of the national government and to the state governments. Serving as a means for protecting and defining the rights of individuals against the claims of executive and legislative government, the courts play a unique role in advancing democratic values. At the same time, by continually reinterpreting the Constitution, the judiciary permits the other branches and levels of government to accommodate themselves to the challenges of changing times. By providing individuals and groups with an impartial decision-making center for resolving their private controversies, the courts contribute to the orderly, peaceful resolution of conflict in society. And, by claiming the ultimate power to define the Constitution, the courts have imposed judicially defined limits upon the powers of the President, Congress, and state governments.

The national judiciary is clearly an independent and powerful unit of government. But it is not absolutely independent and powerful. It, too, is subject to the checks and balances of Congress and the President,

From *Herblock's Special for Today*, (Simon & Schuster, 1968)

"Can you see me now?"

and it may be frustrated by the state governments. Separately or in combination, these other governmental units have at times overruled or ignored the decisions of the national courts. Ours is a political system in which no unit of government is unlimited in its power.

THE NATIONAL JUDICIARY
COMPARED WITH THE PRESIDENT AND CONGRESS

In some important ways the national judiciary shares certain characteristics with the other branches of the national government. In other respects, the judiciary is absolutely unique.

Similarities

It is the similarities that usually escape us, for most Americans tend to distinguish between judges on the one hand and legislators and executive officials on the other. The distinctive garb of the judges, their flowing black robes, seems to imply that judges are fundamentally different from the President and members of Congress. And yet this is very misleading, for the judiciary, too, is a political institution that operates in a political manner.

Courts decide policy; courts are political.   Like the President and Congress, the judiciary is essentially a political institution. That is one major aspect of the courts that most people fail to recognize. But political it is! Just as conflicts among individuals and groups are brought to the executive and legislative branches for policy decisions, so too are they brought to the courts for policy resolution. The judges are not just umpires who decide how to apply the rules of the game for the contestants before them. They also help write and interpret the rules.

The courts, like the other branches of government, authoritatively resolve conflict over the allocation of values, goods, and services in American society. And courts impose sanctions and punishments. Each branch is a source of power for making binding decisions on those involved in conflict. If any group feels it can better advance or protect its interests in the courts, it will try to shift the struggle from the executive and legislative branches to the judiciary. Conflicts over power among states or between a state and the national government are often brought to the courts for resolution. So too are conflicts between the legislative and executive branches and conflicts between private people or groups and units of government.

In resolving these conflicts, the courts often do more than determine in favor of one claimant against another. They may also spell out what public policy should be or define guidelines within which public policy may be made. In so doing, judges make political choices, which are inevitably based on their own values and philosophy of government.

Just as Congress fashions laws in responding to the wishes of the people and the needs of the country, so too do courts fashion laws. There is no absolute right or wrong in the American political system. The Constitution, the supreme law of the land that is the source of judicial power, is itself ambiguous in many ways. It may be read differently by different officials. In interpreting the Constitution, the courts are, in fact, making constitutional law. In interpreting the laws of Congress, judges help shape the very meaning as well as the implementation of statutory law.

The modern courts' decisions on racial segregation by state governments afford us an excellent example of judicial policy making. The judges concluded that such segregation was unconstitutional, that its practice must cease, and that busing could be used in some local school systems to overcome the effects of previous, official segregation practices. Through these rulings the national judges radically reversed the public policies of many states and local governments. Like all major decisions by the courts, these were recognized to be political, or policy, decisions. They overrode the values and powers of certain individuals and governmental units while advancing the values and powers of other individuals and groups. Such court-designed policy was fought by some state and local governments and by private individuals and groups as bad policy; some even resorted to violence in an effort to prevent its implementation. In repudiating official segregation, the judges also repudiated a policy decision made by judges in an earlier era. In doing so they changed the very meaning of the equal protection clause of the Fourteenth Amendment.

In the late nineteenth and early twentieth centuries, decisions of the national courts, striking down national and state regulations of business, incorporated into the law of the land a preference for a particular philosophy of economics (free enterprise capitalism). Such policy preferences then became binding on the policy determinations of the Congress and many state legislatures. Similarly, when in the 1950s a majority on the Supreme Court held that abstract, theoretical teaching and discussion of revolution was permissible under the Smith Act and protected by the Constitution, these judges were interpreting both congressional legislation and the Constitution. The views of this majority also overruled the preferences of national executive officials who wanted to destroy the Communist party.

A judicial decision in the 1960s that abortions could not be legally prohibited by states in the first six months of a women's pregnancy overruled the laws of state legislatures that banned abortions as criminal acts. In a similar fashion, the Supreme Court's decision that local and state governments could not constitutionally support or sponsor prayers in the public schools represented the supremacy of judicial policy making over that of state and local officials.

Note that in these examples the national judiciary substituted its judgment for that of executive and legislative officials of the national government and for executive, legislative, and judicial officials at the state or local levels of government. The policy preferences of these other officials were struck down as invalid and unenforceable according to judicially determined preferences at the national level of government. The federal or national judges were themselves making laws, laws relating to very controversial subjects.

Judges decide issues by a vote.   In the courts above the lowest level of the national judiciary, a number of judges sit together as decision-making bodies. As in multimember legislatures, these judges arrive at their decisions by the political process of counting votes. A majority vote is necessary for appellate courts to overrule the decisions of lower courts. Minority views may be and are often expressed in **dissenting opinions** but, as in legislative determinations, the majority at the time of a vote prevails over the minority. Should a tie vote occur among the judges of the appeals court, the judgment of the lower court prevails.

Just as each member of Congress is equal in voting power to every other member, each judge has an equal vote. The chief justice of an appellate court may be in a position to exert more influence than the others, but not more power. When putting together a majority to swing the decision of the court, judges resemble politicians in the legislature. Judges also try to influence each other's views in order to attract enough votes to achieve that majority. The politics of persuasion and compromise, therefore, are not unknown to judicial decision making.

Interest groups are involved in judicial decision making. Judges, like legislators and executive officials, permit interest groups to intervene in their decision-making process. The very permission they grant to interest groups to file *amicus curiae* briefs (written arguments offered by "friends of the court" to influence its members) testifies to the policy-oriented political nature of much of judicial decision making. Interest groups petition the judges to be heard in legal cases even though they are not the parties immediately in conflict, because they recognize that their own policy preferences are at stake. By filing *amicus curiae* briefs, interest groups try to help judges arrive at decisions favorable to these policy views.

Dissimilarities

In many ways the judiciary is distinctly different from the executive and legislative branches. Judges are, in fact, a different type of public official.

Courts consider only conflict that adversaries bring before them. Unlike executive and legislative officials who take the initiative, who look for problems to solve or adopt policies to anticipate problems, the judiciary is passive. Courts respond only to the initiative of others. Unless an issue is brought to them, they do not consider it. Legislators and executive officials stimulate political activity in society so as to force policy issues on their agendas or those of others. Judges do not. They do not seek out interest groups or work with them to influence the decisions of their fellow judges.

For judges to consider an issue, an adversary, or a conflict, relationship between specific individuals or among specific groups or governments must have led one of these adversaries to challenge the others

[handwritten in margin: only consider issues brought before themselves]

before a court. It is not the policy issue per se that comes to the court for its determination, but a specific conflict between two adversaries. Each tries to persuade the court to reach a decision in its favor. In the process of articulating their interests that are in conflict, they may raise policy issues for the court to decide.

One of the adversaries forces the other into court, reaching out to the jurisdictional authority of the court to resolve the controversy. The adversary party who initiates the legal suit is the plaintiff. The defendant is the one who is being challenged in the judicial sphere of power. Either may be a private individual or group, an executive, a judicial or legislative official or agency, or a foreign government.

National courts do not issue advisory opinions to public officials or to private individuals and groups. That is, these courts will not respond to someone who merely asks of them what would the law be or how would the courts decide in view of a given set of facts. National judges have decided they will only respond to an actual conflict in which adversary parties argue before a court and subject themselves to its authority and power.

Judges are appointed; their tenure is for life or good behavior. Judges of the Supreme Court and the national "inferior courts" are all appointed. They are nominated by the President and must win a vote of approval in the Senate. They serve for life or good behavior, which means their term of office is relatively secure. Since none are elected by popular vote, these judges have no special sets of constituents who can make demands on them and to whom they feel responsible. As a result national judges are the most independent officials in the governmental system of the United States.

Because they have no constituents, national judges are free to make whatever decision, in their judgment, is appropriate to the case before them. They have no need to concern themselves with public opinion, with what is popular; no need to temper their judgment by the necessities of campaigns, raising money, or winning popular elections against a competitor. Once in office, they never again have to seek a renewal of their mandate to serve. Unless they wish to be appointed to a higher court, they need not look over their shoulder at what the President, the Senate, interest groups, or public opinion think of their decisions. If they may be said to have any constituency at all, it is the U.S. Constitution. It is true that lower courts must defer to the U.S. Supreme Court since it can overrule their decisions. But the national judges on the lower courts continue to serve, no matter their record of reversal by the Supreme Court.

In contrast, members of Congress, the President, and the Vice President serve limited terms of office. They are elected to their offices,

no constituency other than Constitution

and all must return to their electoral constituencies for a renewal of their mandates to serve. Since a popular electorate may vote them out of office, such officials must pay special attention to public opinion in their electoral constituencies. They cannot afford to deviate too far, or at least not too often, from that public opinion. And they must constantly reach into that constituency to generate support for their policies. Because the President and Congress are dependent upon each other, they must cultivate each other as additional constituencies. This further constrains their freedom of action and affects their policy positions.

Judges are supposed to be impartial and nonpartisan.   Although many judges have been active party leaders before their appointment to the national courts and have served as elected or appointed executive or legislative officials, once in office they don the robe of nonpartisanship. This is what is expected of them. The fact that one member of the Supreme Court was impeached early in the history of the republic for partisan behavior in his handling of court cases was a lesson that did not go unnoticed in the American judiciary. Judges avoid all partisanship in their court proceedings.

The senior executive leaders and the legislators in Congress, on the other hand, are virtually all strong party partisans. They often take party positions on issues, opposing their party adversaries and helping their party allies. The President acts as a national party leader, and both houses of Congress have their own party organizations and leaders. In addition, party determines the committee memberships and the official committee leaders in Congress.

Judges, who hold themselves above political party in conducting court and arriving at decisions, also respect the rule of impartiality. This is expected of them and they expect it of each other. In the absence of constituencies, they need not be partial to anyone. As for their own self-interests, the operating rule is for a judge to withdraw from any case in which a question of personal conflict of interest arises. Not all judges are as absolutely scrupulous in this respect as others. Nevertheless, it is the judicial norm. If they violate it, they run the risk of impeachment.

Supreme Court Justice Abe Fortas felt compelled to resign from the Court in 1968 when it was revealed that he may have allowed a conflict of interest to affect his judgment. And one of the charges that damaged the chances of a Nixon appointee to win Senate approval to the Supreme Court—he was at the time a lower-court federal judge—was that he had failed to withdraw from a case in which he might possibly have benefited financially from a decision. For this, among a number of reasons, he was rejected by the Senate.

Senior executive officials and legislators are not impartial. They are committed to the advancement of their constituents' interests in the decisions of government. They are allies of various interest groups in the shaping of public policy. In the Congress legislators do not abstain from voting on issues that might benefit them financially. Only recently has Congress begun wrestling with the complicated issues inherent in the conduct of its own members. Ethical standards are much higher in the executive branch, in good part because Congress has insisted on it. National judges, on the other hand, have the highest ethical standards in the government of the United States.

Although the judges are supposed to dissociate themselves from their political party positions when they put on their judicial robes, this does not mean they are necessarily excluded from all partisan activity. Privately and behind the scenes, some members of the Supreme Court have served as unofficial advisers to Presidents. Justice Fortas, for example, after his appointment to the Supreme Court, continued acting as an adviser to President Lyndon B. Johnson, with whom he had previously enjoyed a close association as a Democrat.

Other differences.   The use of juries introduces private individuals directly as official decision makers at one level of the national courts. Congress, on the other hand, allows only its elected officials to make its decision. Similarly, in the executive branch virtually all decisions are made by its partisan leaders or its bureaucrats.

Two types of juries are used in the judicial branch. Grand juries ascertain whether executive officials have marshalled sufficient evidence to bring charges against someone before the courts. A unanimous vote is not necessary for a grand jury to bring in an indictment. Common, or petit, juries are integral parts of the lowest courts of the national judiciary. They need not be used if the accused party waives the right to a jury trial, in which case the judge alone becomes the entire court. A jury in a national court must consist of twelve individuals (except in noncriminal cases where the jury size may be smaller) selected from the general public to give a defendant a jury of his or her peers. Such a jury must reach its conclusions—whether the defendant is guilty or innocent—by a unanimous vote.

Another difference between the national judiciary and both the legislative and executive branches is the hierarchical structure of the judiciary. Higher courts may overrule the decisions of lower courts. At the top of the pyramid is the Supreme Court. It is superior to the rest of the judiciary, and its decisions must be accepted by all the other courts.

In Congress the two equal chambers may check and balance each other, but neither is supreme. Both Congress and the President also share a checks-and-balances relationship. Within the executive branch itself, the President as chief executive does not have final or superior authority over the policy decisions of the independent regulatory agencies. Even units within the departments that are responsible to the President may make their own policy arrangements with congressional committees and allied interest groups to circumvent the decisions of their executive superiors.

In the judiciary the lower courts do not try to reverse or negate the decisions of higher courts by appealing to allied legislators or interest groups. The judges accept as legitimate the decisions of higher courts and incorporate these into their own judicial thinking and decisions. This is the norm they respect.

Judges differ also from members of Congress and from the President in having to meet no constitutional qualifications to hold their positions. House and Senate members must reside in the states they represent, and they must meet specific age qualifications. To occupy the presidency, one must be at least thirty-five years of age and a native-born citizen of the United States. Surprisingly, the Constitution makes no reference to any qualifications for those who serve as federal judges. It is true that all such judges have always been trained as lawyers, but a legal background is only an informal qualification. No previous experience as a judge is necessary for appointment to even the highest court, the Supreme Court. Indeed, some of the great chief justices of the Court had previously made their reputations in politics as executive and legislative officials and had never served as judges.

Although the Constitution lists specifically the powers of Congress and the President, it merely states that "the judicial Power" shall be vested in a Supreme Court and in the inferior courts Congress may establish. What this judicial power is the Constitution does not say—only that it extends to certain cases and controversies.

Finally, the judiciary makes its decisions in secret sessions, although it hears arguments in a public trial and publicly announces the decisions of the courts and the opinions on which these decisions are based. In the multimember appeals courts, judges in the majority on a decision may each write **concurring opinions** if they employ different reasons to reach the same conclusions. Judges in the minority may do the same. Never are the meetings in which they convene to discuss and vote on the case open to the public. The curtain of secrecy with which they or the other judges in the federal judiciary shield their deliberations is not lifted except insofar as the written opinions and votes reveal what has occurred. This secrecy contrasts sharply with the practice of Congress today. Virtually all of its decisions, whether in committee or on the floor of the House or Senate, are now arrived at in open or public sessions.

ORGANIZATION, JURISDICTION, AND POWER

Both the Constitution and the Congress define the jurisdiction and organization of the national courts. Below the Supreme Court, the national, or federal, judiciary is entirely a creation of congressional statutes. The power of the judiciary to decide whether decisions of the executive or legislative branches are constitutional or not is found neither in the Constitution nor in congressional statutes. The Supreme Court itself created this power.

Jurisdiction

Only certain cases and controversies may come to the national courts. This is spelled out essentially by the language of the U.S. Constitution. All other types of cases must, therefore, be heard in state courts. Federal, or national courts, can *only* be used to settle conflict if either of two conditions is met. One pertains to the subject matter of the issue in controversy. The other, the nature of the adversaries or parties to the conflict.

The *subject matter* at conflict that permits federal courts to be used by adversary parties includes anything pertaining to the U.S. Constitution, the laws and treaties of the Congress, or maritime or admiralty matters. The *nature of the adversaries* permits the federal courts to consider (irrespective of the issues) cases involving the following: the U.S. Government; foreign diplomats; states in conflict with other states; a citizen of one state in conflict with a citizen of a different state; a citizen of a state or a state government in conflict with a foreign government or one of its citizens; a state initiating a suit against a citizen of another state.

In essence, the Constitution endeavors to confine federal courts to cases involving the U.S. Constitution, treaties, and national laws; to conflicts on the seas or oceans (clearly being outside state boundaries); to foreign diplomats and countries; and to conflicts that cross state lines. The national courts, therefore, operate within jurisdictional limits.

Citizens + State

U.S. District Courts

Almost all federal cases start in district courts. They are trial courts of **original jurisdiction.** That is, the cases are initially fought out by the adversary parties before these courts. No cases come to them on appeal.

In these trial courts of original jurisdiction, lawyers representing the plaintiff and the defendant present their arguments, introduce witnesses, and cross-examine them. All the drama we associate with personal testimony, veracity and character, and the establishment of the facts of a case characterize the trial courts. If juries are used, they are responsible for determining the matter of guilt or innocence. Otherwise, the judge in a district court assumes this responsibility, in addition to responding to legal questions and imposing sentence if a defendant is found guilty.

In almost all cases, one judge presides over a district court. A panel

break federal law ⟹ go before District Court

of three judges is used when questions about the constitutionality of national or state law arise. Each state has at least one federal district court; some have more. Most of the federal cases start and end in these courts.

U.S. Circuit Courts of Appeals

handle appeals

The circuit courts are the latest addition (1891) to the regular federal court system. Originally, Supreme Court judges "rode circuit" to hear appeals from the district trial courts that Congress had created. Subsequently, a set of intermediary appellate courts was established between the district courts and the Supreme Court, which relieved the Supreme Court of much of its workload and enabled it to concentrate only on the most important appeals cases.

Geographically the United States is divided into eleven judicial circuits. Three to fifteen judges are assigned to a court of appeals in each circuit. Usually, three judges sit together to hear and decide a case.

Circuit courts are basically courts of *appellate* jurisdiction. That is, they are not original trial courts; they only hear appeals from decisions of the district courts. They also hear appeals from the orders and decisions of independent regulatory commissions of the executive branch.

As **appellate courts** they sit without a jury. Although they give lawyers for the adversary parties an opportunity to present brief oral arguments, they confine themselves principally to a study of the written record of the district courts or the administrative agencies. To arrive at a decision, the judges must vote among themselves. It takes either a unanimous or a majority vote to overrule a decision of a lower court or executive agency.

Most appeals begin and end in the circuit courts. Only a very few are considered by the next and highest appellate court, the Supreme Court.

The United States Supreme Court

The **U.S. Supreme Court** is unique even within the federal judiciary. It alone is specifically called for by the Constitution. Unlike the other courts below it, there is only one Supreme Court. Moreover, it is the only one that has both original and appellate jurisdiction.

Its original jurisdiction covers cases that may be initiated at the Supreme Court itself. In these instances it sits as a trial court, determining facts as well as law. The Constitution allows cases in which a foreign diplomat or a state is an adversary to come initially to the Supreme Court. However, very few cases come to the Supreme Court on the basis

Can strike down state laws

of its original jurisdiction. Virtually all arise from appeals from the highest courts of the states or the lower federal courts. The appellate jurisdication of the Supreme Court is determined, in accordance with the Constitution, by the laws of Congress.

Essentially, the Supreme Court is an appellate court for the judicial systems of the states and for the national government. Unlike the lower federal courts, it basically determines its own agenda; that is, in most instances it chooses which among the cases that are appealed to it will be considered. It hears only those that, in the opinion of at least four of its justices, raise issues of fundamental importance regarding the Constitution and the laws and treaties of Congress. The Supreme Court exercises its discretion by agreeing to or disallowing requests for it to issue writs of certiorari. These are orders to lower courts directing them to send the records in a case up to the Supreme Court for its review. Each year the Supreme Court hears only a few hundred of the thousands of cases that adversary parties seek to bring to its attention.

Some cases, however, must be considered by the Supreme Court. It has no choice because the losing party in the lower courts has an automatic right under the laws of Congress to a decision by the Supreme Court. Such cases involve those in which a district judge strikes down a federal law; a U.S. Court of Appeals for a circuit strikes down a state law relied upon by one of the parties; the highest court of a state strikes down a federal law. In 1978 all nine judges on the Supreme Court supported a bill in Congress to permit the Supreme Court to refuse to consider *any* case presented to it; in other words, to extend its discretionary power to cover all appeals cases.

The U.S. Supreme Court differs in other ways from the rest of the regular federal courts. One is in size. It is a nine-member court and has been so since 1869. Since the Constitution makes no reference to size, Congress determines the number of judges who sit on the Supreme Court. Its size has varied from five to ten in accordance with congressional decisions.

More important, it is superior to all the other courts in prestige and power. Most ambitious judges, in both the national and state courts, and most lawyers and politicians who would prefer to be judges aspire to sit on the U.S. Supreme Court. And the most respected position on it is that of chief justice. Just as each presidential administration is referred to by the name of its President, so each Supreme Court is known by the name of its chief justice. The present Court is called the Burger Court, after Warren Burger, the chief justice appointed by President Richard M. Nixon. Its immediate predecessor was known as the Warren Court, after Chief Justice Earl Warren, appointed by President Dwight D. Eisenhower.

Despite the title and prestige, a chief justice has only one vote, the same as each of the other judges. Nevertheless, the chief justice is in an influential position to unify and possibly influence the other justices.

His influence (no woman has yet served on the Supreme Court, although some now serve on district and circuit courts of appeals) stems from his personality, intellectual prowess, and vigor, and from his persuasive ability to convince others and bridge the differences that characterize the highly individualistic members of the Court.

When the justices convene to discuss a case and to vote, the chief justice is always the first to speak. Hence, he is in a favorable position to influence the approach other judges may take to the case. Moreover, he is always the last to vote; the justices vote in ascending order of seniority, which affords the chief justice another opportunity to affect the outcome, especially if a tie seems imminent. If the chief justice is in the majority, he may write the Court's opinion or choose the justice on the majority side who will speak for the court. Should the chief justice be in the minority, the next senior judge on the majority side designates who will speak for the Court on the case.

The Supreme Court is the most powerful of all the courts in the nation. At the pinnacle of the American judiciary, state as well as national, its decisions are final. A decision by the Supreme Court may overrule those of the district and circuit courts and those of the highest courts in the states. The reverse is not true. Its instructions are accepted by the lower courts as superior orders. Its opinions and the reasons expressed therein are adopted by the lower courts as their own in dealing with their cases. Not only the other judges in both the national and state courts, but the adversary parties and the public officials in the United States accept the judicial supremacy of the Supreme Court.

At the core of its judicial powers are two components: It is the highest appellate court; and it makes the final authoritative interpretation of the U.S. Constitution. Moreover, it can declare unconstitutional and therefore unenforceable laws of Congress and the rules and actions of the President and other national executive officials as well as laws and actions of state legislatures, state executive officials, and the decisions of state courts.

Not just the U.S. Supreme Court, but all the national and state courts share the power to interpret the Constitution and determine when laws and actions of executive and legislative officials and the decisions of even lower courts are or are not constitutional. The point to be kept in mind is that the U.S. Supreme Court's decisions are the final, authoritative ones. Its logic must be accepted as the grounds on which other judges will proceed. Its decisions and opinions represent the end of the judicial road in the United States. They may be challenged, as we shall see, elsewhere in the political system, and the issues at stake may be raised again in the judicial system in the hope the Supreme Court will reverse itself. But within the judiciary there is no place else to appeal. No other court may overrule the decisions of the U.S. Supreme Court.

The Supreme Court itself carved out for the judiciary this important power to strike down executive and legislative acts as being unconstitutional. There is absolutely no reference in the Constitution to judicial review—the power of the judiciary to decide the constitutionality of legislative laws and executive acts as the legitimate, ultimate interpreter of the Constitution. What the Court declares unconstitutional is illegal and therefore unenforceable.

Judicial review elevates the judicial branch to a position of supremacy over the actions of the other two branches of the national government with regard to the Constitution. This power was asserted by the Supreme Court in deciding the case of **Marbury v. Madison** in 1803. The controversy that came to the Court in that case was a political one. The Court's assumption of this power of judicial review in resolving the controversy was equally political. Its consequences for the American political system were momentous.

Having lost the presidency and control of Congress in the election of 1800, the Federalist party attempted to retain control over the judicial branch of government. Before leaving office the defeated Federalist President, John Adams, appointed many Federalist politicians to judicial positions. Unfortunately for one, William Marbury, a signed presidential commission appointing him justice of the peace in the District of Columbia was still in the hands of the Federalist secretary of state when the authority of the Adams administration ended and the Republicans took over the executive.

The new Republican President, Thomas Jefferson, and his secretary of state, James Madison, refused to give Marbury his commission. Marbury directly requested the Supreme Court for a writ of mandamus (a court order to a person to perform some act) to compel Madison to deliver to him the commission of office. A provision of the Judiciary Act of 1789 authorized such a procedure.

Presided over by a Federalist Chief Justice, John Marshall, the Supreme Court faced a serious dilemma. If it ordered the Jefferson administration to give Marbury his commission, the Republican executive officials might refuse. This would seriously embarrass the Supreme Court; it had no explicit constitutional authority to compel a President and his secretary of state to obey. In addition, a refusal on the part of leaders of the executive branch to comply with the order could weaken considerably the independent authoritity of the Supreme Court and the judiciary under the Constitution. If, on the other hand, the Court declined to issue the writ, it was both supporting a Republican President against the wishes of the Federalist party leaders and apparently agreeing with the Republican position at the time that the judiciary had no authority over the executive branch.

In speaking for a unanimous Court, Chief Justice John Marshall arrived at a solution that allowed the Court to escape this predicament and, at the same time, assert the supremacy of the judiciary on constitutional matters. Yes, the Court agreed, Marbury had a right to the commission. Yes, a judicial writ of mandamus was the proper remedy to obtain the commission. But the Court could not issue the writ, for it had no authority to do so! Congress, asserted the Court, had violated the Constitution in providing, under the Judiciary Act of 1789, that a person could go directly to the Supreme Court for such an order. The Constitution only permitted the Supreme Court to exercise original jurisdiction in cases affecting foreign diplomats and where a state was a party. Through the Judiciary Act of 1789 Congress had itself extended that original jurisdiction and illegally changed the Constitution.

The Constitution, declared the Court, was superior to all the branches of government. Therefore, a law that went contrary to the Constitution was not a binding law. It was void and unenforceable. Since the judiciary was sworn to enforce the Constitution, the judges were obligated to refuse to enforce any law that conflicted with it. Thus, by a decision of the Supreme Court, the doctrine of judicial review was built into the constitutional system very early in the history of the Republic. At the time Republican politicians were furious at what they considered to be a judicial usurpation of constitutional power. Today it is simply accepted as a matter of fact that judicial review is a proper and essential power of the judiciary.

Marbury v. *Madison* and the doctrine of judicial review that emerged out of it fundamentally transformed the nature of the American governmental system. It raised the judiciary, and ultimately the Supreme Court, to be the superior and authoritative interpreter of the Constitution. It enabled the judiciary to serve as a powerful political check on the powers and actions of both the President and Congress.

Judicial review of the laws and acts of the other branches of the national government is only one of the power bases of the judiciary. Another is the authority of the courts to interpret the laws and treaties of Congress when adversary parties bring cases before them. A third is the courts' authority under the "supremacy clause" of the Constitution to strike down acts of state government officials when such state actions violate the U.S. Constitution or national laws or treaties. A fourth is the authority of the courts to resolve social and economic conflict between private parties from different states as well as conflict among the states themselves and conflict between citizens or states and foreign governments or their citizens. A fundamental characteristic of the courts in all these instances is that they do not initiate policy decisions of their own. They do not reach out to check and balance, to solve problems, to give justice. They may only respond when cases in conflict are brought before them.

As the highest appeals court of the land, and one which can select among the cases brought to it, the Supreme Court has a wide range of policy questions it can choose to consider. But it can do so only because Congress, in accordance with a constitutional provision empowering it to determine the appellate jurisdiction of the Supreme Court, has permitted the Supreme Court to act as an appellate court. Without a congressional grant of authority to hear appeals, the Supreme Court would be restricted solely to the very limited areas of conflict defined by its origiral jurisdiction.

Special Courts

Outside the regular court system—district courts, circuit courts of appeals, and the Supreme Court—Congress has created a number of **special courts.** Each is responsible for helping resolve conflict over a particular subject area.

The U.S. Court of Claims considers various financial claims brought by citizens against the U.S. government. Those who object to the import duties levied by federal customs collectors and to their evaluation of imports may turn to the U.S. Customs Court. Appeals from the decision of this court may be taken to a U.S. Court of Customs and Patent Appeals, which also reviews decisions of the U.S. Patent Office. A civilian set of judges sits as the U.S. Court of Military Justice, which acts as the final appeals court for the military services. Appeals may be taken to the U.S. Supreme Court from the Court of Customs and Patent Appeals, and the Supreme Court has reviewed certain types of cases considered by the Court of Military Justice.

These special courts are composed of a varying number of judges. All are appointed by the President with the consent of the Senate. Except for those serving on the Court of Military Justice, whose terms of office are limited to fifteen years, the judges on the special courts are as secure in their lifetime service as are the judges of the regular courts.

POLITICAL RESTRICTIONS ON THE NATIONAL JUDICIARY

The national judiciary is not absolute in its powers. It is vulnerable in a number of ways to the powers of other governmental units in the American system. Just as it may check the executive and legislative branches, so they have the means to blunt its actions, reduce its authority, reverse its policy decisions, and change its personnel. Even the states may play a role in challenging the courts.

True, the national judiciary has reserved for itself supreme authority to interpret the U.S. Constitution as it applies to national and state powers and to individual rights, to declare legislative statutes and executive acts unconstitutional, and to interpret the laws and treaties that Congress adopts. And normally this supremacy is accepted, no matter the discontent a particular policy decision of the courts may engender among the other governmental officials. But when federal judicial policy decisions have proved extremely unpopular or have deeply challenged the political judgment or independence of other public officials, the judiciary has at times found itself challenged by others in the political system and even overruled.

Congress as a Political Restraint

Since Congress has the power to determine the size of the Supreme Court, the legislature may reduce the number of judges who sit on it. In accordance with Congress' wishes in the past, the Supreme Court has varied in size from five to ten judges; for over a hundred years, it has stood at nine. Reducing the number of judges on the Court today would severely strain the ability of the remaining justices to cope with the heavy load of cases brought to it.

Congress also has available a number of very potent weapons for reducing the importance of the Supreme Court. The national legislature could reduce the Court's appellate jurisdiction or completely cut it off from hearing appeals; in effect, it could limit the Court to those few cases arising under its constitutional grant of original jurisdiction. Because the judges on the Court would be precluded from ruling on substantive issues of controversy brought to the lower federal and the state courts, Congress would thereby have effectively nullified much of the present power of the Supreme Court.

Totally eliminating the Supreme Court's appellate jurisdiction is a most unlikely step for Congress to take. But Congress has in the past prohibited the Supreme Court from hearing certain types of cases. A very recent attempt to limit the national judiciary's power was embodied in an amendment to a judiciary bill offered by a Republican senator from North Carolina in 1978. If his amendment had passed, it would have prevented the federal courts from ruling on cases involving voluntary prayers in the public schools.

Since the Constitution authorizes Congress to establish "inferior" courts, the national legislature could abolish all or any of the regular and special courts. Such a radical change is highly improbable, but it is entirely within Congress' prerogative. In the event Congress took such action and the President agreed, the national judiciary would be reduced to the one court that the Constitution specifically authorized, the Supreme Court.

Congress est. courts → limits courts etc.

Congress has more practical alternatives, however, for asserting its powers to check the courts. Should Congress disagree with the interpretation by the courts of one of its laws, the legislature could negate such an interpretation by adopting a new law that made its policy initiatives absolutely clear. The courts would have no recourse then but to abide by the congressional intent and meaning of the law. Should the courts, in interpreting the Constitution, expand the power of Congress or the executive and reduce the rights of individuals, Congress could refuse to exercise that power, or it could adopt legislation limiting the executive's power.

In 1978 Congress was asked by the American Civil Liberties Union and interest groups representing virtually all the daily newspapers in the country to adopt a law overriding the Supreme Court's decision authorizing executive officials to conduct unannounced searches of news offices and the homes and offices of citizens believed to be in possession of material relevant to the investigation of a crime. In response to these appeals, members of Congress introduced a number of bills to restrict the search-warrant power of federal and state law enforcement officers, to protect the privacy of all citizens not suspected of a crime, and to protect the interests of the press.

Congress and the States as a Political Restraint

Since the courts are obligated to operate within the confines of the Constitution, Congress and the states can overrule a constitutional interpretation by amending the Constitution. A number of such amendments have been added to the Constitution.

The Eleventh Amendment (1798) nullified a Supreme Court decision that a citizen of one state could sue the government of another state without its consent. The Fourteenth Amendment, adopted in 1868 after the Civil War, gave United States and state citizenship to anyone born in this country, overturning an earlier Supreme Court decision that blacks of slave descent could not become citizens. In 1913 the Sixteenth Amendment permitted Congress to tax incomes and reversed an 1895 Supreme Court decision that Congress could not constitutionally levy an income tax.

The 1960s and 1970s witnessed a number of unsuccessful attempts to overrule particular Supreme Court decisions by adding amendments to the Constitution. One such effort centered on cancelling the Supreme Court's decision that representation in both houses of state legislatures had to be based principally on population. Another, sought by antiabortionists, centered on an amendment that would overrule the Supreme Court decision that state governments could not constitutionally prohibit women from having abortions in the first six months of pregnancy. Neither amendment was ever proposed to the states by Congress.

The President as a Political Restraint

can refuse to obey a court order

nominates judges

A President has the power to check the courts by refusing to implement their decisions or by refusing to comply with their direct orders. Such a course of action is extremely rare, however. First, almost all Presidents have shared in the general consensus that the courts legitimately exercise the power of judicial review. Second, by flatly refusing to comply with a direct court order, a President would be creating a constitutional crisis, which carries with it serious political risks for the President. Presidents are also aware that to refuse to support the courts in their decisions is to set a dangerous precedent, one that legitimates the future opposition of other governmental as well as private opponents to judicial decisions.

Early in the history of the federal republic, there was much less of a consensus on the supremacy of the courts. Confronted by a decision of the Supreme Court that protected the rights of American Indians against the actions of the state of Georgia, President Andrew Jackson is reported to have said: "John Marshall [the Chief Justice] has made his decision; now let him enforce it." The President made no attempt himself to enforce the Court's decision when Georgia openly refused to comply with it.

Two more recent examples of presidential responses are much more characteristic of the disposition of Presidents to accept the Supreme Court's decisions as legitimate. In a case challenging the authority of President Harry S Truman to use his commander-in-chief powers to seize private steel mills to avert a national steel strike during the Korean War, the Supreme Court, in a five to four decision, ordered the President to return the mines to their owners. The President deferred to the Court, accepting its authority and obeying its decision, despite his conviction that the strike would adversely affect the country's war effort.

In 1974 the federal judiciary ordered President Richard M. Nixon, then struggling desperately to hold on to the presidency in the face of the Watergate scandal, to turn over to it tapes of personal conversations between the President and his aides. Despite the President's initial refusal and his assertion that as head of an independent branch of government he was constitutionally protected by executive privilege from obeying the courts, in the end he reluctantly complied with the decision of the Supreme Court. Had the President, already in serious political trouble, refused to obey the Supreme Court's unanimous decision to turn the tapes over to a district judge for use in a criminal trial,

his refusal would in all likelihood have immediately led to his impeachment in the House of Representatives. As it was, those portions of the
tapes that the district judge did release in the course of the criminal trial
ultimately helped topple Nixon from the presidency.

Invested with the power to nominate judges, Presidents have sought
to shape the policies of the courts by filling vacancies on them with
judges who shared their political orientations. Given the preeminence of
the Supreme Court in the judicial system, Presidents have been especially concerned with appointing judges who were sufficiently sympathetic to their political views to ensure their expression in the Court's
approach to policy questions.

While it is true that some 90 percent of all federal judges have
shared the same political party affiliation as the Presidents who appointed them, not all judges have decided cases as these Presidents would
have preferred. President Eisenhower, for example, was so disgusted with
the opinions of former Republican governor of California, Earl Warren,
whom he had appointed Chief Justice of the Supreme Court, that he is
reported to have referred to the appointment as the "worst mistake" he
ever made as President. The decision of a unanimous Supreme Court
ordering President Nixon to turn over the famous White House tapes to
a district judge was written by the Chief Justice whom Nixon had
appointed. On the whole, however, the judges appointed by a President
have tended to share in a President's general political orientation to
issues. Hence, Presidents have been able to move the Court in the
direction they favored.

A President's ability to place judges of his persuasion on the
Supreme Court is limited by the countervailing power of the Senate,
which may refuse to give its consent to such nominations. The Senate,
however, is disposed to defer to presidential preferences. Since 1894,
when two presidential nominees to the Supreme Court were rejected,
the Senate has refused to confirm only five such appointees. Two of
these five were nominated by President Nixon as part of his political
strategy toward reorienting the Court in a more conservative direction
and strengthening the Republican party in the South. President Nixon
was, however, able to appoint a Chief Justice and three other judges to
the Court.

One President, Franklin D. Roosevelt, was so frustrated in his first
term by Supreme Court decisions striking down major portions of his
economic program, which Congress had adopted to deal with the Great
Depression of the 1930s, that he urged Congress to expand his appointing
powers. Since none of the Supreme Court judges were his appointees, he
requested Congress to empower the President to appoint one new judge
for everyone seventy years of age and over who continued to sit on the

Court, up to a maximum of fifteen judges. Despite the President's overwhelming reelection in 1936 and the fact that Democrats dominated the Congress, the Senate refused in 1937 to accept such a blatant attempt to "pack" the Court with judges of his political persuasion. Only when one member on the Court began shifting his positions and when vacancies opened up appointments in the traditional manner did the President succeed in gaining a Court that fully coincided with his political point of view.

Presidents are also very influential in filling vacancies on the circuit courts of appeals. In contrast, when district court vacancies occur, local interests and the patronage concerns of senators severely intrude on presidential discretion in nominating federal judges. In 1978 Congress authorized the President to appoint 152 new judges—117 to the district courts and 35 to the circuit courts of appeal. This greatly expanded Democratic President Carter's power to shape the composition and approach of the lower national judiciary. The politics surrounding this appointment process immediately became intense.

Other Political Restraints

State and local officials may try to prevent the implementation of unpopular decisions by the national judiciary. Alabama Governor George C. Wallace resisted court-ordered desegregation of the University of Alabama, and the governor of Arkansas refused to be responsible for preventing violence against black children seeking to attend Little Rock Central High School under a court order. In both instances, Presidents supported the courts and used troops to back up their decisions.

At other times, state and local officials can effectively frustrate the decisions of the federal courts by simply refusing to obey them. For approximately ten years after the Supreme Court had decided in 1954 that racial segregation in public schools was unconstitutional, many southern school systems continued to practice segregation. Similarly, the Supreme Court's decisions banning school-supported prayers and bible readings continue to be ignored in a number of school districts where officials and parents want their public schools to incorporate these religious practices in their official activities. As long as no one in the community takes the issue to the courts, challenging such practices as violating the law of the land, prayers and bible readings will continue in these school districts. Thus, local citizens and officials who ignore the Court's decisions can sometimes succeed in nullifying the impact of the Court's policy decisions, at least in their communities.

As a consequence of American federalism, two sets of courts exist in the United States: national, or federal, courts and state courts. Each of the fifty states has its own hierarchy of lower trial courts, intermediary appellate courts, and one court, supreme over the others, called the state supreme court in most states. Unlike their counterparts in the federal judiciary, state judges may initially be appointed or elected to office. They serve for a limited term before their office must be filled through a popular election. Also, unlike the U.S. Supreme Court, the highest state courts have been willing to offer advisory opinions when they have been requested to do so by state officials.

State courts deal principally with cases arising under their own constitutions, the laws of their legislatures, the acts of their executive officials, and with cases involving conflict between private adversary parties. Should the powers and rights spelled out in the national Constitution or a congressional law be at issue in a case before a state court, the adversaries may appeal from that system to a national court. On the other hand, Congress has diverted certain cases from the national courts to the state courts. By law of Congress, suits between citizens of different states must involve $10,000 or more to be initiated in a federal court. Below this sum the contending parties must take their cases to state courts.

Both national and state courts are bound by the supremacy of the U.S. Constitution and the decisions of the U.S. Supreme Court. The U.S. Constitution declares that it and the national laws and treaties adopted under its authority shall be the supreme law of the land. It also specifically states that state judges are bound by such superior laws, regardless of their own state laws or state constitutions. American judicial federalism, therefore, involves an ongoing set of relationships between national and state court systems.

Concepts To Study

checks and balances	hierarchy	minority
democracy	judicial review	separation of powers
federalism	majority	

Special Terms To Review

advisory opinion
amicus curiae (friend of the court)
appellate courts
appellate jurisdiction
concurring opinions
constitutional law
defendant

dissenting opinions
executive privilege
inferior courts
Marbury v. Madison
original jurisdiction
plaintiff
rule of impartiality
rule of nonpartisanship

special courts
supremacy clause
trial courts
U.S. circuit courts of appeals
U.S. district courts
U.S. Supreme Court
writ of certiorari

CHAPTER 15

12/1

CIVIL RIGHTS AND THE FIRST AMENDMENT

Government has power. Individuals and groups have rights. How to accommodate the two is a major issue in our political system and constitutes the focus of this chapter on First Amendment rights and the two succeeding chapters on **civil rights**.

Government has power over everyone within the boundaries of the society under its jurisdiction, but power to do what? It has power to provide services, obviously; but it also has power to make binding rules that affect our lives, liberty, and property and to impose sanctions that may deprive us of these precious possessions.

Individuals have rights against the power of government and even against the actions of other individuals and groups, but rights for what purposes? Rights to operate freely in pursuing our conceptions of happiness, to disagree with government or others in society without the fear of losing liberties, to be treated with respect and consideration when governmental power does impinge upon life, liberty, or property.

BOTH POWER AND RIGHTS ARE PROTECTED
BY THE CONSTITUTION

The design of government embodied in the United States Constitution recognizes the necessity and usefulness of both power and rights. Granted specific powers, the national government has gained additional powers of tremendous importance through its necessary and proper and general welfare clauses. The states, as you will recall, have a vast amount of reserve powers.

Originally the Constitution imposed only a few specific restrictions on government in behalf of rights. Both state and national governments, for example, were forbidden to pass *ex post facto* (retroactive criminal)

340

laws and bills of attainder (legislative punishment of individuals). To protect people from the abuse of power, the framers relied more heavily on structural arrangements in the national government—checks and balances and separation of powers—to act as built-in limitations on its use of power. The addition of a Bill of Rights was designed to guarantee a broad array of personal rights to the people against the exercise of national power. Subsequent amendments in behalf of the rights of the people also restricted the powers of state governments.

Rights as well as power, therefore, are integral parts of the same Constitution. Both are recognized by the supreme law of the land as being valuable and necessary. Because the assertion of rights limits the uses of power and the exercise of power threatens the protections afforded by rights, clashes between the two are inevitable. Reconciling their conflicting claims is difficult, for each asserts that its demands are proper and legitimate.

CONFLICT BETWEEN RIGHTS AND POWER

Governmental power is always imposed in the name of official authority. It proclaims the importance and priority of law and order, stability, and the public interest. In a democratic republic such as ours, the legislature and the executive speak as the legitimate voice of the people, as representatives of majority rule.

Constitutional rights, or liberties (the terms are interchangeable), are claimed in the name of freedom. They affirm the importance and priority of individual uniqueness, the contribution of private insights into truth, and the value of diversity and conflict. In a democratic republic such as ours, constitutional rights protect the minority by serving as legitimate restraints on the power of public officials and the majority.

Conflict comes about when public officials, in the interest of maintaining law, order, and stability, adopt a law or engage in behavior that threatens the civil rights guaranteed our people by the Constitution. This is especially true in times of crisis, when fear and uncertainty are magnified in the minds of officials or popular majorities.

You must understand that public officials are chosen to govern. That is their primary responsibility. The very thrust of officialdom is to use the power that is placed in their hands. They are responsible to their constituents and the Constitution to exercise the power of government. But they are also responsible to a different set of mandates—to respect constitutional rights, to ensure that the use of power does not violate or undermine the civil liberties of people.

Resolving this dilemma is not easy. The demands for order, stability, and services tend to exaggerate the importance of using power and to depreciate the importance of protecting rights. The use of power may also coincide with the wishes of the majority. It may appear politically more attractive than concern for rights, especially those rights that challenge the wisdom, authority, or interests of public officials or the popular majority. The problem posed for public officials is to exercise necessary powers in a way that respects civil rights, to reject the politically expedient and the popular clamor that leads to the bypassing of rights.

Conflict also occurs between power and rights when public officials become corrupted by power. We have argued that power tends to corrupt, not just in the monetary sense but in the sense that officials may feel they are above the law and may bend it as they wish. Not all officials are so corrupted, but enough are to make us wary. Individuals who place themselves above the law or consider themselves as embodying the law are under little or no self-restraint to consider the rights of others. Wrapped in the cloak of flag and country, acting under the authority of officialdom and supposedly speaking for the popular will, they are in a preeminent position to trample the civil rights of individuals and groups in the name of the law and public good.

Private groups and individuals may also pose threats to the rights guaranteed us in the Constitution. Government, however, is our primary concern, for it represents the highest concentration of power in our society. Confronted with the use of that power, the individual—the ultimate minority—is essentially weak. That government is an indispensable necessity to us as individuals is a lesson we learned in Chapter 1. But just as government is potentially very constructive, it is also potentially very destructive. Not just dictators but officials in democracies are capable of destroying the freedoms of people, belittling their dignity, stripping them of their self-respect.

A number of key questions about power and rights are offered for your consideration at this point. They are pertinent to the different sets of rights discussed in this and the next two chapters. Keep them in mind as you explore the major issues and use them to help formulate your own answers.

KEY QUESTIONS ABOUT CIVIL RIGHTS

How Should We Draw the Line between the Power of Government and the Rights of the Individual and Private Group?

Power and rights are both essential to democratic government, but they often conflict. Therefore, a line must be drawn between the two to keep them in proper balance. Excessive concentration on power at the expense of rights diminishes the individual, weakens the private group, and destroys democracy. Excessive regard for the rights of the individual and the group at the expense of the proper use of power may weaken government and lead to chaos and anarchy. The proper balance between the two should permit them to operate so that we gain the advantages of both: effective government as well as freedom and protection against the abuse of power.

A number of standards have been proposed by judges on the Supreme Court, which serves as the ultimate institutional umpire between rights and power. We will begin our general discussion with the most extreme position favoring rights—the **absolutist standard.** Other standards will be presented as we discuss particular issues and cases that confront the Court. Each standard generates a number of problems. Try both to grasp the essence of the standard and to weigh its advantages and disadvantages in comparison with the others.

The absolutist standard rejects the proposition that power and rights have to be properly balanced, for it asserts the absolute importance of rights over power. Under the absolutist standard, constitutional rights should always prevail. Even to consider drawing a line that accommodates the claims of power as well as rights would virtually concede that no rights were absolute.

Many Americans believe they have constitutional rights that government may not restrict. The Declaration of Independence helps foster this belief. It holds that all men "are endowed by their Creator with certain unalienable Rights, among these are Life, Liberty and the Pursuit of Happiness—That to secure these Rights, Governments are instituted among Men. . . ." If we are so endowed with rights by God, you might logically ask, can government legitimately deprive us of these natural, God-given rights?

Those who adopt an absolutist position based on the Declaration of Independence ignore the fact that this document is not part of the law of the land. A revolutionary statement by the American colonists in 1776, it is praised by our leaders as epitomizing the ideals of our political system. But a statement of ideals does not automatically convert into law. The Declaration is not binding on governments in our federal system. It guarantees nothing and imposes no legal restraints on power.

The language of the Constitution does support the notion that some rights are absolutely protected against action by government. The First Amendment states that Congress may make "no law" respecting freedom of speech, press, assembly, and petition, or one that interferes with the free exercise of, or that supports the establishment of religion. "No law" is an absolutist statement. Former U.S. Supreme Court Justice Hugo Black was one of the strongest advocates of this position:

> It is my belief that there are "absolutes" in our Bill of Rights, and that they are put there on purpose by men who knew what words meant and meant their prohibitions to be "absolutes."

My view is, without deviation, without exception, without any ifs, buts, or whereases, that freedom of speech means that you shall not do something to people either for the views that they have or the views they express or the words they speak or write. . . .

I believe with Jefferson that it is time enough for government to step in to regulate people when they *do* something, not when they say something. . . .

The absolutist judges have never been able to convince a majority on the Court that the rights of speech, press, assembly, petition, or religion were totally immune or protected from governmental regulation. As the ultimate interpreter of the supreme law of the land, the Court has held in case after case, so that it now is the accepted interpretation of the Constitution, that our rights are *relative*, not absolute.

Consider for yourself some practical problems inherent in the position that we have an absolute right to speak or to practice religion. Suppose someone falsely yelled "fire" in a crowded theater. Surely you can visualize the terror on the part of the theatergoers and the death and injury that might result from their rush toward the exits. Exercising our right to speak in this manner dangerously threatens the physical safety of others.

As for making "the free exercise of religion" absolute, imagine a religion calling for the sacrifice of human victims to the gods. This is not as far-fetched as it sounds. The Bible mentions such practices among those who worshipped idols in Canaan. Inca priests in Mexico and Druids in England both sacrificed humans as part of their religious practices. Should similar religious practices be permitted on the grounds that the First Amendment guarantees "the free exercise of religion"? Or is it reasonable and proper for government to prevent killing, even in the name of religion?

Of course these are very extreme examples. But they are cited to illustrate the point that we cannot afford to consider rights *absolute*, despite the wording of the Constitution. At some point in time, under some conditions, the power of government may legitimately restrict our rights.

If rights are not absolute, then how do we balance rights and power to gain the advantages of a free society along with the order and security we desire? To achieve this proper balance, we must have acceptable standards for drawing the line between rights and power. Such a line is difficult to draw, as we will see when we discuss specific areas of conflict between rights and powers. You will discover that there are no definitive standards; rather, there are a number of alternatives. Moreover, you will also discover that the line does not remain fixed; it changes in different times and places. Sometimes it shifts to restrict governmental power and to expand the areas of freedom; at other times and in other areas of controversy, the line cuts into the rights that are protected by the Constitution.

Rights that seem clearly stated in the Constitution actually need to be clarified. What does "speech" include? Is picketing for political or economic reasons or wearing a black armband to show one's opposition to our country's participation in war protected as forms of speech? Are motion pictures also protected by the free speech and press guarantees of the First Amendment?

Another set of questions arises from the vague or ambiguous wording of other rights. What is a "fair" trial? How and by what standards does one define *fair?* A few hundred years ago persons accused of witchcraft were tossed into ponds after having stones tied around their necks. If they sank and drowned, which invariably occurred, they were obviously guilty. Referred to as "trial by ordeal," this procedure was considered fair at the time.

The same vagueness characterizes such phrases as *cruel and unusual punishment* and **due process.** Is the death penalty cruel punishment and therefore prohibited by the Constitution? It was considered permissible throughout our entire history until 1972; thereafter, it was constitutional only under certain conditions. If government may not deprive individuals of life, liberty, or property without due process, then clearly such governments may do so with due process. But what does the term *due process* mean?

Which Constitutional Rights Protect Us against National Action and Which against State Action?

This question might at first appear unnecessary, for the first ten amendments were designed to restrain the national government and a number of later amendments were designed to limit state power. Amendment Fourteen, for example, forbids states to deprive any person of life, liberty, or property without due process of law. But since *liberty* and *due process* are not defined in the Constitution, may the courts read restrictions placed by the Bill of Rights against the national government into the Fourteenth Amendment's due process clause? which of these restrictions? all or some? And by what standards should this be decided?

Should Government Assume a Positive Obligation to Assure the Rights of Individuals against the Private Actions of Others?

This question was raised with regard to the national government immediately after the post-Civil War amendments were adopted, and the Court answered in the negative. The question reemerged recently when some Americans protested that they were being denied their constitutional rights because of discrimination by other Americans on the basis of sex, race, color, religion, or age. As a consequence, national, state, and local governments today are being confronted by demands to protect individuals from discrimination by other individuals.

FIRST AMENDMENT RIGHTS

According to the First Amendment, "Congress shall make no law respecting an establishment of religion, or prohibiting the free exercise thereof; or abridging the freedom of speech, or of the press; or the right of the people peaceably to assemble, and to petition the Government for a redress of grievances."

The importance of the First Amendment should be evident in terms of the basic freedoms it protects. It assumes that religion, speech, press, assembly, and petition are intrinsically private options, areas in which Congress should not intervene. The Supreme Court has expanded the protection of these rights to limit executive and judicial officials as well.

"If there is any fixed star in our constitutional constellation," pointed out Supreme Court Justice Robert H. Jackson, "it is that no official, high or petty, can prescribe what shall be orthodox in politics . . . religion . . . opinion or force citizens to confess by word or act their faith therein." The First Amendment is designed to ensure that the government will not interfere with or penalize our personal search for meaning in areas vital to our private lives and fundamental to a democratic system. If ideas in religion, politics, literature, art, or economics are to win acceptance in our society, this acceptance should emerge from the competitive marketplace of ideas, where people are free to espouse and debate their views. Neither governmental edict nor a popular vote may terminate the search or ban the ideas themselves.

The importance attached to First Amendment freedoms is also evident in the priority assigned to them by the Supreme Court. The Court has held that they are superior to the constitutions, laws, and actions of state and local governments. Initially, the First Amendment restrained only national power. That it was never intended as a limit on the states is clear from its language: "Congress shall not" and by the first Congress's refusal to propose, as part of the Bill of Rights, an amendment specifically prohibiting states from infringing on "rights of conscience . . . freedom of speech or of press." The Supreme Court itself at one time flatly rejected the proposition that the Bill of Rights limited state power.

In the 1920s, however, the Supreme Court began reading the First Amendment into the liberty–due process clause of the Fourteenth Amendment, which forbids states to deprive a person of life, liberty, or property without due process of law. Because of judicial interpretation, you may consider the Fourteenth Amendment to read as if it were written that "No state may make any law abridging freedom of religion, speech, press, assembly, or petition."

Let us now examine the civil rights covered by the First and Fourteenth Amendments. What do they mean? What standards have been devised to draw the line between rights and power? Keep in mind an earlier point: These rights are not absolute. Government *may* interfere with them, but only under certain conditions defined by the Court.

You should decide for yourself whether you favor more rights and freedom or more governmental power and restrictions. The Court itself frequently divides on specific issues and on the standards to apply. New majorities on the Court may disagree with rulings of earlier majorities. So you too may agree or disagree with the definitions, the restrictions, the standards. They are always open to reexamination and to reformulation.

Rights of Speech, Press, and Assembly

Freedom of speech and press especially, but also freedom of assembly, are absolutely critical to the exercise of almost all the other rights we possess. This is what Supreme Court Justice Benjamin N. Cardoza had in mind when he wrote that freedom of thought and speech is "the indispensable condition of nearly every other form of freedom."

Think this proposition through as it applies to religion, art, political parties, interest groups, elections, or holding government accountable. How can we preach a religion or worship as we wish unless we have freedom of speech, press, and assembly? Art, literature, and music cannot develop spontaneously unless the writer, musician, or artist is free to express the truth as he or she sees it. How can candidates compete meaningfully for public office in our democratic republic unless they are free to appeal to us on their own terms or free to criticize each other, including those who already wield governmental power? We cannot hold government responsible, point out the failures and inadequacies of public officials, or move them in new directions, unless we are free to express our criticism. Freedom of speech and press are absolutely crucial to democratic government as well as to the quality of our society.

Restricting criticism and dissent as a threat to government. If we are free to disagree with and criticize government, how far can we go in this criticism? For what reasons may government limit this freedom? The answers to these questions are not clear and are always controversial. Despite the obvious importance of freedom of expression and the constitutional restraints of the First and Fourteenth Amendments, national and state governments *may* restrict our civil rights if their exercise poses a sufficient threat to the functions for which government is responsible: peace, order, and safety. To determine what is dangerous and when these rights may constitutionally be restrained demands a reasonable standard that public officials must follow and by which their actions may be judged.

Unfortunately, reasonable standards are not always employed by those who wield power. Public officials may be tempted to designate as dangerous the speech and press of those whom they or the popular majority fear and dislike. It is very easy to view opponents as enemies. Restricting freedom of expression may be rationalized, moreover, on the grounds that criticism subverts government by undermining the people's confidence in its leaders and policies, weakening their obedience to the law, and destroying governmental effectiveness. But, you should ask, are fear and dislike a reasonable standard? Or does this standard merely substitute the personal self-interest and prejudice of those who hold power for the rights of those who disagree with them? In fact, it offers us no criteria for ascertaining whether public officials are acting properly or constitutionally.

The standard of *fear* and *dislike* has underwritten a number of governmental infringements on First Amendment freedoms. As early as 1798 the national government adopted a sedition act, which severely limited freedom of the press. Pushed through by a Federalist-controlled Congress and aimed at their Republican party rivals, the Sedition Act of 1798 made it a crime, punishable by fine or imprisonment, for anyone to write or publish "any false, scandalous or malicious" statement condemning the Congress or the President or bringing them into "contempt or disrepute."

Some twenty-five persons were arrested and ten convicted under this law, most of them Republican editors or politicians. Fortunately, the Sedition Act of 1798 expired in accordance with its own provisions only two years after it was adopted. A new President, Thomas Jefferson, pardoned all who had been convicted, and a Republican Congress provided monetary compensations to those who had been forced to pay fines.

The language of this sedition law was broad enough to entrap almost anyone critical of our governmental leaders. Officials in a democracy operate in the public arena, where their actions are constantly subject to analysis and attack. Leaders are sensitive to such criticism; it is not only embarrassing but it may impair their political effectiveness and threaten their careers. Therefore, public officials are tempted at times to view criticism of themselves as scandalous and malicious, whatever its intent.

The press, opposition politicians, and interest groups often play a major role in helping to expose mistakes or corruption in Congress, in the executive, and in the judiciary. Thus a sedition law preventing malicious or scandalous remarks against governmental leaders, one supported by strong enforcement and stiff penalties, can stifle the investigative reporter and the editorial writer, silence the opposition politicians, and intimidate the ordinary citizen who might otherwise protest some action or decision by a public official.

As for "bringing [the Congress or President] into contempt or disrepute," such language could be used against any of us who ever called a President inept or a member of Congress an idiot. Whether well-founded or not, criticism *may* actually weaken a leader's reputation or lead others to be contemptuous of our political institutions. But if we treasure freedom of speech and press, this is a price we and our leaders must be prepared to pay.

During World War I, fear of robust open criticism and dissent led Congress to pass the second sedition law in our history. The Sedition Act of 1918 made it a crime for a person to utter or write any disloyal, scurrilous, or abusive language; or language intended to cause contempt, scorn, or disrepute regarding the Constitution, the government of the United States, the armed forces, or the flag; or language calculated to interfere with the sale of war bonds or with war production. Penalties ranged up to $10,000 in fines and twenty years in prison.

Note that acts of disloyalty were not the focus of the sedition law, but rather critical dissent, the expression of free speech and press. During wartime, public officials tend to become especially sensitive to criticism and are likely to equate it with disloyalty and support for the enemy. Over 1,500 persons were arrested for so-called disloyal speech under the Sedition Act of 1918. Under national and state sedition laws, individuals were indicted for such "criminal" activities as advocating increased taxes rather than raising money through war bonds, for calling conscription unconstitutional, for urging a popular vote on the issue of war, even for claiming that war violated the teachings of Christ.

Contrast this curtailment of rights with the freedom from governmental restraint Americans enjoyed during the recent Vietnam War in which we were involved for over ten years. Although our engagement in Vietnam originally evoked little domestic dissent, eventually a vociferous opposition developed. Major newspapers became very critical of our part in the war. Television commentators and reporters helped expose some of the false claims of our military and civilian leaders. Organizations and individuals from all spectrums of our society—religious, economic, social, and political—engaged in an open and often acrimonious debate on the value and constitutionality of our participation. American military involvement in Vietnam was subject to open and constant debate. Yet no one was prosecuted or imprisoned for exercising his or her freedom of speech and press, although a number of demonstrators in Washington, D.C., were temporarily jailed on one occasion for allegedly posing a threat to safety and order in the streets, and some individuals were imprisoned for criminal acts, such as destroying their draft cards.

Should the critics have been silenced? The dissent, strongly expressed and widely based, did encourage doubt about our part in the war and helped lead people to conclude that we should withdraw. Is that not one of the prices we pay, or advantages that accrue to us (depending on your point of view about our role in Vietnam), if we treasure freedom? Unity and stability are important, but surely not at the expense of our learning about the facts, the fallacies involved in an official policy, and the alternative policies that can be adopted. The price of suppression may be far costlier in the long run than the price of freedom of expression.

The Sedition Act of 1918 never affected our debates over Vietnam for, although upheld as constitutional by the Supreme Court, it was repealed in 1921. Our national decision makers were unwilling to tolerate in peacetime the heavy-handed restraints on freedom that fear and dislike had led them to accept during World War I. Since that time and despite our participation in World War II and our involvement in undeclared wars in Korea and Vietnam, we have never adopted a sedition law as sweeping in its effect on First Amendment freedoms as the act of 1918 or, for that matter, the Sedition Act of 1798. We did adopt sedition laws, but they aimed specifically at advocacy of revolution or violent overthrow of government rather than at criticism or contemptuous expression toward government.

The significance of the sedition laws of 1798 and 1918 is two-fold. First, they demonstrate how far public officials will go in reducing freedom of expression when they view criticism and dissent as dangerous to themselves, government, and society. The lines they drew tremendously expanded the power of government at the expense of constitutional rights. Even in a democratic republic such as ours, public officials may be tempted to suppress freedom and not only during time of war, for the Sedition Act of 1798 was a peacetime measure.

Second, the Sedition Law of 1918 together with a companion piece of wartime legislation, the Espionage Act of 1917, which still remains on the books, provided the basis for the first major standard that the Supreme Court developed to deal with the conflict between the power of government and the rights of the people guaranteed in the First Amendment: the **clear and present danger doctrine.**

The First Amendment and the clear and present danger doctrine.   The clear and present danger doctrine is one judicial test for deciding when and if legislative or executive action may infringe upon freedom of speech, press, and assembly. Since Justice Oliver Wendell Holmes devised this standard, we use his definitive statement: "The question in every case is whether the words are used in such circumstances and are of such a nature as to create a clear and present danger that they will bring about substantive evils that Congress [may] prevent." Implicit in this standard is the belief that rights are not absolute, but may be subject to reasonable restraint.

Note that what is at stake is strictly expression of speech or publication. It is not just the content of the words, but also the circumstances in which they are used. In some situations words may be fully protected by the First and Fourteenth Amendments; in different situations the same words may be legitimately prohibited by government. Holmes insisted that words had to create dangers that were "clear and present" (immediate) and that the "evil" had to be substantive before government could constitutionally interfere with First Amendment freedoms.

How useful is this standard? It protects freedom of speech and press by restricting governmental intervention to a special set of circumstances. It recognizes that speech and press are not absolute rights. And it leaves to the Court the final determination as to whether government has acted properly or rights have been unconstitutionally denied. It is not a precise guideline, for it is open to different interpretations of the terms *clear, present,* and *danger.* Given the same set of facts members of the Supreme Court may come to different conclusions as to whether a clear and present danger has been posed by speech or press.

In a Sedition Act case involving some individuals who had circulated a leaflet in 1918 exhorting ammunition workers to strike in order to prevent American military forces from interfering with the revolutionary Russian government in Siberia, the Court's majority concluded that the leaflets presented a clear and present danger. Justice Holmes, on the other hand, could find no clear and present danger to the government or to its pursual of the war against Germany in a few leaflets calling for opposition to our involvement in Siberia. It is only when the words present danger of an immediate substantial evil, he contended, that government was justified in imposing limits on freedom of expression.

Can libel or slander laws protect officials against criticism? Some public officials have sought to silence their critics by suing them in the courts for libel or slander (written or oral damage to reputation). The probability that the payment of significant monetary compensation might be ordered by the court for damage inflicted upon an official's reputation can have a chilling effect on the willingness of the press, opposition leaders, and the citizenry to utilize their First and Fourteenth Amendment rights.

In 1964 the Supreme Court drew the line to favor free speech and press rather than to protect official reputations. An Alabama state official had sued *The New York Times* for $500,000, claiming that his reputation had been damaged by an advertisement containing false statements regarding his official actions. Rejecting his claim, the Court asserted that our commitment to the principles of uninhibited debate on public issues allowed "vehement, caustic and sometimes sharp attacks on government and public officials." The constitutional protection afforded freedom of speech and of press did not depend on the *truth* of the ideas or statements expressed. Erroneous statements were deemed inevitable and in need of protection if such freedoms were to have "breathing room."

The Court designed a standard that balanced protection for official reputations with protection for freedom of speech and press. Public officials could recover monetary damages for defamatory falsehoods pertaining to their official conduct, but only if such officials could prove that the statements were made with "actual malice"—the person expressing them had to know that what was said was false—or "with reckless disregard for whether it was false or not." A "good faith" critic cannot be penalized even if what the critic says or prints about the official turns out to be false. On the other hand, critics who knowingly use false statements or recklessly disregard the truth may be successfully sued for defamatory damages.

Freedom of speech and press: advocating revolution. Criticism of government, no matter how savage or abusive, is one thing; revolution is something else. No one has a constitutional right to engage in revolution, to use violence to overthrow our government. Revolution or violence are substantive evils that government is empowered to prevent.

But what about *advocating* revolution? Should advocacy be protected as part of constitutionally guaranteed freedom of speech and press? Or should government punish such advocacy as speech that borders too closely on dangerous action?

We have already discussed the standard of fear and dislike as well as two judicial standards that allow us to resolve these questions. If fear and dislike were the determining criteria, there would clearly be no right to advocate revolution. In contrast, the absolutist judicial standard would protect all freedom of expression against governmental intervention. As long as nothing more than speech or publication was involved—not an overt act—this standard would fully protect the right to advocate revolution. The clear and present danger standard would justify governmental interference if revolution was clearly imminent as a result of speech or press. In the absence of a clear and present danger, advocating the violent overthrow of government would be a right protected by the Constitution.

The Supreme Court has set forth additional standards in trying to resolve the conflict between those who claim a constitutional right to advocate revolution and the government that claims its power permits it to punish such expression. The American Communist party has been the principal focus for this controversy, although the Ku Klux Klan and other groups advocating violence or revolution have also been involved. The Communist party teaches that a revolution is both inevitable and necessary to bring about a dictatorship of the proletariat and the destruction of capitalism so as to lay the foundation for a future communist society.

The political and economic theories of the Communist party have evoked extremely hostile responses among our people, and some of our governmental leaders have made a determined effort to destroy the party and prevent its ideas from being freely expressed. Advocating Communist economics and even the concept of dictatorship, however, are protected by the Bill of Rights and the Fourteenth Amendment, as are the doctrines of monarchists, Nazis, Ku Klux Klanners, Socialists, and Vegetarians. Advocacy of revolution is another matter altogether.

Both state and national governments have adopted laws that aim specifically at revolutionary speech, punishing the advocacy of violent overthrow of government by force. Under the authority of such a New York state law, a number of Communists were sentenced to prison in 1920 for distributing a manifesto stressing, in part, that violent overthrow of the government was an essential aspect of a Communist revolution. In considering their appeal, the majority of the U.S. Supreme Court refused to apply the clear and present danger standard. It was enough for them that the New York legislature had made a determination that certain expressions would themselves create a danger of a substantive evil. They deemed it reasonable for government to protect itself from revolution that *might* arise in the future as a result of such advocacy.

Note how far the Court's majority was willing to go in expanding the power of government and contracting the right of freedom of expression. As long as the legislative act appeared to be reasonably related to government's power to protect itself, they were willing to accept a **dangerous tendency standard.** Government was to be allowed to punish any expression which had a *tendency,* however remote, to bring about dangers that government was empowered to prohibit. In contrast, the minority on the Court argued that they could find nothing in the manifesto that constituted a clear and present threat to the safety of government. The advocacy of revolution in some indefinite time in the future did not, in their eyes, warrant interfering with freedom of expression.

In 1940 Congress adopted what is popularly referred to as the Smith Act, which made it unlawful for anyone to "advocate, advise or teach the necessity, desirability or propriety of overthrowing any governments in the United States by force or violence." This law also made it a crime to print and circulate any literature with that intent, to help organize any group preaching such doctrines, or to be a member of such a group, knowing its purposes. Note that acts to overthrow government or conspiracies to make a revolution were not the concern of Congress. It was teaching or advocacy, expression rather than overt action.

Although the Smith Act was declared constitutional, the Supreme Court has at times interpreted its provisions quite differently. In *Dennis* v. *United States* (1951), eleven Communist party leaders were sent to jail for having advocated the overthrow of government by force. The Court concluded that a danger clearly existed in the presence of a disciplined party whose members were ready to follow their leaders should the latter believe the time propitious for action. The standard of the judges in upholding the Smith Act was "whether the gravity of the evil, discounted by its improbability," justified government's invasion of free speech. Advocacy of revolution did not have to represent a present danger; its being a *probable danger* was enough to justify governmental repression **(probable danger standard)**.

Here was another significant retreat from the protection of speech and press under the clear and present danger doctrine. "Probable" is an elastic test that allows considerable discretion to government since the time element is read out of the clear and present danger standard. The Court's judgment did not go uncontested. A minority of the judges argued that the Smith Act was unconstitutional as a prior restraint on freedom of speech and press and that a clear and present danger had not been demonstrated.

Despite its opinion, the Court did say in an aside that if the Communists were involved only in the peaceful study, discussion, or teaching of revolution in the *realm of ideas*, then the Smith Act did not apply. It was on this exact point that a subsequent Court refused to accept the government's claims that another set of Communist leaders had violated the Smith Act.

In *Yates* v. *United States* (1957), the Supreme Court concluded that advocacy of revolution was not prohibited if it were taught as an abstract doctrine. In other words, Communists who merely advocated or taught their members to believe in the importance or inevitability of revolution were free to express themselves without hindrance from government. Should leaders urge their members to *do* something about revolution "now or in the near future rather than merely to believe in something," said the judge who spoke for the Court, they would then be guilty of violating the law. And in 1969 the Court struck down an Ohio law that prohibited advocacy of violent means to achieve political change. "Mere advocacy," contended the Court, had to be distinguished from "incitement to imminent lawless action." The government could constitutionally forbid only the latter type of advocacy. The First and Fourteenth Amendments guarantee the right to advocate the idea of revolution or violence against government. Speech or press that is oriented to belief in revolution or violence is legitimate, but expression that points to immediate action is not.

In the 1950s the United States was engaged in both "hot" and "cold" wars with Communist countries. It was also gripped by an hysteria of fear concerning American Communists. In this supercharged atmosphere Congress adopted a number of laws aimed specifically at crippling the Communist party and eventually destroying it completely. Although only one law was ever held unconstitutional as violating First Amendment rights, the rest were effectively nullified by Court action.

A law making it a crime for Communist party members to serve as officers of labor unions was struck down as unconstitutional in 1965. The Court saw the law as a bill of attainder—legislative rather than judicial punishment of individuals—which is specifically forbidden by the Constitution. Despite the fact that the Internal Security Act of 1950, which required the Communist party and Communist organizations to register with the U.S. Attorney General, was declared constitutional, its enforcement was made impossible. The Supreme Court held that any individual registering for the party would be incriminating himself as guilty of active membership under the Smith Act. (The Fifth Amendment prohibits actions by national laws or officers leading to self-incrimination by individuals.) The Justice Department gave up trying to enforce the registration requirements because of the strong possibility the Court would rule such action contrary to our Fifth Amendment rights. A provision of the Internal Security Act that prohibited the issuance of passports to American Communists was also struck down as violating the liberty guaranteed in the due process clause of the Fifth Amendment.

Fear of the Communists led the national government to adopt even more extreme measures. In 1950 Congress authorized the President to declare an internal security emergency. Under it he was empowered to detain, without regard for a person's constitutional rights, anyone whom the government suspected might engage in sabotage or espionage. All that was required to deprive a person of his or her constitutional rights was a *suspicion* on the part of government officials that the person *might* do something that was a substantive evil. No overt acts of sabotage or espionage had to occur. Although a number of special detention camps were established, the law was never invoked, and it was repealed in 1971. By that time Americans were sufficiently removed from the hysteria of the previous period to recognize the danger to constitutional rights in granting such unlimited power to executive leaders.

Congress also adopted a Communist Control Act in 1954 that

declared the party to be both an agency of a hostile foreign country and a clear and present danger to the government and security of the United States. Communist party candidates were forbidden to compete for public office in national, state, and local elections. The law was so vaguely written and was of such doubtful constitutionality that it was never enforced. Despite this law, Communist party candidates continue to compete openly in elections for public offices ranging up to that of the President of the United States.

Prior restraint and constitutional rights.   Up to this point we have dealt with governmental attempts to punish expression *after* the fact. But government has also attempted to impose *prior* restraints. By prior restraints we mean prepublication control—licensing, banning, or censoring in advance, before people speak or publish their views.

Prepublication censorship by government is clearly constitutional in time of war. In legitimizing restraints on freedom of the press under the Espionage Act of 1917, Justice Holmes made the following observation about rights during wartime: "When a nation is at war many things that might be said in time of peace are such a hindrance to its efforts that their utterance will not be endured as long as men fight, and that no court could regard them as protected by any constitutional right."

Does this apply in peacetime? May government then impose in *advance* restraints on what the press may print? The answer seems to be a qualified no. In 1931 the Supreme Court struck down a Minnesota law which permitted government to prevent the publication of any newspaper or magazine as a public nuisance because it was "malicious, scandalous and defamatory." A weekly newspaper, obviously a scandal sheet, had been banned from publishing because in the past it had charged the Minneapolis police chief with graft and with engaging in illegal relations with gangsters and it had charged the mayor with inefficiency and dereliction of duty. Arguing that its rights under the First and Fourteenth Amendments had been violated, the paper appealed. The U.S. Supreme Court struck down the Minnesota law on the grounds that a chief purpose of the constitutional guarantee of freedom of press was to prevent just such laws, ones that imposed prior restraints on publications. The Court was acutely aware of the danger to free expression in allowing executive officials discretionary power to suppress the press for fear of what it *might* publish.

A later case concerning the national government and the press was less uncompromising in its rejection of prior censorship. In 1971, during our participation in the war in Vietnam, a major confrontation occurred between the freedom of the press to publish what it wished and the power of national officials to suppress publications in the name of the national interest. A Pentagon study spelling out the history of the policy process by which we had become committed to that war had been leaked to the press, although it had been officially classified "secret." Both the *New York Times* and the *Washington Post* published articles based upon this study as well as verbatim portions of it.

The attorney general requested the courts to suppress any further articles. The government argued that publication of this 1967 study of our decision-making process would irreparably damage our national security. The press contended that the government could not prove its charge and asserted that prior restraint on its publication of future articles violated its First Amendment rights.

The Supreme Court split six to three in favor of the press and against the government. Any system of prior restraints of expression was declared to carry a heavy presumption against its constitutional validity. Therefore, the government was obligated to show sufficient justification for the enforcement of a restraining order. The Court concluded that the government had not met this responsibility.

In effect, the Court *was* conceding that prior restraints on freedom of expression, although presumably unconstitutional, might be permitted. But only if the government could demonstrate to the Court's satisfaction that the use of these freedoms actually resulted in direct, irreparable damage to our national security. Since the government could not prove its case, the Court was unwilling to interfere with freedom of the press.

This case illustrates one of the basic tensions in our democracy: the conflicting claims of constitutional rights and governmental powers. To resolve the clash between the two we must consider the costs of liberty and authority as well as the benefits. After all, national security can be threatened by our exercising constitutionally guaranteed rights. And secrecy and the stamp of national security can be used to camouflage ineptness and irresponsibility. For example, the Nixon White House repeatedly used the cloak of national security and secrecy in trying to deny to the courts, the press, and the Congress evidence that would have incriminated its executive leaders as engaging in criminal activities.

Until very recently, one type of prior restraint on press and speech seemed permissible during peacetime. In the criminal justice system the judges, as distinct from executive or legislative officials, imposed censorship to protect the right of a defendant to a fair trial. Here we have an interesting conflict of two rights—the right to a free press and the right to a fair trial—and censorship being imposed in behalf of the latter by the judiciary.

Some trial judges had imposed "gag" rules prohibiting the press, under penalty of imprisonment for contempt, from publishing news stories or editorials on what occurred during criminal trials. By the time the U.S. Supreme Court considered the constitutionality of this practice, it had been increasingly resorted to in lower courts. In June 1976 the Court for the first time expressed its opinion. The press had challenged a Nebraska judge's gag rule as violating First and Fourteenth amendment rights. This judge had forbidden news reporting of a sensational murder trial. A unanimous Supreme Court struck down his gag rule, although the judges disagreed among themselves on whether such judicial restraints on the press were absolutely prohibited. Some argued that judicial gag rules were to be presumed unconstitutional, even if a trial judge concluded that forbidding the press to publish information would help assure a defendant a fair trial. But they conceded that an extraordinary showing would override this presumption. Some judges took the absolutist position: Prior restraint of the press could never be constitutional. In 1979 the Supreme Court did hold, in a split decision, that trial judges might constitutionally bar the press from pretrial hearings for individuals who were accused of crimes.

Actions by local governments that have presumed to determine in advance who may or may not use their rights to speech and assembly have also been held to be unconstitutional "prior restraints." The Court has concluded that local laws giving city officials unlimited discretion to grant to or withhold permits from those seeking to solicit membership in organizations requiring dues or from those desiring to rent a hall for a public meeting or speech imposed unconstitutional "prior restraint." Making the opportunity for speech, assembly, or solicitation dependent on the discretionary power of public officials meant that they could easily deny First and Fourteenth Amendment rights to individuals and groups whose views or actions they disliked.

If, on the other hand, reasonable and definite standards control the decisions of such officials, local governments may constitutionally require permits for speech or assembly on public property where competition may arise over the use of a location. The permit requirement must be nondiscriminatory and only for the purpose of the orderly scheduling of public meetings. Officials may not deny a permit to someone on the basis of the nature of the group or individual who applies. The same holds true for requiring persons to obtain a permit from the police in order to conduct a parade down public streets.

Freedom of the press and the issue of obscenity. Freedom of expression and governmental power have sharply clashed on the issue of obscenity. In this instance power is not used to protect public officials or ensure the safety of the government, but rather to guard the morality and social order of the community—to protect private individuals from being "degraded" and to keep the cultural environment of the community "clean."

Obscenity is not protected by our freedom of speech and press;

majorities on the Supreme Court have never deviated from that position. Since obscenity lies outside the protection of the First and Fourteenth Amendments, it is a form of expression that government may regulate and ban. But what is obscene? That is difficult to answer. One member of the Court exclaimed in exasperation that he could not define obscenity, "but I know it when I see it." But knowing it when one sees it is not a reasonable standard. Different people and different judges often arrive at diametrically opposite conclusions about whether or not a book, magazine, or motion picture is obscene.

To permit the banning of obscene material in the absence of reasonable standards is to open the door for public officials to ban anything dealing with sex merely because they find it personally shocking or because some people in their community disapprove of it. Fear and prejudice then become the basis for determining what books may be distributed or read and what motion pictures may be shown or viewed. This is not only dangerous to the development and expression of science, art, and literature, but it cuts deeply into the private right of the individual reader or viewer to determine personally which ideas or images to examine.

The problem in defining obscenity and devising adequate standards for governmental intervention arises in good part because the Court has consistently held that sex and obscenity are not synonymous. "The portrayal of sex . . . in art, literature and scientific works," the Court pointed out in its first major case on the subject, "is not itself sufficient reason to deny material the constitutional protection of freedom of speech and press."

If obscenity is more than the portrayal of sex, what other elements must be present to legitimize government's using its power to censor? On this question, which is actually one of drawing a line between power and liberty, the judges have been highly divided. Some have favored standards that expand greatly the area of freedom of expression. Others support standards allowing considerable discretion to government officials. Still another group has figuratively thrown up its hands in despair at the possibility of drawing any reasonable line. A few judges have insisted on the absolutist position, that the Constitution forbids all governmental restraint on freedom of expression, no matter the treatment of sex.

The conflict within the Court and the difficulty of devising standards may best be illustrated by reference to some recent cases. In 1966 Massachusetts tried to ban the sale of a fiction book that dealt very explicitly with sexual acts. In rejecting the constitutionality of that state's action, the Court laid down a three-fold test, each element of which had to be met before a state could constitutionally ban a work as obscene: (1) The dominant theme of the material, taken as a whole, appeals to the prurient interest in sex; (2) the material, taken as a whole, is patently offensive to contemporary community standards; and (3) the material is *"utterly* without redeeming social value."

Note the severity of the test the majority of the judges had devised to protect freedom of expression against official censorship. The material had to be judged in its entirety; isolated objectionable passages did not make it obscene. Moreover, if it had even the slightest redeeming social importance, the material—no matter how shocking or obnoxious it might be—did not meet the test of being obscene. Of course, there still remained the determination of contemporary community standards and whether the material as a whole appealed to prurient interests (lascivious or obsessively interested in sexual matters). In subsequent cases, the majority of the Court held that contemporary community standards meant national standards.

In 1973, by a five to four vote, the Court retreated from these standards and expanded the power of government to limit treatment of sexual themes in publications or motion pictures. The Court dropped entirely one of the most rigorous tests, that the material must be *"utterly* without redeeming social value,"* and the Court also altered the other two tests so as to make it easier to impose censorship.

The new standards were again three in number and all had to be met before officials could declare any publication or movie obscene: (1) The average person applying local contemporary community standards finds that the material taken as a whole appeals to prurient interests; (2) the material presents in a patently offensive manner sexual conduct prohibited by state law; (3) the work as a whole "lacks serious literary, artistic, political, or scientific value." The majority suggested that under these new standards only hard-core pornography would be banned, permitting all other treatment of sexual themes. And, although the Court expanded the discretion provided local authorities in determining obscenity, the Court still insisted on its authority to check whether local authorities had complied with its standards.

In 1974 the Court overruled a local decision on a motion picture that had been based on its new standards. It refused to rely on the determination of obscenity by local Georgia authorities. Making its own review of the motion picture, the Supreme Court drew totally different conclusions from that of a Georgia jury and ruled that the motion picture was not obscene.

A number of judges have contended that the Court should cease reviewing each motion picture and book to determine obscenity every time a governmental unit imposes a ban and someone challenges it. The courts, Congress, and the states should give up any attempt to distinguish between sexually oriented material that is protected by the Constitution and material that is not, for it constitutes an impossible task. Consenting adults, but not juveniles, should be free to read or see what they wish. So far this view has been rejected by the majority on the Court.

Lately we have undergone a sexual revolution in this country; the topic of sex is treated more explicitly in literature and on the motion picture screen than ever before. In many communities no effort is any longer made to censor obscenity. Consenting adults, but not minors, are free to make up their own minds on what they wish to read or view. In other communities public officials continue to apply local values in using the standards of the Court to ban what they consider obscene. Ask yourself how you think government should proceed in your community. Which standards, if any, should be followed?

Freedom of Religion

The Constitution thrice draws a line between government and religion or church. Article IV forbids any religious tests for holding national public office. That line is absolute. The First Amendment contains two additional prohibitions against Congressional action with regard to religion. Congress is forbidden to adopt laws "prohibiting the free exercise of religion" or "respecting an establishment of religion." As with other First Amendment rights, these lines have turned out to be ambiguous and have generated extensive public policy debate throughout our political system.

Before you consider the problems and issues relating to First Amendment provisions on religion, keep two important points in mind. First, the prohibitions against congressional action in the sphere of religion today apply equally to state and local governments. Since the 1940s the U.S. Supreme Court has read the First Amendment provisions on religion into the Fourteenth Amendment. The prohibition against laws fostering an establishment of religion or interfering with the free exercise of religion is now part of that liberty which the due process clause of the Fourteenth Amendment forbids states to abridge. Relying on its interpretation of these two amendments, the Supreme Court in 1961 also extended Article IV's prohibition against religious tests for public office to the state and local levels of government as well.

Second, the First Amendment does not totally separate government and religion. Governmental intervention under certain circumstances is permissible just as it is in the areas of speech, press, and assembly. And the same type of question presents itself: How does one draw a line that recognizes the legitimate use of governmental power and, at the same time, respects the religious rights of individuals? Moreover, a new set of questions altogether unique to religion and government arises out of the prohibition against "an establishment of religion." Does this prohibition mean merely that government may not create an official religion or church? Or does it mean that government may not support any religion or church? Or that it may not favor one religion but may support them all? "An establishment" is a very vague phrase.

Free Exercise of Religion

A person's right to believe or disbelieve in religion is absolutely protected. In the area of belief—ideas—our rights are absolute. Government may not interfere. On this point the Supreme Court is united and adamant. Government may interfere, however, with the advocacy and practice of religion.

Drawing the line in favor of governmental intervention. On what grounds may government intervene? If religious practices violate criminal or moral laws, government may punish those who engage in them in the name of religion. The Supreme Court in 1878 upheld a national law prohibiting polygamy (multiple wives) in the territories of the United States. A Mormon who practiced his religion's belief that polygamy was proper and necessary was convicted of violating that law. Rejecting the contention that his First Amendment rights had been violated, the Court concluded that *actions* based on religious beliefs could legitimately be regulated by government to prevent unlawful antisocial behavior. Under the impact of this decision and because Utah could not become a state unless it made polygamy a crime, the Mormon Church changed its religious beliefs to eliminate polygamy.

Government may also legitimately interfere in the advocacy or practice of religion if the disadvantages that accrue to religion are only minimal in effect. In other words, the costs, in terms of limitations on religious liberty, are slight compared with the needs of government and the benefits to society. Thus state child labor laws may be validly enforced to protect young children who sell religious literature on the streets. So too the Court has held reasonable the imposition of local government fees to cover police services for groups holding public parades, even those advocating a particular religion. Christian Science parents, whose religion holds that illness is spiritual rather than physical, may be required to comply with a law that all children entering local public schools be vaccinated against smallpox. State Sunday-closing laws may legitimately be enforced against the claims of Orthodox Jewish merchants who assert such laws place an economic burden on them because of their religion; they cease doing business on Saturday (their

Sabbath). The Court decided that Sunday-closing laws were not intended to discriminate against particular religions and had only an indirect impact on religion.

Drawing the line in favor of the individual's religious rights. Government may *not* interfere with religious advocacy and practices if such intervention imposes *an undue burden* on people for their religious beliefs or practices. A series of cases illustrating this restraint on government were brought to the Court by Jehovah's Witnesses, members of an evangelical Protestant denomination whose doctrines were very unpopular in many communities. In going from door-to-door to sell their literature and convert others to their faith, Jehovah's Witnesses strongly condemned other religions. A number of cities and towns tried unsuccessfully to collect from them a license fee usually imposed on all outsiders who peddled this way. Jehovah's Witnesses claimed interference with their First and Fourteenth amendment rights. The Court held that local governments could not apply their usual license fee requirement to those who evangelized for their religion in this manner. Requiring such fees had the effect of seriously inhibiting religious minorities from disseminating their beliefs.

Similar attempts by states and local communities to prevent Jehovah's Witnesses from evangelizing from door to door by denying them permits were also declared unconstitutional. A Connecticut law, for example, required any person soliciting for religious causes to obtain prior permission from a local official who was authorized to determine whether the cause was legitimately religious. The Court held that empowering the official to decide what was and was not religious transformed him into a censor of religions.

The Court has held that the practice of religious beliefs is not predicated on its approval by popular or legislative majorities. In the 1940s, for example, a number of state legislatures adopted compulsory flag salute laws for children in public schools. Jehovah's Witness children refused to pledge allegiance to the American flag, contending that such a pledge violated the biblical injunction against worshipping idols and false images. As a result the children were expelled from school. The claims of the popular majority and its public officials on the need to teach patriotism in the public schools conflicted dramatically with the claims of an unpopular minority to the free exercise of its religion.

Although the Court initially concluded, eight to one, that the government's claim took precedence over freedom of religion, within a very short period a number of judges changed their minds. A new majority on the Court struck down the compulsory flag salute and pledge laws as violating First and Fourteenth amendment rights to freedom of speech and conscience and to the implied right to remain silent.

The "paramount state interest—no alternative means" standard. In 1963 the Court spelled out a standard that broadened the protection of free exercise guarantees and restricted the power of government. South Carolina's Unemployment Compensation Commission had ruled that a Seventh Day Adventist was ineligible for benefits because she would not accept jobs requiring her to work on Saturday, her Sabbath. By a seven to two vote, the Court decided that the state's action imposed an unconstitutional burden on her free exercise of religion. The state was forcing her to choose between obeying her religious convictions and losing the unemployment compensation benefits or abandoning her basic religious belief in order to accept work. "Only the greatest abuses endangering paramount [state] interest," concluded the judge who wrote the Court's opinion, "give occasion for permissible limitation" of the free exercise of religion. For its regulation to be constitutional insofar as it affects religion, a state must show that it has no alternative means to achieve its objective.

The **paramount state interest—no alternative means standard** became the basis of a 1972 decision upholding the right of a religious minority, the Amish, against the authority of a state government to compel public school attendance of children through high school. The Amish, a Protestant sect, seek to live a simple rural life in religious communities of their own, cut off from the social and technological aspects of society. Refusing to send their children to school beyond the eighth grade, they argued that the values to which their children would be exposed seriously conflicted with their religious beliefs and endangered their salvation.

The Amish offered an alternative to compulsory high school attendance: sending their children to an Amish vocational school three times a week and having them work in their homes and on their farms during the remainder of the week. A unanimous Supreme Court ruled in favor of the Amish and against the state. The judges applied the paramount state interest—no alternative means standard in agreeing that enforcement of the compulsory school attendance law against the Amish violated their free exercise of religion. "Only those interests of the highest order," said the judges, "and those not otherwise served can overbalance legitimate claims to the free exercise of religion."

Religion vs. government: compulsory military service. One of the Ten Commandments orders: "Thou Shalt Not Kill." May an individual refuse to serve his country in the armed services on the basis of a belief in God and the religious proscription against killing? In this conflict between the national interest and the individual religious conscience, the Court held that the First Amendment does *not* protect the individual.

As part of its compulsory military service law, however, Congress provided conscientious objector status for those who felt they were being forced to violate their religion by complying. According to this law a person would not be subject to combat service in the military if that person:

> ... by reason of religious training and belief, is consciously opposed to participation in war in any form. Religious training and belief in this connection means an individual's belief in relation to a Supreme Being ... , but does not include essentially political, sociological or philosophical views or merely a personal moral code.

In conscientious objector cases, the judges have interpreted this legislative language so as to afford the broadest definition of the religious beliefs of individuals. Faced with a conscientious objector who would neither affirm nor deny belief in a "Supreme Being," but who held deep, conscientious scruples about taking part in wars, considering them unethical and immoral, the Court held that Congress did not intend to give preference only to those who believed in a conventional God and held formal religious principles. The test of belief was whether it was a "sincere and meaningful one which occupied in the life of its possessor a place parallel to that filled by the God of those admittedly qualifying for the exemption."

In 1967 Congress eliminated any reference in the conscientious objector provision of the selective service law to "belief in relation to a Supreme Being." An appeal came to the Court from an individual denied conscientious objector status because he had originally characterized his belief as nonreligious, but subsequently declared that his beliefs were "certainly religious in the ethical sense of that word." His conscientious objection to war was also based, in part, on his perception of world politics. The Court took the broadest point of view, concluding that the law did not exclude those whose objections were largely based on considerations of public policy. Exemptions had to be granted, concluded the Court, to those "whose consciences, spurred by deep held moral, ethical or religious beliefs, would give them no rest or peace if they allowed themselves to become part of an instrument of war." Nevertheless, the Court has refused to grant conscientious objector status to anyone who objected to a particular war rather than to all wars.

Establishment of Religion

What does the First Amendment prohibition against "an establishment of religion" mean? The prevailing view is that the establishment clause means government may neither create nor directly help or hinder religion or church. But may government give indirect aid? Indeed, what constitutes indirect aid? On these questions the Court has developed a number of standards which have led it to arrive at different conclusions. The judges differ among themselves in responding to three distinct public policy questions that concern the establishment clause: May government support education in private religious schools? May government encourage religious instruction in public schools? May government exempt religious institutions from the payment of state or local property taxes?

Government and religious education: disagreement over standards. The fundamental position of the U.S. Supreme Court on establishment of religion, one to which judges holding different views repeatedly return, *Everson* v. *Board of Education* (1947), produced two different types of approaches to the establishment clause. A New Jersey law had authorized local school boards to arrange for transportation of children to and from school. One board reimbursed parents to cover the costs of transporting their children to school—parochial as well as public—on the local bus system. In a five to four decision, the majority upheld the reimbursement policy as a valid "public welfare" measure but interpreted the establishment clause as building a "wall of separation between Church and State." (*State* in this phrase means all levels of government, just as *Church* means all religions.)

According to Justice Hugo Black who wrote the Court's opinion, the establishment clause meant at the least that:

> Neither a state nor the Federal Government can set up a church. Neither can pass laws which aid one religion, aid all religions, or prefer one religion over another. Neither can force nor influence a person to go to or to remain away from church against his will or force him to profess a belief or disbelief in any religion. No person can be punished for entertaining or professing religious beliefs or disbeliefs, for church attendance or non-attendance. No tax in any amount, large or small, can be levied to support any religious activities or institutions, whatever they may be called, or whatever form they may adopt to teach or practice religion. . . . In the words of Jefferson, the clause against establishment of religion by law was intended to erect a "wall of separation between Church and State."

The majority on the Court concluded, however, that New Jersey officials could constitutionally spend tax funds to pay the costs of transporting children to religious schools because the money was being spent to benefit the children, not the schools. The government's financial support had not breached the wall of separation, because the money was being spent for a secular purpose in behalf of the public welfare. Thus, in addition to the **wall of separation standard,** other standards for deciding establishment questions were contained in the *Everson* decision: a "child benefit" standard, a "public welfare" standard and a "secular purpose" standard.

Four judges dissented, claiming that the school board had in fact breached the wall of separation: Compelling taxpayers to provide funds to transport children to church schools constituted aid to religion. In their eyes, the establishment clause was intended to create a complete separation, forbidding any form of public aid or support to religion.

On the basis of the *Everson* decision, the Court later ruled, in an Illinois case, that government could not permit religious instruction in the public schools. The school board of Champaign, Illinois, had permitted the teaching of religion in its public schools. Children voluntarily attended these classes, which were taught by representatives of different religious faiths. Religious classes held on public property and constituting part of the compulsory school day, concluded the Court, violated the establishment clause as spelled out in *Everson*. The local school board was aiding religious groups to spread or reinforce their faith.

The Court retreated from a strict wall of separation standard four years later in *Zorach* v. *Clauson*, which involved a challenge to New York City's policy of releasing public school children from the last period of a compulsory school day to attend religious school if they wished. The majority on the Court took the position that the establishment clause did not require a separation of church and state *in all respects*. Writing for the majority, Justice William O. Douglas contended:

> We are a religious people whose institutions presuppose a Supreme Being. . . . When the state encourages religious instruction or cooperates with religious authorities by adjusting the schedule of public events to sectarian needs, it follows the best of our traditions. For it then respects the religious nature of our people and accommodates the public service to their spiritual needs. To hold that it may not would be to find in the Constitution a requirement that the government show a callous indifference to religious groups. That would be preferring those who believe in no religion over those who do believe.

Although the majority concluded that governmental action widening the scope of religious influence was permissible, it warned that government might not finance religious groups or blend secular and sectarian education. The dissenters, led by the judge who had written the *Everson* opinion, protested that using the public school system to implement released-time religious education clearly violated the wall of separation.

It is clear from these three important cases that the Supreme Court agrees that the establishment of religion clause erected some kind of a wall between government and religion. But the key question remained: exactly what kind of wall? Some judges believe it should absolutely separate the two; others do not. Certain aid to religion, both groups agree, is totally forbidden. But as they begin to diverge over what government may constitutionally do, the wall of separation standard becomes less useful.

Even the standards of "secular purpose," "child benefit," "public welfare" and Zorach's "accommodating the public service to [the people's] spiritual needs" have not proved entirely satisfactory. Increasingly, the Court has examined them critically to observe their *effect* and tested them against another standard—**excessive entanglement.** If they lead to an excessive entanglement of government with religion, then government has violated the wall of separation in the establishment clause. If the effect of governmental aid or accommodation is not excessive entanglement, it is constitutional.

In 1968 the Court, by a seven to two vote, decided that a New York state law requiring local school boards to loan textbooks to children attending parochial schools was constitutional. Its effect was to benefit financially the children and their parents, contended the Court, and not the religious schools. Since funds or books were not given to the parochial schools but to the children, the law met the secular purpose and public welfare standards. In 1971, however, the Court rejected the laws of Pennsylvania and Rhode Island that gave extensive financial support to religious schools in the form of teacher salary supplements and other instructional aid. This support, concluded the Court, required the public government to continually supervise the use of its funds by the religious schools and therefore constituted excessive entanglement.

On the other hand federal financial aid for the construction of buildings in religious institutions of higher education was upheld in 1971 as not bringing about excessive entanglement between Church and State. The Court's majority pointed out that the physical facilities would be religiously neutral and that the grant of money would be a one-shot affair. National aid did not require continuous government surveillance of (therefore, excessive entanglement with) the religious colleges and universities. The Court also concluded there was less danger of religious indoctrination of students in colleges and universities than in elementary and secondary schools. The dissenting judges maintained that the Constitution prohibited all aid to sectarian schools at whatever level of education and that construction grants constituted excessive entanglement.

A number of states continued to adopt laws allocating public tax money to support religious schools. In 1973 the Supreme Court nullified Pennsylvania and New York laws that provided public grants of money for maintenance and repair of religious schools and for tuition reimbursements and tax credits to parents whose children attended such schools. In both cases the majority examined the state aid programs in terms of their *intent* and *effect* and found them flawed. Their *purpose* and *primary effect* were found to advance religion since they directly subsidized the religious activities of parochial elementary and secondary schools. Parents, concluded the Court, could not constitutionally serve as conduits for religious school aid by receiving and using public tax credit and reimbursements.

The minority on the Court, reaching back to the *Everson* and *Zorach* decisions, claimed the state laws had a secular purpose and were for the general welfare. These judges argued that the tax credit and reimbursements of tuition did not grant direct aid to the religious institutions but represented general aid to individual families, which moved the aid outside the limits of the establishment clause.

Prayers or Bible reading in public schools: an establishment of religion?   The practice of requiring prayer or Bible reading before starting the school day or during elementary and secondary class periods has been extremely widespread in our country's public schools. In almost all cases students who did not wish to participate were excused. Many religious leaders, parents, and schoolteachers contend that such school-prescribed religious practices are good for the children—morally, spiritually, and psychologically. Other religious leaders, parents, and school-teachers believe that the public schools should not officially sponsor or encourage prayer or Bible reading on the ground that it is not government's business to support religion. The child's private right to pray voluntarily during school hours is not at issue. Rather it is the authority of government officials to encourage prayers and Bible readings in tax-supported, compulsory, public elementary and secondary schools. Are such practices "an establishment of religion" prohibited by the First and Fourteenth Amendments?

A nondenominational prayer, one composed to avoid offending different religious groups, was designed by the New York State Board of Regents for daily opening exercises in the public schools. Participation by the children was voluntary. The Supreme Court decided in 1962 that an officially prescribed prayer violated the establishment clause. That children could voluntarily abstain from the prayer was irrelevant; government had no business composing prayers for its people. The one dissenter on the Court argued that the prayer did not constitute "an establishment of religion." He claimed that those who wished to say the prayer were being denied the free exercise of their rights by the Court.

A year later the Supreme Court extended the reach of the establishment clause to prohibit any and all prayers encouraged by the public schools, including readings from the Bible for religious purposes. Maryland and Pennsylvania had required the use of the Lord's Prayer and readings from the Bible at the beginning of the public school day. The Court held that for government to encourage prayer and Bible reading was a violation of the prohibition against an establishment of religion.

For a state law not to violate the establishment clause, concluded the majority of the judges, the state had to demonstrate that its law had a "secular legislative purpose and a primary effect that neither advances nor inhibits religion." The Court concluded that laws or administrative rules ordering public schools to use the Lord's Prayer or readings from the Bible had no secular purpose, but were intended to advance religion. Government should be basically neutral. The minority again relied on the free exercise clause to justify voluntary compliance with school rules on prayer and Bible reading.

Tax exemption for religious organizations: an establishment of religion? As with school-sponsored prayers and Bible readings, our state and local governments have a long-standing practice of affording religious institutions a property tax exemption. In 1970 the Supreme Court for the first time came to grips with this issue. Under the authority of New York State's constitution, the New York City Tax Commission had granted tax exemptions to religious institutions for property used solely for religious purposes. The Court confronted an interesting paradox: A tax on church property might be construed as interfering with the free exercise of religion; a tax exemption, as helping or supporting religion. Voting eight to one, the Court held that the tax exemption was constitutional, that it neither advanced nor inhibited religion.

The majority argued that no perfect or absolute separation was possible between religion and government; separation did not mean absence of all contact. As long as no religion was "sponsored or favored, none commanded and none inhibited," the majority found that there was room for "benevolent neutrality" on the part of government. The tax exemption was declared to represent such a "benevolent act," since government granted this protection to all private nonprofit groups assumed to be beneficial to society. The Court contended that a property tax exemption did not aid religion but merely spared the exercise of religion "from the burden of property taxation levied on private profit institutions." Testing the tax exemption against the standard of "excessive governmental entanglement," the Court concluded that, although a direct subsidy would have failed the test, the tax exemption did not. Through it the government merely abstained from demanding that "church support state."

One judge dissented strongly. He argued that a tax exemption was a subsidy, which meant that nonbelievers as well as believers were supporting churches under the compulsion of state law. Maintaining that government was required to be neutral not only between religious groups but between believers and nonbelievers, he saw the tax exemption as a "long step down the establishment path."

WHERE DO YOU STAND?

Controversy lies imbedded in the First Amendment. Not only are its provisions open to many interpretations, but different standards lead our judges to different conclusions regarding the power of government and the liberties and rights of people. The American people themselves do not agree on the meaning of the First Amendment or on how far they would go in implementing it. How far are you personally willing to limit government in the areas of religion, speech, press, assembly, or petition? Which standards do you think the most appropriate to apply? How much freedom and liberty are you prepared to tolerate on the part of those whom you or popular majorities find objectionable? What role should government play regarding the free exercise of religion? Should a solid wall separate government and religion, or may government aid religion? Ask yourself what the costs and benefits are to our society in your search for answers to these questions.

Concepts To Study

checks and balances	minority	separation of power
civil rights (liberties)	obscenity	standards
conflict	power	
majority	prior restraint	

Special Terms To Review

absolutist standard	Dennis v. United States	general welfare clause
bill of attainder	due process	Internal Security Act of 1954
child benefit standard	an establishment of religion	
clear and present danger doctrine	excessive entanglement standard	libel and slander laws
		necessary and proper clause
Communist Control Act of 1954	ex post facto law	"paramount state interest–no alternative means" standard
	fear and dislike standard	
contemporary community standards	First Amendment	
	Fourteenth Amendment	probable danger standard
dangerous tendency standard	free exercise of religion	prurient interest
	"gag" rule	public welfare standard

reserve power
Sedition Act of 1798
Sedition Act of 1918

Smith Act of 1940
U.S. Supreme Court

wall of separation standard
Yates v. United States

CHAPTER 16

12/8

CIVIL RIGHTS:
Due Process
and Other Rights

We have important rights besides those spelled out in the First Amendment. They are found in the main body of the Constitution, in the Bill of Rights, and in some of the later amendments. This chapter will concentrate primarily on due process rights, which are among the most important protections we have against the arbitrary, unfair exercise of governmental power.

Due process rights are concerned with procedures and with substance. **Procedural due process** defines the steps or processes government must follow when it threatens our lives, liberty, and property. Our procedural rights guarantee that government will afford us certain protections should we be caught up in its criminal justice system. These rights are designed to give us a fair chance to defend ourselves against the enormous power of government.

Virtually all the procedural due process rights that protect us against the national government are contained in the Bill of Rights. Most of these protections now restrict state power as well. The Supreme Court has read them into the provision of the Fourteenth Amendment, which prohibits states from depriving a person of life, liberty, or property "without due process of law."

The same clause of the Fourteenth Amendment has also been interpreted by the Court to guarantee us **substantive due process**. As opposed to restricting the procedures of government, substantive due process restricts the power of state government to determine social or economic policy. The Court has decided that certain social and economic regulations by state government violate rights that are inherent in the liberty protected by the due process clause. These rights are called substantive due process rights because they protect us against the substantive focus of legislation rather than against unfair, arbitrary procedures. What our substantive due process rights are at any period depend entirely on the decisions of the Supreme Court.

PROCEDURAL DUE PROCESS RIGHTS

Take a minute to think through the following question. If you were accused of a crime or arrested, how capable would you personally be of defending yourself? Confronted by the authority, power, and experience of both the police and the public prosecutor, you would be at a tremendous disadvantage. Unless you possessed rights that public officials had to respect, you would run a very high risk of losing your life, liberty, or property. Procedural rights are designed to reduce that risk by limiting the arbitrariness and power of government and by guaranteeing you fair procedures.

Procedural rights stem from a belief in certain democratic values. These values assert the importance, uniqueness, and inherent worth of the individual. Whoever the person, whatever the accusation, that person is intrinsically valuable and deserves to be treated with respect, consideration, and fairness. Keep these democratic values in mind when you study the procedural rights that the Constitution and the Supreme Court have developed for us.

Procedural rights stem also from lessons learned by the English and later by the American colonists through bitter experience with governmental power. Those who designed the Bill of Rights knew how government could abuse individuals accused of breaking its laws; they understood just how vulnerable the individual was. They were determined that their new national government would be carefully restrained by procedural rights written into the supreme law of the land.

Procedural due process in the American criminal justice system rests upon a right that is not even written in the Constitution. It is the right to be *presumed innocent until proven guilty.* When government brings its powers to bear on someone believed to have broken a law, the burden of proof is on the government, not on the individual. Government must prove the person's guilt rather than the person prove his own innocence. Because the powers of government are enormous and the individual relatively weak, government is required by procedural rights to equalize the contest between the two. It must treat an individual fairly, placing in his hands the means by which to protect and defend himself.

Limitations are imposed on governmental power even before the criminal justice system begins. The Constitution forbids the national and state governments to adopt *ex post facto* laws. These are laws which make criminal an act that was legal when it was performed or laws which increase the punishment for a crime over and above the punishment called for at the time the crime was committed. We are only responsible for conforming to rules *after* they have been adopted. We do not have to anticipate what might become illegal.

To help you better understand our procedural rights, we will examine them as they apply to the three phases of the criminal justice system: pretrial; trial; and punishment, appeal, and prison. Certain rights apply only to a single phase, others to two or all three.

Rights in the Pretrial Phase

Pretrial rights not only help determine whether an individual goes to trial, but they affect the rights of that individual at the trial itself. Pretrial rights protect individuals against unreasonable searches and seizures, enable individuals to remain silent, to have the aid of a lawyer, to obtain a writ of habeas corpus, and to request bail that is not excessive. Moreover, they require the national government (but not the states) to obtain an indictment from a grand jury to bring a person to trial. And these rights guarantee that officials of both levels of government will inform an accused person of the specific charges against him.

Rights against unreasonable searches and seizures. Convictions at trials are often based on evidence that police officers uncover before or during an arrest. Against the power of these officers to seize such evidence stands the right of a person to the protection of self, home, and possessions. The Fourth Amendment protects the "right of the people to be secure in their persons, houses, papers, and effects, against unreasonable searches and seizures." It also guarantees that search warrants will not be issued except "upon probable cause, supported by Oath or affirmation, and particularly describing the place to be searched and the persons or things to be seized."

The Court has insisted that, before being allowed to break into someone's house or property, law officers must secure approval from a judicial official. They must demonstrate to that official probable cause for such an invasion of privacy and must indicate what they are looking for and where they expect to find it. Once this system of judicial checks on executive power (law enforcement being an executive responsibility) is satisfied, a search warrant may be authorized. Note where the burden of proof is placed. The arresting and prosecuting side of government must demonstrate to the judiciary sufficient reasons for invading a person's privacy.

The Supreme Court has recognized that there are times when

obtaining a search warrant does not make sense—when it clearly thwarts and unfairly burdens the law enforcement process in protecting society. The immediate danger of the commission of a crime or the destruction of evidence clearly overrides the fundamental right of privacy of person and home. Thus, certain warrantless searches and seizures are permitted. For example, the police may search an automobile without a warrant if they have probable cause to believe it contains illegal goods. Or they may stop and search someone on the street if they suspect that person is armed and dangerous. Why are these reasonable? Because the automobile is highly mobile and may be quickly driven away, and the suspect may injure someone if not apprehended.

But, ordinarily, police may not frisk anyone whenever they wish, or break into someone's home or office at will or, once there, search and seize material at random. These are considered unreasonable acts, and any evidence uncovered in such a manner, even if it points to or confirms a criminal act, is inadmissible at a trial. Not only does such evidence violate the Fourth Amendment, but the Court has held that to admit it at a trial would also violate the Fifth Amendment's prohibition against self-incrimination.

Special problems in interpreting the Fourth Amendment's prohibition against unreasonable searches and seizures arise from the technology of the twentieth century. Electronic devices now enable law officers to listen to and "seize" private conversations without physically violating a person's privacy. Are such electronic intercepts of oral communications unreasonable searches and seizures? The Congress and the Court have at various times taken different positions on this question.

At present, the Omnibus Crime Control and Safe Streets Act of 1968, adopted by Congress and interpreted by the Supreme Court, defines the use of electronic surveillance by law officers. It authorizes national and state officers to wiretap and intercept oral communications for a long list of offenses. But, in almost all such instances, a court order must first be obtained. In other words, executive officers cannot act on their own; they must demonstrate to judicial officials the necessity for using a tap or bug. The court has the authority to grant or deny the order. This 1968 law does recognize that a need for emergency action might make obtaining court permission an unreasonable burden on law enforcement. Therefore, the police are authorized to bug or tap for up to forty-eight hours before applying for a court order. In the event the order is later denied, no evidence obtained through electronic surveillance would be admissible in court or at any other hearing.

In 1972 the Surpeme Court rejected the U.S. attorney general's contention that the language of this law exempted the President from going to the courts for authority to wiretap in cases involving foreign and domestic threats to national security. Although recognizing the executive's need to employ wiretaps to protect national security, the Court insisted that the Fourth Amendment made it mandatory for the President to obtain prior court permission in the case of *domestic* threats and that the 1968 act did not waive this obligation. The Court pointed out that the Fourth Amendment did not contemplate relying entirely on executive discretion in guarding the private lives of individuals and, therefore, required prior judicial judgment. This coincides with a basic American constitutional principle: Freedom is best preserved through a system of checks and balances.

Unfortunately, checks and balances do not always prevent abuses. Agents of the national and state governments have participated in illegal searches and seizures in the past and no doubt have continued to resort to these activities. The Nixon White House imposed wiretaps on some of its top officials to shut off policy leaks to the press, and its agents engaged in burglary in an effort to destroy the political effectiveness of some of its domestic opponents to the Vietnam War. More recently it was revealed that the FBI had engaged in illegal buglaries and wiretaps on Americans belonging to a variety of political and social groups.

The Court can declare what the Constitution means in defending our civil liberties against executive abuse. And it can prevent illegally seized evidence from being introduced against a defendant in a trial. But it cannot absolutely prevent law officers from resorting to illegal searches and seizures or using the material obtained in this manner to damage an individual. In the end the quality of our system of justice and the protection of our rights against unreasonable searches and seizures largely depend on the quality of our public officials. If they hold to the standard of obeying the law, even though it restricts their activities, they will defer to and defend our civil liberties.

The right to remain silent and to have counsel during police interrogation. The Fifth and Sixth Amendments are designed to protect during a trial the rights of persons accused of crimes. They have recently acquired new significance in the pretrial phase of the criminal justice system. Note the extensive protection of rights covered by each of these amendments.

> No person shall be held to answer for a capital, or otherwise infamous crime, unless on a presentment or indictment of Grand Jury ... nor shall any person be subject for the same offense to be twice put in jeopardy of life or limb; nor shall be compelled in any criminal case to be a witness against himself, nor be deprived of life, liberty, or property, without due process of law; nor shall private property be taken for public use, without just compensation.
>
> **Amendment V**

In all criminal prosecutions, the accused shall enjoy the right to a speedy and public trial, by an impartial jury of the State and district wherein the crime shall have been committed, which district shall have been previously ascertained by law, and to be informed of the nature and cause of the accusation; to be confronted with the witnesses against him; to have compulsory process for obtaining witnesses in his favor, and to have the Assistance of Counsel for his defense.

Amendment VI

The Fifth Amendment guarantees, among other things, that an accused person will not be compelled to "be a witness against himself" (right to remain silent). The Sixth Amendment includes the assurance that a person shall have the right to counsel "for his defense." The reach of these amendments has now been expanded by the Supreme Court to protect the rights of persons in the custody of the police immediately after an arrest and in the period before a trial.

Traditionally, the Supreme Court has rejected evidence obtained by the police through third-degree methods. Forced confessions—whether by physical or psychological mistreatment or deception—clearly violate the Fifth Amendment prohibition against involuntary confession (self-incrimination). The Court has also recognized that many people easily become bewildered and intimidated when taken into custody by the police. Without a trained lawyer to advise them, they can unwittingly waive (give up the protection of) their rights. In the 1960s, the Supreme Court took major steps to strengthen the procedural rights of persons in the hands of the police. Two famous decisions (which remain controversial today)—*Escobedo* v. *Illinois* (1964) and *Miranda v. Arizona* (1966)—made drastic changes in the required relations between the police and accused persons in their custody.

Before *Escobedo* in 1964, the Supreme Court had been gradually extending the right of an accused to have a lawyer, even at the state's expense, from the trial proceedings back to the occasion of arraignment on charges before a court, and, still earlier in the process, to the preliminary hearing stages. The Court considered these to be "critical stages" in the criminal justice system where arrested individuals might say or do something that could seriously prejudice their cases.

The *Escobedo* decision extended still further this right to counsel. It affirmed the right of a suspect to have a lawyer during a police interrogation. The Court held that, by refusing Escobedo's request to talk with his lawyer during their interrogation of him, the police had denied him his Sixth Amendment right to counsel. This right was binding on the states through the Supreme Court's interpretation of the Fourteenth Amendment, which prohibits the states from depriving any

gave right to have attorney present

person of life, liberty, or property "without due process." The right to a lawyer during police interrogation was declared to be part of that due process. Escobedo's murder conviction, based on his statement during interrogation, was therefore reversed.

Despite the bitter attacks on the Supreme Court by those who felt this decision had seriously handicapped the police in their efforts to protect society against criminals, a majority on the Court moved even further to protect the rights of the accused in *Miranda* v. *Arizona* two years later. Two questions relating to police procedures that were never covered in *Escobedo* lay at the heart of *Miranda* in 1966: Are the police responsible for informing suspects of their constitutional rights? Can a suspect intelligently waive his rights without the advice of counsel?

In *Miranda*, the Court held that unless the government could demonstrate that the police, at a "custodial interrogation," had employed effective safeguards to secure an accused his or her constitutional rights, statements made by that person during the interrogation could not be used against him or her in a trial. *Miranda* imposed strict procedural requirements on the police. Before questioning an accused person, the police had to warn that person of his or her right to remain silent and that any statement made by the accused could later be used as evidence against him or her. During the interrogation the police were obligated to inform the accused of his or her right to have a lawyer present if one was wanted, and that, if he or she could not afford a lawyer, the government would provide one. If the accused person wished to proceed without a lawyer, any waiver of that right had to be made "voluntarily, knowingly and intelligently."

The *Miranda* rules originally applied to both national and state criminal offenses (under the Fifth and Fourteenth Amendments). These protections were made inapplicable in national cases by a provision of the Omnibus Crime Control and Safe Streets Act of 1968. Thereafter, evidence of voluntary confessions was admissible in national courts even if a suspect had not been given the *Miranda* warnings of his constitutional rights by national law enforcement officers. And in the 1970s, a new majority on the Supreme Court began chipping away at the *Miranda* rules as they applied to state law officers. Nevertheless, *Miranda* represents a high watermark of procedural protections, enabling an arrested person to remain silent and to have a lawyer in the pretrial phases of the criminal justice proceedings.

Writ of habeas corpus: protection against arbitrary imprisonment. A *writ of habeas corpus* is a court order directing executive officials to produce before that court a person who has been jailed and to demonstrate just cause why that person should be held. If the executive officials cannot justify the imprisonment, the judge orders the release of the

Congress can't imprison somebody for nothing (no reason)

prisoner. Remember, at this point the person has not been tried in the courts and so is presumed innocent. Should legitimate charges be spelled out to the court, the person acquires two distinct advantages. He learns why he has been jailed and can begin preparing a defense. And he can, except in special circumstances, apply for bail, thereby securing a period of freedom until the time of the trial.

Habeas corpus is a fundamental right, one guaranteed in the main body of the Constitution rather than in the amendments. The Constitution does authorize the suspension of this right by Congress, but only in time of rebellion or invasion, when the public safety may require it.

guaranteed in constitution

Right to bail that is not excessive.   The Eighth Amendment protection of the right to **bail** and its prohibition of excessive bail balance the right of the individual against the power of government and the protection of society. They protect the individual's right to liberty, to be free from incarceration in jail while he is still presumed innocent. At the same time, they permit government to require a sufficiently high bail, or even to refuse bail altogether, to ensure that a defendant will not try to escape trial or inflict further damage on others in society.

Bail is a monetary sum set by the court as a condition for a person's release from jail or police custody. An individual must pledge that sum to guarantee his subsequent appearance before the court. The amount will vary with the nature of the alleged crime and with other considerations, such as the past record of the defendant and his social and economic position. Permission to post bail may be refused by the court in instances of capital (death penalty) or other very serious crimes, if it is feared that the defendant will try to escape trial. Excessive bail is a sum disproportionate to what is required to ensure the subsequent appearance of a defendant in court. It puts too much of a financial burden on the defendant and leads to his confinement in jail before any judicial determination of guilt.

Right to indictment by a grand jury: sufficiency of evidence.   The Fifth Amendment places still another restriction on the power of the national government in the pretrial phase. National law officers may not bring a person to trial without first having convinced a neutral group of citizens (a grand jury) that sufficient evidence exists to warrant one. For not only does a trial involve a possible threat to the life, liberty, or property of the accused, but it imposes heavy psychological and monetary strains, and it may damage that person's social and economic reputation.

not covered by 14th

By calling for a grand jury indictment (bringing charges), the Bill of Rights attempts to protect the individual against arbitrary and vindictive actions by executive officials. These officials are required to prove that sufficient evidence really exists to charge an individual with a crime.

grand jury made up of 23 members

Neither innocence nor guilt is determined by the grand jury; it considers only the sufficiency of evidence. If the prosecutor cannot persuade its members that there is enough evidence to warrant a trial, the grand jury will refuse to indict.

The grand jury is much larger in size (twenty-three persons) than a trial jury, and its decisions require only a majority vote. Moreover, the Fifth Amendment grand jury requirement does not apply to state officers. It is one protection in the Bill of Rights that the Supreme Court has refused to read into the due process clause of the Fourteenth Amendment. State constitutions, however, may themselves call for the use of grand jury indictments.

Right to know specific charges. The Sixth Amendment obligates the government to inform the accused of the "nature and cause of the accusation" before he can be brought to trial. This right lets the accused know the specific charges he must face so that he has a chance to prepare a defense and to weigh his options. Imagine just how frightening and difficult it would be if a person had to defend himself in court without knowing the exact charges leveled against him.

Not only must the executive side of the government provide the accused with a copy of an indictment, but it must bring the person before a judge for a preliminary hearing on those charges. Here the accused has a right to the presence of a lawyer in responding to the charges. A response of guilty as charged makes a trial unnecessary. All that remains is for the judge to impose sentence. Frequently an accused may respond by pleading guilty to a lesser charge that the prosecution and the defense have agreed upon (plea bargaining). It, too, leads to sentencing rather than a trial. A response of not guilty means that the government must then prove the charges in an open trial.

Rights at a Judicial Trial

Judicial trials determine the legal innocence or guilt of an accused person. Unless a trial takes place before the judicial branch of government, no punishment may be imposed upon an individual. Legislatures may not try or punish individuals, for the Constitution explicitly forbids bills of attainder (legislative punishment of individuals).

The Sixth Amendment to the United States Constitution, whose provisions now apply almost equally to state and national criminal prosecutions, was designed to guarantee the accused a fair trial. A fair trial is a contest between a government and an individual in an impartial judicial arena—an environment conducive to a careful and nonpartisan consideration of the charges and the facts—where the rights of the accused are fully protected. The prosecution must prove guilt; the defendant need not prove innocence. A judge presides as an impartial umpire to whom both prosecution and defense may appeal. In a jury trial the judge also instructs the jury on matters of law and rights.

Right to a speedy and public trial. The Sixth Amendment's guarantee of a speedy and public trial is binding on the national government. By reading it into the due process clause of the Fourteenth Amendment, the Supreme Court has made it binding on state governments as well.

A *speedy* trial is considered by the Court to be inherent in the very concept of a *fair* trial. The failure by government to provide a speedy trial places an accused person at a severe disadvantage. Not knowing when the government will compel him to defend himself may cause the person great anxiety and disrupt his life. Moreover, his witnesses may die or their memories may fade. For the individual who cannot post bail, failure to obtain a speedy trial means a loss of liberty for an indeterminate period.

The Court has refused to spell out in exact detail what *speedy* means. Nevertheless, it has been willing to penalize the executive side of government for failing to move quickly, dismissing indictments where unreasonable delay was attributed to the government. In 1974 Congress recognized the seriousness of the problem for defendants and passed a Speedy Trial Act which, over a period of five years, gradually reduced the permissible time period between arrest and trial. By the fifth year, an accused had to be brought to trial within one hundred days of arrest (except in certain special circumstances); otherwise, the court was to dismiss the charges upon a motion of the defense. This law applies only to the national courts. In the event states do not give a defendant a speedy trial, the Supreme Court can still find that they have violated the due process protection of the Fourteenth Amendment.

Right to a jury trial. Article III and Amendment Six of the Constitution guarantee a jury trial in criminal cases. This right has now been read into the Fourteenth Amendment's due process clause. The Supreme Court has held that the right to a jury trial in serious criminal cases (determined by the maximum sentence possible) is a "fundamental" right. Thus, state prosecutions that could involve punishment of a year or more in jail entitle the accused to a jury trial.

A jury is a group of people from within the defendant's local community who deliberate on the facts and decide for the court whether the accused is innocent or not. A jury of the defendant's peers is a safeguard against corrupt and overzealous prosecutors and a biased or eccentric judge. In addition, a jury brings to the case the common sense judgment of a group of laymen.

Almost any adult can be considered a potential juror. The Supreme Court has held that no person may be systematically excluded from juries because of race or sex. Otherwise, defendants may legitimately complain that they have been denied a fair trial. In 1968 the Court prohibited the practice of excluding prospective jurors who said they had conscientious scruples against the death penalty. Such a practice, the Court held, leads to "prosecution-prone" juries, those more likely than the average to find a defendant guilty and to impose the death penalty. And in 1973 the Court insisted that, in examining potential jurors, the trial judge was required, upon request from a defendant, to inquire into possible racial prejudice on the part of the prospective jurors.

Juries in national courts must come to a unanimous decision on the guilt or innocence of an accused person. If they are unable to do so, they are dismissed by the judge, and the prosecution must then decide whether to retry the defendant with another jury. The same standard does not apply to state prosecutions. In 1972 the Court divided five to four in upholding state laws permitting nonunanimous verdicts in noncapital prosecutions (those not involving the death penalty); such split verdicts do not violate Fourteenth Amendment due process. Consequently, unless a state's law calls for it, jury unanimity is not a necessity for due process in state trials, except for capital crimes.

There is no proper or constitutional mandate regarding the size of the jury in our federal system. Juries in national courts dealing with criminal cases must be composed of twelve people, but the Supreme Court has concluded that in civil cases a six-member jury is permissible. State laws may call for less than twelve-member juries, even in criminal cases, and still satisfy the Fourteenth Amendment.

A jury trial is not mandatory if a defendant waives this right. He may ask for a trial by a judge alone if he feels that this is more advantageous to his case.

Right to change of venue (location) to ensure a fair trial. Wide-spread local publicity in the press or on television or radio may create a climate of opinion that prevents a person from having a fair trial. Although the Sixth Amendment calls for an impartial trial in the district where the crime was committed, a change of location may be necessary to preserve impartiality and therefore due process.

Right to counsel (legal assistance). You have already noted the importance attached by the Supreme Court to the presence of a lawyer at various "critical stages" before the trial. The Sixth Amendment recognizes the absolute importance of a lawyer during a trial itself, where innocence or guilt is determined and punishment may be imposed.

Originally, this Sixth Amendment right applied solely to defendants in national courts. Starting in 1932 the Supreme Court began reading the right to counsel into the Fourteenth Amendment, so that it became a right states also had to guarantee on the ground that right to counsel was a "fundamental ingredient of a fair trial." Today the right to counsel is fully guaranteed—in state courts by the Supreme Court's interpretation of the due process clause of the Fourteenth Amendment and in national courts by the Sixth Amendment.

Right to confront and cross-examine witnesses. This Sixth Amendment protection for defendants in national criminal proceedings was finally made obligatory upon the states in 1965. A person who had been convicted in a Texas court had not been allowed to cross-examine the hostile witnesses. The Court ruled that the right of the defendant to confront witnesses was a "fundamental" right to a fair trial, and the right to cross-examine them was included in the confrontation guarantee. In 1967 the Supreme Court extended to defendants in state courts another Sixth Amendment right. A defendant could use the power of the state courts to compel the presence of favorable witnesses at a trial.

You can easily see the importance of these protections to an individual and to his obtaining a fair trial. Confronting and cross-examining hostile witnesses affords the defendant a better chance to refute the prosecution's case. Granting a defendant the right to use the court to compel the appearance of witnesses helps balance the power of the defense against that of the prosecution.

The right to remain silent: no self-incrimination. The Fifth Amendment guarantees the right of a defendant to remain silent during a trial. This denies to the prosecution the power to compel an accused to testify against his will. The right is so crucial that it is protected during the pretrial stages as well. In 1964 this Fifth Amendment right of defendants in national courts was made obligatory upon states through the Supreme Court's interpretation of due process in the Fourteenth Amendment. No adverse interpretation may be drawn by the prosecution when a defendant prefers to remain silent. In fact, the judge must warn the jury not to construe the defendant's refusal to take the stand as an admission of guilt.

Under special conditions—if the government agrees to grant a person immunity from prosecution—the prosecution may force testimony from a defendant or a witness. On the grounds that the Fifth Amendment protection against self-incrimination would no longer be relevant, since the person could not be hurt by his testimony, the Court has agreed to compel the giving of such testimony. Individuals given this immunity must testify or risk being jailed in contempt of court if they refuse, because they would then be interfering with the course of justice.

Can be forced to testify but given immunity

Constitutional rights to guarantee fairness and to protect a person from arbitrary governmental action extend beyond the decision of guilt or innocence at a trial. They cover rights against double jeopardy and cruel and unusual punishment as well as the right to counsel and to fair treatment in prisons.

No double jeopardy.   The Fifth Amendment states that no person shall be twice put in jeopardy of life or limb for the same offense. Once found innocent, a person may never again be forced by a government to stand trial on the same charge. The individual is free therefore to continue his life without worrying about being constantly hounded by government. A "hung" jury, on the other hand, one that does not come to a decision of innocence or guilt, does permit government to retry the individual for the same offense.

Can't be tried for same crime twice

In the process of breaking the law, a person may actually commit a number of offenses. If a person is found innocent of one set of charges at a trial, the government may still prosecute that person for other offenses stemming from that person's action. This is not considered double jeopardy—endangering in court a person's life, liberty, or property more than once for the same offense. Moreover, one action may simultaneously violate both national and state laws. This means that a verdict of innocent at one level of the federal system does not preclude a government at the other level from prosecuting the defendant for violating its identical law.

If a defendant appeals a conviction to a higher court, the appeals trial also would not be considered double jeopardy because the defendant initiates it. Due process rights are designed to protect people, not to handicap them in seeking a reversal of their conviction or a lesser penalty.

No cruel and unusual punishment.   The Eighth Amendment prevents the infliction of cruel and unusual punishment on a person who has been found guilty after a fair trial. The U.S. Supreme Court has held that this right also extends to punishment by state governments.

But what is cruel and unusual? Obviously, cutting off the hand of a thief or stoning a person who commits adultery—punishments still used in certain Islamic countries—would be considered cruel and unusual in our country. Any form of deliberate torture or mutilation of the body would be prohibited under this amendment.

In 1962 the Court declared that a California law making drug addiction itself a punishable crime violated the prohibition against cruel and unusual punishment. But the Court refused to hold that jailing a chronic alcoholic for public drunkenness was also cruel and unusual punishment. The Court differentiated this case from the one punishing drug addicts by reasoning that the drunkard was punished for behavior, while the addict was punished for an illness. The dissenters on the Court argued that alcoholism was also a disease, one that deprived a person of the will to stay sober. Hence, jailing a person for a condition he could not change should be considered cruel and unusual punishment.

Probably the greatest controversy regarding the prohibition of cruel and unusual punishment today revolves around the death penalty. In 1972 the Supreme Court for the first time held that the death penalty, as prescribed by the laws of Georgia and Texas, was cruel and unusual punishment, in violation of the Eighth and Fourteenth Amendments. The majority on the Court could not agree on a common reason for their conclusion. Some judges faulted the Georgia and Texas laws because they did not require mandatory death penalties for specific crimes; instead, they allowed juries considerable discretion in applying the punishment. These judges concluded that this led to discriminatory application of the death penalty or its imposition in an arbitrary manner. Other judges in the majority felt the death penalty was in itself a cruel and unusual punishment. The dissenters on the Court concluded that since the Eighth Amendment's prohibition of cruel and unusual punishment did not explicitly ban the death penalty, the Fourteenth Amendment did not prevent the states from imposing one.

Since only two judges within the majority had concluded that the death penalty per se was essentially cruel and unusual punishment, the Court's decision still left to the state legislatures the option of assigning capital punishment for specific crimes. As a result, many states adopted new capital punishment laws. Some made the penalty mandatory for certain offenses. Others removed all discretion from juries or judges in imposing the sentence. And still others separated the determination of guilt or innocence from the sentencing process and provided explicit standards to guide juries or judges in helping them decide whether to impose the death penalty.

In 1976 a new majority on the Supreme Court ruled that the death penalty was not in itself cruel and unusual punishment. The Court did continue to hold that the death penalty could not be imposed in an arbitrary and capricious manner. It upheld the death penalty laws of Florida, Georgia, and Texas and ruled unconstitutional the laws of Louisiana and North Carolina. What differentiated the death penalty laws that were upheld from those that were nullified? The only difference was whether or not the judge or jury responsible for sentencing was required to consider the records and characters of the persons being punished and the circumstances of the particular crime. "In capital cases the fundamental respect for humanity underlying the Eighth Amendment" requires this consideration, said the Court, "as a constitutionally indispensable part of the process of inflicting the penalty of death."

Two dissenters in this case, who had been members of the majority in the previous decision, continued to maintain that the death penalty itself was cruel and unusual punishment. Criminals, they contended, were human beings who deserved to be treated with dignity and respect. Moreover, death was an excessive penalty, one which did not promote the deterrence of crime.

Right to counsel for an appeal. A verdict of guilty and the pronouncement of a sentence do not mean that a defendant has lost futher recourse to the courts. An appeal may be taken to a higher court. The Supreme Court has declared that at the first appeals stage the defendant continues to have the right to a lawyer. If the individual cannot afford counsel, government must provide one.

Supreme Court interpretation

Right to be treated fairly in prison. Even a convicted person serving time in prison has certain constitutional rights. The Supreme Court has said that prisoners continue to retain rights under the due process clause of the Fourteenth Amendment. These rights are admittedly not as complete as those protecting a defendant in a judicial trial. Nevertheless, prison disciplinary proceedings must not be arbitrary. Prison officials must provide written notice of the charges to an inmate not less than twenty-four hours before a disciplinary hearing so that the inmate can prepare his case. The inmate must be allowed to call witnesses and present documentary evidence in his defense. The court has refused, however, to afford inmates the right to confront and cross-examine witnesses in the proceedings or to have counsel.

Clause in 14th Amendment

SUBSTANTIVE DUE PROCESS RIGHTS

Substantive due process refers to the essence or substance of a law. It has nothing to do with the procedures or steps government must take in the criminal justice system. Nevertheless, our substantive due process rights are based on the identical due process provision guaranteed us by the Fourteenth Amendment to the Constitution, that no state governments "shall deprive any person of life, liberty, or property without due process of law." *basically found*

Recall our earlier discussion of First Amendment rights. The First Amendment prohibits the national government from interfering with freedom of speech, press, religion, petition, or assembly. These rights deal with the substance or essence of the law, not with the processes that government must follow. In this century the Supreme Court has read First Amendment rights into the liberty part of the due process clause of the Fourteenth Amendment. In effect, then, the Court was expanding the substantive areas of our lives into which state governments could not constitutionally intervene except in special circumstances. *deals w/ economic area*

"Economic" Due Process

For a long time the Supreme Court read "economic rights" into the liberty protected by the Fourteenth Amendment's due process clause. The Court held unconstitutional certain state laws regulating wages and hours of employment and prices of goods or services. These regulations were forbidden because they were considered to interfere with the economic liberty of the private employer and employee to make their own decisions. Up until the Great Depression of the 1930s the majority on the Court insisted that economic liberties were protected by the due process clause. The term *economic due process* was used at times to indicate the substance that was being protected.

Economic due process is now dead; the Supreme Court has absolutely repudiated that concept. State governments may and do regulate economic matters. Private property is still constitutionally protected, but basically it is protected against improper procedural steps by government. The Constitution specifically prohibits national and state governments from confiscating private property for public use without just compensation to the owner. The procedure that is guaranteed is one of "just compensation," and this legitimates the taking of private property.

Personal Privacy as a Substantive Right

In recent years the Supreme Court has articulated a new substantive right—the constitutional right to personal privacy, particularly as it relates to the institution of marriage. If you read the main body of the Constitution, the Bill of Rights, or any of the later amendments, you will find no reference to a right to personal privacy. Yet it has been the basis for the Court's striking down state laws that prevented women from obtaining advice on contraception and from having recourse to abortions if they wished. It has also been one of the grounds for nullifying state laws prohibiting interracial marriage.

Although the Court is convinced that the right to privacy exists, the judges differ among themselves as to its constitutional source. In 1972 in *Roe* v. *Wade* the Court definitively read the right to privacy into the liberty protected by the Fourteenth Amendment's due process clause. That is, the Court expanded the substantive protection of due process to

after 1937 after abortion case

violation of due process Amendment 4

include the private right of a woman to abort without governmental interference.

Texas was one of a number of states that had adopted criminal statutes prohibiting abortion except to save a mother's life. In holding the Texas law unconstitutional, the majority (seven to two) of judges conceded that privacy was not explicitly mentioned in the Constitution. However, they pointed out that the roots of this right had been found by previous Courts in parts of the Bill of Rights and the Fourteenth Amendment. Past Court decisions had made it clear that this right "has some extension to activities relating to marriage." The majority now concluded that the right of privacy, whether based on the Fourteenth Amendment's concept of liberty, which they believed, or whether protected by the Ninth Amendment, "is broad enough to protect a woman's decision whether or not to terminate her pregnancy."

Personal privacy is therefore a substantive constitutional right inherent in the liberty protected by the due process clause. It may be considered a new right that has been added to those protecting individuals against state governments. Like our other rights, a woman's right to privacy is not absolute. This is explicit in the conclusion reached by the Court. Only in the first trimester of pregnancy is the decision to abort left entirely to the pregnant woman and her physician. States may regulate abortion procedures in the second and third trimesters since they "may properly assert their interests in safeguarding health, in maintaining medical standards and in protecting potential life." These interests, said the Court, become "sufficiently compelling" to sustain state interference with the substance of a woman's rights. In the third trimester, states may even prohibit abortions in the interest of promoting the potentiality of human life. What they may still not do in this period is prohibit an abortion considered necessary for the life or health of the mother.

MISCELLANEOUS RIGHTS IN CONTEMPORARY AMERICA

Two less significant amendments in the Bill of Rights offer a contrast between a traditional right that today is noncontroversial and one that is very controversial. Both these amendments, the Second and the Third, arise out of the personal experiences of Americans in the eighteenth century.

Amendment Three reflects the outrage our people experienced when they were compelled to keep British troops in their homes against their will. This amendment protects the right of Americans to refuse to have troops quartered in their houses during peacetime. During wartime the requirement of obtaining the owner's consent is dropped, but government is still obligated to act "in a manner to be prescribed by law" rather than arbitrarily. The old saying, "A man's home is his castle," lies at the heart of this amendment, which is no longer controversial.

Considerable controversy does revolve around Amendment Two, which deals with the right of the people to bear arms. Because numerous attempts have been made to restrict or abolish the private possession of guns, we should examine the exact wording of the amendment:

> A well regulated Militia, being necessary to the security of a free State, the right of the people to keep and bear Arms, shall not be infringed.

The advocates of gun control contend that this amendment was designed solely to guarantee the existence of a well-regulated militia. In revolutionary America soldiers brought their own weapons with them into battle, and the various state militias, composed of these citizen-soldiers, played a role in defeating the British. Today, each state guard or militia is armed with weapons supplied by the national government and is merely supplementary to a strong, standing national army. Since a well-armed militia already exists, the intent of the amendment has been realized. Inasmuch as the possession of weapons by individual citizens is no longer necessary to protect the nation or states, these governments may legitimately control or ban the ownership of guns by private citizens.

Those who favor private ownership of guns also make a constitutional argument. They stress the part of the Second Amendment that guarantees Americans "the right to keep and bear Arms." Some within this group argue that only a constitutional amendment cancelling the Second Amendment could legitimately allow the national and state governments to ban the ownership of guns. Nevertheless, the national government does already ban the sale of sawed-off shotguns and machine guns through the mail and the importation of cheap "Saturday night specials." A few states also have adopted laws limiting the ownership of handguns.

COMMON DENOMINATORS IN DUE PROCESS RIGHTS

A number of common denominators run through our consideration of all these rights. They not only tie these rights into the rest of the political system, but they should orient you to the dynamic relationships between our rights and our political system as they will confront you in the future.

1. *Our rights protect us against governmental power, but they are not absolute.* We are guaranteed life, liberty, and property, but govern-

ment may take them away if it uses due process. Even substantive due process rights are not sacred. Government may prescribe rules regulating abortions in the second trimester of pregnancy and even ban them in the third trimester, despite a woman's substantive right to personal privacy.

2. *Because the lines between power and rights are often imprecise and ambiguous, the U.S. Supreme Court plays a major role in defining them.* Although the procedural due process protections in the Bill of Rights pertaining to jury trials, searches and seizures, and rights to counsel and bail, for example, seem very specific, they turn out in the end to be vague and in need of clarification. Even more imprecise is the term *liberty.* The Court has tremendous discretion in reading substantive meaning into the liberty–due process combination. References by some judges to the Ninth Amendment, in protecting the right to privacy, show that this amendment may be a reservoir of additional unspecified rights. This amendment states that: "The enumeration in the Constitution, of certain rights, shall not be construed to deny or disparage others retained by the people." To what "others" does this amendment refer? Only the Court can decide.

3. *Our rights can always change.* Witness the division in the Supreme Court recently over whether government's use of the death penalty is cruel and unusual. The new technology of electronic surveillance forces a reconsideration of rights relating to searches and seizures by police officers. And the power of the states to prevent abortions diminishes as the right to privacy acquires new meaning and importance.

4. *Conflict over the meaning, expansion, or restriction of rights is inevitable.* This conflict can become intense because opposing values confront each other. Those who assert the right of the embryo or child to life conflict with those who assert the right of the pregnant woman to abort. Those who would ban or strictly license the ownership and use of weapons conflict with those who insist they have a constitutional right to bear arms.

Expanding or restricting the protection of procedural civil rights raises critical questions of costs pertaining both to the quality of justice and the peace and safety of our society. Greater procedural rights favor the individual. At the same time, they curtail government's power to enforce the law and to guarantee peace and security for its citizens. Both the police and the prosecuting attorney are more restricted on how they may proceed. Narrowing the meaning of procedural rights makes it easier for law enforcement officers to operate. It also diminishes the ability of individuals to defend themselves against unfair and arbitrary actions by such officers. Which price do we want to pay? Which benefit is the more desirable one? Can we balance the benefits and at the same time minimize the costs?

5. *Questions of federalism are inherent in resolving procedural*

and substantive due process issues. Should the entire Bill of Rights, designed to protect us against the national government, be read into the Fourteenth Amendment to protect us against state governments? If not, which rights should be imposed as restrictions on the states and which should not? By what standards are these decisions to be made?

6. _Rights exemplify democracy._ Although the emphases of these various sets of rights are different, virtually all relate to the realization of the values of democracy. In their different ways, they address themselves to the importance and dignity of the individual as crucial to our political system. Whatever the conflict over the meaning or extension of these rights, never fail to keep in mind that they help keep democracy alive. They exemplify and protect the basic values that democracy places on the individual and the restrictions that democracy places on the majority and the power of government.

Concepts To Study

checks and balances
democratic values
due process rights
economic due process

fair trial
federalism
power
procedural due process

rights v. power
substantive due process
unanimity

Special Terms To Review

bail
Bill of Rights
counsel
cruel and unusual
  punishment
double jeopardy
ex post facto law

fair trial
Fourteenth Amendment
grand jury
indictment
Miranda rules
personal privacy
Roe v. Wade

self-incrimination
speedy, public trial
supreme law of the land
trial jury
writ of habeas corpus

CHAPTER 17

CIVIL RIGHTS:
Protecting and
Advancing Equality

In 1776 our Declaration of Independence proudly proclaimed the revolutionary belief that "all men are created equal." Today, over two hundred years later, we are still struggling to live up to that ideal.

You will not find any right to equality in the original Constitution. Nor is it guaranteed in the Bill of Rights. Not until 1868, when a post-Civil War amendment was adopted to guarantee that freed slaves would be treated like all other Americans, did the Constitution restrain the states from denying any person "equal protection of the law." Congress was empowered to implement by appropriate means the Fourteenth Amendment, which embodied this policy change, but it was not effectively realized for many decades. At various times private individuals and governments at different levels of our federal system were able to treat blacks, American Indians, women, and members of other minority groups as if they were inherently inferior and not entitled to equal treatment.

Only recently have we seriously begun trying to implement the principle of equality embodied in the Declaration of Independence and the Fourteenth Amendment. It has been and continues to be a difficult and controversial battle. Why has it taken so long to win acceptance for the concept of equality? There are at least two reasons. First, from the earliest days of the American colonies, many of our people have felt that neither they nor their government should extend equal consideration and treatment to others in society. These people were convinced they were inherently superior to "others" who were inherently inferior. Frequently they practiced these beliefs in their private social and economic relations and incorporated these private prejudices into public law. Deep-seated attitudes and the long-established social customs and laws that reflect them are highly resistant to change. When change does come, it often arouses great anxiety, fear, and resentment among those who have accepted inequality as normal and legitimate. This, in turn, tends to limit the scope as well as the rate of change.

A second reason why we are still grappling with the realization of equality is that the concept is very ambiguous. We differ among ourselves as to what we mean by equality and what, if anything, should be done to support or extend it. Does equality mean that all people should share equally in everything? Or does it mean only that individuals should be treated equally by government, irrespective of their race, religion, sex, or color? Does the right to equality mean that government should assure all people an equal opportunity to live a good life? If so, should government assume a positive obligation to intervene in private relations to limit the adverse effects of private discrimination on the opportunities of individuals? Does realizing equality mean that government should guarantee not just equality of opportunity, but of results as well? If so, how far into our social and economic life should government intervene to assure that people are equal?

In this chapter we will deal with three aspects of the drive for equality, a concept central to democracy. First, we will examine efforts to halt government-imposed inequality. Second, we will examine how governmental power is being employed to limit private discrimination. And third, we will look at the approach which insists that government help individuals achieve equality. The first calls for *limits on governmental power*. The next calls for governmental *limits on private economic power*. The last calls for *government to assume a positive obligation* to compel others to advance the rights of those who have suffered discrimination.

LIMITING GOVERNMENT'S POWER TO DISCRIMINATE

Governments at different levels of our federal system have at times adopted as public policy the prejudices of those who feared or disliked some group and ascribed to its members qualities of inferiority. By writing these convictions into law, governments officially sanctioned inequality and sought to perpetuate it.

State and local governments have been the most active in denying equality of rights. In breaking down their barriers to equality, the U.S. Supreme Court has relied upon the Fourteenth and Fifteenth Amendments, which explicitly restrain state power in favor of human rights. Because these amendments expanded the power of Congress by authorizing it to enforce their provisions through appropriate means, Congress has also played a part in striking down state laws and practices that legitimated inequality.

Under our federal system, the states are empowered to set voting requirements, within the limits established by the Constitution. The Fifteenth Amendment (1870) prohibited states from denying anyone the right to vote because of race, color, or previous condition of servitude. It was deliberately designed to enable the new black citizens to participate in the political system after the Civil War by giving them a voice in the selection of their governmental leaders.

In the southern states—the epicenter of the old slave economy and culture and of the country's black population—many blacks did originally try to take advantage of their Fifteenth Amendment right. They participated as voters and competed successfully for seats in the state legislatures and the Congress. By the 1890s, however, many southern white leaders made a determined effort to deprive blacks of the right to vote. One objective was to prevent black citizens from having an equal opportunity with white citizens to select their governmental leaders. Another was to remove any incentive for candidates and public officials to appeal to black Americans for their support. With blacks shut out of (segregated from) the voting process, their interests could not be reflected in election politics or government policies.

Despite the Supreme Court's striking down a number of devices designed to disfranchise blacks in the South, the movement to circumvent the Fifteenth Amendment was until recent times very successful. The number of black voters declined drastically; by the 1930s only a minute fraction of the black people in the region voted. Legal barriers by government were reinforced by private economic and social sanctions against voting, often backed up by physical violence. Only the massive intervention of the national government through the Congress, the President, and the Supreme Court finally broke the back of voting segregation.

The Fifteenth Amendment forbids the states to use race or color as classifications in making distinctions between those who can or can not vote. This meant that those whites who drew up the laws depriving blacks of their right to vote had to use subterfuge to get around the Constitution. Impelled by their prejudice, they developed the most ingenious devices for excluding blacks, devices which have now been outlawed by Supreme Court decisions and congressional legislation.

The literacy test and the "grandfather clause."   Imposing a literacy test to qualify voters was one such device adopted by southern state legislatures. Literacy—the ability to read or write—ostensibly made no racial distinction and did not violate the Fifteenth Amendment. All potential voters were required to demonstrate literacy to vote. This device backfired at first, because illiteracy was originally very high among whites as well as blacks, which meant many whites were also prevented from voting. Since race and not illiteracy was the real classification which these state legislatures wanted to exclude, they devised a way for illiterate whites to vote.

The states modified their laws to adopt what was called a **grandfather clause.** It exempted from the literacy test all those who were descendents of people who had voted before a certain date (usually 1866). Although the grandfather clause still made no reference to race, the date selected was a complete giveaway. It antedated the Fifteenth Amendment, which forbade states to deny the right to vote to anyone because of race or color. Few blacks had fathers or grandfathers who were eligible to vote before that date, but almost all the illiterate whites did. As a consequence, the grandfather clause automatically exempted illiterate whites, but not blacks, from the literacy test. Eventually, the grandfather clause was struck down in the courts as a blatant attempt to nullify the Fifteenth Amendment.

The white primary. Another device for disfranchising blacks was the adoption of laws allowing only whites to vote in the Democratic primaries. In the **white primary,** southern whites explicitly relied on race to deprive blacks of the right to vote in the only meaningful elections in the South at the time, the Democratic party primaries. These primaries were elections to choose the Democratic candidates for public office. Before 1952 the Republican party was not a real contender for power in southern states, except in a few areas. Republicans either did not run candidates for public office or, if they did, such candidates had little chance of winning. As a result, whoever was chosen in the Democratic primaries almost always won the regular November elections. In other words, who would hold public office was really decided in the Democratic primaries.

If race or color were explicitly built into the party primary election, how did southern legislatures expect to get around the Fifteenth Amendment? The answer lay in the distinction between a primary and a regular election. The former was merely a nominating election within a private political party, not a regular election. Because public officials were legally chosen in the regular elections—and blacks could still vote in these—white segregationists felt they had effectively circumvented the Fifteenth Amendment.

Nevertheless the white primary laws were struck down by the Supreme Court as violating the Fifteenth Amendment's prohibition against states using race or color as a test for voting. The distinction between primary and final elections was irrelevant; state governments could not constitutionally bar anyone from voting on the basis of race, even in private party elections. Subsequent state legislative actions authorizing the Democratic parties themselves to bar black citizens from their primaries were also held to be violations of the Fifteenth Amendment. Thereupon, southern legislatures dropped all references to white primaries.

Since it was official state action that was forbidden by the Fifteenth Amendment, the Democratic parties, on their own initiative, undertook to exclude blacks from participating in their nominating elections. This time the Supreme Court decided that such white party primaries did not violate the Fifteenth Amendment, on the grounds that a political party was a private group and that primaries were not the final official elections for public office.

Not until 1944 was the white primary, as devised by a political party itself, declared unconstitutional by the Supreme Court. When a party held a primary, declared the Court, that party was acting as an instrument of the state, because the primary election was called for by state law and paid for by state money. Just as the state government was prohibited from preventing people from voting in primaries because of race or color, so too was the political party when it operated through state-mandated and financed primaries.

One southern legislature attempted to circumvent this decision by abolishing all its primary rules, enabling the Democratic party in the state to claim it was strictly a private group with the unqualified right to determine who could participate in the selection of its candidates. This too failed to satisfy the courts. Since those who won their party nominations had to compete for public office in the official elections run by the state, the private primary was still intimately tied to official state election machinery. From this time on, the white primary, with its explicit racial bias, was as dead as the grandfather clause, which had never referred to race.

Poll taxes. The poll tax was another device employed in some southern states to get around the Fifteenth Amendment and deprive black Americans of their equal right to vote. A poll tax required a person who wanted to vote to pay a special tax. This tax had no explicit racial basis; it discriminated equally against poor whites and poor blacks. By 1964, when use of the poll tax to disqualify people from voting in national elections was finally prohibited by the Twenty-fourth Amendment to the Constitution, most southern states had already repealed their poll tax laws. The Supreme Court terminated the poll tax as a requirement for voting in state elections in 1966 on the grounds that it violated the right of people to equal protection of the law as guaranteed them by the Fourteenth Amendment.

Abolishing the literacy test. Ironically, the device which survived longest and was most effective in disfranchising blacks was the literacy test. Its longevity can be explained by the fact that on its face it was not discriminatory: officially it affected blacks and whites equally. However, although the literacy test was applied fairly to blacks and whites in some parts of the South, in many other areas it was so administered as to discriminate against blacks: Illiterate whites were allowed to become voters; both literate and illiterate blacks were disqualified under the same tests. In states where this test called for an interpretation of the Constitution, those public officials who administered the tests had almost unlimited discretion to carry out their prejudices.

In a number of civil rights laws adopted in the 1960s, Congress began limiting the use of literacy tests, even to the extent of sending in national officers to register voters in areas where discrimination had been practiced. Eventually, through the Voting Rights Acts of 1970 and 1975, Congress completely forbade states to use literacy tests for determining who was eligible to vote.

The official state walls against equality in voting because of race have now been torn down. Equality in voting did not come quickly or easily. In its final stages this change was resisted in some parts of the South with violence and intimidation. Nevertheless, black Americans today are no longer segregated out of the election system in the South; they register and vote by the millions (see Table 17–1). An increasing number of blacks have been elected to serve in southern legislatures and as mayors, sheriffs, judges, and city councilmen at the local level of government. In the last few years, black congressmen have been elected from Georgia, Tennessee, and Texas with the support of white and black

Table 17–1
Black Voter Registration in the South, 1940–1973

	Estimated Number of Black Registrants	Percentage of Black Voting-age Population Registered
1940	250,000	5
1947	595,000	12
1952	1,008,614	20
1956	1,238,038	25
1960	1,414,052	28
1964	1,907,279	38
1968	3,312,000	62
1970	3,357,000	54*
1973	3,560,856	59*

*Includes eighteen-year-old voters.

SOURCE: David Campbell and Joe R. Feagin, "Black Politics in the South: A Descriptive Analysis," *Journal of Politics*, Vol. 7, No. 1 (Feb. 1975), p. 133.

Figure 17–1
The Rising Black Vote in the South

1960
1,463,000

1964
2,164,000

1968
3,112,000

1972
3,576,639

1976
4,000,000

VA.
N.C.
ARK. TENN.
S.C.
MISS.
TEXAS LA. ALA. GA.
FLA

SOURCE: *The New York Times*, Nov. 14, 1976, p. 4E.

voters. The intent of the Fifteenth Amendment has now been fully realized—state governments will not use race or color to deny people the right to vote, and black Americans will have an equal opportunity to elect public officials.

Breaking Down Governmental Barriers to Equality in Public and Private Life

The Fourteenth Amendment to the Constitution specifically forbade states to deny any person "equal protection of the law." But this clause is vague and open to various interpretations. It is little wonder that the Supreme Court, at different times in our history, arrived at different conclusions about laws that segregated (separated) people according to their race. In the 1890s the Court accepted segregation as legitimate under the equal protection clause. By 1954, however, the Court rejected all segregation by law as unconstitutional.

In the intervening sixty years segregation had not only been legal, but it had become deeply embedded in our culture, both in the South and in parts of the North. Many whites accepted segregation as the customary, proper, and legitimate way of life. For much of our history a number of states ordered and practiced segregation in both the public and private sectors of life. State laws demanded that blacks and whites attend separate public schools and that separate public facilities—water fountains, toilets, waiting rooms—be provided for the different races. Moreover, blacks were forbidden to serve on juries. In the private sphere, some state governments forbade marriages between blacks and whites; they required buses and theaters to seat blacks and whites in separate sections and required railroads to maintain separate cars for the two races. A few cities even tried to segregate blacks and whites in separate residential sections.

These laws were adopted by state legislatures and city councils to keep blacks from mixing with whites. Blacks were officially treated as if they were unequal, inferior to whites. To a certain extent the national government also practiced racial segregation. The military was segregated until the 1950s, and Washington, D.C., which is governed by Congress, was for a long time fully segregated by law.

In 1954 the Supreme Court determined that governmentally imposed segregation was itself unequal and unconstitutional. This decision generated a tremendous outcry. Resistance to the abolition of segregation was massive, deeply emotional, and occasionally violent. Today, more than twenty years later, much progress has occurred, but the fight over adjusting to that decision is still extremely emotional and occasionally violent.

Breaking Down Official Segregation in the Public Schools

You should be familiar with _Plessy_ v. _Ferguson_ (1896), because this case first gave constitutional blessing to segregation by state governments, although it did not deal with schools. Louisiana law required separate accommodations for blacks and whites traveling by railroad. When this law was challenged as violating the equal protection rights guaranteed by the Fourteenth Amendment, it was upheld by the U.S. Supreme Court. Both the logic and size of that majority had far-reaching consequences for segregation as a governmental practice in the United States.

Eight judges agreed that laws compelling whites and blacks to separate by race were constitutional. The mandate of the Fourteenth Amendment was met as long as facilities afforded the two races were equal. In other words, official racial segregation was constitutional if black and whites were given similar facilities. Only one judge dissented, arguing that the Constitution was colorblind and that state segregation by race was, therefore, unconstitutional.

The "separate but equal" doctrine that emerged out of *Plessy* v. *Ferguson* legitimized governmentally imposed racial segregation. For decades, relying upon this decision, all southern states and some northern cities lawfully practiced segregation in their public school systems, forbidding black and white children to attend the same schools. Southern states went a step further and segregated their colleges and universities by race. The dual school systems established, financed, and operated by states and local governments were, however, rarely if ever equal. Black schools were almost always decidedly inferior.

In **Brown v. Board of Education of Topeka,** the Supreme Court, in 1954, reconsidered its position on governmental segregation in the public schools. In a revolutionary decision—almost sixty years of legal segregation was overruled—the Court held that laws separating people on the basis of race violated the equal protection clause of the Fourteenth Amendment. State governments that practiced school segregation were found to be fostering a sense of inferiority among black children. Segregation could, therefore, never be equal, even if all the physical educational facilities of dual school systems were identical. "Separate but equal" was repudiated by a unanimous Supreme Court, which concluded that *segregation was itself inequality.*

All state and local laws based on racial segregation were undermined by the *Brown* decision. *Brown* sounded the critical trumpet call in the fight against compulsory inequality. Like the walls of Jericho, the official walls of segregation eventually came tumbling down.

They did not collapse all at once. The Court gave the offending governments time to move with deliberation so as to absorb the social and political shock that would result from removing governmental discrimination against blacks. State and local governments were ordered to move with "all deliberate speed" in dismantling the walls of school segregation; the lower national courts were instructed to monitor their action. Some ten years later, in the face of almost total resistance to its order that segregation in schools be dismantled, the Court held that "all deliberate speed" was no longer constitutionally permissible. Dual school systems based on race had to be terminated at once. Today the courts are still engaged in the process of compelling some cities to abolish their segregated school systems.

Breaking Other Governmental Barriers to Equality: In Juries, Housing, Marriage

That racial segregation actually reflected a governmental policy of fostering racial inferiority was most clearly illustrated in the laws preventing blacks and members of other groups from serving on juries.

Juries are supposed to be composed of people who are our peers, our equals. Permitting blacks or Mexican-Americans to sit with whites as jurors or to share in determining the guilt or innocence of white defendants meant accepting them as equals. Hence some states and communities barred them from any opportunity to serve as jurors. The Court eventually recognized that excluding people on the basis of color or national origin reflected an official judgment that they were not the peers or equals of other Americans. State laws or practices that systematically excluded blacks or Mexican-Americans from participating on juries have therefore been held to violate the equal protection clause of the Fourteenth Amendment. The same prohibition applies in the selection of grand juries.

As for segregation in housing, some southern cities have in the past attempted by law to separate blacks and whites so that they could not live in the same residential areas. The Supreme Court has concluded that this, too, violated the Fourteenth Amendment's due process protection of liberty.

The most intimate social group in our society is the family. Yet some states used race as a classification to prevent certain individuals from marrying. For many years all southern and some western states forbade marriages that crossed racial lines. Whites and blacks could not intermarry in the southern states; often it was orientals and caucasians who could not intermarry in the western ones. Since 1967, when the Court struck down a Virginia law prohibiting interracial marriages as violating both the equal protection and the due process clauses of the Fourteenth Amendment, all such laws have been unconstitutional. The Court unanimously condemned such white supremacy legislation as "odious to a free people whose institutions are founded upon a doctrine of equality."

Determining Constitutionality
of Unequal Treatment by Government

All laws that treat people unequally are *not* automatically unconstitutional. The Supreme Court has continued to recognize that the "Fourteenth Amendment does not deny to States the power to treat classes of persons in different ways . . . . "Consider the following: States are permitted to deny those below the age of eighteen the right to vote while guaranteeing this right to those eighteen and over. States may grant marriage licenses to applicants who have reached a specific age and have passed a venereal disease test, but may deny them to individuals who do not meet the age test or pass the health test. States may tax people with larger incomes at a rate higher than those with lesser incomes. And states may zone land for various uses, a governmental practice that affects differentially the economic interests of those owning the land. Moreover, the Supreme Court recently upheld a Florida law that gives widows, but not widowers, an annual property tax exemption and a California disability insurance program that excludes normal pregnancy from its protection coverage. None of these differences in the treatment of people by state governments violate the equal protection clause.

To help it decide whether the Fourteenth Amendment's prohibition against states depriving persons of equal protection of the law has been violated, the Court has developed certain tests, or standards, for determining whether unequal treatment by government is or is not permissible. None of these tests is absolute, but two of them, the *suspect classification test* and the *fundamental rights test,* weigh very heavily against state governments. Should governmental distinctions between people violate either test, unequal treatment is presumed to be unconstitutional. In such cases government carries a heavy burden in trying to demonstrate that its laws have not violated the Fourteenth Amendment. Under the *irrational-unreasonable test,* on the other hand, government is given more leeway by the Court. Laws are presumed to be constitutional unless the complaining party can prove otherwise.

Special suspect classifications. By labeling certain governmental classifications of people automatically suspect, the Supreme Court has sharply restricted state power to discriminate. It might help you understand the Court's view of suspect classifications if you read Judge Lewis F. Powell, Jr.'s, definition. Suspect classifications cover persons who are "saddled with such disabilities, or subject to such a history of purposeful unequal treatment, or relegated to such position of political powerlessness as to command extraordinary protection from the majoritarian political process." Justice Powell is saying that persons in certain groups need special consideration or protection against laws that majorities adopt. The Court has so far found race, national origin, and alienage (status as an alien) to be such suspect classifications. Laws differentiating among people on the basis of these classifications are presumed to be unconstitutional.

Race, national origin, and alienage may still be used, however, by state governments as classifications for dealing with people, but only if such governments can show a "compelling public interest" for their use. And the burden of proof is a demanding one. To justify the use of one of these suspect classifications, a state must "show that its purpose or interest is both constitutionally permissible and substantial, and that its use of the classification is necessary . . . to the accomplishment of its purpose or the safeguarding of its interest." In the absence of such a justification, these classifications are considered to violate the equal protection clause of the Fourteenth Amendment.

Recent court cases illustrate the Supreme Court's stern insistence that alienage is a suspect classification. In 1971 laws of Arizona and Pennsylvania that barred welfare payments for resident aliens but not for resident citizens were declared unconstitutional. The judges held that "classifications based on alienage, like those based on nationality or race, are inherently suspect and subject to close judicial scrutiny. Aliens as a class are a prime example of a . . . minority . . . for whom such heightened judicial solicitude is appropriate." And in 1973 the Court used this reasoning to strike down a Connecticut rule that denied aliens permission to practice law.

The same restriction regarding the classification of aliens does not apply to the national government. True, in 1976 the Court nullified a regulation of the U.S. Civil Service Commission barring aliens from employment in the national civil service. This was held to violate the liberty–due process guarantee of the Fifth Amendment. The Court implied, however, that if Congress or the President had imposed citizenship requirements, such action would be valid. And in 1976, that same year, the Court upheld an act of Congress which placed a condition on the eligibility of permanent resident aliens for medicare supplemental insurance: They had to have resided in the country for five continuous years. The Court concluded that this law did not constitute insidious discrimination against aliens as a class or deprive the ineligible aliens of their rights under the Fifth Amendment.

Two controversial classifications that have not yet been declared inherently suspect are sex and age. So far, only four judges (one short of a majority) on the Supreme Court have come to accept the argument that sex as a classification is suspect. Should the proposed Twenty-seventh Amendment to the Constitution—the Equal Rights Amendment—be ratified, discrimination on the basis of sex would be constitutionally prohibited. In an upsurge of resentment against the compulsory retirement built into state and local government employment practices, many middle-age and older Americans are now asking that age be included within the suspect classification. At present, age, like sex, remains outside the Court's forbidden list. But Congress has now responded to the complaints of older Americans by passing a law that prohibits the compulsory retirement of employees before age seventy by private and governmental employers.

Classifications dealing with "fundamental rights" are suspect. A second test that applies to unequal treatment is that of "fundamental rights." Using the equal protection clause of the Fourteenth Amendment, the Court has struck down a number of state laws that deprived some individuals of rights while affording those rights to others. Note that in this instance it is not the classification of persons per se that is forbidden but the denial of the equal opportunity to "fundamental rights."

The Court has stated, for example, that individuals have a fundamental right to travel from one state to another. State laws that denied welfare assistance to those who had not resided in a state for at least one year have been declared unconstitutional as violating the right to travel. The purpose of these laws, said the Court, was to inhibit the migration of needy people into the state. The classification of people so as to deny them the exercise of a fundamental right is unconstitutional, unless it can stand the test of "a compelling public interest." "Fundamental rights," therefore, have special protections.

The Supreme Court has also included within the list of "fundamental rights" the right to vote. In 1972 the Court nullified a one-year residence requirement for voting in Tennessee because of an absence of a "compelling public interest." The judges rejected Tennessee's claim that the requirement furthered a compelling state interest to have more intelligent and knowledgeable voters. "Knowledge or competence has never been a criterion for participation in Tennessee's election process for long-time residents," the Court said. Therefore, if the state wanted to assure intelligent use of the ballot, "it may not try to serve the interest only with respect to new arrivals."

Equal protection prohibits "irrational" or "unreasonable" state distinctions. Virtually all laws discriminate in the sense that they make distinctions among people. But if the particular distinction is deemed *irrational* or *unreasonable*, it violates the Fourteenth Amendment's equal protection clause. A law fails the irrational or unreasonable test if the distinction that the law draws between two groups of people does not reasonably relate to the objective sought by that law.

Until the 1970s the Supreme Court held that states did not violate the Fourteenth Amendment's mandate for equal protection by providing different treatment for men and women. But in 1971 the Court invoked the equal protection clause to hold such laws unconstitutional as discriminating against women by using the irrational-unreasonable test. The case concerned an Idaho law that gave fathers preference over mothers in the appointment of administrators for the estates of minor children. The judges unanimously agreed that this difference in the treatment of sexes bore no rational relationship to the objectives of the law. Mothers could reasonably be assumed to be as capable as fathers to look after their children's estates. Certainly fathers could not be presumed to be more capable.

Equal protection for the sexes means, of course, that males as well as females will be protected. A majority of the Court in 1972 struck down an Illinois statute which discriminated in favor of unwed mothers in custody cases for illegitimate children. Presuming the fathers to be unfit, the law did not even allow them a hearing to determine whether they should have custody of the children. This sex discrimination did not reasonably relate to the purpose of the law.

Increasingly, the Court has struck down as irrational and unreasonable state laws that differentiate between the sexes. In 1975 it rejected a Utah law that responsibility for child support payments after a divorce stopped at age eighteen for female dependents, but continued to age twenty-one for male dependents. The Court rejected Utah's argument that females tended to marry earlier than males and that males needed more education and training because they were responsible for providing homes for their families. And in 1976 the Court rejected, as violating the equal protection clause, an Oklahoma law permitting females to be served beer at age eighteen while denying males that privilege until the age of twenty-one. In both cases the Court found that the distinctions were irrational and unreasonable. Do you agree?

PROHIBITING PRIVATE DISCRIMINATION IN ECONOMIC AFFAIRS

Acceptance of the equality concept has now greatly accelerated. Walls of inequality erected by governmental discrimination are not the only ones coming down. Private walls—economic discrimination by private individuals and groups—are also crumbling as a result of governmental intervention at all levels of our federal system. In fact, we have been undergoing an "equality revolution" in the United States. Why do we use the term *revolution*? First, the Court and Congress have moved radically and extensively to abolish government-imposed inequality. Second, this concern with abolishing governmental rules that foster inequality has now been carried over to a concern with eliminating private barriers to equality. We have shifted our view of government from one in which it was a potential violator of rights to one in which it uses its power to protect rights.

Traditionally, Americans have looked upon their rights almost entirely as needing protection *against* governmental power. The drafters of the Constitution, the first ten amendments, and the later civil rights amendments were concerned with restraining the power of government; at first only the national government but later including state governments. Our rights had to be protected against those who, in the name of the public, had tremendous power to control life, liberty, and property. The modern equality revolution, on the other hand, also includes a concern with protecting individuals from the prejudice of private power, that of businessmen and labor unions.

Preventing Private Discrimination in Accommodation Businesses

The extent of the equality revolution is revealed in part in the changed attitude of the Supreme Court toward Congress' efforts to deal with economic discrimination. Originally, the Court rejected the proposition that Congress could constitutionally intervene in private economic relations to prevent inequality. On the basis of its power to enforce the Fourteenth Amendment, Congress in 1875 had adopted a Civil Rights Act. This law made it a crime to deny any person, on the basis of race or color, access to inns, transportation, and theaters. The Supreme Court declared the law unconstitutional on the grounds that the Fourteenth Amendment prohibited only state discrimination, not racial discrimination practiced by private individuals.

By the 1960s the Supreme Court concluded that Congress could prohibit unequal treatment by private individuals in economic relations. Congress's broad power to regulate interstate commerce was sufficient authority to prohibit such private discrimination. Under the Civil Rights Act of 1964, the Congress banned discrimination on the basis of race, color, religion, or national origin by a number of accommodation businesses—hotels, motels, gas stations, restaurants, theaters, and large places of entertainment—whose operations affected interstate commerce. Congress's power to promote interstate commerce, said the Court, extends to the prohibition of private discrimination that may have a "substantial and harmful effect upon that commerce." Individuals who wished to purchase services or products from such businesses could not be discriminated against because of their race, color, religion, or national origin.

Preventing Private Discrimination in Employment

Another provision of the Civil Rights Act of 1964 prohibited discrimination in employment practices by businesses and unions affecting interstate commerce. This section of the law was much broader than the one that called for equality of accommodations. It covered a greater part of the economic sector relating to interstate commerce: *all* businesses and unions with twenty-five or more employees or members, rather than just certain kinds of accommodation enterprises. It also added sex to the forbidden classifications. By relying on its interstate commerce power, the national government was able to assume responsibility for regulating private business and labor union practices to ensure people the right to equal employment opportunities, irrespective of race, color, religion, national origin, or sex. Congress expanded the coverage of the 1964 law and improved its enforcement provisions in the Equal Employment Opportunity Act of 1972.

Congressional prohibitions against employment discrimination had been preceded much earlier by presidential action. President Franklin D. Roosevelt, by executive order, had prohibited discrimination in employment in defense-related industries as early as 1940. And President Harry S Truman had banned discrimination in the employment of people by the national government itself by an executive order in 1945.

Some businesses and unions are still permitted to discriminate by race, color, religion, sex, or national origin. Small businesses are specifically exempt from the coverage of the 1964 and 1972 laws. However, the number of such exempt businesses has decreased sharply since the 1972 Equal Employment Opportunity Act extended its coverage to those with fifteen or more employees. Sex, religion, or national origin (but not race) may continue to be used if the classification is "a bona fide occupational qualification reasonably necessary to the operation of that particular business or enterprise." A religious school, for example, may hire only employees of a particular faith if the curriculum is directed toward propagating that faith.

Preventing Private Discrimination in Housing

Housing is the third economic area that has now come under the national prohibition against private discrimination. In the past, state courts had been willing to enforce restrictive covenants in private contracts—agreements forbidding individuals to sell houses to people of certain races, religions, or national origins. In 1948 the Supreme Court stopped this practice; the Court contended that state courts were lending the authority and legitimacy of public government to private discriminatory practices. Since states were forbidden by the Fourteenth Amendment to discriminate on the basis of race, their actions in enforcing private restrictive covenants were also illegal.

In 1968 Congress passed a national fair housing law which prohibited discrimination in the advertising, financing, sale, and rental of housing units. This law exempts certain people in housing from the prohibition against discrimination. Owners of single-family homes, whose sale or rental does not involve the use of real estate agents, may still discriminate. Exempt also under these rules are owner-occupied dwellings with four housing units or less.

The scope of the equality revolution in housing can also be measured by a 1968 Supreme Court decision that finally legitimated Congress' power to prevent private discrimination on the basis of race in matters of housing. The overwhelming majority of judges (eight to two) agreed that the Thirteenth Amendment, which prohibited slavery, constitutionally supported the following provision of the Civil Rights Act of 1866 as it applied to private discrimination:

> All citizens of the United States shall have the same right, in every State and Territory, as is enjoyed by white citizens thereof to inherit, purchase, lease, sell, hold, and convey real and personal property.

In 1976 the Supreme Court again relied on the Thirteenth Amendment and a provision of the same Civil Rights Act of 1866 to prohibit other types of private economic discrimination. The Civil Rights Act of 1866 had also provided that all persons within the country should have the same right to "make and enforce contracts" and to enjoy "full and equal benefit of all laws and proceedings for the security of persons and property as is enjoyed by white citizens. . . . " In one case the Court insisted that this provision prohibited commercially operated nonsectarian schools from refusing to admit black applicants because of their race. In another case the Court unanimously concluded that this provision of the Civil Rights Act of 1866 also prohibited racial discrimination against whites in private employment. "All persons" was held to apply equally to members of all races; therefore, it protected whites as well as blacks against job discrimination based on racial grounds.

Many city, county, and state governments have now adopted fair employment and housing laws to eliminate economic inequality based on private prejudice. Such laws show that support for fair employment and fair housing is not solely a national policy. State house, city hall, and Washington, D.C., have begun to march together in the same equality revolution.

Private Noneconomic Discrimination Is Still Permissible

Privately imposed inequality has been prohibited by government only in the economic sphere. In the social and religious spheres of our private lives, we retain the right to choose our friends, guests, club members, and religious colleagues. But if state or local governments become "significantly involved" in supporting private social discrimination, it would transform permissible private action into unconstitutional public action.

In our social and religious but not our economic relations, we may discriminate on whatever grounds we wish. These are strictly private decisions. Should government prohibit discrimination in private (noneconomic) relations? That is a matter for you and others to decide. Can government do so constitutionally? That is a matter for the Supreme Court to decide. You now confront a basic question that was raised in your first chapter: How far into the private sphere of society and our personal lives should government extend its power in order to protect and advance the right to equality?

SHOULD GOVERNMENT MAKE PEOPLE EQUAL?

Should government try to guarantee equality? That, in essence, is the controversial equality issue facing us today. The battle has moved far beyond knocking down the walls of discrimination created by governmental rules or by private practices. Should government actively intervene to help people achieve equality when they are unable to achieve it themselves? Should government give or allow others to give special advantages to members of minority groups who have suffered from discrimination and its effects? These questions lie at the heart of the latest phase of the equality revolution.

A reversal in our approach to race, national origin, and sex is occurring. Until recently, such categories for dealing with people were considered (except for sex) constitutionally suspect. Now using these very same categories is being advanced as legitimate, *if* they are used to help members of these groups overcome the disadvantages of past discrimination.

In education the original equality approach concentrated on abolishing segregation. The new approach calls for integration, the deliberate mixing of students from different racial, ethnic, or sexual groups. It also calls for giving special advantages to members of minority groups.

A similar reversal characterizes government's attempt to deal with inequality in private employment. The original equality approach concentrated on prohibiting governmental and private employment rules based on race, religion, sex, and national origin. The new approach—affirmative action—is for government to help women and members of minority groups secure jobs and promotions and to demand that employers and unions make special efforts in their behalf.

Education and Equality

Desegregation, the initial approach to overcoming racial inequality in the schools, lasted for about fifteen years after the *Brown* case. It collapsed in good part because many communities and states made little or no real effort to desegregate. Thereafter, the Supreme Court moved away from its emphasis on desegregation toward a policy of integration.

In *Brown* v. *Board of Education of Topeka* (1954), the Supreme Court unanimously decided that segregated schools were automatically unconstitutional. One year later, lower national courts were ordered to ensure that state and local governments complied with the Supreme Court's mandate for a prompt and reasonable start "to effectuate a transition to a racially nondiscriminatory school system." On the whole very little progress took place and, when desegregation was officially adopted, most minority students and white students continued to attend separate sets of schools.

In 1968 the Supreme Court took a stronger stand, one that moved the lower courts into employing integration as a policy position. A county in rural Virginia had officially discontinued its segregated schools but continued to assign students to the same schools they had previously been attending along racial lines. Although students were permitted to request a change in school assignment, no white child was assigned or requested a transfer to a "black" school and only a few black children requested a change to a "white" school.

Calling attention to the fact that 85 percent of all black students in that county were still in traditionally black schools, the Supreme Court completely rejected the pupil assignment solution. In effect, said the Court, the county was still operating a dual school system based on race, contrary to the *Brown* decision. The fact that segregation was no longer compulsory did not end the dual, racially segregated school system. Only a united nonracial school system of public education, the Court concluded, was the ultimate end to which *Brown* pointed. The Court, therefore, ordered a new plan that would convert the school system into one "without a 'white' school and a 'Negro' school, but just schools. . . ." Following these guidelines, lower courts throughout the nation began ordering localities operating dual school systems to integrate; that is, the courts began using race as a classification for assigning students to schools in order to ensure the operation of integrated systems. Race was now used to mix students, not to separate them.

Busing became an intensely emotional and political issue in the North and the South in the late 1960s and 1970s as transfers of children were ordered to ensure that schools were not white or black. In 1971 the Supreme Court itself dealt specifically with this issue: Was busing or the transfer of school children along racial lines in order to abolish dual school systems a constitutionally acceptable remedy?

A lower court had ordered an extensive school busing plan in Charlotte, North Carolina. When that plan was challenged, the Supreme Court held that busing was one legitimate judicial means for eliminating vestiges of state-imposed segregation. The Court did point out that, in the absence of a history of state-imposed segregation in the schools, there "would be no basis for judicially ordered assignment of students on a racial basis." In such instances, the school board could integrate or not as it wished, but there would be no constitutional responsibility for doing so. The Court also recognized that population could shift considerably within many communities. It held, therefore, that neither the lower courts nor the school authorities were constitutionally required to make yearly adjustments in the racial composition of the student body, once "the affirmative duty to desegregate has been accomplished and racial discrimination through official action is eliminated from the system."

On the basis of these criteria, the Supreme Court rejected lower court orders compelling school systems that had not resorted to segregation to link up in school busing plans with those that had. Schools in Detroit, Michigan, which had been desegregated, had become resegregated in fact (not law) because many whites had moved to areas beyond the city limits. To abolish this new form of segregation, a lower national court ordered schools in the suburbs around Detroit to consolidate with city schools. Busing was to be used to achieve this objective. In 1974 the Supreme Court rejected the plan. The judiciary, it held, could not impose a multidistrict, areawide plan to remedy segregation in the city when there was no proof that the suburbs had themselves practiced segregation.

In 1976, again on the basis of its new criteria, the Supreme Court held (six to two) that a lower national court could not require Pasadena, California, school authorities to readjust their attendance lines each year to keep up with population shifts. Pasadena authorities had initially complied with a court order to revise their school attendance zones and to enact a "racially neutral" system of student assignments. The Supreme Court concluded that the lower court had, therefore, already fulfilled its function of providing the necessary remedy; the school authorities could not be ordered to do more.

Later in 1976 the Supreme Court went a step further in limiting the power of lower national courts to impose broad school integration plans on a community. A lower court had found illegal discrimination against both blacks and Mexican-Americans in the Austin, Texas, school system. The Supreme Court held it was not enough to prove that official laws or acts place a "substantially disproportionate" burden on a racial group. To prove a violation of the Constitution's ban on racial discrimination, it was also necessary to prove a "racially discriminatory purpose." Discriminatory *effect* was insufficient; discriminatory *intent* had also to be demonstrated. The case was sent back to the lower courts for a reexamination of the facts in light of this criterion.

Although the push in the equality revolution seems to have reached its limits in the area of public schools, it has taken a different direction in higher education. Public colleges and universities, like public schools that discriminated in the past, have been compelled by court order to admit women and members of minority groups who meet regular admission standards. But a number of these schools, on their own initiative, moved far beyond desegregation. Some set aside special quotas for members of minority groups to guarantee their entrance. And some lowered their standards so that members of minority groups could be assured admission. These quotas and lower standards were justified by school authorities on the grounds that past discriminatory practices so handicapped individuals in minority groups that, without such special advantages, minority students could not compete effectively for entrance into institutions of higher education.

May public colleges and universities legally use special admissions programs with quotas or different standards for minority students? Should colleges and universities judge minority applications separately or by lower standards to assure them entrance if such individuals cannot meet the usual standards? The questions go to the heart of the equality revolution today: How far should governmental institutions go in fostering equality? And if special quotas or lower standards are used for certain minority students, is this not racial discrimination in reverse?

Are not other students discriminated against if those who have higher marks or scores on entrance examinations are excluded from professional schools because of the favoritism afforded minority students?

The charge of **reverse discrimination** is now before the courts and the nation. Here we face two conflicting values: equality for all, meaning the same standards for all, as against inequality, meaning special advantages for minority students so they can catch up in economic and social equality with the rest of the population. Does the drive for equal opportunity for some have to result in the denial of equal opportunity for others? This is the ironic question that the equality revolution has posed in the schools of higher education.

The reverse discrimination issue first reached the Court in 1974 when a white student, Marco DeFunis, charged that he had been deprived of equal protection under the Fourteenth Amendment. He had been denied admission to the law school at the University of Washington, a public university, while thirty-six of the forty-four minority applicants who were accepted had lower grades and entrance scores than he. The issues raised by DeFunis were never resolved because, by the time the case came to the Supreme Court, he had already been admitted to and graduated from the law school on an order from a lower court.

The issue of reverse discrimination, or the validity of special advantages for minority students in higher education, was raised anew in 1976. A white male, Allan Bakke, who wanted to become a physician, was twice rejected by the medical school of the University of California at Davis, which reserved sixteen of one hundred places in its entering class for members of minority groups. Maintaining he was better qualified for admission than some of these minority students, having scored higher on tests than they, he charged discrimination on the basis of race, which violated his right to equal protection under the Fourteenth Amendment. His position was upheld in the state's supreme court and subsequently by a sharply divided U.S. Supreme Court (five to four). The Court was so divided in its opinion that all one can conclude from its decision is that the university's quota for the admission of minorities was an unconstitutional violation of Bakke's right to equal protection, but that race can still legitimately be used as a factor in determining the admission of students. The Court's decision left unanswered as many if not more questions than it answered. How far the equality revolution advances in the field of higher education still remains to be fought out in the political system.

Employment and Equality

Government originally intervened to break down private discrimination in employment by making it illegal for employers and unions to discriminate against individuals in employment practices because of race, sex, religion, or national origin. Now it has adopted the approach of ordering employers and unions to act affirmatively in seeing that women and members of minority groups are hired and promoted. A 1965 executive order by President Lyndon B. Johnson laid the legal foundation for affirmative action, It required contractors working for the national government to formulate plans for the employment and promotion of women and members of minority groups. Universities and colleges receiving money from the national government were later brought under this order. In the $4 billion public works law that it adopted early in 1977, in an effort to create job possibilities for about one million people, Congress moved a step further in affirmative action. One provision of this law required that 10 percent of the dollar amount of public works projects be earmarked for minority building contractors.

In 1976 the Supreme Court accepted the affirmative action approach. It ordered that blacks who had earlier been denied jobs in violation of the Civil Rights Act of 1964 be awarded retroactive seniority with all its benefits and rights. In other words, the employers were obligated to move them to the position of equality they might have achieved had they not illegally been discriminated against in the first place. What about the rights of those white workers who had innocently benefited as a result of past discrimination against blacks? The Court observed that, as it had noted in the area of public education, whites had to share with blacks "the burden of past discrimination" in the area of employment.

In 1976 the U.S. Department of Justice sued the City of Boston, Massachusetts, on the charge that it practiced discrimination against blacks and Spanish-surnamed individuals in its Public Works Department. In addition to asking the lower national courts to forbid future discrimination, the U.S. government requested that the city be ordered to start recruiting blacks and Spanish-surnamed employees and to compensate the victims of past discrimination.

Affirmative action programs elsewhere call for the recruitment and promotion of women and minority group members, even to the point of demanding that the employer or union show progress in meeting certain target goals. Such guidelines have also been imposed by the U.S. Department of Health, Education and Welfare on those universities and colleges receiving national financial support for research and other activities.

Another dimension of the new emphasis upon equality in employment centers on the constitutionality of tests for hiring employees. Should government nullify employment tests used by businesses that contain no references to race but which are failed disproportionately by members of one race? In 1971 the Supreme Court held such examinations unconstitutional under the Civil Rights Act of 1964. On the other hand, the Court did agree that an employer who could demonstrate a sufficient relationship between the abilities tested and the job for which the examination was designed could still administer the examination.

By 1976 the Court began moving away from a reliance upon discriminatory impact to one based on purpose or intent as well. A higher proportion of blacks than whites had failed the examination for employment on the Washington, D.C., police force. A challenge to this test was dismissed by the Court (seven to two) on the grounds that a law or other official act was not unconstitutional merely because it places a disproportionate burden on one race. Proving a violation of the constitutional ban against racial discrimination requires proof of "a racially discriminatory purpose" in addition to a discriminatory effect. Discriminatory effect alone is insufficient to prove racial bias.

In 1979 civil rights organizations favoring special preference job quotas for blacks scored a victory. In what is commonly referred to as the Weber Case, the Supreme Court ruled, five to two, that a voluntary employer-union plan reserving to black employees 50 percent of the openings in a job-upgrading program *did not* violate the Civil Rights Act of 1964, which specifically prohibited racial discrimination in employment. Weber, a white employee who had been rejected although he had more job seniority than one of the black workers accepted in the program, argued that the racial quotas imposed reverse discrimination against him as a white.

Note that this case did not involve a state government or call for an interpretation of constitutional rights. The Court simply ruled that the plan under attack did not violate the law; the prohibition against racial discrimination in employment in the Civil Rights Act of 1964 did "not condemn all private, voluntary, race-conscious affirmative action plans." However, the Court made no attempt to differentiate between permissible and nonpermissible plans.

Housing, Zoning, and Equality

Private and public discrimination on the basis of race in the rental or sale of houses is now prohibited. Should government, in addition, take the initiative and push for equality in housing? In other words, should it order remedial action in housing to compensate minority groups for past patterns of inequalities against them?

In 1976 the Supreme Court agreed with lower courts that the City of Chicago and the U.S. Department of Housing and Urban Development had discriminated illegally against blacks in building public housing only in certain low-income, black residential areas. Since some of Chicago's suburbs had also been involved in such discriminatory practices, the lower courts concluded that the entire metropolitan area was the relevant locality for locating low-cost housing; a plan for the city alone would not remedy the situation. The Supreme Court concurred in the propriety of a comprehensive metropolitan plan that required both local and national governments to fund housing beyond Chicago's city limits.

But in 1977 the new "intent rather than discriminatory effect alone" standard was used by the Court to cancel remedial affirmative action ordered by a lower court for a particular suburb of Chicago. This suburb had refused to change its zoning restriction that limited buildings to single-family houses. A firm wanting to build a low-income housing project claimed that this failure to rezone was unconstitutional because it had a discriminatory effect on members of one race, most of whom could not afford to purchase single-family houses. The suburban government argued that its zoning law was not intended to bar blacks, but rather to maintain its low-density population character.

The Supreme Court held that this refusal to rezone was not unconstitutional just because it had a "racially disproportionate impact." For governmental action to be unconstitutional, there must also be an "intent" or "purpose" to discriminate. The suburb could only be forced to rezone if it were shown that the refusal to do so was based on a desire to exclude minority group members. Since intent of discrimination had not been demonstrated, the Court refused to place on the suburb an affirmative obligation to allow low-cost multidwelling housing to be built within its limits. The Court explained, however, how intent could be proven: by examining the background and legislative history of the zoning policy and by determining whether the policy was a departure from normal procedures used by the government involved.

Although some state supreme courts have invalidated suburban zoning laws on the sole ground that they have the effect of excluding members of a minority group, the U.S. Supreme Court has adopted an additional standard of its own. It has now taken the position that, under the national Constitution, intent of prejudice as well as discriminatory effect must be shown before affirmative action to require equality may be imposed.

Thus far this new standard has been applied in the education field with regard to compelling the mixing of races, in the employment field with regard to tests, and in the housing field with regard to suburban zoning. It seems clear, therefore, that at least for the near future one major limit has been placed on the equality revolution.

Is it a reasonable limit? How far should we go in using the power of government in our society to impose equality? These are policy considerations that will continue to confront us and our state and national governments. They are extremely controversial and not easy to decide, since they end up forcing a confrontation between different sets of values and rights.

Concepts To Study

affirmative action
democracy
discriminatory effect
discriminatory intent
equal protection of the law

equality
"equality revolution"
federalism
governmental
  discrimination

private discrimination
quotas
reverse discrimination
segregation
separate but equal doctrine

Special Terms To Review

Bakke case
Brown v. Board of Education
  of Topeka (1954)
Civil Rights Act of 1964
Declaration of Independence
Equal Employment
  Opportunity Act of 1972

Equal Rights Amendment
fundamental rights test
grandfather clause
irrational–unreasonable test
literacy test
Plessy v. Ferguson (1896)

poll taxes
suspect classification test
Voting Rights Acts
  of 1970 and 1975
Weber case
white primary laws

THE CONSTITUTION
OF THE UNITED STATES

We the People of the United States, In Order to form a more perfect Union, establish Justice, insure domestic Tranquility, provide for the common defence, promote the general Welfare, and secure the Blessings of Liberty to ourselves and our Posterity, do ordain and establish this Constitution for the United States of America.

Article I

Section 1. All legislative Powers herein granted shall be vested in a Congress of the United States, which shall consist of a Senate and House of Representatives.

Section 2. The House of Representatives shall be composed of Members chosen every second Year by the People of the several States, and the Electors in each State shall have the Qualifications requisite for Electors of the most numerous Branch of the State Legislature.

No Person shall be a Representative who shall not have attained the Age of twenty five Years, and been seven Years a Citizen of the United States, and who shall not, when elected, be an Inhabitant of that State in which he shall be chosen.

Representatives and direct Taxes shall be apportioned among the several States which may be included within this Union, according to their respective Numbers, which shall be determined by adding to the whole Number of free Persons, including those bound to Service for a Term of Years, and excluding Indians not taxed, three fifths of all other Persons. The actual Enumeration shall be made within three Years after the first Meeting of the Congress of the United States, and within every subsequent Term of ten Years, in such Manner as they shall by Law direct. The Number of Representatives shall not exceed one for every thirty Thousand, but each State shall have at Least one Representative; and until such enumeration shall be made, the State of New Hampshire shall be entitled to chuse three, Massachusetts eight, Rhode-Island and Providence Plantations one, Connecticut five, New-York six, New Jersey four, Pennsylvania eight, Delaware one, Maryland six, Virginia ten, North Carolina five, South Carolina five, and Georgia three.

When vacancies happen in the Representation from any State, the Executive Authority thereof shall issue Writs of Election to fill such Vacancies.

The House of Representatives shall chuse their Speaker and other Officers; and shall have the sole Power of Impeachment.

Section 3. The Senate of the United States shall be composed of two Senators from each State, chosen by the Legislature thereof, for six Years; and each Senator shall have one Vote.

Immediately after they shall be assembled

in Consequence of the first Election, they shall be divided as equally as may be into three Classes. The Seats of the Senators of the first Class shall be vacated at the Expiration of the second Year, of the second Class at the Expiration of the fourth Year, and of the third Class at the Expiration of the sixth Year, so that one third may be chosen every second Year; and if Vacancies happen by Resignation, or otherwise, during the Recess of the Legislature of any State, the Executive thereof may make temporary Appointments until the next Meeting of the Legislature, which shall then fill such Vacancies.

No Person shall be a Senator who shall not have attained to the Age of thirty Years, and been nine Years a Citizen of the United States, and who shall not, when elected, be an Inhabitant of that State for which he shall be chosen.

The Vice President of the United States shall be President of the Senate, but shall have no Vote, unless they be equally divided.

The Senate shall chuse their other Officers, and also a President pro tempore, in the Absence of the Vice President, or when he shall exercise the Office of the President of the United States.

The Senate shall have the sole Power to try all Impeachments. When sitting for that Purpose, they shall be on Oath or Affirmation. When the President of the United States is tried, the Chief Justice shall preside: And no Person shall be convicted without the Concurrence of two thirds of the Members present.

Judgment in Cases of Impeachment shall not extend further than to removal from Office, and disqualification to hold and enjoy any Office of honor, Trust or Profit under the United States: but the Party convicted shall nevertheless be liable and subject to Indictment, Trial, Judgment and Punishment, according to Law.

Section 4. The Times, Places and Manner of holding Elections for Senators and Representatives, shall be prescribed in each State by the Legislature thereof; but the Congress may at any time by Law make or alter such Regulations, except as to the Places of chusing Senators.

The Congress shall assemble at least once in every Year, and such Meeting shall be on the first Monday in December, unless they shall by Law appoint a different Day.

Section 5. Each House shall be the Judge of the Elections, Returns and Qualifications of its own Members, and a Majority of each shall constitute a Quorum to do Business; but a smaller Number may adjourn from day to day, and may be authorized to compel the Attendance of absent Members, in such Manner, and under such Penalties as each House may provide.

Each House may determine the Rules of its Proceedings, punish its Members for disorderly Behaviour, and, with the Concurrence of two thirds, expel a Member.

Each House shall keep a Journal of its Proceedings, and from time to time publish the same, excepting such Parts as may in their Judgment require Secrecy; and the Yeas and Nays of the Members of either House on any question shall, at the Desire of one fifth of those Present, be entered on the Journal.

Neither House, during the Session of Congress, shall, without the Consent of the other, adjourn for more than three days, nor to any other Place than that in which the two Houses shall be sitting.

Section 6. The Senators and Representatives shall receive a Compensation for their Services, to be ascertained by Law, and paid out of the Treasury of the United States. They shall in all Cases, except Treason, Felony and Breach of the Peace, be privileged from Arrest during their Attendance at the Session of their respective Houses, and in going to and returning from the same; and for any Speech or Debate in either House, they shall not be questioned in any other Place.

No Senator or Representative shall, during the Time for which he was elected, be appointed to any civil Office under the Authority of the United States, which shall have been created, or the Emoluments whereof shall have been encreased during such time; and no Person holding any Office under the United States, shall be a Member of either House during his Continuance in Office.

Section 7. All Bills for raising Revenue shall originate in the House of Representatives; but the Senate may propose or concur with Amendments as on other Bills.

Every Bill which shall have passed the House of Representatives and the Senate, shall, before it become a Law, be presented to the President of the United States; If he approve he shall sign it, but if not he shall return it, with his Objections to that House in which it shall have originated, who shall enter the Objections at large on their Journal, and proceed to reconsider it. If after such Reconsideration two thirds of that House shall agree to pass the Bill, it shall be sent, together with the Objections, to the other House, by which it shall likewise be reconsidered, and if approved by two thirds of that House, it shall become a Law. But in all such Cases the Votes of both Houses shall be determined by Yeas and Nays, and the Names of the Persons voting for and against the Bill shall be entered on the Journal of each House respectively. If any Bill shall not be returned by the President within ten Days (Sundays excepted) after it shall have been presented to him, the Same shall be a Law, in like Manner as if he had signed it, unless the Congress by their Adjournment prevent its Return, in which Case it shall not be a Law.

Every Order, Resolution, or Vote to which the Concurrence of the Senate and House of Representatives may be necessary (except on a question of Adjournment) shall be presented to the President of the United States; and before the Same shall take Effect, shall be approved by him, or being disapproved by him, shall be repassed by two thirds of the Senate and House of Representatives, according to the Rules and Limitations prescribed in the Case of a Bill.

Section 8. The Congress shall have Power To lay and collect Taxes, Duties, Imposts and Excises, to pay the Debts and provide for the common Defence and general Welfare of the United States; but all Duties, Imposts and Excises shall be uniform throughout the United States;

To borrow Money on the credit of the United States;

To regulate Commerce with foreign Nations, and among the several States, and with the Indian Tribes;

To establish an uniform Rule of Naturalization, and uniform Laws on the subject of Bankruptcies throughout the United States;

To coin Money, regulate the Value thereof, and of foreign Coin, and fix the Standard of Weights and Measures;

To provide for the Punishment of counterfeiting the Securities and current Coin of the United States;

To establish Post Offices and post Roads;

To promote the Progress of Science and useful Arts, by securing for limited Times to Authors and Inventors the exclusive Right to their respective Writings and Discoveries;

To constitute Tribunals inferior to the supreme Court;

To define and punish Piracies and Felonies committed on the high Seas, and Offences against the Law of Nations;

To declare War, grant Letters of Marque and Reprisal, and make Rules concerning Captures on Land and Water;

To raise and support Armies, but no Appropriation of Money to that Use shall be for a longer Term than two Years;

To provide and maintain a Navy;

To make Rules for the Government and Regulation of the land and naval Forces;

To provide for calling forth the Militia to execute the Laws of the Union, suppress Insurrections and repel Invasions;

To provide for organizing, arming, and disciplining, the Militia, and for governing such Part of them as may be employed in the Service of the United States, reserving to the States respectively, the Appointment of the Officers, and the Authority of training the Militia according to the discipline prescribed by Congress;

To exercise exclusive Legislation in all Cases whatsoever, over such District (not exceeding ten Miles square) as may, by Cession of particular States, and the Acceptance of Congress, become the Seat of the Government of the United States, and to exercise like Authority over all Places purchased by the Consent of the Legislature of the State in which the Same shall be, for the Erection of Forts, Magazines, Arsenals, dock-Yards, and other needful Buildings;- And

To make all Laws which shall be necessary and proper for carrying into Execution the foregoing Powers, and all other Powers vested by this Constitution in the Government of the United States, or in any Department or Officer thereof.

Section 9. The Migration or Importation of such Persons as any of the States now existing shall think proper to admit, shall not be prohibited by the Congress prior to the Year one thousand eight hundred and eight, but a Tax or duty may be imposed on such Importation, not exceeding ten dollars for each Person.

The Privilege of the Writ of Habeas Corpus shall not be suspended, unless when in Cases of Rebellion or Invasion the public Safety may require it.

No Bill of Attainder or ex post facto Law shall be passed.

No Capitation, or other direct, Tax shall be

laid, unless in Proportion to the Census or Enumeration herein before directed to be taken.

No Tax or Duty shall be laid on Articles exported from any State.

No Preference shall be given by any Regulation of Commerce or Revenue to the Ports of one State over those of another; nor shall Vessels bound to, or from, one State be obliged to enter, clear, or pay Duties in another.

No Money shall be drawn from the Treasury, but in Consequence of Appropriations made by Law; and a regular Statement and Account of the Receipts and Expenditures of all public Money shall be published from time to time.

No Title of Nobility shall be granted by the United States: And no Person holding any Office of Profit or Trust under them, shall, without the Consent of the Congress, accept of any present, Emolument, Office, or Title, of any kind whatever, from any King, Prince, or foreign State.

Section 10. No State shall enter into any Treaty, Alliance, or Confederation; grant Letters of Marque and Reprisal; coin Money, emit Bills of Credit; make any Thing but gold and silver Coin a Tender in Payment of Debts; pass any Bill of Attainder, ex post facto Law, or Law impairing the Obligation of Contracts, or grant any Title of Nobility.

No State shall, without the Consent of the Congress, lay any Imposts or Duties on Imports or Exports, except what may be absolutely necessary for executing its inspection Laws; and the net Produce of all Duties and Imposts, laid by any State on Imports or Exports, shall be for the Use of the Treasury of the United States; and all such Laws shall be subject to the Revision and Controul of the Congress.

No State shall, without the Consent of Congress, lay any Duty of Tonnage, keep Troops, or Ships of War in time of Peace, enter into any Agreement or Compact with another State, or with a foreign Power, or engage in War, unless actually invaded, or in such imminent Danger as will not admit of delay.

Article II

Section 1. The executive Power shall be vested in a President of the United States of America. He shall hold his Office during the Term of four Years, and, together with the Vice President, chosen for the same Term, be elected, as follows

Each State shall appoint, in such Manner as the Legislature thereof may direct, a Number of Electors, equal to the whole Number of Senators and Representatives to which the State may be entitled in the Congress; but no Senator or Representative, or Person holding an Office of Trust or Profit under the United States, shall be appointed an Elector.

The Electors shall meet in their respective States, and vote by Ballot for two Persons, of whom one at least shall not be an Inhabitant of the same State with themselves. And they shall make a List of all the Persons voted for, and of the Number of Votes for each; which List they shall sign and certify, and transmit sealed to the Seat of the Government of the United States, directed to the President of the Senate. The President of the Senate shall, in the Presence of the Senate and House of Representatives, open all the Certificates, and the Votes shall then be counted. The Person having the greatest Number of Votes shall be the President, if such Number be a Majority of the whole Number of Electors appointed; and if there be more than one who have such Majority, and have an equal Number of Votes, then the House of Representatives shall immediately chuse by Ballot one of them for President; and if no Person have a Majority, then from the five highest on the List the said House shall in like Manner chuse the President. But in chusing the President, the Votes shall be taken by States, the Representation from each State having one Vote; A quorum for this Purpose shall consist of a Member or Members from two thirds of the States, and a Majority of all the States shall be necessary to a Choice. In every Case, after the Choice of the President, the Person having the greatest Number of Votes of the Electors shall be the Vice President. But if there should remain two or more who have equal Votes, the Senate shall chuse from them by Ballot the Vice President.

The Congress may determine the Time of chusing the Electors, and the Day on which they shall give their Votes; which Day shall be the same throughout the United States.

No Person except a natural born Citizen, or a Citizen of the United States, at the time of the Adoption of this Constitution, shall be eligible to the Office of President; neither shall any Person be eligible to that Office who shall not have attained to the Age of thirty five Years, and been fourteen Years a Resident within the United States.

In Case of the Removal of the President from Office, or of his Death, Resignation, or Inability to discharge the Powers and Duties of the said Office, the Same shall devolve on the Vice President, and the Congress may by Law provide for the Case of Removal, Death, Resignation or Inability, both of the President and Vice President, declaring what Officer shall then act as President, and such Officer shall act accordingly, until the Disability be removed, or a President shall be elected.

The President shall, at stated Times, receive for his Services a Compensation, which shall neither be encreased nor diminished during the Period for which he shall have been elected, and he shall not receive within that Period any other Emolument from the United States, or any of them.

Before he enter on the Execution of his Office, he shall take the following Oath or Affirmation:- "I do solemnly swear (or affirm) that I will faithfully execute the Office of President of the United States, and will to the best of my Ability, preserve, protect and defend the Constitution of the United States."

Section 2. The President shall be Commander in Chief of the Army and Navy of the United States, and of the Militia of the several States, when called into the actual Service of the United States; he may require the Opinion, in writing, of the principal Officer in each of the executive Departments, upon any Subject relating to the Duties of their respective Offices, and he shall have Power to grant Reprieves and Pardons for Offences against the United States, except in Cases of Impeachment.

He shall have Power, by and with the Advice and Consent of the Senate, to make Treaties, provided two thirds of the Senators present concur; and he shall nominate, and by and with the Advice and Consent of the Senate, shall appoint Ambassadors, other public Ministers and Consuls, Judges of the supreme Court, and all other Officers of the United States, whose Appointments are not herein otherwise provided for, and which shall be established by Law; but the Congress may by Law vest the Appointment of such inferior Officers, as they think proper, in the President alone, in the Courts of Law, or in the Heads of Departments.

The President shall have Power to fill up all Vacancies that may happen during the Recess of the Senate, by granting Commissions which shall expire at the End of their next Session.

Section 3. He shall from time to time give to the Congress Information of the State of the Union, and recommend to their Consideration such Measures as he shall judge necessary and expedient; he may, on extraordinary Occasions, convene both Houses, or either of them, and in Case of Disagreement between them, with Respect to the Time of Adjournment, he may adjourn them to such Time as he shall think proper; he shall receive Ambassadors and other public Ministers; he shall take Care that the Laws be faithfully executed, and shall Commission all the Officers of the United States.

Section 4. The President, Vice President and all civil Officers of the United States, shall be removed from Office on Impeachment for, and Conviction of, Treason, Bribery, or other high Crimes and Misdemeanors.

Article III

Section 1. The judicial Power of the United States, shall be vested in one supreme Court, and in such inferior Courts as the Congress may from to time ordain and establish. The Judges, both of the supreme and inferior Courts, shall hold their Offices during good Behaviour, and shall, at stated Times, receive for their Services, a Compensation, which shall not be diminished during their Continuance in Office.

Section 2. The judicial Power shall extend to all Cases, in Law and Equity, arising under this Constitution, the Laws of the United States, and Treaties made, or which shall be made, under their Authority;-to all Cases affecting Ambassadors, other public Ministers and Consuls;-to all Cases of admiralty and maritime Jurisdiction;-to Controversies to which the United States shall be a Party;-to Controversies between two or more States;-between a State and Citizens of another State;-between Citizens of different States;-between Citizens of the same State claiming Lands under Grants of different States, and between a State, or the Citizens thereof, and foreign States, Citizens or Subjects.

In all Cases affecting Ambassadors, other public Ministers and Consuls, and those in which a State shall be Party, the supreme Court shall have original Jurisdiction. In all the other Cases before mentioned, the supreme Court shall have appellate Jurisdiction, both as to Law and Fact, with such Exceptions, and under such Regulations as the Congress shall make.

The Trial of all Crimes, except in Cases of Impeachment, shall be by Jury; and such Trial shall be held in the State where the said Crimes shall have been committed; but when not committed within any State, the Trial shall be at such Place or Places as the Congress may by Law have directed.

Section 3. Treason against the United States, shall consist only in levying War against them, or in adhering to their Enemies, giving them Aid and Comfort. No Person shall be convicted of Treason unless on the Testimony of two Witnesses to the same overt Act, or on Confession in open Court.

The Congress shall have Power to declare the Punishment of Treason, but no Attainder of Treason shall work Corruption of Blood, or Forfeiture except during the Life of the Person attainted.

Article IV

Section 1. Full Faith and Credit shall be given in each State to the public Acts, Records, and judicial Proceedings of every other State. And the Congress may by general Laws prescribe the Manner in which such Acts, Records and Proceedings shall be proved, and the Effect thereof.

Section 2. The Citizens of each State shall be entitled to all Privileges and Immunities of Citizens in the several States.

A Person charged in any State with Treason, Felony, or other Crime, who shall flee from Justice, and be found in another State, shall on Demand of the executive Authority of the State from which he fled, be delivered up, to be removed to the State having Jurisdiction of the Crime.

No Person held to Service or Labour in one State, under the Laws thereof, escaping into another, shall, in Consequence of any Law or Regulation therein, be discharged from such Service or Labour, but shall be delivered up on Claim of the Party to whom such Service or Labour may be due.

Section 3. New States may be admitted by the Congress into this Union; but no new State shall be formed or erected within the Jurisdiction of any other State; nor any State be formed by the Junction of two or more States, or Parts of States,

without the Consent of the Legislatures of the States concerned, as well as of the Congress.

The Congress shall have Power to dispose of and make all needful Rules and Regulations respecting the Territory or other Property belonging to the United States; and nothing in this Constitution shall be so construed as to Prejudice any Claims of the United States, or of any particular state.

Section 4. The United States shall guarantee to every State in this Union a Republican Form of Government, and shall protect each of them against Invasion; and on Application of the Legislature, or of the Executive (when the Legislature cannot be convened) against domestic Violence.

Article V

The Congress, whenever two thirds of both Houses shall deem it necessary, shall propose Amendments to this Constitution, or, on the Application of the Legislatures of two thirds of the several States, shall call a Convention for proposing Amendments, which, in either Case, shall be valid to all Intents and Purposes, as Part of this Constitution, when ratified by the Legislatures of three fourths of the several States, or by Conventions in three fourths thereof, as the one or the other Mode of Ratification may be proposed by the Congress; Provided that no Amendment which may be made prior to the Year One thousand eight hundred and eight shall in any Manner affect the first and fourth Clauses in the Ninth Section of the first Article; and that no State, without its Consent, shall be deprived of its equal Suffrage in the Senate.

Article VI

All Debts contracted and Engagements entered into, before the Adoption of this Constitution, shall be as valid against the United States under this Constitution, as under the Confederation.

This Constitution, and the Laws of the United States which shall be made in Pursuance thereof; and all Treaties made, or which shall be made, under the Authority of the United States, shall be the supreme Law of the Land; and the Judges in every State shall be bound thereby, any Thing in the Constitution or Laws of any State to the Contrary notwithstanding.

The Senators and Representatives before mentioned, and the Members of the several State Legislatures, and all executive and judicial Officers, both of the United States and of the several States, shall be bound by Oath or Affirmation, to support this Constitution; but no religious Test shall ever be required as a Qualification to any Office or public Trust under the United States.

Article VII

The Ratification of the Conventions of nine States, shall be sufficient for the Establishment of this Constitution between the States so ratifying the Same.

done in Convention by the Unanimous Consent of the States present the Seventeenth Day of September in the Year of our Lord one thousand seven hundred and Eighty seven and of the Independence of the United States of America the Twelfth in witness whereof We have hereunto subscribed our Names.

[The first 10 Amendments were ratified December 15, 1791, and form what is known as the Bill of Rights]

Amendment 1

Congress shall make no law respecting an establishment of religion, or prohibiting the free exercise thereof; or abridging the freedom of speech, or of the press; or the right of the people peaceably to assemble, and to petition the Government for a redress of grievances.

Amendment 2

A well regulated Militia, being necessary to the security of a free State, the right of the people to keep and bear Arms, shall not be infringed.

Amendment 3

No Soldier shall, in time of peace be quartered in any house, without the consent of the Owner, nor in time of war, but in a manner to be prescribed by law.

Amendment 4

The right of the people to be secure in their persons, houses, papers, and effects, against unreasonable searches and seizures, shall not be violated, and no Warrants shall issue, but upon probable cause, supported by Oath or affirmation, and particularly describing the place to be searched and the persons or things to be seized.

Amendment 5

No person shall be held to answer for a capital, or otherwise infamous crime, unless on a presentment or indictment of a Grand Jury, except in cases arising in the land or naval forces, or in the Militia, when in actual service in time of War or public danger; nor shall any person be subject for the same offence to be twice put in jeopardy of life or limb; nor shall be compelled in any criminal case to be a witness against himself, nor be deprived of life, liberty, or property, without due process of law; nor shall private property be taken for public use, without just compensation.

Amendment 6

In all criminal prosecutions, the accused shall enjoy the right to a speedy and public trial by an impartial jury of the State and district wherein the crime shall have been committed, which district shall have been previously ascertained by law, and to be informed of the nature and cause of the accusation; to be confronted with the witnesses against him; to have compulsory process for obtaining witnesses in his favor, and to have the Assistance of Counsel for his defence.

Amendment 7

In suits at common law, where the value in controversy shall exceed twenty dollars, the right of trial by jury shall be preserved, and no fact tried by a jury, shall be otherwise reexamined in any Court of the United States, than according to the rules of the common law.

Amendment 8

Excessive bail shall not be required, nor excessive fines imposed, nor cruel and unusual punishments inflicted.

Amendment 9

The enumeration in the Constitution, of certain rights, shall not be construed to deny or disparage others retained by the people.

Amendment 10

The powers not delegated to the United States by the Constitution, nor prohibited by it to the States, are reserved to the States respectively, or to the people.

Amendment 11

[RATIFIED FEBRUARY 7, 1795]

The Judicial power of the United States shall not be construed to extend to any suit in law or equity, commenced or prosecuted against one of the United States by Citizens of another State, or by Citizens or Subjects of any Foreign State.

Amendment 12

[RATIFIED JULY 27, 1804]

The Electors shall meet in their respective states and vote by ballot for President and Vice-President, one of whom, at least, shall not be an inhabitant of the same state with themselves; they shall name in their ballots the person voted for as President, and in distinct ballots the person voted for as Vice-President, and they shall make distinct lists of all persons voted for as President, and of all persons voted for as Vice-President, and of the number of votes for each, which lists they shall sign and certify, and transmit sealed to the seat of the government of the United States, directed to the President of the Senate;-The President of the Senate shall, in the presence of the Senate and House of Representatives, open all the certificates and the votes shall then be counted;- The person having the greatest number of votes for President, shall be the President, if such number be a majority of the whole number of Electors appointed; and if no person have such majority, then from the persons having the highest numbers not exceeding three on the list of those voted for as President, the House of Representatives shall choose immediately, by ballot, the President. But in choosing the President, the votes shall be taken by states, the representation from each state having one vote; a quorum for this pupose shall consist of a member or members from two-thirds of the states, and a majority of all the states shall be necessary to a choice. And if the House of Representatives shall not choose a President whenever the right of choice shall devolve upon them, before the fourth day of March next following, then the Vice-President shall act as President, as in the case of the death or other constitutional disability of the President.-The person having the greatest number of votes as Vice-President, shall be the Vice-President, if such number be a major-

ity of the whole number of Electors appointed, and if no person have a majority, then from the two highest numbers on the list, the Senate shall choose the Vice-President; a quorum for the purpose shall consist of two-thirds of the whole number of Senators, and a majority of the whole number shall be necessary to a choice. But no person constitutionally ineligible to the office of President shall be eligible to that of Vice-President of the United States.

Amendment 13

[RATIFIED DECEMBER 6, 1865]

Section 1. Neither slavery nor involuntary servitude, except as a punishment for crime whereof the party shall have been duly convicted, shall exist within the United States, or any place subject to their jurisdiction.

Section 2. Congress shall have power to enforce this article by appropriate legislation.

Amendment 14

[RATIFIED JULY 9, 1868]

Section 1. All persons born or naturalized in the United States, and subject to the jurisdiction thereof, are citizens of the United States and of the State wherein they reside. No State shall make or enforce any law which shall abridge the privileges or immunities of citizens of the United States; nor shall any State deprive any person of life, liberty, or property, without due process of law; nor deny to any person within its jurisdiction the equal protection of the laws.

Section 2. Representatives shall be apportioned among the several States according to their respective numbers, counting the whole number of persons in each State, excluding Indians not taxed. But when the right to vote at any election for the choice of electors for President and Vice President of the United States, Representatives in Congress, the Executive and Judicial officers of a State, or the members of the Legislature thereof, is denied to any of the male inhabitants of such State, being twenty-one years of age, and citizens of the United States, or in any way abridged, except for participation in rebellion, or other crime, the basis of representation therein shall be reduced in the proportion which the number of such male citizens shall bear to the whole number of male citizens twenty-one years of age in such State.

Section 3. No person shall be a Senator or Representative in Congress, or elector of President and Vice President, or hold any office, civil or military, under the United States, or under any State, who, having previously taken an oath, as a member of Congress, or as an officer of the United States, or as a member of any State legislature, or as an executive or judicial officer of any State, to support the Constitution of the United States, shall have engaged in insurrection or rebellion against the same, or given aid or comfort to the enemies thereof. But Congress may by a vote of two-thirds of each House, remove such disability.

Section 4. The validity of the public debt of the United States, authorized by law, including debts incurred for payment of pensions and bounties for services in suppressing insurrection or rebellion, shall not be questioned. But neither the United States nor any State shall assume or pay any debt or obligation incurred in aid of insurrection or rebellion against the United States, or any claim for the loss or emancipation of any slave; but all such debts, obligations and claims shall be held illegal and void.

Section 5. The Congress shall have power to enforce, by appropriate legislation, the provisions of this article.

Amendment 15

[RATIFIED FEBRUARY 3, 1870]

Section 1. The right of citizens of the United States to vote shall not be denied or abridged by the United States or by any State on account of race, color, or previous condition of servitude.

Section 2. The Congress shall have power to enforce this article by appropriate legislation.

Amendment 16

[RATIFIED FEBRUARY 3, 1913]

The Congress shall have power to lay and collect taxes on incomes, from whatever source derived, without apportionment among the several States, and without regard to any census or enumeration.

Amendment 17

[RATIFIED APRIL 8, 1913]

The Senate of the United States shall be composed of two Senators from each State, elected by the people thereof for six years; and each Senator shall have one vote. The electors in each State shall have the qualifications requisite for electors of the most numerous branch of the State legislatures.

When vacancies happen in the representation of any State in the Senate, the executive authority of such State shall issue writs of election to fill such vacancies: *Provided,* That the legislature of any State may empower the executive thereof to make temporary appointments until the people fill the vacancies by election as the legislature may direct.

This amendment shall not be so construed as to affect the election or term of any Senator chosen before it becomes valid as part of the Constitution.

Amendment 18

[RATIFIED JANUARY 16, 1919]

Section 1. After one year from the ratification of this article the manufacture, sale, or transportation of intoxicating liquors within, the importation thereof into, or the exportation thereof from the United States and all territory subject to the jurisdiction thereof for beverage purposes is hereby prohibited.

Section 2. The Congress and the several States shall have concurrent power to enforce this article by appropriate legislation.

Section 3. This article shall be inoperative unless it shall have been ratified as an amendment to the Constitution by the legislatures of the several States, as provided in the Constitution, within seven years from the date of the submission hereof to the States by the Congress.

Amendment 19

[RATIFIED AUGUST 18, 1920]

The right of citizens of the United States to vote shall not be denied or abridged by the United States or by any State on account of sex. Congress shall have power to enforce this article by appropriate legislation.

Amendment 20

[RATIFIED JANUARY 23, 1933]

Section 1. The terms of the President and Vice President shall end at noon on the 20th day of January, and the terms of Senators and Representatives at noon on the 3d day of January, of the years in which such terms would have ended if this article had not been ratified; and the terms of their successors shall then begin.

Section 2. The Congress shall assemble at least once in every year, and such meeting shall begin at noon on the 3d day of January, unless they shall by law appoint a different day.

Section 3. If, at the time fixed for the beginning of the term of the President, the President elect shall have died, the Vice President elect shall become President. If a President shall not have been chosen before the time fixed for the beginning of his term, or if the President elect shall have failed to qualify, then the Vice President elect shall act as President until a President shall have qualified; and the Congress may by law provide for the case wherein neither a President elect nor a Vice President elect shall have qualified, declaring who shall then act as President, or the manner in which one who is to act shall be selected, and such person shall act accordingly until a President or Vice President shall have qualified.

Section 4. The Congress may by law provide for the case of the death of any of the persons from whom the House of Representatives may choose a President whenever the right of choice shall have devolved upon them, and for the case of the death of any of the persons from whom the Senate may choose a Vice President whenever the right of choice shall have devolved upon them.

Section 5. Sections 1 and 2 shall take effect on the 15th day of October following the ratification of this article.

Section 6. This article shall be inoperative unless it shall have been ratified as an amendment to the Constitution by the legislatures of three-fourths of the several States within seven years from the date of its submission.

Amendment 21

[RATIFIED DECEMBER 5, 1933]

Section 1. The eighteenth article of amendment to the Constitution of the United States is hereby repealed.

Section 2. The transportation or importation into any State, Territory, or possession of the United States for delivery or use therein of intoxicating liquors, in violation of the laws thereof, is hereby prohibited.

Section 3. This article shall be inoperative unless it shall have been ratified as an amendment to the Constitution by conventions in the several States, as provided in the Constitution, within seven years from the date of the submission hereof to the States by the Congress.

Amendment 22

[RATIFIED FEBRUARY 27, 1951]

Section 1. No person shall be elected to the office of the President more than twice, and no person who has held the office of President, or acted as President, for more than two years of a term to which some other person was elected President shall be elected to the office of the President more than once. But this Article shall not apply to any person holding the office of President when this Article was proposed by the Congress, and shall not prevent any person who may be holding the office of President, or acting as President, during the term within which this Article becomes operative from holding the office of President or acting as President during the remainder of such term.

Section 2. This article shall be inoperative unless it shall have been ratified as an amendment to the Constitution by the legislatures of three-fourths of the several States within seven years from the date of its submission to the States by the Congress.

Amendment 23

[RATIFIED MARCH 29, 1961]

Section 1. The District constituting the seat of Government of the United States shall appoint in such manner as the Congress may direct:

A number of electors of President and Vice President equal to the whole number of Senators and Representatives in Congress to which the District would be entitled if it were a State, but in no event more than the least populous State; they shall be in addition to those appointed by the States, but they shall be considered, for the purposes of the election of President and Vice President, to be electors appointed by a State; and they shall meet in the District and perform such duties as provided by the twelfth article of amendment.

Section 2. The Congress shall have power to enforce this article by appropriate legislation.

Amendment 24

[RATIFIED JANUARY 23, 1964]

Section 1. The right of citizens of the United States to vote in any primary or other election for President or Vice President, for electors for President or Vice President, or for Senator or Representative in Congress, shall not be denied or abridged by the United States or any State by reason of failure to pay any poll tax or other tax.

Section 2. The Congress shall have power to enforce this article by appropriate legislation.

Amendment 25

[RATIFIED FEBRUARY 10, 1967]

Section 1. In case of the removal of the President from office or of his death or resignation, the Vice President shall become President.

Section 2. Whenever there is a vacancy in the office of the Vice President, the President shall nominate a Vice President who shall take office upon confirmation by a majority vote of both Houses of Congress.

Section 3. Whenever the President transmits to the President pro tempore of the Senate and the Speaker of the House of Representatives his written declaration that he is unable to discharge the powers and duties of his office, and until he transmits to them a written declaration to the contrary, such powers and duties shall be discharged by the Vice President as Acting President.

Section 4. Whenever the Vice President and a majority of either the principal officers of the executive departments or of such other body as Congress may by law provide, transmit to the President pro tempore of the Senate and the Speaker of the House of Representatives their written declaration that the President is unable to discharge the powers and duties of his office, the Vice President shall immediately assume the powers and duties of the office as Acting President.

Thereafter, when the President transmits to the President pro tempore of the Senate and the Speaker of the House of Representatives his written declaration that no inability exists, he shall resume the powers and duties of his office unless the Vice President and a majority of either the principal officers of the executive department or of such other body as Congress may by law provide, transmit within four days to the President pro tempore of the Senate and the Speaker of the House of Representatives their written declaration that the President is unable to discharge the powers and duties of his office. Thereupon Congress shall decide the issue, assembling within forty-eight hours for that purpose if not in session. If the Congress, within twenty-one days after receipt of the latter written declaration, or, if Congress is not in session, within twenty-one days after Congress is required to assemble, determines by two-thirds vote of both Houses that the President is unable to discharge the powers and duties of his office, the Vice President shall continue to discharge the same as Acting President; otherwise, the President shall resume the powers and duties of his office.

Amendment 26

[RATIFIED JUNE 30, 1971]

Section 1. The right of citizens of the United States, who are eighteen years of age or older, to vote shall not be denied or abridged by the United States or by any State on account of age.

Section 2. The Congress shall have the power to enforce this article by appropriate legislation.

Proposed Amendment 27

[PROPOSED MARCH 22, 1972]

Section 1. Equality of rights under the law shall not be denied or abridged by the United States or by any State on account of sex.

Section 2. The Congress shall have power to enforce, by appropriate legislation, the provisions of this article.

Section 3. This amendment shall take effect two years after date of ratification.

GLOSSARY

absentee ballot A ballot requested by an individual who will be away from his or her voting district on election day.

absolutist standard A guideline advocated by some judges that First Amendment rights are totally and always protected against governmental power.

amicus curiae (friend of the court) An individual, or group, not an immediate party to a case in court, who is permitted to file a legal brief advising the judges how to decide.

appellate courts Courts that are responsible for hearing appeals from lower courts.

appropriations bill A legislative bill legitimizing the spending of money that has initially been authorized by the legislature.

Articles of Confederation The basic rules defining the American confederacy of 1781–1788.

authorization bill A legislative bill giving the initial permission for the expenditure of money.

bail Money or property put up as security by an accused to obtain release from jail while awaiting trial.

bicameral (congress) A legislature composed of two houses or chambers.

bill of attainder A legislative act that imposes a punishment upon some individual.

Bill of Rights The first ten amendments to the Constitution.

block grants Money offered by the national government to state or local governments to perform services in broadly defined policy areas within which they have discretion to spend the money.

Brown v. Board of Education of Topeka A case in which the Supreme Court ruled that laws separating schoolchildren on the basis of race violated the equal protection clause of the Fourteenth Amendment.

bureaucratic executives Members of the executive branch who are the appointed, day-to-day, long-term administrators of government programs.

bureaucracy A hierarchical system of organization staffed by career employees and characterized by routine and impersonal performance.

cabinet An advisory group to the President made up of the heads of the executive departments.

candidate elections Elections in which candidates compete for public office.

capitalism *See* free enterprise capitalism.

categorical grants-in-aid Money offered by the national government to state or local governments on the condition that they undertake specific, narrowly defined programs of activity.

cause parties Minor parties organized to promote special causes or unique solutions to society's problems.

checks and balances A principle of government in which each branch of a government shares in the powers of the other branches and can therefore limit or stop their exercise of power.

civil rights or liberties The basic rights of individuals, protected by the Constitution.

clear and present danger doctrine A judicial test that permits government to violate freedom of speech, press, and assembly only when the danger to society is substantive, clear, and immediate.

closed rule A rule in the House of Representatives that prohibits any amendments to a bill.

cloture A Senate device for compulsorily terminating a filibuster.

Committee of the Whole House The entire House of Representatives meeting as a committee to consider a bill.

concurrent powers Powers belonging to both the national and the state governments.

concurring opinions The written views of judges who agree with a court's official majority or minority opinions but who develop a somewhat different argument.

Confederate Congress The national legislature established by the Articles of Confederation.

confederation An alliance among independent states that establishes a minimal degree of unity (central government) among them while enabling each state to retain maximum powers to itself.

conference committee A joint committee set up by the House and Senate to resolve differences in their respective versions of proposed legislation.

Connecticut or Great Compromise The agreement on congressional representation worked out between the large and the small states at the Constitutional Convention.

consent The permission or agreement of those who are governed, which legitimates the operation of government.

constituency In a broad sense, any group to whom a leader has a set of obligations. In a narrow sense, the people of an election district whom a legislator or executive official represents.

constitutional (limited) government A principle that public officials are as much obligated to obey the laws as are the rest of the people.

Continental Congress The ad hoc or temporary national legislature in which the new, independent states were represented during the American Revolution.

cooperative federalism A system of financial and policy arrangements between the national government and state or local governments in which resources and power are shared in order to accomplish common ends.

crisis parties Minor parties that arise in response to a drastic deterioration in social or economic conditions.

dangerous tendency standard A judicial test under which government may interfere with freedom of speech or press or assembly when the exercise of these freedoms is judged to have a dangerous tendency to create substantive evils for society.

delegated powers Those powers assigned to the national government by the Constitution.

delegate role Representational behavior in which a legislator tries faithfully to mirror the views of his or her election district.

democracy A set of values and principles that emphasizes the importance, equality, and freedom of individuals and that calls for government to respect the rights of the people and to be chosen by and responsive to the popular majority.

Democratic caucus A meeting of all the Democrats in the Senate or in the House.

direct democracy A system of government in which the people themselves make their own rules.

direct lobbying Personal interaction by lobbyists with government officials.

dissenting opinions The written views of those judges voting in the minority in a case.

due process *See* procedural due process and substantive due process.

elections The choosing of leaders or the deciding of policy issues by a vote.

electoral college All the electors who vote for President and Vice President.

electorate All the people entitled to vote in an election.

enumerated powers Those powers expressly assigned to the Congress by the Constitution.

equality A value premise in democratic theory that each person is inherently as important as all other persons and as deserving of the right to freedom.

excessive entanglement standard A judicial test to determine whether or not government is involved in the "establishment of religion."

executive agreements Agreements between a President and leaders of other countries that do not require Senate approval.

executive oversight Supervision of the activities of the executive branch by the legislature.

executive privilege A doctrine that certain presidential decisions and behavior are immune from congressional and judicial inquiry.

ex post facto law A law that retroactively makes some act a crime or increases the punishment for a crime.

extradition A constitutional obligation that states comply with the demands of other states for the return of escapees from their criminal justice systems.

federalism A system of government in which power is divided between central and state governments, each ruling the people directly and each deriving its powers from a superior set of fundamental laws.

filibuster Attempting to kill a bill in the Senate by talking long enough to prevent it from coming up for a vote.

freedom A basic value in democracy and capitalism that individuals have to make their own decisions, without limits imposed by others.

free enterprise capitalism A self-regulating, self-motivating economic system based on private profit, private property, and competition.

friend of the court *See* amicus curiae.

full faith and credit A constitutional requirement that states accept as legitimate the civil decisions, official records, and judicial proceedings of other states.

general elections Elections that are open to the entire electorate and that determine the winners of public offices or the adoption of policy proposals on the ballot.

general revenue sharing Money allocated by the national government without any restrictions to states or local governments.

general welfare clause The constitutional provision that authorizes Congress to tax and spend for the general welfare.

gerrymandering Drawing election district lines so as to favor or discriminate against certain groups in their legislative representation.

government Human machinery for making authoritative rules and regulations that affect the behavior of all of us.

grandfather clause A law adopted by southern states allowing illiterate whites but not illiterate blacks to vote by exempting potential voters from a literacy test if their fathers or grandfathers had voted before 1866.

habeas corpus A judicial order removing a person from jail and compelling the executive to inform him or her before a court of the charges against him or her.

impeachment The official charging, by the House of Representatives, of executive or judicial officials with misconduct.

implied powers National powers read by the courts into vague constitutional clauses defining the powers of Congress.

implied powers clause A constitutional provision that authorizes Congress to adopt laws necessary and proper to carry out its other powers.

independent regulatory agencies Semi-independent executive agencies that supervise and regulate special areas of the economy.

indirect lobbying The use by lobbyists of other political actors to influence government officials.

individualism A belief underlying both democracy and capitalism that holds individuals to be intrinsically valuable and capable of knowing what is best for themselves.

inferior courts Regular courts that Congress creates on the basis of Article III in the Constitution.

initiative A proposed law or constitutional amendment placed on the ballot by popular petition for a vote by the people.

interest groups (political) Groups of individuals or organized units that share common attitudes and seek to advance their objectives through political means other than running their own candidates for public office in popular elections.

interstate compacts Formal agreements between or among states to solve common problems, but which require congressional approval.

joint committees Legislative committees on which members of both chambers serve.

judicial interpretation Determining the meaning of constitutional and statutory law by the courts.

judicial review The doctrine that the courts have the legitimate and final authority to decide the constitutionality of acts of the executive and legislative branches.

laissez faire A belief that government should stay out of the private economic system, allowing its participants to make their own decisions and to compete freely among themselves.

legislative veto The nullifying of presidential action by a vote of one or both houses of Congress.

legitimate power Power that is recognized as properly belonging to someone.

liberty A basic value in democracy and capitalism that individuals should have maximum choices to determine the course of their lives.

majority At least one more than half.

majority floor leader The elected floor leader of the majority party in a congressional chamber.

majority rule A democratic principle that decisions should be determined by the votes of at least one more than half those participating and that public officials should be chosen by and responsible to popular majorities.

Marbury v. Madison The case in which the Supreme Court first asserted its power of judicial review.

minority Less than half.

minority leader The elected floor leader of the minority party in a congressional chamber.

minority rights A democratic principle that individuals not in the majority still have basic rights and are entitled to be treated with respect and consideration by government.

modern federalism Today's federal system, which incorporates a tremendous expansion in national government powers and an extensive network of cooperative relations among national, state, and local governments.

multistate-national compact An agreement between a group of states and the national government to cope with common problems that cross the states' boundaries.

national regional government A special unit of the national government empowered to deal with the problems of a specific region in the country.

national supremacy A principle of the

U.S. Constitution that it as well as the laws and treaties of the national government are supreme over the laws and constitutions of the states.

necessary and proper clause The constitutional clause giving Congress the power to make all laws necessary and proper for the execution of its other powers. Referred to as the implied powers, or elastic, clause.

New Jersey Plan The plan of government advanced by the small states at the Constitutional Convention.

nonpartisan elections Elections in which candidates compete for public office without any political party designations on the ballot.

one man–one vote The principle that all units of representation in a legislature should represent equal units of population in election districts.

open rule A House of Representatives rule that permits amendments to be offered to a bill.

original jurisdiction The authority of a court to hear a case at its initial stage when the defendant and plaintiff first argue their points.

paramount state interest–no alternative means standard A judicial test that holds that only if there is an overriding interest of government and no other alternatives are available may government restrict certain constitutional rights.

parliamentary government A governmental system that concentrates power in the legislative branch, its members choosing the executive leaders who are responsible to the legislative majority.

partisan elections Elections in which candidates run under party labels.

partisan executives The senior elected leaders of the executive branch or those appointed by these partisan officials and whose tenure depends on the wishes of the elected executives.

party-in-the-electorate Those individuals who merely identify with or register as members of a party.

party-in-the-government Those party leaders who win election to public office and comprise a separate unit of their party in a legislative chamber or in the executive branches.

party-in-the-organization The leaders at all levels of the internal organization of a political party who are responsible for keeping its machinery operating.

party platforms Sets of policy proposals adopted by political parties at their conventions.

plurality A number of votes that is less than half the total cast, but that is larger than any other number of votes.

pocket veto A presidential refusal to sign a bill, which kills the bill when Congress adjourns within ten days of its having sent the bill to the President.

political action committees (PACs) Campaign committees set up by interest groups that raise money to support candidates and policy issues in elections.

political culture The framework of accepted values, attitudes, and practices within which government operates and politics takes place.

political parties Voluntary political organizations that seek to capture the power of government by offering their candidates in general elections for public office.

political system Everything in society that relates to the shaping and implementing of government policy, whether it occurs within or outside the framework of government.

politico role Representational behavior in which a legislator sometimes follows the views of the people in his or her election district and sometimes acts according to what the legislator personally feels should be done.

poll taxes Fees required by some state governments of those who wanted to vote in public elections.

power The ability to determine the behavior of others.

presidential electors A special group of elected public officials authorized by the Constitution to vote for the President and Vice President.

presidential primary A party primary that either chooses delegates from state parties to presidential nominating conventions or that helps determine how these delegates will vote.

primaries Popular elections in which candidates are chosen to compete for public office.

privileges and immunities Those rights provided by states to their own citizens, and which, according to the Constitution, they must also provide to citizens from other states.

probable danger standard A judicial test that permits government to violate freedom of speech, press, or assembly if the exercise of these rights represents a probable danger to law and order.

procedural due process A judicial doctrine, based on the due process clauses in the Fifth and Fourteenth Amendments, that government must use fair, reasonable, and predictable means when it threatens the life, liberty, or property of any person.

project grants Money made available by the national government to state or local governments in nationally determined policy areas in response to particular projects for which those governments request aid.

proportional representation An election system in which a party's candidates are elected to public office in proportion to the percentage of the total vote cast for that party.

public interest group An interest group whose policy goals are designed, not primarily to benefit its members, but rather to benefit society as a whole.

reapportionment Redistributing units of representation in a legislature in accordance with population changes.

referendum A law or constitutional amendment that is either referred by a legislature to the electorate for its decision or is prevented from going into effect by a popular petition that requires a vote by the electorate.

registration A requirement of most states that individuals wishing to vote in elections must first officially enroll their name and, in most cases, their party affiliation, if they have one.

representative democracy A government system in which the people choose representatives in free elections to rule in their name.

representative or republican government A government composed of elected public leaders who at regular intervals must compete in popular elections for public office.

reserved powers Those powers not stated in the Constitution as belonging to the national government or denied to the states are reserved to the states.

reverse discrimination Discrimination against members of one group in the interest of advancing the equality of other groups that have been discriminated against.

roles Sets of behavior patterns expected of anyone occupying any particular position.

seniority rule An unwritten rule in Congress that official committee leadership go to those members in each party with the longest continuous service on the committee.

separation of powers A principle that calls for the division of power at any level of government into separate branches.

silent gerrymandering Deliberately allowing election districts and units of legislative representation to remain the same even though population shifts have occurred that have the effect of giving some districts representation disproportionate to their population.

socioeconomic status A measure for differentiating among people in society according to their income, occupation, and education.

socialism A political-economic system in which the economic means of production and distribution are owned by the government and public profit is substituted for private profit.

Speaker of the House The constitutional presiding officer of the House of Representatives.

special or select committees Temporary committees established by a legislature to study or investigate specific matters.

special courts Courts created by Congress to resolve conflicts in particular subject matter areas.

special interest groups Interest groups that advocate government action that directly benefits their members.

special revenue sharing Money allocated by the national government to state or local governments to be spent at their discretion within a number of broadly defined policy areas.

splinter parties Minor parties created as a result of splits in the major parties.

standing committees The permanent committees in Congress.

state delegations All the members in a congressional chamber who come from the same state, irrespective of party.

state-to-state obligations Constitutional requirements that states behave in certain ways toward one another or one another's citizens.

substantive due process A judicial doctrine, based on the due process clauses of the Constitution, that government may not adopt certain laws interfering with people's behavior or beliefs.

suffrage The right to vote.

Supreme Court (U.S.) The highest court of the national government and the only one specifically called for by the Constitution.

Three-fifths Compromise The agreement at the Constitutional Convention between northern and southern states to count a slave as three-fifths of a person for representative and taxation purposes.

traditional federalism The arrangements of power between national and state governments originally called for in the U.S. Constitution.

treaty A formal agreement between the United States and a foreign country, which the President must submit to the Senate for its approval.

trustee role Representational behavior in which a legislator personally decides what is in the best interest of his or her constituency rather than following exactly its wishes.

two-party system A political system in which competition for elected leadership in government is virtually monopolized by two political parties.

unanimity (rule of) A rule that everyone who is voting must agree before a decision can be taken.

unanimous consent A Senate device for determining conditions of floor debate on a bill and for holding a vote on it that requires the consent of all senators concerned with the bill.

unicameral (congress) A one-chamber legislature.

unit rule A requirement that a majority in a delegation cast the entire delegation's votes, thereby preventing a minority from having its votes count.

veto A formal rejection by the President of legislation adopted by Congress.

Virginia Plan The plan of government advanced by the large states at the Constitutional Convention.

wall of separation standard A judicial doctrine, first advanced by Thomas Jefferson, that the First Amendment absolutely separates church and state.

whips Assistant party leaders in both chambers of Congress who help keep the avenues of communication open between senior party leaders and their rank and file legislative party members.

white primary A device used in southern states to disfranchise blacks by restricting those who could vote in Democratic party primaries to whites only.

winner-take-all rule An election rule that a candidate who receives the most votes wins the office being contested, and that other candidates with smaller numbers of votes win nothing.

INDEX